Aristotle's Physics

By the same author

Aristotle's Metaphysics (1966)
Aristotle's Nicomachean Ethics (1975)
Aristotle's Categories and Propositions (1980)
Aristotle's Posterior Analytics (1981)
Aristotle's On The Soul (1982)
Aristotle: Selected Works-with Lloyd P. Gerson (1983)

ARISTOTLE'S PHYSICS

Translated with Commentaries
and Glossary by
HIPPOCRATES G. APOSTLE

THE PERIPATETIC PRESS
Grinnell, Iowa

Copyright© 1969 by Indiana University Press
Copyright© 1980 by H. G. Apostle
cl. ISBN 0-9602870-2-7
pa. ISBN 0-9602870-3-5
Library of Congress catalog card number: 80-80037
Manufactured in the United States of America

To Dr. Nathan Silberstein

Contents

Preface

In the translation of the *Physics* the principles which are used are the same as those in the translation of the *Metaphysics,* and those needed for an accurate reading will be repeated here.

Briefly, they are principles of terminology and of thought. We have indicated in the Preface of the *Metaphysics* why an accurate translation requires a terminology which is consistent, adequate, familiar, and clear. Usage of a term in many senses does not lessen consistency in terminology, as long as the various senses are listed. Confusion arises when the translator or the reader selects the wrong sense or when he has the mistaken notion that the meaning of a term depends only on the context in which it is used. Aristotle, we may add, is using Greek terms very accurately, even when he argues dialectically.

On the whole, the Glossary in the *Physics* is the same as that in the *Metaphysics.* Some terms proper to physics have been added, like "accelerate" and "displacement"; others have been omitted because they are not used in the *Physics*; and some minor changes have been made to accord with the principles of translation. For example, the term "consecutive" is used instead of "contiguous", "*Gap*" instead of "*Chaos*", and "refer" instead of "reduce".

To distinguish in writing a vocal or written expression from what it signifies, we enclose it with double quotation marks. For example, "Socrates" is a term and not a man; it signifies Socrates, who was a man and not a term. Similarly, "four is a square integer" is an expression, and it signifies a fact. Thoughts are analogous to expressions, and they too are enclosed with double quotation marks. For example, we may say that the thought "five is an even number" is false. We also use the conjunction "that" instead of quotation marks, as in "the thought that five is even is false". Expressions in Greek are not enclosed by quotation marks, for this is not necessary. For example, we may write: The word ποιόν is a Greek term and is translated as "quality".

Terms in italics with initial capital letters signify principles posited by philosophers other than Aristotle. For example, the *One* and the *Dyad* are posited by Plato as the two principles from which all the other things are generated; *Water* is posited as the material principle by Thales.

Expressions in italics without initial capital letters are used in two ways. (1) For emphasis. (2) For terms used also in roman type, for two reasons: (a) Aristotle uses some terms in two senses, generically and specifically; for example, αὐτόματον is used as a genus and also as a species, and we use "chance" for the genus but *"chance"* for the species. (b) Rather than use a strange term or introduce a new one, we often use a term in roman type for one meaning and in italics for a meaning somehow allied to the first or narrower than the first. For example, we use "reason" and *"reason"*, "composite" and *"composite"*, "clear" and *"clear"*. The meanings of such terms appear in the Glossary.

Expressions appearing in brackets are added for the sake of the reader and are not translations from the Greek. For example, in line 189b1 the term "principle" has been added in the expression "it would be necessary for us to assume a third [principle]" for the sake of the reader, for here Aristotle is talking about a principle which is necessary in understanding motion.

Students who wish to get the thought accurately should make full use of the Glossary. Many Greek terms have no equivalents in English, and the English terms chosen for them are given meaning in more elementary terms. For example, there are no exact English equivalents for προαίρεσις, ὕδωρ, and ἐμπειρία, and the English terms chosen for them (*"choice"*, "water", and "experience"), though close in meaning, still leave room for apparent inconsistency or falsity and for unfair criticism unless the reader uses the Glossary. In addition, in the case of a few terms, we have chosen the terms used by most or all of the translators, even if more technical terms could have been used. For example, for the term ἀριθμός we are using "number" instead of "natural number" or "whole number", although the usual meaning of "number" is closer to the term ποσόν than to the term ἀριθμός.

In the margins of the translation we have inserted the pages and lines of the Bekker text, which are standard. The various works of Aristotle and the Bekker pages containing each of them are listed at the beginning of the Commentaries. The meanings given to a few terms in the Glossary were arrived at by induction, comparison, deduction, or in some other way, for no definitions of those terms appear in the extant Greek text. Whenever we disagreed with the Greek text and the variants, we translated as we thought best, with a commentary, when desirable.

Book H has two versions of Sections 1, 2, and 3, and certain problems have arisen in connection with it. Did Aristotle write it? Is it a part of the *Physics* as defined by Aristotle? Is it an *excrescence* on the main plan of the *Physics* and an early work under Platonic influence, as Mr. Ross believes? Is it elementary for tyros, as Mr. Hoffman believes? Which of the versions of Sections 1, 2, and 3 came later or is more authentic?

Mr. Ross in his *Aristotle's Physics* (Oxford, 1936) has given an adequate historical account of the various opinions about the Book by commentators. The above questions, however, may be adequately answered by the use of internal evidence. All indications of the work (terminology, style, thought, arguments, etc.) point to the fact that it is Aristotle's work. The Book is concerned with problems of (a) a first mover not moved by another mover, (b) the togetherness of a mover and the thing moved, (c) the comparability of motions, for motions as a whole do not come under a single genus, and (d) some simple but fundamental and not wholly quantitative aspects of movers in relation to things moved. Clearly, these are problems coming under physics as defined by Aristotle and not under any other science. Is the Book an excrescence or for tyros? The doctrines of a first mover not moved by another, of the togetherness of mover and object moved (motion by contact is presupposed by lines 267b7–9), and of the comparability of motions are not trivial, and tyros would find it very hard to understand Book H. Is it true, as Mr. Ross says, that there is nothing in the contents of this and the first six Books of the *Physics* that implies much departure from the Platonic ways of thinking? One who is familiar with Plato's and Aristotle's position on the four causes, time, place, the infinite, etc., would find it difficult to agree with Mr. Ross. As for the two versions of Sections 1, 2, and 3 of Book H, they are quite close in all respects, although there is a discrepancy in completeness. Perhaps the more complete came later.

I am indebted to Professor John M. Crossett for editing in detail many aspects of this work; to Father Joseph Owens for a number of important philosophical corrections; to Professor Sheldon P. Zitner for his help in the proper choice of added English terms. I am grateful also to my assistants Mrs. Eva Gardebring Christiansen; Mr. and Mrs. Paul Jones; Misses Elizabeth L. Alexander, Mariana F. Alwell, Susan A. Grow, Eleonore A. Spiegel, Judith H. Wallace, and Messrs. Lloyd P. Gerson, Stephen W. Grow, and James R. Holbrook for their secretarial and other assistance.

H. G. A.

Grinnell College

Aristotle's Physics

Summary of the Physics

Book A

1. The first concern in physics is the principles of its objects, and the method will be to proceed from what is better known to us to what is better known by nature. 184a10–b14.
2. Whether one principle exists or many, and in either case, whether movable or immovable. But physics is concerned with movable being, which is evident by induction. 184b15–5a17.
3. Criticism of those who say that all things are one and that this is immovable. 185a17–7a11.
4. Statement and criticism of the doctrines of the physicists. 187a12–8a18.
5. Two of the principles of motion or of change are contraries; and all thinkers are in agreement in principle, but they differ in detail. 188a19–9a10.
6. Contraries do not act on each other but on something else, on a subject, so the principles required in a change are three; and this is evident by an analysis of generation or of change. 189a11–191a22.
7. The three principles solve the problems raised and avoid the errors committed by both those who do away with generation and those who posit it but in terms of inadequate principles. 191a23–2b4.

Book B

1. What nature is, what has a nature, and what exists by nature or according to nature. 192b8–3a9.
2. Nature in things existing by nature is the form, or the matter, but primarily the form. 193a9–b21.
3. Physical bodies are investigated by the mathematician, not qua having a nature, but qua solids with surfaces, lines, and points,

4

and abstracted from motion by thought; but they are investigated by the physicist qua having a nature, and this includes both matter and form, and even final cause. 193b22–4b15.

Book Δ
I: *Place*

1. Discussion of the *difficulties* with respect to the existence and nature of place. 208a27–9a30.
2. Difficulties in regarding place as the matter or the form of a physical body. 209a31–210a13.
3. From the various meanings of "to be in something" it follows that a thing, taken not qua having parts, cannot be in itself, either primarily or accidentally. 210a14–b31.
4. Place is the primary motionless boundary of a containing body. Some attributes that follow. 210b32–2b22.
5. Solution of the *difficulties* stated at the beginning. 212b22–3a11.

II: *Void*

6. Views and arguments of those who assert and those who deny the existence of void. 213a12–b29.
7. The meanings of the term "void". 213b20–4a16.
8. Refutation of the arguments of those who posit the existence of void. 214a16–b11.
9. No void exists as something separate from bodies. 214b12–6b21.
10. No void exists within any body. 216b22–7b28.

III: *Time*

11. Discussion of *difficulties* in believing that time exists. 217b29–8a31.
12. Time is not the sphere of the whole [universe], as some say, nor the motion of it, as others say. 218a31–b20.
13. Time is the number of motion with respect to before and after, and so it is an attribute of motion. 218b21–9b11.
14. Attributes of time. 219b11–223a15.
15. Discussion of the relation of time to the soul and of other problems. 223a16–4a17.

Book E

1. Change is either accidental or essential. 224a21–b26.
2. Essential changes are three in kind, generation, destruction, and motion, and the contrary of generation is destruction. 224b26–5b5.
3. Motions are of three kinds: with respect to quality (alteration), with respect to quantity (increase and decrease), and with respect to place (locomotion); and the contrary of motion is rest. 225b5–6b17.
4. Definitions of being together, being apart, touching, betweenness succession, consecutiveness, and continuity. 226b18–7b2.

12. Refutation of Zeno's four arguments against motion, which falsely assume that time consists of moments and that lines or magnitudes consist of indivisible elements. 239b5–240b7.
13. That which has no parts cannot move (essentially). 240b8–241a26.
14. No infinite change can exist, except a circular locomotion. 241a26–b20.

Book H

1. That which is in motion is moved by something. 241b24–2a19.
2. There is a first mover which is not moved by anything else. 242a19–3a2.
3. The mover and the thing moved are together, i.e., there is nothing between them. 243a3–5b2.
4. Things are altered by sensible objects, and alteration belongs only to things which can be affected by sensible objects. 245b3–8a9.
5. Comparable and incomparable motions. 248a10–9b26.
6. Relations between quantities of force and quantities of motion. 249b27–250b7.

Book Θ

1. Motion always existed and will always exist, and likewise for time, for it is a number of motion. 250b11–2b6.
2. Refutation of objections to eternal motion. 252b7–3a21.
3. There exist things which are sometimes in motion and sometimes at rest. 253a22–4b6.
4. All things essentially in motion are moved by something. 254b7–6a3.
5. The primary mover of a thing essentially in motion is immovable. 256a4–8b9.
6. There exists an eternal immovable mover. 258b10–260a19.
7. Of the kinds of motion, locomotion is the primary. 260a20–1a26.
8. Of the kinds of locomotions, the circular is primary, and it can be continuous and eternal. 261a27–6a9.
9. The eternal primary mover is indivisible, without parts or magnitude, and at the circumference of the universe. 266a10–7b26.

[handwritten margin note: By nature clearer vs. clearer to us]

Book A

1

184a 10 Since understanding and *knowing*[1] in every *inquiry* concerned with things having principles or causes or elements results from the knowledge of these (for we think that we know each thing when we know the first causes and the first principles and have reached the elements),

15 clearly, in the science of nature too we should first try to determine what is the case with regard to the principles.[2]

The natural way to proceed is from what is more known and *clearer* to us to what is by nature *clearer* and more known; for what is known to us and what is known without qualification are not the same.[3] So

20 we should proceed in this manner, namely, from what is less *clear* by nature, though *clearer* to us, to what is by its nature *clearer* and more known. Now the things that are at first plain and *clear* to us are rather mingled, and it is later that their elements and principles become known to those who distinguish them. Consequently, in the case of each thing, we should proceed from its entirety[4] to each of its constituents, for it is

25 the whole that is more known by sensation; and a thing in its entirety,[4]

184b 10 since it includes many constituents as parts, is a kind of a whole. In a sense, a name is related to its formula in the same way, for a name signifies some whole without distinguishing its parts, as in the case of "a circle"; but its definition analyzes the whole into its constituents. Children, too, at first call every *man* "papa" and every woman "mama", but later on they distinguish each of them.[5]

2

15 It is necessary that there be either one principle[1] or many; and if one, then either immovable, as Parmenides and Melissus say,[2] or in motion, as the physicists say—some of the latter asserting that the first principle is *Air*[3] and others that it is *Water*;[4] but if many, then either

8

finite or infinite. If finite, but more than one, then they are two[5] or three
or four[6] or some other number; but if infinite, then they are either
generically one but differ in shape or kind, as Democritus says,[7] or
even contrary.[8]

Also those who inquire into the number of things do so in a similar
way; for they first inquire whether the constituents of things are one or
many, and if many, whether finite or infinite. Thus they inquire whether
the principles or elements are one or many.[9]

Now to inquire whether being is one and immovable is not to inquire
about nature;[10] for just as the geometer has no arguments at all against
one who rejects the principles of geometry, seeing that their discussion
belongs to another science or to a science common to all others,[11] so
too in the case of principles; for if being is only one and is one in this
manner [immovable], no principle exists at all, seeing that a principle
is a principle of some thing or things.[12] Indeed, to inquire whether
being is one in this manner is like arguing against any other paradox
maintained for the sake of argument, such as that of Heraclitus[13] or the
one which might assert that being is one man,[14] or it is like refuting an
eristic argument, such as that of Melissus and that of Parmenides.[15]
(The latter two thinkers assume false premises, and the conclusions they
draw do not follow from the premises; as for Melissus, his argument is
rather crude and presents no problem, for once an absurd premise is
granted, the rest follow, and there is no difficulty at all in this.)

We, on the other hand, make the assumption that things existing by
nature[16] are in motion, either all or some of them; and this is clear by
induction.[17] In addition, we should refute only those conclusions which
are falsely drawn from the principles of the science in question, and no
others. For example, the task of refuting the squaring of the circle by
means of segments belongs to the geometer,[18] but that of refuting the
squaring of the circle by Antiphon's method does not belong to the
geometer.[19] However, since these thinkers discuss problems in physics
even if their subject is not nature, perhaps it is well to go over their
views somewhat; for such inquiry has philosophic value.

The most appropriate starting-point is to raise this question: In what
sense are all things one? for "being" has many senses.[20] Are all things
substances or quantities or qualities; and if substances, are they all one
substance, as, for example, one man or one horse or one soul, or are
they one quality, as, for example, whiteness or hotness or some other
thing of this sort? These alternative answers differ much and cannot all
be true. If, on the one hand, [they say that] all things are substances
and quantities and qualities, then whether these are detached from each
other or not, things will be many.[21] But if [they say that] all things are
qualities or are quantities, then whether substances exist[22] or not, their

statement is absurd, if one is to call the impossible "absurd"; for none of these can exist separately (except substances), since all of them are said of substances as their subjects.

Now Melissus says that being is the *Infinite;* so, it is a quantity, for the infinite exists in quantity.[23] But a substance or a quality or an affection cannot be infinite except in virtue of another attribute, that is, if each of them were at the same time a quantity;[24] for the formula of the infinite[25] uses "quantity" but not "substance" or "quality". So, if being is both a substance and a quantity, then it is two and not one; but if it is only a substance, then neither will it be infinite nor will it have any magnitude, since to have a magnitude it would have to be a quantity.[26]

Next, since the term "one" itself, like the term "being", also has many senses,[27] we should consider in what sense the totality [of things] is *One.*[28] Now to be one is to be (a) the continuous or (b) the indivisible or (c) things whose formula of their essence is the same and one, like what we call "vintage" and "wine".[29]

Accordingly, if (a) the totality is one by being continuous, then the *One* will be many; for the continuous is infinitely divisible.[30] We may add, there is a *difficulty* in the case of the part and the whole, perhaps not with respect to the expressions about them but with respect to the part and the whole themselves, namely, whether the part and the whole are one or many and how they are one or many and if many, how they are many, and the same applies to the parts and the whole if the latter is not continuous;[31] and further, if each part is one with the whole as if undivided from it, then so will the parts be from each other.[32]

Moreover, if (b) the totality is one in the sense of being indivisible, no thing will be a quantity or a quality, and so being will not be infinite, as Melissus says, nor limited, as Parmenides says;[33] for it is the limit that is [34] indivisible and not that which is limited.

Further, if (c) all things are one by having the same formula, like a dress and a garment, then what they are saying is what Heraclitus says; for to be good and to be bad will be the same, and to be not good and to be good, likewise, so that the same thing will be good and not good and a man and a horse. Indeed, what they will be saying is not that things are one but that they are not even one,[35] and that to be such-and-such will be the same as to be so-much.[36]

Even the later ancient thinkers were troubled lest the same thing should turn out to be both one and many. So some of them, like Lyco-phron, omitted the "is", and others changed the form of expression and used, for example, "man grayed" and not "man is gray", "walks" and not "is walking", lest by adding the "is" they should find themselves making what is one to be many, as if "one" and "being" had only one meaning. But beings are many, either in formula (for example, to be

185*b*

white is distinct from to be musical, even if the same thing should turn out to be both white and musical; so the one may be many)[37] or by
division (like the whole and its parts). And in the latter cases they are even raising *difficulties* and admitting that the one is many, as if the same thing could not be one and also many (that is, one and many but not as opposites);[38] for what is one may be potentially one or actually one.

3

If we proceed in this manner, then, it appears that it is impossible for all things to be one, and the statements[1] from which these thinkers establish their doctrine are not difficult to refute. Both Melissus and Parmenides give eristic proofs, since the premises they introduce are false and the conclusions they draw do not follow from the premises; and in the case of Melissus, his argument is rather crude and presents no problem, for once something[2] absurd is granted, the rest follows, and there is no difficulty at all in this.

Clearly, Melissus draws conclusions falsely; for he thinks that from "every generated thing has a beginning" he can conclude "that which has not been generated has no beginning".[3] Then this too is absurd, namely, to grant a beginning to everything, but not to time,[4] and a beginning not [only] to an unqualified generation but also to an alteration, as if a change cannot occur all at once.[5]

Again, why is a thing immovable, if it is one? Like the part (e.g., a part of water) which is one and moves in itself, why cannot the whole too move?[6] Moreover, why should alteration be impossible? Further, being cannot be one in kind, although it may be one in that [e.g., in matter] of which things consist[7] (and even some physicists speak of things as being one in the latter sense,[8] but not in the former); for a man and a horse are distinct in species, and two contraries are distinct in species also.

The way of arguing against Parmenides, too, is the same, though other ways which are proper to him may also be used against him; and one may refute him by saying that this premise is false or that conclusion does not follow from the premises. Insofar as he assumes "being" to have a single meaning when it has many, he posits something false.[9] As for his conclusion not following from the premises, if "white" has one meaning and if only whites are posited, still there will be many whites and not one; for then neither by continuity nor in formula will there be one white. For to be white and to be that which receives whiteness will be distinct, even if nothing apart from the white will exist; for the white and that to which it belongs are distinct not qua being separate but in essence.[10] Yet Parmenides did not perceive this.

Now Parmenides must grant not only that "being" signifies one thing, of whatever it might be predicated, but also that it signifies *just*[11] a being and what is *just* one.[12] For an attribute is predicated of some sub-
35
ject, and so that of which it is an attribute, being distinct from being,
186*b*
would not be [a being]; and then a nonbeing would exist [be a being]. Certainly, then, *just* being could not belong to something else, for the latter would not be a being unless "being" had many senses, in which case each might be some kind of being; but it was assumed that "being" has [only] one meaning.

5
If, on the other hand, *just* being is not an attribute of anything, but something else is an attribute of it, how does "*just* being" signify a be-ing rather than a nonbeing? For if *just* being were to be itself and also white, the essence of white would still not be a *just* being (for even being could not be an attribute of white, since what is not a *just* being is not a being), and so it would be a nonbeing, and not in a qualified sense but
10
entirely a nonbeing. So a *just* being would be a nonbeing, for it would be true to say "*just* being is white", and "white" was just shown to sig-nify a nonbeing. So if "white" too were to signify a *just* being, then "being" would have many senses.[13]

Moreover, neither would "being" have a magnitude, if it were a *just* being, for it would then be distinct in essence from its two parts.[14]
15
That a *just* being will be divisible into another [kind of] *just* being is also evident from the formula. For example, if a man is a *just* being, also an animal and two-footedness must be *just* beings.[15] For if not, they will be attributes, and either in the man or in some other subject. But this is impossible; for an attribute is said to be either that which may or may
20
not belong [to a subject], or that in whose formula is present the thing of which it is an attribute or that to which belongs the formula of the thing of which it is an attribute. For example, in the case of sitting, it is separable from a man,[16] while snubness has the formula of the nose to which snubness is said to belong as an attribute. Further, in the case of the parts which are present in the formula [of a thing] or of which that formula consists, the formula of the whole [of the thing] is not
25
present in the formula of each part; for example, the formula of a man is not in that of two-footedness, and that of a white man is not in that of the white. Accordingly, if this is so and if two-footedness is an attri-bute of the man, then two-footedness must be separable from the man and so a man might not be two-footed; or else, the formula of the man
30
will be present in the formula of two-footedness, which is impossible, for the converse is the case. If, however, two-footedness and animality were attributes of some other thing and each of them were not a *just* being,

then also the man would be an attribute of some other thing.[17] But let us grant (a) that *just* being is not an attribute of anything and (b) that if both of these two are said of something, also each of them and also the composite of the two will be said of it. Then the entire thing[18] [will be] composed of indivisibles.[19]

Some thinkers gave in to both arguments; so to meet (a) the argument that all things will be one if "being" has just one meaning, they posited that nonbeing exists,[20] and to meet (b) the argument proceeding from the dichotomy, they posited *indivisible* magnitudes.[21]

It is also evident that it is not true to say that nonbeing will not exist if "being" has just one meaning and contradictions are impossible; for nothing prevents nonbeing from being a qualified nonbeing and not an unqualified nonbeing.[22]

As for the statement that all things will be one if nothing else exists besides being itself, it is certainly absurd. For who would learn what being itself is if *just* being were not a kind of a thing[23] And if this is so, then, as we said, nothing prevents things from being many.

It is clear, then, that being cannot be one in the manner it is claimed to be.

4

According to the statements of the physicists[1] there are two ways of proceeding [from principles].

Some of them posit being to be one underlying body—either one of the three[2] or something else which is denser than fire but thinner than air[3]—and generate the rest, making them many [in kind] by means of *Density* and *Rarity*,[4] which are contraries or which are excess and deficiency, if taken universally; and these are like Plato's *Great* and *Small*, except that he posits these as matter and the *One* as form,[5] while they posit the *One* as the underlying matter but the contraries as differentiae or forms.

Others say that things come out from the *One*, in which the contraries are present. And this is how Anaximander speaks, and also those who say that what exists is one and many, like Empedocles and Anaxagoras, for these too say that it is from the *Blend*[6] that the rest are generated by segregation. However, these thinkers differ from each other thus: One[7] of them posits a cycle of such changes, but the other[8] posits just one series of change; and one[9] of them posits an infinite number of homogeneous things and pairs of contraries, while the other posits only the so-called "elements".[10] Thus, Anaxagoras seems to regard the principles as infinite because he believes the common doctrine of the physicists, that no thing is generated from nonbeing, to be true, for it is because of this that these thinkers use the expression "all things were together"; and some regard a generation of such-and-such a thing as being an alteration, while others regard it as being a combination or a separation.[11] Moreover, from the fact that one of two contraries comes to be from the other, these thinkers[12] conclude that the first contrary must have existed before; for, since that which is generated must be generated either from being or from nonbeing and generation from nonbeing is impossible (and all physicists are in agreement concerning this doctrine), they regard the other alternative as immediately following of necessity, namely, that things are generated from what are already present but are not sensible to us because of the smallness of their volume. And on account of this they say that everything is blended in everything because they observe everything coming to be from everything and that the different appearance and the different name given to each arises from that thing in the blend of innumerable things which exceeds all the others because of the great number of its particles; for they[12] say that nothing in its entirety is purely white or black or sweet or flesh or bone but that the nature of the thing is thought to be that which the thing has most.

Now if the infinite qua infinite is unknowable, then the infinite with respect to plurality or with respect to magnitude is an unknowable quantity, while the infinite in kind is an unknowable quality. Thus, if the principles are infinite with respect to plurality and in kind, that which is composed of them cannot be understood; for we believe that it is in this manner that we understand a composite, namely, when we understand what its parts are and how many they are.[13]

Again, if each part of a thing can be of any size in the direction of greatness and of smallness,[14] then[15] necessarily the thing itself can be of any size likewise (by "a part" I mean that which is present and into which the whole is divisible).[16] So if an animal or a plant cannot be of any size in the direction of greatness and of smallness, it is evident that neither can any part of it be of any size likewise (or else the whole would be of any size likewise). But flesh and bone and the like are parts of an animal, and fruits are parts of plants; clearly, then, it is impossible for flesh or bone or some other part to be of any size, whether in the direction of greatness or of smallness.[17]

Again, if all such things are present in each other and are not generable but are separable as constituents and if a thing is named after that part which exceeds the other parts in the thing and if any thing may come to be from any other thing (for example, water from flesh or flesh from water, by segregation), then, since every finite body is exhausted by taking away from it repeatedly an [equal] finite magnitude,[18] it is

evident that not every thing can exist in every other thing. For if flesh
be taken away from water and if this be done again from what remains
30   even if what is taken away is always less, still it will not be smaller than
some magnitude. Hence, if this process of separation comes to a stop,
not every thing will be in every other thing (for there will be no flesh in
the remaining water); but if it does not come to a stop but the removal
of flesh continues indefinitely, there will be an infinite number of equal
magnitudes in a finite magnitude—which is impossible.[19]

35   We may also add this: If every body decreases in magnitude when
something is taken away from it and the quantity of flesh is bounded
188a   both in greatness and in smallness, it is evident that no body can be taken
out of the least amount of flesh; for otherwise there would be flesh less
than the least amount of it. And besides, in [each of] the infinite bodies
there would already be infinite flesh and blood and brain, not[20] separate
from each other but nevertheless existing, and each of them would be
5   infinite; and this is unreasonable.

The statement that separation will never take place is made without
being understood, but it is right; for the *attributes* are inseparable. If
colors and possessions were in a blend, then when separated each would
be, for example, a whiteness or health, but neither would each be something else also nor would it be predicated of a subject.[21] So *Intelligence*
10   would be absurd in seeking to do the impossible, that is, if it [*Intelligence*] wishes to separate these but cannot do so[22] according to quantity
or to quality; it can do so neither according to quantity, if there is no
least magnitude,[23] nor according to quality, since *attributes* are inseparable.

Nor is Anaxagoras right in his view concerning the generation of
homogeneous bodies. There is a sense in which mud is divisible into
15   mud, but there is another sense in which it is not; and the manner in
which bricks come from or exist in a house, or a house comes from or
consists of bricks, is not similar to that in which water and air come from
or consist of each other.[24] Also, it is better to posit a smaller or a finite
number of principles, as Empedocles does.[25]

5

All thinkers posit contraries as principles, e.g., (a) those who say that
20   the universe is one and motionless (even Parmenides posits the *Hot* and
the *Cold* as principles[1] and calls them *"Fire"* and *"Earth"*) and (b) those
who speak of the *Rare* and the *Dense* and (c) Democritus, who posits
the *Solid*[2] and the *Void*, calling them *"Being"* and *"Nonbeing"*, respectively, and who uses [as differentiae] *Position, Shape,* and *Order* as

25 genera of contraries (for example, in the case of position, these are *up* and *down,* and also *in front* and *behind;* but in the case of shape, they are the *angular* and the *non-angular,* and also the *straight* and the *circular*).

It is clear, then, that in a sense[3] all thinkers posit contraries as principles, and with good reason; for (a) neither must one principle be composed of another principle, (b) nor should they be composed of other things but the other things should be composed of them. Now the primary[4] contraries possess both these attributes: (b) They are not com-
30 posed of other things because they are primary, and (a) neither of them is composed of the other because they are contraries. However, we should attend to an argument as well in order to see how this turns out to be the case.

First we must grant that no thing by nature acts on, or is acted on by, any other chance thing, nor does any thing come to be from any other [chance] thing, unless one grants that this takes place in virtue of
35 of an attribute.[5] For how could the white come to be from the musical unless the musical were an accident of the not-white or the black? But the white does come to be from the nonwhite, not from any nonwhite[6]
188*b* but from black or some intermediate color; and the musical comes to be from the nonmusical, not from any nonmusical but from the unmusical[7] or something between the musical and the unmusical, if there is such.

Nor again does any thing, when destroyed, change into any chance thing. For example, the white is destroyed not into the musical,[8] unless
5 it be in virtue of an attribute, but into the nonwhite, not into any chance nonwhite but into black or some other intermediate color; and the musical is similarly destroyed into the nonmusical, not into any chance nonmusical but into the unmusical or some intermediate between the two, if there is such.

It is likewise with all other cases, since the same formula applies even
10 to things which are not simple but composite; but we fail to notice this happening because no names have been given to the opposite dispositions. For the harmonious must come to be from the inharmonious,[9] and the inharmonious, from the harmonious; and the harmonious must be destroyed into something which is not harmonious, not into any chance
15 thing but into that which is opposed[10] to the harmonious. It makes no difference whether we speak of harmony or of order or of composition, for evidently it is the same formula which applies to them. Again, the generation of a house and of a statue and of any other thing takes place in a similar way. For a house is generated from objects which exist not in composition but are divided in a certain way, and likewise for a statue
20 or anything that has been shaped from shapelessness;[11] and what results in each of these are order in one case and a composition in the other.

If, then, all this is true, every thing that is generated or destroyed is so from or to a contrary or an intermediate. As for the intermediates, they are composed of contraries;[12] the other colors, for example, are composed

25   of white and black. Thus every thing which is generated by nature is a contrary or composed of contraries.

Up to this point most of the other thinkers were quite close in following this line of thinking, as we said before; for they all said that the elements, also called "principles" by them, are contraries, as if compelled by

30   truth itself even if they gave no reason. However, they differed from each other thus: Some of them used prior[13] contraries, while others used posterior, and some used contraries more known in formula, while others used contraries more known according to sensation; for some posited as causes of generation the *Hot* and the *Cold*, others, the *Moist* and the *Dry*, while others posited the *Odd* and the *Even*, and still others, *Strife*

35   and *Friendship*;[14] and these differ from each other in the way stated. So the principles which they used are in one way the same but in another distinct. They are distinct in the manner in which most thinkers took

189*a*   them to be; but they are the same insofar as they are analogous, for they are taken from the same two sets of contraries, some of them being wider while others narrower in extent.[15] In this way, then, they spoke of them in the same and also in a distinct manner, some in a worse and others in a better way,[16] and, as we said, some posited them as more

5   known according to formula while others as more known according to sensation. For the universal is known according to formula but the individual according to sensation, since the formula is of the universal but sensation is of the part; for example, contrary principles according to formula are the *Great* and the *Small*,[17] those according to sensation are the *Dense* and the *Rare*.[18]

10   It is evident, then, that the principles should be contraries.

6

Next, we should consider whether the principles are two or three or more than three.

There cannot be just one principle, since there cannot be just one contrary,[1] nor can the principles be infinite, since otherwise being will not be *knowable*.[2] Also, in every genus there is just one contrariety, and "substance"[3] is one genus. Besides, it is possible for things to be gener-

15   ated from a finite number of principles; and it is better if they come to be from a finite number, as Empedocles[4] says, than from an infinite number (for Empedocles thinks that from his finite principles he can give an account of all that Anaxagoras can from his infinite principles). Again,

some contraries are prior to others,[5] and some come to be from others, as in the case of the sweet and bitter and of the white and black, but the principles must always remain.[6] So it is clear from all these arguments that the principles are neither one nor infinite.

Since the principles, then, are finite, there is some reason in positing them to be not only two; for one might raise the problem as to how density can by nature act on rarity, or rarity on density, so as to produce something.[7] The problem is similar in the case of any pair of contraries; for it is not *Strife* that *Friendship* brings together and makes something out of, nor does *Strife* make something out of *Friendship*, but both act on a third and distinct object.[8] Some thinkers use even more such objects from which they construct the nature of things.[9]

In addition to the above, if no nature distinct from the contraries is assumed, one might also raise another *difficulty*, for among things, we observe no contrary as being a substance.[10] Now a principle should not be a predicate of any subject, since there would then be a principle of a principle; for the subject is a principle and is thought to be prior to what is a predicate of it.[11] Moreover, we maintain that no substance is contrary to a substance.[12] So how can there be a substance which is composed of nonsubstances? Or, how can a nonsubstance be prior to a substance?[13]

In view of all this, if we were to grant as true both the previous statement[14] and this [argument],[15] then, to preserve both, it would be necessary for us to assume a third [principle], like the one held by those who say that the universe is of one nature, i.e., of water or fire[16] or an intermediate between them. This principle seems to be rather an intermediate; for fire and earth and air and water are already composites with contraries.[17] And on account of this, those who posit as an underlying subject something distinct from these four elements do so not without good reason. Other thinkers choose air from the four elements; for of these, air has sensible differences to the least degree. Then water comes next. Yet all these thinkers regard this one principle [or, the *One*] as taking on a shape by means of contraries, i.e., by *Density* and *Rarity,* and in varying degrees. Now such contraries, considered universally, are clearly excess and deficiency, as stated previously.[18] And the doctrine that the *One*[19] and *Excess* and *Deficiency* are principles of things, we may add, seems to be an old one, except that it is not stated in the same manner; for the early thinkers said that the two [contraries] act but the *One* is acted upon, whereas some of the later thinkers[20] stated rather the contrary, namely, that the *One* acts while the two [contraries] are acted upon.

From a consideration of these and other such arguments, then, it would seem that there is some reason in maintaining that the elements are three,[21] as we said before; but there is no reason in maintaining that they are more than three, for one element is sufficient [as a subject] to be acted upon. If with four [elements] there are two contrarieties, a distinct intermediate nature will be needed for each contrariety; and if, being two, they[22] can generate[23] from each other, one of the two contrarieties will be superfluous.[24] And along with this, the primary contrarieties cannot be many; for "substance" is a single genus of being, so the principles can differ in priority and posteriority and not in genus (for in a single genus there can be only one contrariety, and all other contrarieties [in that genus] are thought to be referred to one).[25]

It is evident, then, that there can be neither only one nor more than two or three elements; but, as we said before, there is much *difficulty* as to whether there are two or three.

7

We shall now give our own account by first going over generation universally, for in proceeding according to nature we should first investigate what is common and then what is proper in each case.[1]

We say that something comes to be[2] from something else or that some one thing is coming to be from some other thing by speaking either of simple or of composite things.[3] By this I mean the following: (a) A man becomes musical or the not-musical becomes musical, and (b) the not-musical man becomes a musical man. In (a), I call "simple" the man or the not-musical, which is becoming something else, and also the musical, which is what the former [the man or the musical] becomes; and in (b), when we say that the not-musical man becomes a musical man, we call "composite" both the thing generated and that which is in the process of becoming.[4]

Now of these, in some cases we say not only "A becomes B" but also "B comes to be from A", as in "the musical comes to be from the not-musical"; but we do not speak likewise in all cases, for we do not say "the musical came to be from the man" but "the man became musical".

Of simple things that come to be something, some of them persist throughout the generation but others do not. For when a man becomes musical, he persists during the generation and is still a man [at the end of it], but the not-musical or the unmusical does not so persist, whether as a simple thing or when combined with the subject.[5]

With these distinctions granted, then from all things which are being generated one may gather this, if he is to attend carefully to the manner of our statement—that there must always be something which underlies that which is in the process of becoming and that this, even if numerically one,[6] in kind[7] at least is not one (and by "in kind"[7] I mean the same thing as by "in formula") for "to be a man" and "to be unmusical" do not have the same meaning). And one part of that which is being generated persists but the other does not, that is, what is not an opposite persists[8] (for the man persists) but the musical[9] or the unmusical does not, and neither does the composite persist, i.e., the unmusical man.[10]

We say "B comes to be from A" rather than "A becomes B" of things which do not persist, i.e., we say "the musical is generated from the unmusical" but not "the musical is generated from the man"; but occasionally we do likewise also of things which persist, for we say "a statue comes to be from bronze" but not "bronze becomes a statue".[11] As for the generation from the opposite which does not persist, it is stated in both ways: We say both "B comes to be from A" and "A becomes B", for we say both "the musical comes to be from the unmusical" and "the unmusical becomes musical"; and in view of this, we do likewise in the case of the composite, for we say both "from being an unmusical man he becomes musical" and "the unmusical man becomes musical".

Now "becoming" has many senses: (a) In certain cases a thing is said to become a *this* in a qualified sense, while (b) a becoming without qualification exists only of substances.[12] And it is evident that in the former cases something underlies that which is in the process of generation; for in the generation of some quantity or some quality or some relation or sometime or somewhere, there is some underlying subject, because only a substance is not said of [predicated of] some other underlying subject whereas all others are said of substances. However, it will become evident on further examination that also substances and all other unqualified beings[13] are generated from some underlying subject,[14] for there is always some underlying subject from which the thing generated comes to be, e.g., plants and animals from seeds.[15]

Things in the process of generation without specification may be generated by the changing of shape, as a statue from bronze; or by addition, like things which increase; or by the removal of something, like the statue *Hermes* from stone; or by composition, like a house; or by alteration, like things which alter with respect to their matter. It is evident that all things which are being generated in this manner are generated from an underlying subject. So it is clear from what has been said that the thing in generation is always a composite, and there is that [say, A] which is generated, and what comes to be that [i.e., A] is something else, and this in two senses, either the subject or the opposite. By "the opposite" I mean, for example, the unmusical; by "the subject" I mean the man; and the shapelessness and the formlessness and the disorder are opposites, while the bronze and the stone and the gold are underlying subjects.[16]

Thus if, of things by nature, there are causes or principles[17] of which those things are composed primarily and from which they come to be not accidentally, but come to be what each of them is called according to its *substance,* then everything which is generated is generated from a subject and a *form;* for the musical man is composed, in a sense, of a man and the musical, since one would be analyzing the formula [of the musical man][18] by giving a formula of each of these two. Clearly, then, things in generation come to be from these [causes or principles].

Now the subject is in number one but in kind two;[19] for a man or gold or matter in general can be numbered, for it is rather this [the subject] which is a *this,* and it is not as from an attribute that the thing in generation comes to be from this, but what is an attribute is the privation or the contrary; and the form is one, as in the case of order or music or some other such predicate. So in a sense the principles may be spoken of as being two, but in another sense as being three;[20] and they may also be spoken of as being the contraries,[21] for example, if one were to say that they are the musical and the unmusical or the hot and the cold or the harmonious and the inharmonious; but in another sense they may not be so spoken of, for the contraries cannot be acted upon by each other. And this problem[22] is solved because there is a subject which is distinct [from the contraries], for it is not a contrary. So in some sense the principles are not more than the contraries but are two in number, so to speak; yet on the other hand, they are not entirely two but are three because in each of them there is a distinction in essence;[23] for the essence of a man is distinct from the essence of the unmusical,[24] and the essence of the unshaped is distinct from that of bronze.

We have stated, then, the number of the principles concerning the generation of physical objects and how they are so many, and it is clear that there must be something which underlies the contraries and that the contraries are two. Yet in another sense this is not necessary, for one of the contraries is sufficient to produce the change by its absence or presence.

As for the underlying nature,[25] it is *knowable* by analogy. Thus, as bronze is to the statue or the wood is to the bed or the matter or the *formless* object prior to receiving a *form* is to that which has a *form,* so is this [underlying nature] to a substance or to a *this* or to being. This then is one of the principles, though it is not one nor a being in the manner of a *this;* another [principle] is the formula; then there is the contrary of the latter, and this is the privation.

In what sense these [principles] are two and in what sense more than two has been stated above. First it was stated that only the contraries are principles, then it was stated that there must be something else, an underlying subject, and so the principles must be three. From the pre-

ceding statements it is evident how the contraries differ, how the principles are related to each other, and what the underlying subject is. As
to whether it is the form or the underlying subject that is a substance,
this is not yet clear.[26] But that the principles are three and how they
are three and what their manner of existence is, this is clear.

Concerning the number of the principles and what they are, then, let
the above be our investigation.

20

8

We will now proceed to state that the *difficulty* of the early thinkers,
too, is solved only in this manner.

In seeking the truth and the nature of things from the philosophical
point of view, the first thinkers, as if led astray by inexperience, were
misled into another way of thinking by maintaining the following: No
thing can be generated or be destroyed because a thing must be generated either from being or from nonbeing; but both of these are impossible, for being cannot become something since it already exists, and a
thing generated cannot come to be from nonbeing since there must be
some underlying subject [from which it is to be generated]. And
exaggerating the consequences in this manner, they concluded by saying
that there is no plurality of things, but that only *Being* itself exists. This
is the doctrine they adopted, then, and for the *reasons* stated.

Our position, however, is that, in one way, the expressions "to be
generated from being or from nonbeing" or "nonbeing or being acts upon
or is acted upon by something, or becomes a *this*, whatever this[1] may
be" do not differ from "a doctor acts upon or is acted upon by something"
or "from a doctor something else is or comes to be"; hence, since each of
these expressions has two senses, it is clear that also each of the expressions "from being [or nonbeing]" and "being [or nonbeing] acts upon
or is acted upon" has two senses. Thus, the doctor builds [a house] not
qua a doctor but qua a builder, and he becomes grey-haired not qua a
doctor but qua black-haired; but he heals or becomes a nondoctor qua
a doctor. So since, in saying "a doctor acts or is acted upon by something,
or from a doctor he becomes something else", we do so mainly when it
is qua a doctor that he acts upon or is acted upon by something or that
he becomes something else; it is clear that also "to become something
from nonbeing" means this, namely, to become something qua not-
being.[2]   which distinction?

It is the failure to make this distinction that led those thinkers astray,
and through their ignorance of this they added so much more as to
think that nothing else is generated or exists [besides *Being*], thus doing
away with every [kind of] generation. Now we too maintain, as they do,

25

30

35

191*b*

5

10

that nothing is generated from unqualified nonbeing,[3] yet we do maintain that generation from nonbeing in a qualified sense exists, namely,
15   with respect to an attribute;[4] for from the privation, which in itself is a
not-being, something which did not exist is generated. Such generation
from nonbeing, of course, is surprising and is thought to be impossible.
In the same way, we maintain that being is not generated from being,
except with respect to an attribute; so this generation too takes place in
20   the same manner, as if an animal were to be generated from an animal,
or an animal of one kind from an animal of another kind, i.e., if a dog
were to come to be from a horse. For the dog would then come to be not
only from an animal of another kind, but also from an animal, but not
qua an animal since this is already there.[5] But if an object is to become
an animal not with respect to an attribute, then it will do so not from
an animal,[6] and if it is to become a being, then it will do so not from
25   being, nor from nonbeing,[7] since we have stated that "from nonbeing"
means qua not-being. And we may add here that [by this] we do not
reject the truth of "everything either is or is not"[8] — p 2.1

This then is one way [of solving the difficulty]; but there is another,
in view of the fact that we may speak of things with respect to their
potentiality as well as with respect to their *actuality,* and we have settled
this elsewhere with greater accuracy.[9]
30   As we said, then, the difficulties through which some thinkers are compelled to reject some of the things which we maintain are now solved;
for it was because of these [*difficulties*] that earlier thinkers also deviated
so much from the path which leads to the belief in generation, destruction, and change in general. If they had perceived this [underlying]
nature, this would have released them from all their ignorance.

9

35   Other thinkers,[1] too, have perceived this nature, but not adequately.
For, in the first place, they agree that there is unqualified generation
192a   from nonbeing, thus granting the statement of Parmenides as being
right;[2] secondly, it appears to them that if this nature is numerically one,
then it must be also one potentially,[3] and this makes the greatest difference.
Now we maintain that matter is distinct from privation and that one
5   of these, matter, is nonbeing with respect to an attribute but privation is
nonbeing in itself,[4] and also that matter is in some way near to a substance but privation is in no way such.[5]
These thinkers, on the other hand, maintain that the *Great* and the
Small are alike nonbeing, whether these two are taken together as one

or each is taken separately.[6] And so they posit their triad in a manner which is entirely distinct from ours.[7] Thus, they have gone so far as to perceive the need of some underlying nature, but they posit this as being one; for even if someone [Plato] posits the *Dyad*, calling it "the *Great and Small*", he nevertheless does the same since he overlooks the other [nature].[8]

Now in things which are being generated, one of these [two natures] is an underlying joint cause with a *form*,[9] being like a mother, so to speak;[10] but the other part of the contrariety might often be imagined, by one who would belittle it, as not existing at all. For, as there exists an object[11] which is divine and good and something to strive after, we maintain that one of the principles is contrary to it, but that the other [principle],[12] in virtue of its nature, by nature strives after and desires that object. According to the doctrine of these thinkers, on the other hand, what results is that the contrary desires its own destruction.[13] Yet neither would the form strive after itself, because it does not lack it, nor does it strive after the contrary, for contraries are destructive of each other. Now this [principle] is matter, and it is like the female which desires the male and the ugly which desires the beautiful, but it is not by itself that the ugly or the female does this,[14] since these are only attributes.

In one way, this [principle] is destroyed or is generated, but in another way it is not. For, as that[15] which is in something [in the matter], it is this which in itself is being destroyed, since it is the privation in it [in the matter] that is being destroyed; but as that which exists in virtue of its potentiality,[16] this is not being destroyed in itself but is necessarily indestructible and ungenerable.[17] For (a) if the latter were to be generated, it would have to be generated from something else which is present and must be a primary underlying subject; yet its nature is to be just this, so it would then be existing prior to its generation[18] (for by "matter" here we mean the primary underlying subject in a thing, from which [matter], as something present but not as an attribute, something else is generated). And (b) if it were to be destroyed, it would ultimately arrive at this very thing, so it would then be destroyed prior to its destruction.[19]

Concerning the principle with respect to form, whether it is one or many and what it is or what they are, its accurate determination is a task belonging to first philosophy and will be laid aside till then;[20] but as regards the natural and destructible forms, we shall consider them in this treatise later.[21]

That there are principles, what these are, and how many they are, let the above as given so far be our account of them. Next, let us proceed from another starting-point.

"by nature."

Book **B**

1

¹⁹²*b* Of things, some exist by nature, others through other causes. Animals
10 and their parts exist by nature, and so do plants and the simple bodies,
for example, earth, fire, air, and water; for we say[1] that these and other
such exist by nature. Now all the things mentioned appear to differ
from things which are composed not by nature. All things existing by
nature appear to have in themselves a principle of motion[2] and of stand-
15 still,[3] whether with respect to place or increase or decrease or alteration.[4] But a bed or a garment or a thing in some other similar genus,[5]
insofar as each of them is called by a similar predicate and in virtue of
existing by art, has no natural tendency in itself for changing; but
20 insofar as it happens to be made of stone or earth or to be a composite
of these, it has such a tendency and only to that extent.[6] So nature is a
principle and a cause of being moved or of rest in the thing to which it
belongs primarily[7] and in virtue of that thing, but not accidentally. I
say "not accidentally" in view of the fact that the same man may cause
25 himself to become healthy by being a doctor; however, it is not in virtue
of becoming healthy that he has the medical art, but it is an accident
that the same man is both a doctor and becoming healthy,[8] and on account of this, the one is at times separate from the other.[9] Similarly, each
of the other things produced has in itself no principle of producing, but
in certain cases [in most cases] such a principle is in another thing or is
30 outside of the thing produced, as in the case of a house and other manufactured products,[10] while in the remaining cases it is in the thing itself
but not in virtue of that thing, that is, whenever it is an accident in the
thing that causes the production in it.[11]
We have stated, then, what nature is. Things which have such a
principle are said to have a nature; and they are all substances, for
35 each of them is a subject, and nature exists always in a subject.[12] And
they and whatever essentially belongs to them are said to exist according to nature, as, for example, the upward locomotion of fire; for this

193a [locomotion] is not nature, nor does it have a nature, but it exists by nature or according to nature.[13]

We have stated, then, what nature is and what exists by nature and[14] according to nature. As far as trying to prove that nature exists, this would be ridiculous, for it is evident that there are many such things; and to try to prove what is evident through what is not evident is a mark of a man who cannot *judge* what is known through itself from what is known not through itself.[15] That this can take place is clear; for a man born blind may form syllogisms concerning colors, but such a man must be using mere names without conceiving the corresponding things.[16]

Some think that the nature or *substance* of a thing existing by nature is the first[17] constituent which is in the thing and which in itself is without shape, like wood in the case of a bed or bronze in a bronze statue. (According to Antiphon, a sign of this is the fact that if one plants a bed and the moistened wood acquires the power of sending up a shoot, what will result is not a bed but wood, thus showing that the arrangement of the parts according to custom or art belongs to the object planted by accident, but that the substance is that which persists while it is acted upon continuously.) And if each of these is also related to another object in the same way, say bronze and gold to water, bones and wood to earth, and similarly with any others, then it is that other object which is the nature and the *substance* of those things. It is in view of this that some say that the nature[18] of all things is earth; others, that it is fire; others, air; others, water; others, some of these; and others, all of them. For whatever each thinker believed to be of this sort, whether only one object or more than one,[19] he posited this or these as being all that is substance, but all other things as being affections or possessions or dispositions of substances, and also this or these as being eternal (for they said that there is no change from one of them to something else), but the other things [he posited] as being in generation and destruction a countless number of times.

In one way, then, nature is said to be the first underlying matter in things which have in themselves a principle of motion or of change, but in another it is said to be the *shape* or form according to formula;[20] for just as we call "art" that[21] which exists in virtue of art[22] and is artistic,[23] so we call "nature" that which exists in virtue of nature and is natural.[24] Neither in the former case would we say that a thing has something in virtue of art[25] or that there is art[26] if the thing is only potentially a bed but has not yet the form of a bed, nor is it so in things which are *composites* by nature; for that which is potentially flesh or bone has not yet its nature[27] or does not yet exist by nature until it acquires the form according to the formula by which [form] we state what flesh or bone is when we define it. Thus, in another way, the nature of things which have in themselves a principle of motion would be the *shape* or form, which does not exist separately from the thing except according to formula.[28] As for the *composite* of the two, e.g., a man, this is not nature, but [we say] it exists by nature.

Indeed, the form is a nature to a higher degree than the matter; for each thing receives a name when it exists in actuality rather than when it exists potentially.[29] Moreover, it is from a man that a man is generated, but a bed is not generated from a bed (and in view of this they say that nature is not the shape but the wood, since, if it buds, what is generated is wood and not a bed); so if in the latter case it is the art,[30] in the former too it is the form that should be nature, for it is from a man that a man is generated.[31] Again, when we speak of nature as being a generation, this is a process toward nature [as a form]; for the term "nature" as signifying a process is not like the term "doctoring". The latter term signifies a process toward health, not toward the art of doctoring, for doctoring which begins from the art of doctoring cannot be a process toward the art of doctoring; but nature [as a process] is not related to nature [as a form] in the same way, for from something the growing object proceeds to something or grows into something. Into what does it grow? Not into that from which it begins but into that toward which it proceeds. Thus it is the *form* that is nature.[32] "*Form*" or "nature", it may be added, has two senses, for privation, too, is in a way a form;[33] but whether there is a privation or a contrary in an unqualified generation or not must be considered later.[34]

2

Having distinguished the various senses of "nature", we should next investigate how the mathematician and the physicist differ with respect to their objects, for physical bodies have also surfaces and solids and lengths and points, and these are the concern of the mathematician.[1] Moreover, is astronomy a distinct science or a part of physics?[2] For it is absurd that the physicist[3] should understand what the Sun or the Moon is but not what their essential attributes are, not to mention the fact that those who are concerned with nature appear to be discussing the shape of the Moon and of the Sun and to be raising the problem of whether the Earth and the universe are spherical or not.

Now the mathematician, too, is concerned with these, but not insofar as each is a limit of a physical body; nor does he investigate attributes qua existing in such bodies. That is why he separates them, for in thought they are separable from motion; and it makes no difference, nor does any falsity occur in separating them [in thought].[4] Those who

194*a* posit Ideas, too, are doing the same but are unaware of it; for they are separating the physical objects[5][from motion], although these are less separable than the mathematical objects. This becomes clear if one tries to state the definitions in each [science], both of the subjects and of their attributes. For oddness and evenness and straightness and curva-

5 ture, and also a number and a line and a figure, will each be defined without reference to motion; but not so in the case of flesh and bone and a man, for these are defined like a snub nose and not like curva-ture.[6] This is also clear in those parts of mathematics which are more physical, such as optics and harmonics and astronomy, for these are related to geometry in a somewhat converse manner. On the one hand,

10 geometry is concerned with physical lines but not qua physical;[7] on the other, optics is concerned with mathematical lines not qua mathe-matical but qua physical.[8]

Since we speak of nature in two ways, as form as well as matter, we should investigate the whatness [of the objects of physics] as we would the whatness of snubness. Such objects, then, should be investigated

15 neither without matter nor with respect to matter [alone].[9] With regard to this we might also raise another problem. Since there are two natures, with which of them should the physicist be concerned? Or should he be concerned with that which has both natures? Of course, if with both natures, then also with each of the two natures. So should the same science be concerned with both natures, or one science with one and another with the other?

If we turn our attention to the ancients, physics would seem to be

20 concerned with matter, for even Empedocles and Democritus touched upon form or essence only slightly.[10] But if art imitates nature and the same science should understand the form and the matter to some extent (for example, the doctor should understand health, and also bile and phlegm in which health exists; the builder should likewise understand

25 the form of the house, and also the matter, namely, bricks and wooden materials; and similarly in each of the other arts), it should be the con-cern of physics, too, to know both natures.[11]

Moreover, it belongs to the same science to be concerned with the final cause or the end and also with whatever is needed for the sake of the final cause or the end. But nature is [also] an end and a final cause;

30 for if, in that which is in continuous motion, there is some end of that motion, this [end] is the last and the final cause.[12] And it is in view of this that the poet was carried away when he made the ridiculous state-ment "he has an end [death], for the sake of which he was born". For not every last thing tends to be an end, but only the best, seeing that in the case of the arts, too, some of them just make the matter but others

35 make it serviceable and that we use things as if they exist all for our
own sake (since in a certain sense, we too are an end, for "final cause"
194*b* has two senses, as we stated in *"On Philosophy"*[13]). Indeed, there are
two arts which rule over matter and have knowledge of it—the art
which is concerned with the use of it and the art which directs the production of it. Thus the art which uses matter is also in a sense directive,
but as directive it differs from the other insofar as it knows the form,
5 while the art which directs the production knows the matter; for the
steersman knows what kind of form the rudder should have and orders
its production, but the engineer knows from what kind of wood it
should be produced and how it should move.[14] Now in objects produced
according to art, it is we who produce the matter for the sake of some
function,[15] but in natural objects it is there all along.[16]

Again, matter is relative to some thing, for distinct forms require
distinct matter.[17]

10 To what extent should the physicist understand the form or the whatness? Up to a point, just as the doctor understands sinews and the smith
understands bronze, for each of them [sinews and bronze] is for the
sake of something, and the physicist is concerned with what is separable
in kind but exists in matter; for both man and the Sun beget man.[18] As
for a separate form, how it exists and what it is, this is a task to be
15 settled by first philosophy.[19]

3

Having made these distinctions, we should next examine the causes,
their kinds and number. Since our *inquiry* is for the sake of understanding, and we think that we do not understand a thing until we have
20 acquired the *why* of it (and this is to acquire the first[1] cause), clearly
we should do this as regards generation and destruction and every
physical change so that, with an understanding of their principles, we
may try to refer to them each of the things[2] we seek.

In one sense, "a cause" means (1) that from which, as a constituent,[3]
25 something is generated; for example, the bronze is a cause of the statue,
and the silver, of the cup, and the genera of these[4] [are also causes].

In another, it means (2) the form or the pattern,[5] this being the formula of the essence,[6] and also the genera of this; for example, in the
case of the octave, the ratio 2:1, and, in general, a number and the parts
in the formula.[7]

30 In another, it means (3) that from which change or coming to rest[8]
first begins; for example, the adviser is a cause, and the father is the

cause of the baby, and, in general, that which acts is a cause of that which is acted upon, and that which brings about a change is a cause of that which is being changed.

Finally, it means (4) the end, and this is the final cause [that for the sake of which]; for example, walking is for the sake of health.[9] Why does he walk? We answer, "In order to be healthy"; and having spoken thus, we think that we have given the cause. And those things which, after that which started the motion, lie between the beginning and the end, such as reducing weight or purging or drugs or instruments in the case of health, all of them are for the sake of the end;[10] and they differ in this, that some of them are operations while others are instruments.

The term "cause", then, has about so many senses. And since they [the causes] are spoken of in many ways, there may be many nonaccidental causes of the same thing; for example, in the case of a statue, not with respect to something else but qua a statue, both the art of sculpture and the bronze are causes of it, though not in the same manner, but the bronze as matter and the art as the source of motion. There may be also causes of each other; for example, exercise is a cause of good physical condition, and good physical condition is a cause of exercise, although not in the same manner, but good physical condition as an end, while exercise as a principle[11] of motion. Again, the same thing may be a cause of contraries, for if one thing, when present, is the cause of another, then the first, when absent, is sometimes also said to be the cause of the contrary of the second; for example, we say that the absence of the pilot was the cause of the capsizing, while his presence was the cause of safety.[12]

All of the causes just mentioned fall into four most evident types. For, the letters of the syllables, the matter of manufactured articles, fire and all such in the case of bodies, the parts of the whole, the hypotheses[13] of the conclusion[14]—in all of these there are causes in the sense that they are *that of which*[15] the latter[16] consists; and in these,[16] those first mentioned in each case are causes in the sense that they are the underlying subject, as in the case of the parts,[17] but each[18] of the others is a cause in the sense of essence, and this is the whole[19] or the composition or the form. As for the seed and the doctor and the adviser and, in general, that which acts, all these are causes in the sense of the source of change or of standstill or of motion. Finally, each of the rest is a cause as the end or the good of the others; for that for the sake of which the others exist or are done tends to be the best or their end. Let there be no difference here between calling this "the good" or "the apparent good".[20]

These, then, are the causes and their number in kind; but their modes are numerically many, although when summarized they too are fewer.

[handwritten marginal note: why something is there – what is the purpose?]

For causes are spoken of in many ways, and even within the same kind
one cause may be prior[21] or posterior to another; for example, the cause
of health is the doctor or the artist, and the cause of the octave is
the ratio 2:1 or a number, and whatever includes[22] each is always a
cause. Again, there are accidental causes and their genera; for example,
Polyclitus as a cause of a statue is distinct from a sculptor as a cause,
since the sculptor is by accident Polyclitus.[23] Also, whatever includes[24]
the accident would be a cause; for example, a man, or, in general, an
animal, would be a cause of the statue. Even of accidents, some are
more remote or more near than others; for example, this would be the
case if the white or the musical were to be called "a cause" of the
statue.[25]

Of all causes, both those said to be *proper*[26] and those said to be
accidental, some are said to be causes in the sense of being in potentiality, others in *actuality;* for example, the cause of the house to be
built is the builder[27] and of the house that is being built the builder
who is building. Similar remarks will apply to the things caused by the
causes already listed; for example, the cause may be a cause of this
statue or of a statue or of a portrait in general, and it may be a cause of
this bronze or of bronze or of matter[28] in general.[29] Similar remarks may
be made in the case of accidents. Again, both accidental and *proper*
causes and also the objects caused may be spoken of in combination;[30]
for example, not Polyclitus, nor the sculptor, but Polyclitus the sculptor.

However, all these are six in number, and each is spoken of in two
ways. For as a cause or an object caused each may be stated as a particular[31] or as a genus of a particular; as an accident or as a genus of an
accident; in combination or singly taken; and in each of these either in
actuality or in virtue of its potentiality. And there is this difference, that
causes which are in *actuality* and are taken as individuals exist, or do
not exist, at the same time as the things of which they are the causes, for
example, as in the case of this doctor who is healing and this man who
is being healed, and this builder who is building and that building
which is being built.[32] But with respect to potentiality this is not always
so; for the house is not destroyed at the same time as the builder.

We should always seek the ultimate[33] cause of each thing, as in other
cases; for example, a man builds in view of the fact that he is a builder,
and a builder builds in virtue of his art of building; accordingly, this
latter is the prior cause. It is likewise with all other cases. Moreover,
causes generically given should be stated of effects generically given,
and particular[31] causes, of particular effects; for example, a sculptor
[in general] of a statue [in general], and this sculptor of this statue.
Also potential causes should be stated of potential effects, and causes in
actuality of effects in *actuality*.

Let this, then, be a sufficient description of the number of causes and the manner in which they are causes.

30

<hr />

4

Luck and *chance*, too, are said to be causes, and many things are said to exist and to come to be through luck or *chance*. Accordingly, we must inquire (a) in what manner luck and *chance* are causes among those given, (b) whether luck and *chance* are the same or distinct, and, as a whole,[1] (c) what luck is and what *chance* is.

35

Some thinkers even raise the problem of whether luck and *chance* exist or not;[2] for they[3] say that nothing comes by luck, but that in every case in which we say that a thing comes to be by *chance* or luck there is a definite cause. For example, if a man came to the market and met by luck someone whom he wished but did not expect to meet, the cause of this meeting is the wish to come and buy something. Similarly, in the other cases which are said to happen by luck there is always a [definite] cause, and this is not luck; for it would indeed appear strange if luck were something, and one might even raise the question as to why not even one of the ancient wise men, in speaking of the causes of generation and of destruction, said anything definite about luck. So it seems that they, too, thought that nothing could exist by luck. Yet this too is surprising: Many things come to be and exist by luck or by *chance*. And although we know that each of these can be referred to some [definite] cause, like the old argument which eliminated luck, nevertheless all speak of some of these things as being by luck and others as being not by luck; and on this account, this fact should have been touched upon by them in some way or other.

196a

5

10

15

Now none of the ancient thinkers thought that luck was some thing, such as *Friendship* or *Strife* or *Intelligence* or *Fire* or some other such thing. And this is certainly strange, whether they believed that luck does not exist or thought that it does but neglected to discuss it; for they sometimes used it, as in the case of Empedocles, who said that air is not always separated in the highest region but wherever it might chance. Anyway, he did say in his cosmology "it happened to run to that region at that time, but it often ran otherwise";[4] and he also said that most of the parts of animals came to be by luck.[5]

20

There are some[6] who say that chance[7] is a cause both of this heaven and of everything that is in the ordered universe; for they say that the vortex came to be by chance, and so did the motion which separated the parts and caused the present order of the universe. And this is very surprising; for they say, on the one hand, that animals and plants neither

25

30   exist nor are generated by luck but that the cause is nature or intellect
or some other such thing (for it is not any chance thing that is generated
from a given seed, but an olive tree from this kind and a man from that
kind), and, on the other, that the heavens and the most divine of the
35   visible objects were generated by *chance*, which cause is not such as
any of those in the case of animals or plants. Yet if such is the case, it
196b   deserves attention, and it is right that something should be said about it.
For, besides the fact that the statement is absurd in other ways, it is
more absurd to speak thus when they observe nothing generated by
chance in the heavens but many things happening by luck among things
which [according to them] neither exist nor are generated by luck, even
5   if probability would have it the other way around.

There are also others who seem to think that chance is a cause but is
not revealed to human *thought*, that it is something divine and rather
godlike.

Let us inquire, then, what chance is and what luck is, whether they
are the same or distinct, and how they fit into the causes already
described.

5

10   To begin, then, since we observe that some things come to be always
in the same way and others [come to be] for the most part,[1] it is evident
that luck as a cause and what comes to be by luck[2] are none of those
things, neither of what is necessary or eternal nor of what is for the most
part. But since of things that come to be there exist, besides these, also
15   others,[3] which all say exist by luck, it is evident that luck or chance does
exist; for we grant that such things do come to be by luck and that
things which come to be by luck are of such a kind.[4]

Of things that come to be, some do so for the sake of something [else]
but others do not;[5] and of the former, some come to be according to
choice and others not so, but both these are for the sake of something;[6]
20   so it is clear that, besides things which exist necessarily or for the most
part, there are also others[7] to which final cause may belong. Things to
which final cause belongs may be done by *thought* or by nature. Now
when such things come to be by accident, we say that they do so by
25   luck;[8] for just as being exists either essentially or by accident, so may a
cause exist.[9] In the case of a house, for example, a cause which is essential is the art of building, but one that is accidental is the white or the
musical. Thus the essential cause of something is definite, but the accidental cause is indefinite,[10] for a great many accidents may belong to a
thing.

30   As it was stated, then, when this happens in things for the sake of
which there is generation, then it is said to happen by *chance*[11] or by
luck. The difference between these two will be specified later,[12] but for
the present it is evident that both belong to things for the sake of something. For example, a man engaged in collecting contributions would
have gone to a certain place for the sake of getting the money,[13] had
35   he known; but he went there not for the sake of this, and it is by accident that he got the money when he went there; and this happened
197a   neither for the most part whenever he went there, nor of necessity. And
the end, which is getting the money, is not a cause present in him,[14] but
it is something done by *choice* or by *thought*, and he is then said to
have gone there by luck;[15] but if he had gone there by *choice* and for
the sake of this, whether he was getting the money always or for the
5   most part, then he would have done so not by luck.
          It is clear, then, that luck is an accidental cause of things done ac-
cording to *choice* and for the sake of something; and so both *thought*
and luck are concerned with the same thing,[16] for *choice* is not without
thought.
          Now the causes of things which might come to be by luck are of
10   necessity indefinite. In view of all this, (a) luck seems to be something
indefinite or not revealed to man,[17] and (b) there is a sense in which
nothing would seem to come to be by luck;[18] for both these opinions are
right, since there is a good reason for them. For what comes to be by
luck does so in a qualified sense, namely, in virtue of an accident, and
it is as an accident that luck is a cause; but as a cause without qualification, it is a cause of no thing.[19] For example, of a house the builder is
15   the cause, but accidentally it is the flute player; and in going to a place
and getting the money, but not doing so for the sake of getting the
money, the accidental causes might be a great many, such as wishing
to see someone or following someone or avoiding someone or going to
see a play. And it is right to say that luck is contrary to reason; for
20   reason[20] is of what is always or for the most part, while luck is present
in events which are outside of these. So, since such causes are indefinite,
luck too is indefinite.
          In some cases, however, one might raise the problem of whether a
cause as luck may not be any chance thing whatever, as in the case of
health, for example, whether the wind or the heat from the sun is such
25   a cause but not the purge;[21] for, of accidental causes, some are nearer
[to the effects] than others.
          Luck is called "good" when the result is good, but "bad" when the
result is bad; and it is called "good fortune" and "misfortune" when its
goodness and badness, respectively, are of considerable magnitude. In
view of this, even if great goodness or badness is missed by a little, we

are said to have been fortunate or unfortunate; for the small difference
30   seems negligible, and so *thought* regards good fortune or misfortune as
if attained. Further, it is with good reason that good fortune has no
certainty, for luck has no certainy; for what comes to be by luck does so
neither always nor for the most part.[22]

As we stated, both luck and *chance* are causes, but accidental; and
they are among things[23] which come to be neither without qualification
35   nor for the most part, and for the sake of something.

6

The term "chance" differs from "luck" by being a wider predicate; for
every effect by luck is also an effect by chance, but not every effect by
197b   chance is an effect by luck. Luck and an effect by luck belong also to
whatever good fortune and *action* in general belong.[1] It is for this reason, too, that luck is necessarily a cause of what may result by *action*. A
sign of this is the fact that good fortune seems[2] to be either the same as
5   happiness or close to it; and happiness is a kind of *action*, for it is a good
action. Hence, whatever is incapable of *acting* is also incapable of doing
anything by luck. And it is because of this that inanimate things and
brutes and children, having no *choice*,[3] cannot do anything by luck;
and neither good nor ill fortune can belong to them, except in virtue of
10   some similarity, as in Protarchus' statement that the stones of which
altars are made are fortunate, for they are honored, while those leading
to the altar are walked upon. Of course, even these things[4] are affected
by luck, but in a sense, that is, when one *acts* on them by luck, but in no
other way.[5]

As for chance, it exists also in the other animals and in many inani-
15   mate things. For example, we say that the horse who came is a chance
[cause],[6] that is, his coming saved him, but he did not come for the
sake of being saved; and the tripod which fell [on its feet] is a chance
[cause], for though its being on its feet is for the sake of being sat on, it
did not fall for the sake of being sat on.[7]

Thus it is evident that in things which come to be without qualification for the sake of something, when the effects, whose causes are
20   outside of them, do not come to be for their own sake, then we say that
they come to be by chance; and of these, those *chosen* by those who
have *choice* are said to come to be by luck.[8] A sign of this is the use of
the phrase "in vain"[9] when that for the sake of which something is done
does not result, as in walking which is for the sake of bowel movement;
25   if the movement does not result after one has walked, we say that he
has walked in vain and that the walking was futile, thus regarding as

futile that which was by nature for the sake of something that did not result, although by nature it does result (for it would be ridiculous to say that a man had bathed in vain if as a consequence the Sun was not eclipsed, seeing that the bathing was not for the sake of the Sun's

30 eclipse). So chance, as its name also indicates, exists when something occurs in vain,[10] so to speak, for the stone that fell did so not for the sake of striking the man, but by chance, seeing that it might have been thrown by someone for the sake of striking the man.

Things occurring by *chance* are most distinct from those occurring by luck in things generated by nature; for when something has been gen-

35 erated contrary to nature, then we say that it did so not by luck but rather by *chance*. And there is another distinction, for in the one case the cause is outside, in the other it is inside.[11]

198a We have stated, then, what chance[12] is, what luck is, and in what they differ from each other. As for the manner in which they are causes, each of them is a source which begins motion; for each is always a cause of what results either by nature or by *thought,* and each of them

5 as a cause may vary indefinitely in number.

Now, since *chance* and luck are causes of effects caused either by the intellect or by nature, when each of them comes to be an accidental cause of such an effect, then it is clear that, since nothing that is acci- dental is prior to what is essential, no accidental cause is prior to an

10 essential cause. Thus *chance* and luck are posterior to intellect and nature.[13] Hence, however true it may be that chance is the cause of the heavens,[14] intellect or nature is of necessity a prior cause of many other things and of this [whole] universe.[14]

*Can only read chance
backward?*

7

It is clear, then, that there are causes and that there are as many

15 [in kind] as we have stated;[1] for the *why* of things includes just so many [in kind]. For the *why* in referred either (a) ultimately to the whatness[2] in the case of what is immovable, as in mathematics (for it is ultimately referred to the definition of a straight line or of commensurability or of something else[3]), or (b) to the first mover[4]—for example: Why did they

20 declare war? Because they were raided—or (c) to a final cause:[5] [in declaring war] for the sake of ruling the enemy, or (d) to matter, as in things generated. Evidently, then, the causes are those stated and are as many in number.

Since the causes are four, it is the task of the physicist to understand all of them; and as a physicist he should state the *why* by referring it to all of them—the matter, the form, the mover, and the final cause. The

4 different "why" questions

25   last three often amount to one; for both the whatness and the final cause
      are one, and the first[6] source of motion is the same in kind as these[7]
      (for man begets man), and, in general, this is so in the case of a movable
      mover. But a mover that is not movable is not a cause within physics,[8]
      for it moves without having in itself motion or a principle of motion[9] but
30   is immovable. Accordingly, there are three disciplines: one concerning
      immovable things, a second concerning things which are in motion but
      are indestructible, and a third concerning destructible things.[10]
          The *why*, then, is given by being referred to matter, to the whatness,
      and to the first mover,[11] for in generations causes are sought mostly in
35   this manner: "What comes after what?",[12] "What was the first thing
      that acted or was acted upon?", and at each step always in this way.
      Now the principles that cause physical motion are two: One of these
198b is not physical, for it has no principle of motion in itself,[13] and such is
      that which moves another without itself being moved, as in the case of
      that which is completely immovable and primary among all;[14] and
      such is also the whatness or the *form*, for this is the end or final cause.
      So, since nature is a final cause, we should also understand this [cause].
5   So the *why* must be given in all [four] ways, namely, (1) that this must
      follow from that[15] (the phrase "this from that" to be taken either without
      qualification or for the most part[16]); (2) that if this is to be, then that[17]
      will be (as in the case of premises, from which conclusions follow); (3)
      that this was the essence; and (4) because it is better in this way (not
      without qualification, but relative to the *substance*[18] of each thing).[19]

                              8

10   We must discuss first (a) why nature is a cause for the sake of some-
      thing;[1] then (b) how necessity exists in physical things,[2] for all thinkers
      make reference to this cause by saying, for example, that since the hot
      and the cold and each of such things are by nature of such-and-such a
15   kind, certain other things must exist or come to be (for even if they
      mention some other cause—one of them mentions *Friendship* and
      Strife,[3] another mentions *Intelligence*[4]—they just touch upon it and let
      it go at that).
          The following question arises: What prevents nature from acting, not
      for the sake of something or for what is better,[5] but by necessity, as in
      the case of rain, which does not fall in order that wheat may grow. For,
20   one may say, what goes up must be cooled, and the resulting cold water
      must come down, and when this takes place, the growth of corn just
      happens; similarly, if a man's wheat is spoiled on the threshing floor,
      rain did not fall for the sake of spoiling the wheat, but this just hap-

Empidocles argument by necessity implies it would always be that way

pened.[6] So what should prevent the parts in nature, too, from coming to be of necessity in this manner, for example, the front teeth of necessity coming out sharp and so fit for tearing but the molars broad and useful for grinding food, not however for the sake of this but by coincidence? A similar question arises with the other parts in which final cause seems to exist. If so, then whenever[7] all the parts came together as if generated for the sake of something, the wholes which by *chance* were fitfully composed survived, but those which came together not in this manner,[8] like the man-faced offspring of oxen mentioned by Empedocles,[9] perished and still do so.[10]

This is the argument, then, or any other such, that might cause a *difficulty*. Yet it is impossible for things to come to be in this manner; for the examples cited and all things by nature come to be either always or for the most part, but none of those by luck or *chance* do so likewise.[11] It is not during the winter that frequent rain is thought to occur by luck or by coincidence, but during the summer, nor frequent heat during the summer, but during the winter. So if these be thought to occur either by coincidence or for the sake of something and if they cannot occur by coincidence or by chance, then they occur for the sake of something. Besides, those who use the preceding arguments, too, would admit that all such things exist by nature.[12] There is, then, final cause in things which come to be or exist by nature.[13]

Moreover, in that which has an end, a prior stage and the stages that follow are done for the sake of that end. Accordingly, these are done in the manner in which the nature of the thing disposes them to be done; and the nature of the thing disposes them to be done in the manner in which they are done at each stage, if nothing obstructs.[14] But they are done for the sake of something; so they are by nature disposed to be done for the sake of something.[15] For example, if a house were a thing generated by nature, it would have been generated in a way similar to that in which it is now generated by art.[16] So if things by nature were to be generated not only by nature but also by art, they would have been generated just as they are by nature disposed to be generated. So one stage is for the sake of the next.[17] In general, in some cases art completes what nature cannot carry out to an end,[18] in others, it imitates nature.[19] Thus, if things done according to art are for the sake of something, clearly also those according to nature are done for the sake of something; for the later stages are similarly related to the earlier stages in those according to art and those according to nature.

This is most evident in those of the other animals which make things neither by art nor by having inquired or deliberated about them; and from this latter fact arise discussions by some thinkers about the problem of whether spiders and ants and other such animals work by intel-

25

30

35

199a

5

10

15

20

lect or by some other power. If we go a little further in this direction,[20]
25   we observe that in plants, too, parts appear to be generated which contribute to an end, for example, leaves for the sake of protecting the fruit.
So if it is both by nature and for the sake of something that the swallow
makes its nest and the spider its web and that plants grow leaves for
the sake of fruit and send their roots not up but down for the sake of
30   food, it is evident that there exists such a cause[21] in things which come
to be or exist by nature. And since nature may be either matter or *form*,
and it is the latter that may be an end while all the rest are for the sake
of an end, it is *form* that would be a cause in the sense of a final cause.

Now error occurs even with respect to things produced according to
art, for example, a grammarian did not write correctly and a doctor did
35   not give the right medicine; so clearly this may occur also in things that
199*b*   come to be according to nature. If then there are (a) things produced
according to art in which there is a right final cause and (b) also things
done erroneously when the final cause has been aimed at but failed, a
similar situation would exist also in natural things, and monstrosities in
5   these would be failures of final causes. So too must have been the case
in the original formation of the offspring of oxen, if they could not attain
a certain limit or end; for there must have been some corruption in the
source from which their generation started, like that in the seed nowadays.[22] We might add, too, that the seed must have come into being first
and not the animals all at once, and the expression "first the whole-
10   natured" meant the seed.[23] And final cause exists also in plants, though
it is less capable of being articulated. So did olive-headed offspring of
vines [24] come into being just as man-faced offspring did from oxen, or
not? It would seem absurd; but they must have, if indeed this was also
the case in animals. Again, any chance thing might otherwise be
generated from a seed.

15   In general, he who asserts this rejects things existing by nature as well
as nature itself.[25] For what exists by nature is a thing which, having
started from some principle in itself, finally arrives by a continuous motion at a certain end; and neither is the end the same from every principle,[26] nor does any chance end come to be from a given principle,[27] but
from the same principle the same end comes to be, if nothing obstructs.
As for the final cause or what acts for the sake of the final cause, it might
20   take place by luck. (For example, we say "the stranger came by luck
and departed after paying the ransom" if he would have come for the
sake of doing this [had he known], not that he came for the sake of this;
and this happened by accident,[28] for luck is an accidental cause, as we
25   stated earlier.[29]) But if it takes place always or for the most part, it is not
an accident nor does it come to be by luck; and in natural things it takes
place always, if nothing obstructs.

It is absurd to think that nothing comes to be for the sake of something if the moving cause is not observed deliberating (and we may add, even art does not deliberate [30]); and if the ship-building art were in the wood, it would have produced results similar to those produced by nature. So if there is a final cause in art,[31] so also in nature. This is most clearly seen in a doctor who heals himself; nature is like that.[32]

It is evident, then, that nature is a cause and that it is a cause also in this manner, namely, for the sake of something.

9

As for that which is necessary, does it exist by hypothesis or also simply?[1] Nowadays it is thought that what exists by necessity does so in generation, as if one were to consider the wall as having been constructed by necessity, since what is heavy travels down by its nature and what is light travels up by its nature, and so the stones and the foundations are down, then earth right above because it is lighter, and finally wood at the very top since it is the lightest. However, although a wall is not constructed without these, still it is constructed not because of these (except in the sense that they are causes as matter[2]) but for the sake of sheltering or preserving certain things. Similarly, in all other cases in which there is a final cause, although what is generated could not have been generated without a nature which is necessary for it, still it is not because of what is necessary (except as a material cause) but for the sake of something. For example, why is a saw such-and-such? So that this may come to be or for the sake of this. But this final cause cannot come to be unless the saw is made of iron. So if there is to be a saw capable of doing this work, it is necessary that it be made of iron. What is necessary, then, exists by hypothesis[3] and not as an end; for it exists in matter, while final cause is in the formula.[4]

The necessary in mathematics is in some way parallel to that in things generated according to nature. Since this is what a straight line is, it is necessary for a triangle to have its angles equal to two right angles, but the converse is not the case; but if the angles of a triangle were not equal to two right angles, neither would a straight line be what it is said to be. In things generated for the sake of something, this parallelism proceeds in a reverse manner. If the end will exist or exists, what precedes it also will exist or exists; but if what precedes the end will not or does not exist, then, just as in the other case the starting-point is not what it is posited to be if the conclusion is not true, so here, the end or final cause will not or does not exist if what precedes it will not or does not exist. The final cause here, we may add, is also a starting-point, not of *action,* but of reasoning;[5] but in the other case [e.g., in mathematics], it is the whatness that is the starting-point of reasoning, for no *actions* exist there. Thus, if there is to be a house, certain things must be made or be available or exist (or the matter in general, which is for the sake of something, such as bricks and stones in the case of a house); but the end does not exist because of these things, except in the sense that they are a cause as matter, nor will the house come to be because of these. In general, then, if there are no stones, there can be no house, and if there is no iron, there can be no saw; whereas in mathematics, if the angles of the triangle are not equal to two right angles, the principles from which the equality to two right angles follows cannot be such as are posited.

It is evident, then, that the necessary in natural things is what we call "matter" and also the motions of matter.[6] We may also add that both causes must be stated by the physicist, and the final cause more so than the cause as matter, for it is the former which is the cause[7] of the latter, not the latter, of the end; and we may also add that the end is the final cause and that the starting-point is the definition or the formula, as in the case of things produced according to art. For example, if a house is such-and-such a thing, such other things must be produced or be available; and so in the case of a man: If he is such-and-such, then such other things must be or come to be, and if these, then such others likewise. Perhaps the necessary exists also in the formula; for, if one has defined the operation of sawing as being such-and-such an act of division, then this cannot take place unless the saw has teeth of such-and-such a kind, and these cannot be of such-and-such a kind unless they are made of iron. Indeed, even in formulas there are some parts which are parts as if they were the matter of these formulas.[8]

Book Γ

1

200b   Since nature is a principle of motion or[1] of change and our *inquiry* is about nature, we should not neglect to inquire what a motion is; for
15   if we are ignorant of what a motion is, we are of necessity ignorant of what nature is. When we have explained motion,[2] then we shall try in the same manner to take up what follows.[3]

Now a motion is thought to be one of those things which are continuous, and it is in the continuous that the infinite first appears;[4] and for this reason, it often happens that those who define the continuous use
20   the formula of the infinite, that is, they say that the continuous is that which is infinitely divisible.[5] Again, a motion is thought to be impossible without place and void and time.[6] Clearly, then, because of all this and because of the fact that these[7] are common and belong universally to all the others, we must first undertake to inquire about each of these;
25   for the investigation of what is specific should come after that of what is common.[8]

As we said, then, our first inquiry is about motion. To begin, there is (a) that which exists in actuality only[9] and also (b) that which exists both potentially and in actuality,[10] and this may be a *this* or a *so-much* or a *such* or, likewise, any of the other categories of being. As for that which is relative to something, it may be stated with respect to excess
30   or deficiency or with respect to its being able to act or be acted upon or, in general, with respect to its being able to move or be moved;[11] for that which is able to move is able to move that which can be moved, and that which can be moved can be moved by that which can move.

Now no motion exists apart from things; for that which changes always does so either with respect to substance or with respect to quantity
35   or with respect to quality or with respect to place, and there can be no thing common to these which is not, as is our manner of speaking, a *this*
201a   or a quantity or a quality or some one of the other categories.[12] Thus

42

neither a motion nor a change can exist apart from these [categories] if nothing else exists but these.

In all cases, each of these [categories] may exist in two ways; for example, with respect to a *this*, it may be the *form* or the privation of that *form*, with respect to quality it may be whiteness or blackness, and with respect to quantity it may be the complete or the incomplete. Similarly, with respect to locomotion the thing may be up or down or it may be heavy or light. Thus there are as many kinds of motion or of change as there are kinds of being.[13] In view of this distinction between the actual and the potential in each genus, a motion is [defined as] the actuality of the potentially existing qua existing potentially.[14] For example, the actuality of the alterable qua alterable is an alteration, the actuality of what can be increased or (its opposite) what can be decreased [qua such] is an increase or decrease (no name exists which is a common predicate of both),[15] the actuality of the generable or destructible [qua such] is a generation or a destruction, and the actuality of the movable with respect to place [qua such] is a locomotion.

That a motion is what we have stated it to be is clear from the following. When the buildable, insofar as it is said to be such, exists in actuality, it is then [in the process of] being built, and this is [the process of] building; and similarly in the case of learning, healing, rolling, leaping, ripening, and aging.

Since, in some cases, the same things exist both potentially and actually, but not at the same time nor with respect to the same thing (as in the case of that which is potentially hot but actually cold), many of them will eventually both act and be acted upon by each other; for each of them has the potentiality both of acting and of being acted upon. Consequently, that which causes a motion physically[16] is also movable, for every such thing which causes a motion is itself moved. There are some who think that every thing that moves another is itself moved; now what the situation is with respect to this will be made clear from other arguments (for there exists also something which causes a motion but is itself immovable),[17] but as for a motion, it is the actuality of that which exists potentially when it is in *actuality* not qua itself but qua movable.

By "qua" I mean the following. Bronze is potentially a statue, yet it is not qua bronze that the actuality of bronze is a motion; for to be bronze and to be movable by something are not the same, since if they were the same without qualification or according to formula, the actuality of bronze qua bronze would be a motion.[18] So they are not the same, as stated. This is clear in the case of contraries; for to be capable of being healthy and to be capable of being sick are distinct, for otherwise being sick and being healthy would be the same. It is the underlying subject,

44

be it moisture or blood, which is one and the same, whether in health or in sickness.[19] Since, then, to be bronze and to be potentially something else are not the same, just as to be a color and to be visible are not the same,[20] evidently it is the actuality of the potential qua potential that is a motion.

It is clear, then, that this is what a motion is and that an object happens to be in motion just when this actuality exists, and neither before nor after. For each [such] thing may be sometimes in *actuality* and sometimes not, as in the case of the buildable, and it is qua buildable that the *actuality* of the buildable is [the process of] building. For this *actuality* is either [the process of] building or the house. But when the house exists, it is no longer buildable; and it is the buildable that is being built. This *actuality*, then, must be [the process of] building, and [the process of] building is a [kind of] motion. Moreover, the same argument applies to the other motions.

2

That we have stated the facts well is also clear from (a) what the other thinkers are saying about motion and from (b) the fact that it is not easy to describe it in another way. For (b) one could not place motion or change in some other genus; and (a) an examination of the way in which some thinkers posit motion clearly shows them to be saying that it is otherness or inequality or nonbeing,[1] none of which (whether that which is other or that which is unequal or that which is nonbeing) need be in motion,[2] and besides, a change is no more into these or from these than into or from their opposites.[3]

The cause of positing motion as being some one of these is the fact that motion is thought to be something indefinite;[4] and the principles in one of the two columns of contraries are indefinite because they are privative, for none of them is a *this* or a *such* or any of the other categories.[5] And a motion is thought to be indefinite because of the fact that it cannot be placed in an unqualified way[6] either under the potentiality or under the *actuality* of things; for neither that which is potentially a quantity nor that which is *actually* a quantity is necessarily moved. And although a motion is thought to be an *actuality* of a sort, yet it is incomplete; and the cause of this is the fact that the potential, of which this is the *actuality*, is incomplete.[7] And it is indeed because of this that it is difficult to grasp its whatness; for it must be placed either under privation or under potentiality or under unqualified *actuality*, but none of these alternatives appears possible. What remains, then, is the manner in which we described it, namely, that a motion is a sort of an *actuality* —an *actuality* such as we have stated,[8] difficult to grasp but capable of existing.

The mover too is movable, as has been stated, that is, every mover which is potentially movable and whose absence of motion is rest; for the absence of motion in that which may be in motion is [said to be] rest. For to act on the movable qua such is precisely to move it. But it [i.e., the mover] acts on it by contact; so it is at the same time acted upon.[9] Thus it is of the movable qua movable that a motion is the actuality;[10] and this happens by contact with that which can move, so the latter too is at the same time acted upon. And the mover always has a form, whether a *this* or a *such* or a *so-much*,[11] which is a principle and a cause[12] of motion when the mover moves [something]; for example, a man in actuality begets a man from what is potentially a man.

3

Moreover, the solution to the problem[1] raised concerning a motion is now evident: A motion is in a movable [object], for it is of the movable that it [motion] is the actuality, and it [motion] is caused by that which can move [the movable]. And the *actuality* of that which can cause a motion is not distinct,[2] for there must be one actuality in both; for a thing can cause a motion by its potency, and it [the thing] causes a motion by *actualizing* that potency. But this *actuality* is in the movable, so it is alike one *actuality* [numerically] in both, just as it is the same interval from one to two and from two to one and the same interval from A going up to B and from B coming down to A. For these [two] intervals are [numerically] one, although their formula is not one;[3] and similarly with the mover and that which is moved.

However, there is a logical *difficulty*. Perhaps it is necessary for the *actuality* of that which can act to be distinct from the *actuality* of that which can be affected; in the one, it is [the process of] acting, in the other, it is [the process of] being affected, and the function or end of the first is an action, but that of the second is an affection. Now if both [*actualities*] are motions, in what [subject or subjects] do they exist if they are distinct? Either (a) both are in that which is affected or is moved, or (b) [the process of] acting is in that which acts and [the process of] being affected is in that which is being affected;[4] and if the latter motion, too, were to be called "an acting", then it would be equivocally so called.[5]

Now, if (b), then the motion will be in the mover, for the same argu-

30 ment applies to the mover and to the object moved;[6] so either every mover will be moved,[7] or, having motion, it will not be moved.[8] But in (a), if both motions are in the object which is being moved or is being affected, that is, both [the process of] acting and [the process of] being affected (for example, if both teaching and learning, which are two, are in the learner), then, first, the *actuality* of each will not be in each,[9] and second, it will be absurd for that object to have two motions at the same

35 time (for what will be the two alterations of that which is proceeding toward one form?).[10] But this is impossible; so there will be one *actu-*

202*b* *ality*. But it would be unreasonable for two [motions] which are distinct in kind to be one and the same *actuality*; for if indeed teaching and learning (and in general, acting and being affected) were the same, then also to teach and to learn (and in general, to act and to be affected)

5 would be the same, and so it would be necessary for the teacher to learn everything that he teaches (and in general, for that which acts to be affected by every affection it causes).[11]

Nevertheless, neither is it absurd for the *actuality* of one thing to be in another thing (for teaching is the activity of a man who can teach but it is an activity *upon another man;* it is not cut off but is an activity of A upon B), nor can anything prevent one *actuality* from being the same for two things[12]—not in the sense that the essence is the same for

10 both,[13] but in the sense in which potential being is related to being in *actuality*.[14] So it is not necessary for the teacher to learn, even if to act and to be affected are the same,[15] not however in the sense that the formula which states the essence is one (as in the case of the formula of clothing and of garment),[16] but in the sense that the road from Thebes to Athens and that from Athens to Thebes is the same, as it

15 was stated before;[17] for things are in every way the same not if they are the same in any way whatsoever, but only if to be each [i.e., if their essence] is the same.[18] Nor is to learn the same as to teach, if teaching and learning are [numerically] the same, just as the direction from A to B is not one and the same as that from B to A, if the distance connect-

20 ing A and B is one.[19] In general, however, neither are teaching and learning the same in the main sense,[20] nor are acting and being affected, but that to which they belong, which is motion, is the same;[21] for to be an *actuality* of A upon B and to be an *actuality* of B by A are distinct in formula.[22]

What motion is has been stated both universally and with respect to

25 its parts, for it is not unclear how each of its species will be defined; for example, alteration is the actuality of the alterable qua alterable, or, in more known terms, it is the actuality of that which can act or that which can be affected qua such, whether without qualification or in each par-ticular case[23] (as in [the process of] building and in [the process of]

healing). Each of the other motions will be defined in the same manner.

ד | ד | ס׳

4

30 Since the science of nature is about magnitudes and motion and time
—each of which is of necessity either finite or infinite,[1] even if not every
thing is either finite or infinite (as for example an affection or a point,
for perhaps it is not necessary for such things to be either finite or in-
35 finite)[2]—he who is concerned with nature should investigate whether
the infinite exists or not; and if it exists, what it is.[3] A sign of the fact
203a that the investigation of the infinite is *proper* to this science is this: All
those who are thought to have touched upon this kind of philosophy
in a worthy manner have discussed the infinite, and all of them have
posited it as a principle[4] of things.

5 The Pythagoreans and Plato posit the infinite as a thing by itself,[5] not
as an attribute existing in some other thing but as being itself a substance. But the Pythagoreans say that it exists in sensible things (for they
do not posit numbers as existing apart from sensible things) and that the
infinite exists also outside of the heaven;[6] whereas Plato holds that
outside of the heavens no body exists, not even the Ideas, because these
10 are not even in a place, but that the infinite exists in the sensible things as
well as in the Ideas.[7] Moreover, the Pythagoreans posit the infinite as
being the *Even;* for they say that it is this which, when cut off and
limited by the *Odd,* provides [as matter] for the infinity[8] of things. A
sign of this, they say, is what happens to numbers; for if gnomons are
placed around the one, and apart,[9] in the latter case the form produced

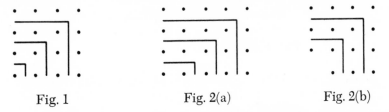

Fig. 1   Fig. 2(a)   Fig. 2(b)

15 is always distinct, but in the former it is unique. Plato posits two infinites, the *Great* and the *Small.*[10]

On the other hand, all those who are concerned with nature always
assign to the infinite a nature [a *substance*] which is distinct[11] from that
of the so-called "elements", such as water or air or something between
these. Of those who posit the elements to be finite, no one makes them
20 infinite. But those who posit the elements to be infinite, like the various
homogeneous elements in the case of Anaxagoras and the seeds of all

kinds of shapes in the case of Democritus, say that the infinite is a continuum by contact.

Now Anaxagoras adds that any part of a whole is a blend just like the whole because anything is observed to be generated from anything. It is from this that he seems to maintain that at one time all things were together, for example, this flesh and this bone and similarly any other thing, and so all of them, and at the same time too. For, according to him, there is a beginning of the separation not only of each thing but also of all; for since it is from such a body that a thing is generated and there is a generation of all things but not at the same time and, further, since there must be some principle of generation[12] (which is one and is called by him "*Intelligence*") and *Intelligence* works by thinking, which begins at some starting-point, it follows that at one time all things were necessarily together and started to be in motion at a certain time.

Democritus, on the other hand, says that of the primary things[13] no one comes from another; yet common body[14] as such is the principle of all of them, although they themselves differ in magnitude and shape.

It is clear from what has been said, then, that it is the task of the physicist to investigate the infinite. Now all thinkers have a good reason for positing the infinite as a principle.[15] For neither would they regard it as capable of existing in vain,[16] nor would they assign to it a power other than that of a principle; for every thing is either a principle or comes to be from a principle, but of the infinite there is no principle, since otherwise the infinite would have a limit.[17] Moreover, as a principle, it should be ungenerable and indestructible; for what is being generated must come to an end, and to every [process of] destruction there is a completion.[18] And so, as is our manner of saying, there is no principle of the infinite, but it itself is thought to be the principle of the other things, to contain all, to rule all (as is asserted by those who, besides the infinite, posit no other cause, such as *Intelligence* or *Friendship*), and to be divine[19] (for it is deathless and imperishable, as Anaximander and most of the natural philosophers say).

Conviction about the existence of the infinite might arise from the following five considerations:[20]

(1) From time, for this is regarded as infinite.

(2) From the division of magnitudes, for the mathematicians also use the infinite.

(3) If generation and destruction are not to come to an end, it will be only if there is an infinite source from which things to be generated can be taken.[21]

(4) From the view that what is finite always has its limits coincide with something [which contains it]; so if the finite is always limited by something, then there can be no ultimate limit.

(5) The greatest and most important point, which gives rise to a

difficulty affecting everyone, is this: Numbers and mathematical magnitudes and [also] what is outside of the heaven are considered to be
infinite because in thought they never come to an end.[22] And if that
which is outside of the heaven is infinite, then it seems that there is also
an infinite body and an infinity of universes; for why should mass be in
one part of the void[23] rather than in another? So if indeed it is in one
part, then it should be everywhere. Also, if void or place is infinite, then
there must be an infinite body, too;[24] for, in the case of eternal things,
that which may be does not differ from that which exists.[25]

Now the investigation of the infinite gives rise to a *difficulty;* for many
impossibilities result whether it is posited to exist or not to exist. Moreover, if existing, how does it exist—as a substance or as an essential
attribute of some nature?[26] Or does it exist in neither of these ways, but
an infinity or an infinite plurality of things nevertheless exist?[27]

Now it belongs most of all to the physicist to inquire whether there
exists a sensible magnitude which is infinite.[28] First, then, let us distinguish the various meanings of the term "infinite". The infinite is

(1) That which cannot be gone through, since it does not by nature
admit of being gone through, as in the case of a voice, which is
invisible.[29]

(2) That which admits of being traversed but without end, either
(a) almost so [i.e., almost without end] or (b) when by nature it admits
of being traversed but it cannot be traversed or it has no limit.[30]

Further, everything considered as infinite may be so either with respect to addition or with respect to division or with respect to both.[31]

5

Now the infinite, being itself just an infinite,[1] cannot exist as something separate from sensible things;[2] for if it is neither a magnitude nor
a plurality[3] but is itself a substance and not an attribute, it will be
indivisible,[4] for what is divisible is either a magnitude or a plurality;
and if it is indivisible, it cannot be infinite, except in the sense in which
the voice is invisible.[5] However, neither those who assert that the infinite
exists speak of it as existing in this manner[6] nor do we inquire about it
as such, but only as something which cannot be traversed.[7]

But if the infinite exists as an attribute, then just as invisibility is not
an element of speech, even if voice is invisible, so the infinite qua infinite would not be an element[8] of things. Moreover, how can the infinite
be itself something if it is not also a number or a magnitude, of which
that infinite is an essential *attribute*?[9] And besides, the infinite will be
of necessity less likely to exist than a number or a magnitude.[10]

It is also evident that the infinite cannot exist as a thing in *actuality* and as a substance[11] and a principle; for, if it can have parts, each part that may be taken would be infinite. For to be infinite and the infinite would be the same[12] if the infinite were indeed a substance[11] and not

25 an attribute of a subject; so it would be either indivisible or divisible into infinites. But the same thing cannot be [in actuality] many infinites;[13] and besides, just as a part of air is air, so a part of the infinite would be infinite, if it were a substance and a principle.[14] The infinite, then, must be without parts and indivisible. But the infinite as a thing in *actuality* cannot be so; for it must be a quantity. It exists, then, as an

30 attribute; but if so, it was stated that it is not the infinite that can be truly called "a principle" but that of which it is an attribute, for example, air or the *Even*. So those who speak like the Pythagoreans do so absurdly, for they posit the infinite both as a substance and as divisible into parts.[15]

35 However, perhaps this is a more universal inquiry, that is, whether
204b the infinite can be in mathematical objects as well as in those which are intelligible and have no magnitude.[16] We are now examining the sensible objects and those with which our *inquiry* is concerned, and we are asking if there is among them a body which is infinite in the direction of increase.

If we consider the problem logically,[17] it would seem from the fol-
5 lowing that no such body can exist; for if the formula of a body is "that which is limited by a surface", no infinite body can exist, whether intelligible or sensible. Moreover, also a number cannot exist as something separate and infinite; for a number or that which has a number is
10 numerable, so if the numerable may be numbered, it would also be possible to traverse the infinite.[18]

If we consider the problem rather from the point of view of physics, it would seem from what follows that no infinite body can be either (1) composite or (2) simple.

(1) If the [kinds of] elements[19] are finite in number, an infinite body cannot exist. For it is necessary that the elements be more than one, that the contraries always balance, and that no one of these be infinite; for
15 however much one contrary in one body falls short in power relative to the other contrary in another body (for example, if fire is finite and air is infinite, but, volume for volume, the power of fire is any multiple m relative to that of air, as long as m is a number), still it is evident that the infinite body will overpower and destroy the finite body.[20] Nor is it
20 possible for each element to be infinite; for (a) a body is that which is extended in all directions, (b) what is infinite would be infinitely extended, and so an infinite body would be infinitely extended in all directions.[21]

(2) Nor can there be an infinite body which is one and simple, whether

(a) as something which exists apart from the elements and from which the elements[22] are generated (as some thinkers say) or (b) as something
25   without any qualification. For (a) there are some who posit the infinite in the first sense, and not as being air or water, since thus there would be no infinite element which might destroy the other finite elements. For these elements have contrarieties relative to each other (for example, air is cold, water is moist, and fire is hot); so if one of them were infinite, it would have already destroyed the others, and so they say that the infinite from which these elements are generated is distinct
30   from them.[23] However, no such body can exist, not in view of its infiniteness (for, in connection with this, something common should be stated which applies to all alike, whether to air or water or whatever this may be), but in view of the fact that no such sensible body exists besides the so-called "elements". For, in all cases, a body is resolved into that of which it consists; so such a body would have existed besides
35   air and fire and earth and water, but no such body appears to exist. Also,
205a it is not possible for fire or for any of the other elements to be infinite. For, in general, even apart from the problem of whether any of them can be infinite, it is impossible for the universe, even if it were finite, to be or to become one of them, as Heraclitus says that at times all things
5   become fire; and the same argument applies to the one [element], which the physicists posit besides the elements; for all things are changing, from one contrary to another contrary, for example, from hot to cold.[24]

Whether an infinite sensible body can exist or not should also be examined from what follows.

That it is impossible, in general, for an infinite sensible body to exist
10   is clear from the following. Every sensible body is by its nature somewhere, and for each such body there is a [proper] place, the same for the whole and for a part of it, for example, the same for all the Earth and a clod, for fire and a spark.[25] So if such an infinite body is alike in kind, either it will be motionless or it will always be in motion with respect to place. But this is impossible; for why should it travel up rather than down or to any other place or *rest* at one rather than at any
15   other of these places?[26] For example, what I mean is that if there is a clod, where will it be moved or where will it rest? For its place is the infinite place of the body which is alike in kind and of which it is a part.[27] Will it[28] then occupy the whole place? And how? Which, then, or where will its [loco]motion or *rest* be?[29] It will either be *resting* everywhere, in which case it will not be in motion, or it will be moving everywhere, in which case it will not be at a standstill.[30]
20   But if the universe is composed of unlike parts,[31] there will also be unlike places;[32] then first, the body of the universe will not be one except by contact, and second, those parts will be either finite or infinite in

kind. They cannot be finite; for if the universe is infinite, some parts[33] will have to be infinite and others not, as in the case of fire and water, and in such a case there will be a destruction by a contrary, as it was stated earlier.[34] And it is because of this that none of the natural philosophers posited the *One* or the *Infinite*[35] to be fire or earth, but either water or air or something between these two,[36] seeing that the place of each of the former [fire, earth] is clearly definite,[37] while each of the latter lies in a place between [up and down].

On the other hand, if the parts are infinite [in kind] and simple, the places will also be infinite [in number], and the elements will be infinite.[38] So if this is impossible and the places are finite [in number], the whole too must be finite; for it is impossible for the places and the corresponding bodies not to fit each other exactly, since neither can each place be larger than the corresponding body it contains (and then the body will not be infinite) nor can the body be larger than its corresponding place[39] (otherwise, either void will exist,[40] or there will be a body whose nature is to be in no place).[41]

Anaxagoras speaks absurdly concerning the *Infinite* as being at *rest* with respect to place. He says the *Infinite* holds itself fixed, and it does this in view of the fact that it is in itself, for nothing else contains it, as if saying that wherever a thing is, it is there by its nature. But this is not true; for a thing might be somewhere by force and not by its nature.[42] So, however true it may be that the whole is not in motion (for that which holds itself fixed and is in itself cannot be in motion), still he should state why it is not its nature to be in motion; for it is not enough to make a statement in this manner and let it go at that. Other things, too, might not be in motion, but nothing would prevent them from being so and yet having a nature to be in motion. Thus the Earth does not move to any place, even if it were infinite; but it is held together at the Center. And it would *rest* at the Center not because there is no other place to which it might travel, but because it is not its nature to move to another place;[43] and we might still say in this case that the Earth holds itself fixed. So if the Earth, assumed infinite, holds itself fixed not because of its being infinite but by the fact that it is heavy, and what is heavy *rests* at the Center and the Earth is at the Center, then in a similar way the *Infinite* too would *rest* in itself through some other cause and not by the fact that it is infinite and holds itself fixed.

It is at the same time clear that any part, too, should remain at *rest*; for just as the *Infinite* keeps itself fixed at *rest*, so will any part of it. For the places of the whole and of a part are the same in kind (for example, the place of the whole earth and of a clod is down and that of the whole fire and of a spark is up); so if the place of the *Infinite* is to have what is in itself, so will the place of a part. Hence, the part will *rest* in itself.[44]

25   In general, if every sensible body is heavy or light and if it goes by
nature towards the Center when heavy but up when light, it is evident
that one cannot truly say both that an infinite body exists and that each
body has a [proper] place. For this must be the case also with the
infinite body, but neither all of it nor each of its halves can be affected
30   in either way.[45] For how will one divide it,[46] or how will one part of the
infinite be up and another down, or one part at the extreme and another
at the Center?[47]

Further, every sensible body is in a place, and the species or differentiae of place are up, down, front, behind, right, and left, and these
are specified not only relative to us or in position[48] but also in the
35   whole[49] itself; yet these cannot exist in the infinite. And, without quali-
206*a*   fication, if no infinite place can exist and if every body is in a place, then
no infinite body can exist. Moreover, that which is somewhere is in a
place, and that which is in a place is somewhere.[50] So if the infinite
cannot be a quantity (for if it were, it would have to be some quantity,
5   e.g., two feet or three feet or the like, since it is these that "quantity"
signifies), then likewise it cannot be in a place; for if it were, it would
have to be somewhere, and this would be up or down or in some other
of the six directions, each of which is a boundary.[51]

It is evident from what has been said, then, that no infinite body
exists in *actuality*.

6

          That many impossibilities result if the infinite, taken without quali-
10   fication,[1] does not exist is clear from what will follow, namely, (a) there
will be a beginning and an end of time, (b) magnitudes will not [always]
be divisible into magnitudes, and (c) there will not be an infinite
number.[2]

If no alternative appears possible when things are stated in this manner, then an arbiter is needed; and clearly there is a way in which the
infinite exists and a way in whch it does not. Indeed, in one sense, "to
15   be" is used for what exists potentially, and in another, for what exists
actually; moreover, the infinite exists by addition and also by removal.[3]
That the infinite does not exist in actuality has already been stated,[4]
but it exists by division; and it is not hard to reject the hypothesis that
indivisible lines exists.[5] Accordingly, we are left with the alternative
that the infinite exists potentially.

However, the potential existence of the infinite must not be taken to
20   be like that of a statue; for what is potentially a statue may come to be
actually a statue, but this is not so for what is potentially infinite.[6] But

it cannot
become actual

since "to be" has many senses, the infinite exists in the sense in which the day exists or games exist, namely, by always coming into being one after another; for these too exist both potentially and actually, e.g., Olympic games exist both in the sense that they *can* come to be and in the sense that they are *occuring*. However, it is clear that there is a distinction in the way in which the infinite exists in time and in men and in the division of magnitudes. For, although in general the infinite exists in the sense that one thing is always being taken after another, each thing so taken being always finite but always another and another (hence, the infinite should not be considered as being a *this*, e.g., a man or a house, but as we speak of a day or a game whose being, even if finite, is always in generation and destruction, not as something which became a *substance*, but always becoming one thing after another), yet in the case of magnitudes the parts taken persist, while in the case of time and of men they are destroyed but not exhausted.[7]

The infinite by addition is in a sense the same as that by division,[8] for in a finite magnitude the infinite by addition occurs in a way inverse to that by division; for as that magnitude is seen to be divided to infinity, the sum of the parts taken appears to tend toward something definite. For if in a finite magnitude one takes a definite part and then from what remains keeps on taking a part, not equal to the first part but always using the same ratio,[9] he will not traverse the original finite magnitude; but if he is to so increase the ratio that the parts taken are always equal, he will traverse it, because every finite magnitude is exhausted by any definite magnitude.[10] Thus it is in this and not in any other way that the infinite[11] exists, namely, potentially and by reduction. And it exists actually in the way in which a day and the games are said to exist,[12] and potentially in the way in which matter exists; and, unlike that which is limited, it exists not by itself.[13]

And the infinite by addition exists potentially in this manner,[14] which as we said is in a sense the same as that by division; for although there is always something outside of it that can be taken, it will not surpass every definite magnitude, unlike the infinite by division, which surpasses in smallness any given definite magnitude and remains smaller thereafter. As to surpassing every magnitude by addition, the infinite cannot do so even potentially if indeed it does not exist actually as an attribute;[15] and this is unlike what the natural philosophers say, namely, that the body which is outside of the world, whose *substance* is air or some other such thing, is infinite. But if no sensible body can be actually infinite in this manner,[16] it is evident that neither can it exist potentially by addition, except in a manner inverse to that by division, as already stated. It is because of this that Plato, too, posited two infinites,[17] namely, in view of the fact that it is thought possible to surpass all

30   magnitudes and proceed to infinity in the direction both of increase and
of reduction. Yet though he posits two infinites, he does not make any
use of them; for neither in numbers does the infinite exist in the direction
of reduction, seeing that the unit is the smallest, nor in the direction of
increase, seeing that he posits Numbers up to Ten only.[18]

207*a*   Now the infinite turns out to be the contrary of what they say it is; for
it is not that outside of which there is nothing, but that outside of which
there is always something. A sign of this is the following: People say
that rings without a bezel are infinite [endless] as there is always some-

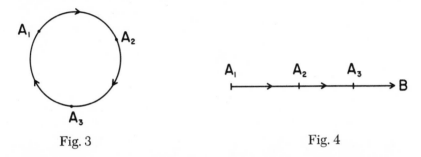

Fig. 3   Fig. 4

thing outside [beyond] that may be taken. But they say this in virtue
5   of some similarity and not in the main sense;[19] for both (a) this[20] must
be the case and (b) the same thing must not be taken again, while in
the circle this is not what happens but [only] (a) the succeeding part is
always distinct.[21] Thus the infinite is that outside of which, with respect
to taking a quantity, there is always some part [yet] to be taken.[22] On
the other hand, that of which there is no part outside is complete or a
10   whole; for this is how we define a whole,[23] namely, that from which no
part is absent, as in the case of a whole man or a whole box. And as in
the case of each individual, so it is when the term "whole" is considered
in the main sense,[24] that is, the whole is that outside of which no part
exists; but, in every case, that from which there is a part absent (whatever that part may be) is not a whole. The whole and the complete are
either entirely the same or quite close in their nature.[25] Nothing is com-
15   plete which has no end, and the end is a limit.
In view of this, Parmenides must be considered to have spoken better
than Melissus; for the latter says that the whole is infinite,[26] while the
former says that the whole is finite and equally balanced from the
middle. For to attach the infinite to the universe or the whole is not
to tie a string to a string,[27] although it is because of some similarity to
the whole that they attribute dignity to the infinite (namely, that of
20   containing all things and of having in itself the universe). For the infinite
is the matter of the completeness of a magnitude and is potentially the

whole and not actually,[28] and it is distinguishable as proceeding in the direction of both reduction and its inverse, which is addition; and as for its being a whole and finite, it is not so in itself but in virtue of something else.[29] And qua infinite it does not contain but is contained; and because of this, it is unknowable qua infinite, for matter has no form.[30] So it is evident that the infinite is in the formula of a part rather than in that of a whole; for the matter [of a whole thing] is a part of the whole, just as the bronze in the case of a bronze statue, since if, we might add, in both sensible and intelligible things the *Great* and *Small* does indeed act as a container, it should contain the intelligibles.[31] But it is absurd and impossible for the unknowable and the indefinite to contain or to limit [something else].

25

30

7

It is according to reason, too, to think that no infinite by addition is such as to surpass every magnitude, but that every magnitude may be surpassed in smallness by an infinite by division; for, like matter, the infinite too is contained inside, while it is the form which contains.[1] It is also reasonable to think that (a) in numbers there is a limit in the direction of the least, but in the direction of the greater every plurality can always be surpassed, (b) while in magnitudes, on the contrary, every given magnitude can be surpassed in the direction of the less, but in the direction of the greater there can be no infinite magnitude.

35

207b

5

The *reason* for this is the fact that the one[2] is indivisible, whatever it is that is just one; for example, a man is one man and not many; but a number is many ones or a quantity of things. Hence, in numbers, there must be a stop in the direction of the indivisible, for "two" and "three" are derivative terms,[3] and the same applies to each term which signifies a number. In the direction of the greater, however, it is always possible to think of a greater number, for the bisections of a magnitude may be infinite, so [in this direction] an infinite number exists potentially and not actually.[4] But this number will always surpass any definite plurality as the parts are taken one after another; yet neither is it separable from that bisection,[5] nor does its infiniteness *rest* but is in the process of becoming, as in the case of time and the number of time.[6]

10

15

With magnitudes, the contrary is the case, for the continuous is infinitely divisible; but there is no infinite in the direction of the greater, for whatever size a [sensible] magnitude may be potentially, it may also be *actually*. Hence, since no sensible magnitude can be infinite, it is not possible to exceed every definite magnitude; otherwise, something greater than the heaven would be possible.[7]

20

The infinite is not the same in magnitude and in motion and in time in the sense that it is one nature, but the infinite which is posterior is named according to the infinite which is prior; for example, the motion of a thing is called "infinite" in view of the fact that the magnitude over which the thing is being moved or is being altered or is growing is infi-
25   nite, and time is infinite because motion is infinite. At present, these are taken for granted, but later we shall try to state what each of them is and why every magnitude is divisible into magnitudes.[8]

Our account, which rejects the infinite as existing in *actuality* and as being untraversible in the direction of increase, does not deprive the
30   mathematicians from investigating their objects; for neither do they need it nor do they use it in this way,[9] but only in the way in which, for example, they extend a finite line as far as they wish, and any magnitude may be divided in the same ratio as that in which the greatest magnitude may.[10] Thus, as far as proofs are concerned, an infinite of this sort makes no difference, but as for the existence of an infinite, it is in existing magnitudes.

35   As there are four senses of "cause", it is evident that the infinite is a
208*a*   cause as matter and that its being is a privation,[11] and the subject in virtue of which it exists is that which is continuous and sensible.[12] All the other thinkers who use the infinite appear likewise to use it as matter;[13] and for this reason, too, it is absurd that they should posit it as containing and not as being contained.

8

5   It remains to meet the arguments according to which the infinite is thought to exist not only potentially but as something definite, for some of them are not necessary, and there are true replies for the others.[1]

(1) If generation is to come to an end, it is not necessary that an
10   infinite sensible body exist in *actuality;* for the destruction of one thing may be the generation of another, while the whole universe remains finite.[2]

(2) To touch and to be limited are distinct. The first is related to something else or is of something else (for every thing that touches does touch something else) and is an accident of something which is finite;[3] but neither is that which is limited [necessarily] related to something else (since its limit is only in itself), nor is it possible for any chance thing to touch any other chance thing.

15   (3) To base our convictions on [just] thinking is absurd, for excess and deficiency here are not in the things but in thinking. For one might think that each of us is becoming many times greater than our [actual]

size and that we might continue doing so to infinity. But because of this, that is, of the fact that one so thinks, it does not follow that we are beyond the city or that we exceed our own size; we are as great as we are, and that one is thinking about it is an accident.[4]

20   (4) Concerning time and motion, they are infinite, and so is thinking, but each part that is taken does not remain.[5]

(5) As for a magnitude, it cannot be infinite [in *actuality*], whether by way of reduction or by increase through thought.[6]

We have stated, then, how the infinite exists, how it does not exist, and what it is.

Book Δ

1

As in the case of the infinite, so in that of place the physicist must
know if it exists or not, how it exists, and what it is; for all believe[1] that
30   existing things are somewhere (nonbeing, on the other hand, is nowhere;
for where is a goat-stag or a sphinx?) and that the most common and
most independent[2] motion, which we call "locomotion", is a motion with
respect to place.

As to what a place is, there are many problems that arise; for if a
place is viewed from all [the attributes] that belong to it, it does not
35   appear to be the same. Moreover, nothing is available to us from the
previous thinkers by way of a statement of the *difficulties* about it or of
a solution.

208b   That a place exists seems clear from the replacement of one thing by
another, for where water is at one time, at a later time air will be there
after the water has gone out as from a vessel; and since it is the same
5   place that is occupied by different bodies, that place is then thought to
be distinct from all the bodies which come to be in it and replace each
other. For *that* in which air is now, in *that* there was water earlier; so,
clearly the place or space[3] into which these came and out of which they
went would be distinct from each of them.

Moreover, the locomotions of physical bodies and of simple bodies
10   (e.g., of fire, earth, and the like) make it clear not only that a place is
some thing, but also that it has some power. For each of those bodies, if
not prevented, travels to its own place, some of them up and others
down;[4] and these (up and down and the rest of the six directions) are
parts and species of place. Now such directions (up, down, right, left,
15   etc.) do not exist only relative to us; for to us a thing is not always the
same in direction but changes according as we change our position,
whichever way we may happen to turn, and so the same thing often is
now to the right, now to the left, now up, now down, now ahead, now
behind. By nature, on the other hand, each of these is distinct and exists

20 apart from the others; for the up-direction is not any chance direction but where fire or a light object travels, and likewise the down-direction is not any chance direction but where heavy or earthy bodies are carried, as if these directions differed not only in position but also in power. Mathematical objects, too, make this clear; for they are not in a place,[5] and with respect to position it is [only] relative to us that they have a

25 right and a left; so the position of each of these has no nature but is only conceived [by the soul].[6]

Further, those who say that a void exists include a place in their statement, since a void would be a place deprived of a body.

Through these arguments one might come to the belief that a place is something existing apart from bodies and that every sensible body is

30 in a place. Hesiod too might be thought to have spoken rightly when he posited the *Gap*[7] first. At least he said:

First of all did the *Gap* come to be, then broad-breasted earth,

as if he held that space should first exist for things to be in it, because he thought, like most people, that all things are somewhere or are in a place. If such is the case, then the power of a place would be something

35 marvelous and prior[8] to all other things; for that without which the

209a other things cannot exist, whereas it can exist without them, must of necessity be first,[8] for a place does not perish if the things in it are destroyed.

Yet even if it exists, there is still a *difficulty* as to what it is, whether a sort of volume of a body or some other nature, for its genus must be sought first.[9]

5 (a) Now it has three dimensions—length, width, and depth—by which every body is bounded. But a place cannot be a body, for then two bodies would be in the same thing.[10]

(b) Moreover, if indeed a body has a place or space, clearly also a surface and each of the other limits have [a place],[11] for the same argu-

10 ment applies to them; for where the bounding surfaces of the water were before, there in turn those of the air will be. But we observe no difference between a point and its place;[12] hence, if the place of a point is not distinct from that point, neither will there be a distinction in the case of the others, and so their place will not be something besides what they are.

(c) What else, then, shall we posit a place to be? Having such a

15 nature, it is neither an element nor composed of elements, whether these be corporeal or incorporeal; for it has a magnitude but no body, and yet the elements of sensible bodies are bodies while from the elements of intelligible things no magnitude at all can be generated.[13]

(d) Further, of which things would one posit a place to be a cause? For it can be no cause in any of the four senses of "cause", whether as matter of things (for no thing consists of it), or as form or formula of things or as end or as a mover of things.[14]

(e) Again, if a place is itself a being, where will it be? Thus, Zeno's *difficulty* must be met with an argument; for if every thing is in a place, clearly a place too is in a place, and this goes on to infinity.[15]

(f) Finally, just as every body is in a place, so also in every place there is a body.[16] How are we then to speak about growing things? For, from what has been said, the place of such things must also grow with them, that is, if the place of a thing is neither less nor greater than that thing.[17]

Because of all this, it is necessary to raise the problem not only as to what a place is, but also if it exists.

2

Since B may be predicated of A either in virtue of A or in virtue of some other thing,[1] in the case of a place, too, there may be a common place in which all bodies are or a proper place in which a given body primarily is.[2] I mean, for example, that you are in the heavens by being in the air, which is in the heavens, and you are in the air by being likewise on the Earth, and similarly you are on the Earth by being in *this* place which contains no more than you.[2]

If, then, the place of each body is what primarily contains it, it would be a boundary; so it would seem that the place of each body is its form or *shape*, by which the magnitude or[3] the matter of the magnitude is bounded, for this is the boundary of each. If we view the problem in this manner, then, a place would be the form of a body; but insofar as a place is regarded as the interval of the magnitude, it would be the matter of a body (for this is distinct from the magnitude), and this is what is contained and is limited by the form, as by a surface or a boundary. Now such are matter and the indefinite; for when the limit and the affections of the sphere are removed,[4] what remains is none other than matter.

This is why Plato says in the *Timaeus* that matter and space are the same; for the receptacle and space[5] are one and the same. Although the manner in which he speaks about the receptacle in the *Timaeus* differs from that in the so-called "*Unpublished Doctrines*",[6] he explicitly states that place and space are the same. And although all the others said that a place is something, he alone tried to say what it is.

In view of all this, it is with good reason that it seems difficult to know what a place is, if indeed a place is any one of the two, whether matter or a form, especially when these require an examination of the highest kind[7] and when it is not easy to know one of them apart from the other.

Nevertheless, it is not difficult to see that a place cannot be either of these two; for neither the form nor the matter exists separately from the thing, but its place can exist separately from it. For, as we said, where air was, there in turn water comes to be, water replacing air; and similarly with other bodies. Thus a place is neither a [material] part nor a possession[8] of the thing but is separable from it; for a place seems to be something like a vessel,[9] which is a transportable place, but the vessel is no part of the thing.[10] Accordingly, qua being separable from the thing,[10] the place of it is not its form, and qua containing [the thing], it is distinct from the matter of that thing. Also, if a thing is somewhere, in every case it is thought that both the thing itself is something and also something else is outside of it.[11] So Plato should have stated, if we may digress, why the Forms or the Numbers are not in a place,[12] if that in which things participate is a place (whether this be the *Great* and the *Small* or matter), as he wrote in the *Timaeus*.

Again, if a place were matter or a form, how would a thing travel to its own place? For it is impossible for that to which neither motion nor up nor down can belong to be a place.[13] So a place should be sought in things to which these can belong.[14] And if a place were in the thing (for it would have to be, if indeed it were a form or matter), then a place would be in a place. For both the form and the indefinite are changing or are moved along with the thing, not always in the same place, but where the thing also is; and so there would be a place of a place.[15]

Again, if water is generated from air, its place perishes; for the body that is generated would not be in the same place. Which of the destructions will this one be, then?[16]

We have given arguments, then, both for the necessary existence of a place and for the *difficulties* that might be raised about its *substance*.

3

We should next enumerate the ways in which one thing is said to be *in*[1] another.

(1) As the finger is in the hand, and in general, as a part[2] is in the whole.

(2) As the whole is in the parts, for the whole does not exist apart from the parts.

(3) As "man" is in "animal", and in general, as a species is in its genus.[3]

20 (4) As a genus is in the species, and in general, as a part of a species is in the formula of the species.[4]

(5) As health is in the hot and the cold,[5] and in general, as the form[6] is in the matter.

(6) As the affairs of the Greeks are in the king, and in general, as things are in[7] the first mover.

(7) As a thing is in the good, and in general, as it is in[8] its end, and this is its final cause.

(8) In the most important[9] sense, as a thing is in a vessel, and in general, in a place.

25 One might also raise the question of whether a thing can be in itself,[10] or nothing can, but a thing either is in no thing or is in some other thing. Now the thing may be said to be in something in two ways, either in virtue of itself or in virtue of something else.[11] For when that which is in something else and that in which it is are parts of a whole, then the whole can be said to be in itself; for a thing can also be stated by its parts, for example, a man is called "white" since his surface is 30 white, and he is called "a scientist" since science is in his reasoning power.[12] Accordingly, a jar will not be in itself, and wine will not be in itself; but the jar with wine will, for both that which contains and that which is contained are parts of the same thing.[13] So it is in the latter sense that a thing may be in itself, and not in the primary sense; for 210b example, whiteness is in the body (for the surface is in the body) and science is in the soul, and it is according to these which are parts of a man that he is spoken of as "white" or a "scientist".[14] In the case of the jar and the wine, if they are separate from each other, they are not parts of a whole, but if they are together, they are parts of a whole. Hence, when a thing has parts, it will be possible for it to be in itself.[15] 5 For example, whiteness is in the man by being in his body, and it is in the body by being in its surface, but it is in the surface in virtue of no other thing;[16] and these two, the surface and whiteness, are distinct in kind and have a distinct nature or power.[17]

If we examine things inductively, then we observe no thing[18] as 10 being in itself in any of the [listed] senses of "in", and clearly this situation is impossible also by argument; for each of two things would have to be both of them, if indeed a thing can be in itself. For example, the jar would have to be a vessel as well as wine, and wine would have to be wine as well as a jar. So, however true it might be that each is in the other, the jar will receive the wine not insofar as the jar is wine

15   but insofar as the wine is wine, and the wine will be in the jar not insofar as the wine is a jar but insofar as the jar is a jar.[19] Clearly, then, with respect to what it is to be each,[20] the two are distinct;[21] for the formula of that which is in something is distinct from the formula of that in which it is.

    Further, neither is it possible for a thing to be in itself by accident,
20   since two things might then be simultaneously in the same thing; for if a thing with a receptive nature can be in itself, then both the jar and that which the jar can receive (the wine, if it is wine) might be in themselves.

    Clearly it is impossible for something to be in itself primarily.

    The *difficulty* raised by Zeno, that if a place were something it would have to be in something, is not difficult to solve; for nothing prevents a
25   primary place from being in another thing, not however in that thing as in a place, but as health is in heat by being a possession of heat and as heat is in the body by being an affection of the body.[22] Thus there is no necessity of proceeding to infinity. In the other case, however, it is evident that since the vessel is no part of what it contains (for what contains primarily is distinct from what is contained primarily), a place
30   cannot be the matter or the form of the thing [contained] but is something else; for these (both matter and *shape*) are parts of what is contained.[23]

    This then may serve as the discussion of the *difficulties* concerning a place.

4

    As to what a place is, this should become evident from what follows. Let us enumerate what is thought truly to belong to it essentially [or primarily]. Our requirements[1] are these:

211a   (1) A place is what contains that of which it is the place, and it is no part of the thing contained.

    (2) The primary place is neither less nor greater than the thing contained.[2]

    (3) A place can be left behind by the thing contained and is separable from it.[3]

    (4) Every place has the attribute of being up or down;[4] and by nature
5   each body travels to or remains in its *proper* place, and it does so in the direction of up or down.[5]

    With these assumed, the rest should be investigated. We should try to make our inquiry in such a way that the whatness of a place is given and in such a way that (a) the *difficulties* raised are solved, (b) what

10   is thought to belong to a place will belong to it, and (c) the cause of the
trouble and of the problems raised concerning it will become clear; for
such would be the best way of presenting each thing.

First, we must bear in mind that there would have been no inquiry
about place if motion with respect to place did not exist; for it is because
of this that we also consider the heaven to be in a place most of all, see-
15   ing that it is always in motion. Of this motion, one kind is locomotion,
the other is increase or decrease;[6] for a thing changes also by increasing
or decreasing, and what was earlier in this place has later passed into
another which is lesser or greater.

Now a thing may be *actually* in motion (1) essentially[7] or (2) acciden-
20   tally; and of things accidentally in motion (a) some can be in motion by
themselves, as in the case of the parts of a body and the nail in the ship,[8]
and (b) others cannot move but do so always as attributes, as in the case
of whiteness and *knowledge,* for these change only in the sense that it
is that to which they belong that changes.[9]

So since, using "in" as "in a place", we say that a thing T is in the
25   heavens because it is in the air and air is in the heavens, and that T is
in the air (but not in all of it) because the innermost part[10] of the air
which contains T is in the air[11] (for if the place [of T] were all the air,
the place of a thing would not be equal to the thing;[12] yet it [the place]
is thought to be equal to it [the thing], and such is the primary place
in which it [the thing] is), (a) when that which contains is not divided
30   from but is continuous with what is contained, the latter is said to be
in the former, not in the sense that it is in a place, but as a part[13] in a
whole, but (b) when that which contains is divided from and touches
that which is contained,[14] then the latter is in the primary and innermost
part[10] of that which contains, and this part[15] is neither a part of nor
greater than the interval of what is contained but is equal to it, for the
extremities of things which touch each other coincide.

35   Moreover, if what is contained is continuous with what contains it,
the former is said to be moving not in the latter but *with* the latter; but
if it is divided from it, then it is said to be moving *in* the latter, regardless of whether the latter is in motion or not.[16]

211b   Further, when that which is contained is not divided from what contains it, the former is said to be in the latter as a part in a whole, for example, as sight in the eye or as a hand in the body,[17] but when it [the
contained] is divided, it is in the latter [the container] as water is in
the vessel or as wine is in the jar;[18] for a hand is moving *with* the body
5   whereas the water is moving *in* the vessel.

It is now evident from what has been said what a place is, for there
are four main things of which it must be one: either (1) the *shape*[19] or
(2) the matter[20] or (3) a sort of interval[21] between the extremities or

else (4) the extremities,[22] if no interval exists apart from the magnitude of the body which is enclosed by the extremities. It is evident that it cannot be three[23] of them:

(1) Because of the fact that a place contains a body, the place of it is thought to be its *shape;* for the extremes of what contains and of what is contained coincide.[24] Now both are limits, but not of the same thing. The one is the form of the thing; the other is the place of the containing body.

(3) Because of the fact that what is contained and is divided can often change (as water does from a vessel), while that which contains stays the same, it is thought that a sort of interval exists between the extremities, as if some thing in addition to the body which is displaced.[25] Yet no such thing exists, but what enters the container[26] is just a chance body which is subject to displacement and is by nature in contact with another body. If the interval were by nature something and at *rest*, then an infinite number of places would be in the same place, for as water and air displace each other, all the parts in the whole will do just what all the water does in the vessel; and in addition, the place too would be subject to change. Thus, a place would be in another place, and many places would be together.[27]

Now when the whole vessel is displaced, the place of a part [of what is contained in it] is the same as and not distinct from that in which it [the part] is moving. For the air and the water, or the parts of the water, replace each other in the place in which they are, and not in the place into which they come to be; and this place is a part of a place which itself is a place of the whole heaven.[28]

(2) Matter too might be thought to be a place, at least if one views something as being in that[29] which is at rest and is continuous but not separate. For just as in a thing[30] which alters there is that which is now white but was formerly black or that which is now hard but was formerly soft (and in view of this we say that matter is something), so a place is thought to exist because people imagine it in a manner such as this, except that in the former case it is because *what* was formerly air is now water, while in the case of a place it is in view of the fact that *where* air was formerly *there* is now water. But matter, as stated earlier, is neither separable from the thing nor contains [something], while a place does both.[31]

Well then, if a place is none of the three, that is, neither the form nor the matter nor yet a sort of interval always present with but distinct from the thing which is displaced, it must be what remains of the four alternatives, namely, the containing body's boundary which is in contact with what is contained[32] (and by "the contained body" I mean the one that is movable with respect to locomotion).

A place is thought to be an object of importance and difficult to grasp, both because it appears to be present with the matter and the shape [of a thing] and because the displacement of a body in locomotion occurs
10   in a container which is at rest; for within [the inner boundary of the container] there appears to exist an interval distinct from the magnitudes in motion.[33] The air, too, which seems to be incorporeal, contributes something to this belief; for a place appears to be not only the [inner] boundary of the vessel but also what is within it as if a void.[34]
15   Now just as the vessel is a place which can be in locomotion, so a place is an immovable vessel.[35] So when something inside is moving or changing in something else which is in motion, as a boat in a river, it uses the containing body as a vessel rather than as a place.[36] Now a place is meant to be something motionless; so in the example it is rather the whole river [basin][37] which is a place, since the whole river is motion-
20   less. A place, then, is this, namely, the primary motionless boundary

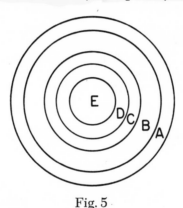

Fig. 5

of that[38] which contains. And it is in view of this that the Center of the heaven and the last [inner surface] of the rotating part of heaven[39] toward us are thought to be, most of all and principally,[40] *down* and *up* respectively, since the first always stays the same,[41] while the last [inner surface] of the rotating part stays in the same condition.[42] Thus,
25   since a light body is that which by nature travels up and a heavy body is that which [by nature] travels down, it is the containing limit[43] in the direction of the center [of the universe] which is down, and the Center itself is down,[44] while it is the part[45] bordering the last [inner surface] which is up, and that last [surface] itself[46] is up. And it is because of this that a place is thought to be a surface and something like a vessel and something which contains.[47] Moreover, a place is together with
30   the thing [contained], for the limit [of that which contains] coincides with that which is limited.[48]

5

A body, then, is in a place if it is contained by another body outside of it, and it is not in a place if it is not so contained. On account of this, even if a body not so contained were to be water, its parts [1] would be in motion (for they are contained by one another); but the universe would be in motion in one sense but not in another. For it would not change if it were taken together as a whole;[2] but it would be moved in a circle, for [in such a motion] its parts[1] would have a place.[3] And although these parts would not be moved up or down, some of them would be moved in a circle; but other parts would be moved up or down, if some of them are dense and others are rare.[4]

As we said, some things are in a place potentially, others *actually*. So, when a homogeneous body is continuous, its parts are in a place potentially,[5] but when these parts are separated[6] yet in contact, like a heap, they are in a place *actually*.

Also, some things are in a place essentially, that is, every body which is movable with respect to locomotion[7] or with respect to increase[8] is somewhere essentially.[9] But the heaven considered as a whole, as stated earlier, is nowhere and in no particular place, that is, if there is no body which contains it; yet with respect to the way in which it is in motion, its parts[10] do have a place, for they are consecutive to each other.

Again, some things are in a place accidentally, like the soul and the heaven,[11] for the parts of the latter [the heaven] are somehow in a place since along the circular direction one part contains another.[12] And so the upper part [of the heaven] moves along a circle, but the universe [as a whole] is not moving anywhere. For if A is somewhere, both A itself is something and also something else must exist in which A exists and which contains A. But nothing besides the universe or the whole exists which is outside the universe, and because of this all things are in the heaven,[13] for the heaven is perhaps[14] all there is. And a place is not the heaven itself, but the innermost boundary of a part of heaven which [boundary] is at rest[15] and in contact with a movable body; and because of this, earth is in water, water in air, air in ether,[16] and ether in the heaven, but the heaven is in no other thing.

It is evident from these remarks that if a place is such as stated, also the problems[17] raised concerning it will be solved. For it is not necessary (f) for the place of a thing to grow along with the thing[18] or (b) for a point to have a place[19] or (a) for two bodies to be in the same place[20] or (c) for a bodily interval[21] to exist (for what is within a place is a chance body but not an interval for a body).[22]

35

212b

5

10

15

20

25

Also, (e) a place too is somewhere, not as something in a place, but as a limit in the limited (for not every being is in a place, but only a movable body).[23]

30   Again, (d) it is reasonable that each body should travel to its own place,[24] for things in succession and in contact but not by force are alike in kind,[25] and they are unaffected by each other when they are by nature together,[26] while they can act on or be affected by each other when they are [just] in contact with each other.[27] And further, it is not without reason that each [body] stays by nature in its *proper* place. For any
35   given part in the whole place is like a divisible part in relation to its
213a   whole, as if one were to disturb a part of water or of air.[28] And it is also in this manner that air is related to water, as if[29] one of them were matter and the other a form, that is, water as if the matter for air and air as if the *actuality* of the other [of water]; for water is potentially air, and it is in another manner that air is potentially water.[30] These
5   distinctions will be made later; but we must mention them now even if *unclearly* because the occasion requires it, and we shall postpone a *clearer* statement of them till then.[31] If, then, it is the same thing that is matter and actuality (for both are water, the one existing potentially
10   and the other in actuality), the relation would be in some manner as that of a part to a whole.[32] And they are in contact, on account of this; but there is a natural unity when both become one in *actuality*.[33]

We have stated, then, both that a place exists and what it is.

_____

6

In the same way, we should believe that it belongs to the physicist to speculate about a void, whether it exists or not and how it exists or what it is, as he does about a place; for, because of what is believed
15   about it, a parallel conviction or lack of conviction holds about a void as about a place. For those who posit a void as existing speak of it as a sort of place or vessel, which is thought to be full when it has the mass which it can receive, but void[1] when deprived of any mass, as if that which is a void[2] or full or a place were the same thing,[3] even though the essence of these is not the same.[4]

20   We should begin the inquiry by taking into account (a) what is said by those who claim that it exists, (b) what is said by those who claim that it does not exist, and (c) the common opinions concerning them.[5]

Those who try to show that no void exists do not refute what people mean by "a void" but use the term erroneously, as in the case of Anaxa-
25   goras[6] and those who refute the existence of a void in this manner; for

by twisting wineskins[7] and showing that air has force and by cutting air off in clepsydras, they show that air is something. But what people mean by "a void" is an interval in which there is no sensible body;[8] and thinking that all beings are bodies, they say a void is that in which there is nothing at all and consequently that[9] which is filled with air is a void.[10] So what needs to be shown is not that air is something, but that no interval can exist, whether separable or in *actuality*, as something which is distinct from bodies and which is so partitioned by the total body[11] as to have its continuity broken (as Democritus[12] and Leucippus and many other natural philosophers say), even if such interval is taken as being something outside of the universe and as being continuous.[13] So it is not these thinkers who meet the problem head-on, but rather those who claim that a void exists.

The latter thinkers[14] say that no motion with respect to place (i.e., locomotion or increase) will otherwise exist; for no motion is thought to exist without a void since what is full cannot receive any more. If it could receive, in which case two bodies could be in the same place, it would be possible for any number of bodies, too, to be in the same place; for one could not point to some number beyond which what has just been said is not true. Now if this were possible, the smallest could receive the greatest,[15] for the great is many smalls; so if many equals could be in the same place, many unequals could likewise so be.[16] (Melissus even proves from all this that the universe is immovable;[17] for, he says, if it can move, it is necessary for a void to exist, but a void for him is not a being.) So this is one way of showing from all this that a void is something that exists.

Another way arises from the fact that some things appear to inter-penetrate or to be compressed; for example, they say that a cask full of wine will also hold the skins,[18] as if the shrinking body contracted into the voids present in it.[19]

Again, it is thought that increase, too, takes place through a void, for food is a body, and two bodies cannot be together.[20] This is also confirmed by what happens to a vessel full of ashes, which can take as much water as it does when empty.[21]

The Pythagoreans, too, said that a void exists, that it enters the heavens from the infinite breath as if the heavens inhaled also the void, that it demarcates the natures of things, as if it were something that separates and brings out the boundaries of things in succession, and that it does this first to numbers, for it is the void that demarcates their nature.[22]

Such and so many, then, are about all the arguments from which some assert and others deny the existence of a void.

7

30   As to which of the two alternatives[1] is the case, we should [first] lay
down the meaning[2] of the term.

A void is thought to be a place with no thing in it. The *reason* for this
is the fact that things are considered to be bodies, every body to be in a
place, a place with no body in it to be a void, hence, a void to exist
214*a*   where there is no body. Moreover, every body is considered to be tangi-
ible, and such would be whatever is either heavy or light. Accordingly,
it follows by a syllogism that a void is that in which there is nothing
heavy or light.

These results then follow syllogistically, as we said before. It is ab-
5   surd to raise the problem of whether a point is a void or not; for in order
to be a place, a point must be an interval for a tangible body.[3]

Thus, in one way, it appears that a void is said to be that which is not
filled with a body that is sensible by touch; and what is sensible by
touch is heavy or light.[4] And in view of this, one might also raise the
10   question: What would one say if an interval were to have [just] a sound
or a color; would it be a void or not? Clearly, if it could receive a tangible body, it would be a void, but if not, it would not.[5]

In another way, a void is [said to be] that[6] in which there is not a
this or a corporeal substance.[7] And in view of this, some say that a void
is the matter of a body, if indeed it [the void] is also the place of it
[the body].[8] But in regarding the two [matter and place] as being the
15   same, they do not speak well; for the matter is not separable from the
thing,[9] yet they inquire about a void as something which is separable.[10]

Now since we have discussed place, and a void if existing must be a
place without a body in it, and since we have stated how a place exists
and how it does not, it is evident that a void does not exist in this man-
20   ner,[11] whether inseparable or separate; for the term "a void" is intended
to mean not a body but the interval of a body. And it is in view of this
that a void is thought to be something, seeing that also a place is thought
to be something, and for the same *reasons*.[12] For motion with respect to
place seems to support both those who claim that a place is something
apart from the bodies which go in it and those who claim that a void is
something apart from those bodies. The latter thinkers think that a void
25   is a cause of motion in this sense, namely, as something in which a body
moves; and this would be the sort of thing which other thinkers call
"a place".

Now there is no necessity for a void to exist if there is to be a motion.
It need not exist for every motion (and Melissus failed to see this), for

30

214b

the full may change with respect to quality;[13] nor is it necessary for a motion with respect to place, for bodies in motion may simultaneously make way for each other although no separate interval apart from them exists. And this is also clear in the whirling of continuous bodies, as in that of liquids.[14] Things may also be condensed, not into any void in them, but because what is in them is squeezed out, as when the air in the water is squeezed out when water is compressed.[15] And things may expand not only when something else enters into them, but also when they are altered, as when water changes to air.[16]

5

In general, the argument about increase conflicts with itself, and so does the one about the water being poured on to the ashes.[17] For either (a) no one[18] part of a body increases,[19] or (b) a body increases but not by a body,[20] or (c) it is possible for two bodies to be in the same place[21] (these thinkers claim to be solving a common *difficulty*, but they do not show that a void exists), or (d) every body is a void if it increases in every part and does so by a void.[22] The same argument may be used also in the case of the ashes.[23]

10

It is evident, then, that it is easy to refute the arguments from which they show that a void exists.

8

Let us again proceed with our argument that no separate void exists in the manner in which some say it does.

15

If each of the simple bodies has a locomotion by nature[1] (for example, the locomotion for fire is upwards, for earth it is downwards or towards the Center), it is clear that the void would not be the cause[2] of that motion. Of what, then, will the void be the cause? For it is thought to be the cause of motion with respect to place, but it is not the cause of this.

20

Again, if it [void] is something like a place deprived of a body, then if a void were to exist, where would a body placed in it go? It will certainly not travel in every direction. The same argument may also be brought against those who think that a place is something separate into which a body travels; for how will a body placed within it travel elsewhere or *rest*? It is reasonable that the same argument will apply to the void, to the place up, and to the place down; for those who declare that a void exists posit it as being a place. And how will something exist in a place or in a void? For when a whole body is placed in it as in a separate place, this is not like something being in a supporting body; for a part of the body, if not placed separately, will be not in a place but in the whole [body].[3] Again, if a place does not exist, neither will a void.[4]

25

As for those who say that a void must exist if there is to be a motion,
on careful examination one finds that what results is the contrary,
namely, that not a single thing can be moved if a void is to exist; for as
with those who say that earth is at rest because of the similarity [of the
surroundings], so a body in a void must likewise be at rest, seeing that
there is no one direction in which it will have a greater tendency or a
lesser tendency to move, for the void qua void has no differentiae.[5]

Then, again, every motion is caused either by force or according to
nature; so if there is a motion by force, there must also be one according to nature, for a motion by force is contrary to nature, and a motion
contrary to nature is posterior[6] to the one according to nature. Hence,
if no motion according to nature can exist in each of the physical bodies,
neither can any of the other motions exist in it. And how can there be a
motion by nature if there are no differentiae with respect to the void or
the infinite? For in the infinite, qua infinite, there can be no place which
is up or down or the center, and in the void, qua void, there can be no
difference between a place up and a place down. For just as there are no
differentiae in nothingness [zero], so there are none in nonbeing; and a
void is thought to be a nonbeing and a privation, while in a locomotion
by nature there is a differentia, and so there will be differentiae in things
which exist by nature.[7] Accordingly, either no object can have anywhere
a locomotion by nature, or if it can so have, there can be no void.

Again, things which are thrown are in motion, though that which
pushed them is not touching them, either because of mutual replacement, as some say,[8] or because the air that has been pushed pushes
[them] with a motion which is faster than the locomotion of the things
pushed,[9] that is, the locomotion with which those things travel to their
proper place. But in a void none of these things can take place,[10] nor can
an object be in locomotion unless it is carried by another.[11]

Again, none of these thinkers could say why a body which has been
caused to be in motion will stop somewhere; for why should it stop in
one place rather than in another? So either it will be resting or it will
of necessity be travelling without an end, unless obstructed by something more powerful.[12]

Again, a body is thought to be travelling into a void because the latter
yields, but in the void such yielding exists alike in all directions and so
a body would be travelling in every direction.[13]

Again, what we maintain is evident also from what follows. We observe that the same weight or[14] body travels faster for two *reasons,*
either because there is a difference in the medium through which it
travels, as through water or earth or air, or because, other things being
the same, the travelling body has an excess of density [or weight] or of
lightness.[15] The medium through which the body travels is a cause by

30   the fact that it obstructs that body, most of all if it [the medium] is travelling in the opposite direction, but even if it is *resting;* and it does so more if it is not easily divisible, and such is a more viscous medium.[16]

215*b*   The body A, then, will travel through medium B in time C and through medium D (which is less viscous) in time E, these [C and E] being proportional to the obstructing medium,[17] if the lengths of B and D are equal. For let B be water and D be air. Then the extent to which

5   air is less viscous or less corporeal than water is proportional to the extent to which A travels faster through D than through B. Let the two speeds have the same ratio as that by which air differs from water. Then if air is half as viscous[18] as water, A will travel through B in twice the

10   time as it will through D, and C will be twice as long as E. And always, the more incorporeal or less obstructive or more easily divisible is the medium, the faster will the body travel through it.

But there is no ratio in which the void is exceeded by a body, just as there is no ratio of zero [nothingness] to a number.[19] For if 4 exceeds

15   3 by 1, and 2 by more than 1, and 1 by still more than it exceeds 2, still there is no ratio by which it exceeds zero; for that which exceeds is of necessity divisible into the excess and that which is exceeded,[20] but in this case 4 would be the sum of that by which it [i.e., 4] exceeds zero and zero. It is in view of this that also a line does not exceed a point, if

20   a line is not composed of points.[21] In a similar way, there can be no ratio of a void to what is full,[22] and so neither can there be a ratio of the motions through these;[23] but if, in a given time, a body travels through the least viscous[24] medium a certain distance, the distance it will travel through a void [in the same time] will exceed the other distance by every ratio.

For let Z be a void, equal in magnitude to that of B or of D. Then if A

25   were to go through and complete it[25] in a certain time H, which is less than E, this would be the ratio [i.e., H:E] of the void to the full. But A traverses a part of D, say K, in a time equal to H; and it also traverses [in time H] any body L differing in viscosity[26] from air in the ratio

30   which time E has to time H. For if body L is as much less viscous than

216*a*   D as E exceeds H, then A, in travelling through L, will traverse it with an inverse speed in as much time as H. Moreover, if there were no body in the magnitude of L, A would traverse it [the magnitude] more quickly. But A was posited as traversing that magnitude[26] [equal to that of Z] in time H.[27] Hence, A would traverse in equal times [equal magnitudes of] what is full[28] and what is void respectively, and this is impossible. So it is evident that if A were to traverse any part of a void in

5   some given time, the impossible result would be this: A would be traversing [equal magnitudes of] what is full and what is void in equal times; for there is a body whose ratio to a given body is as one time is to another time.[29]

To sum up, it is clear that the cause of this result is the fact that there
10   is a ratio of one motion to another motion (for these take time, and any
given time is in a ratio to any other time, if both are finite), but there
is no ratio of the void to the full.

These are the consequences, then, insofar as the differences are in the
media through which bodies travel; but if there is a difference with respect to the excess of one body over the other, then the consequences
are as follows. We observe that bodies which have a preponderance in
15   weight or lightness, if alike in other ways,[30] travel faster over equal
space intervals, and in the ratio which the magnitudes[31] have to each
other. So they should be travelling through the void in the same way.
But this is impossible; for by what cause would they be travelling faster?
For in travelling through what is full they must go faster; for the greater,
by means of its force, divides the medium faster, since a body that
travels or is let go divides the medium either by its shape or by the pre-
20   ponderance of its weight [or density]. So they will all travel with equal
speeds.[32] But this is impossible.

It is evident from what has been said, then, that if a void exists, what
results is contrary to that for the sake of which a void is posited by those
who say it exists. They think that, if indeed there is to be a motion with
25   respect to place, a void must exist and exist as something separate by
itself, and this is the same as to say that a place must exist as something
separate; but it has already been stated that this is impossible.[33]

Even if we examine this [the void] by itself,[34] it will appear that the
so-called "void" will turn out to be something without foundation. For
just as, when one immerses a cube in water, the quantity of water displaced will be as much as that of the cube, so will it be when in air, al-
30   though this is not evident by sensation. And indeed always in the case
of every body capable of displacement, if it is not compressed, it must
undergo displacement in the direction in which it is its nature to do so,
namely, always down if its locomotion is [by nature] downwards, as in
the case of earth, or upwards as in the case of fire, or in both directions,[35] or whatever the case may be,[36] depending on the kind of body
immersed. But in the case of a void this is impossible, for a void is not
35   a body;[37] and it would seem that through the cube there must have
216b   penetrated an interval [of void] equal to that which was formerly in the
[whole] void, as if the water or the air were not displaced by the
wooden cube [immersed in it] but all of that part penetrated into the
cube.

Moreover, the cube too has as much magnitude as that possessed by
5   the void; and this, whether also hot or cold, or heavy or light, is no less
distinct in essence from all changing affections, even if it is not separable,[38] and by "this" I mean the volume[39] of the wooden cube. And so,
even if this [volume] were to be separated from all the other things and

be neither heavy nor light, it would possess an equal amount of void[40] and would be in the same part of the place or of the void, which [part] is equal to itself.[41] Then how would the body of the cube differ from the void or place which is equal to it?[42] And if there are two such things[43] together, why should there not be also any number of them? This, then, is one absurd and impossible consequence.

In addition, it is evident that the cube will have this[44] also when undergoing displacement, and this will be the case with all other bodies too. So, if this does not differ from a place,[45] why posit a place for bodies in addition to their volume, if a volume cannot have any affections? For it contributes nothing, if along with it there is another equal interval of such a kind. (Again, it should be clear from things in motion what sort of thing a void is. In fact, it exists nowhere within the universe; for air is some thing, though it does not seem to exist, nor would the water to fishes, if these were made of iron,[46] for the tangible is *judged* by touch).[47]

From what has been stated, then, it is clear that no void exists as something separate.

9

There are some who regard the existence of a void as evident because rare and dense objects exist. For if no rare or dense things exist, it is not possible for things to interpenetrate or be compressed. And if this cannot be, either (a) no motion at all can exist, or (b) the universe will pulsate,[1] as Xuthus said, or (c) air and water must change into equal volumes (I mean by this, for example, that if a cup of water were to become [a certain volume of] air, then at the same time an equal volume of air would become so much [i.e., a cup] of water), or else void must exist; for compression or expansion cannot take place in any other way.[2]

Now if by "rare" they mean that which has many separate voids, it is evident that if no void can exist separately (just as no place can exist with only an interval in it),[3] neither can a rare object exist in this manner. But if they mean that a void cannot exist separately and yet is present in the rare,[4] this is less impossible. First, a void will be a cause not of every kind of motion but of upward motion (for what is rare is light, and on account of this they say that fire is rare);[5] then again, a void will be a cause of motion not as that in which [things are in motion], but in the sense that it carries things up just as the skins [in water] do which, by going up, carry along what is continuous with them [i.e., heavy things attached to them]. But how can the void have a locomotion or a place? For there will be a void into which this void travels.[6] Then again, how will these thinkers account for the fact that heavy objects travel downwards?[7] It is also clear that if the more rare or more void the object is the quicker it travels upwards, then what is altogether void[8] will travel up the quickest. But perhaps it is impossible for it to move; and just as all things would be immovable when in a void, for the same reason the void would be immovable, for the speeds would be incomparable.[9]

Since we deny that a void exists and the other *difficulties* have been truly stated, namely, that either no motion will exist if there can be no condensation or rarefaction or the heaven will pulsate or the volumes in the change from air to water and from water to air will always be equal (for it is clear that water changes into a greater volume of air), then, if no compression exists, either the body which is pushed outward must cause the extremity of the universe to expand, or somewhere else an equal volume of air must be changing to water if the volume of the whole [universe] is to remain equal, or nothing can be moved; for where something is displaced, this will always happen unless locomotion is circular,[10] and locomotion is not always circular but also rectilinear.[11]

It is indeed because of such arguments that these thinkers might say that a void exists. Our argument, on the other hand, proceeds from what has been laid down, namely, (a) that there is a single matter for contraries, that is, for the hot and cold and the other physical contrarieties, (b) that it is from potential being that actual being is generated, (c) that matter is not separable though it is distinct in being,[12] and (d) that matter may be numerically one, for example, for color and heat and cold.[13]

Now the same [numerical] matter may be matter for a great as well as for a small body. This is clear from the fact that when water becomes air, the same matter becomes something not by adding to itself something else, but that which it itself was potentially comes to be *actually,* and again air becomes water in the same manner; and so the change is sometimes from smallness to greatness in magnitude and sometimes from greatness to smallness. And so, similarly, if a great volume of air becomes smaller or a small volume becomes greater, it is the [same] matter which exists potentially that comes to be both. For just as it is the same matter that changes both from cold to hot and from hot to cold, this being by virtue of the fact that it is potentially both, so also it is when the change is from hot to more hot, this being by virtue of the fact that in the matter no other thing came to be hot which was not hot at the time when the thing was less hot.[14] And just as (a) in the case of the arc and the convexity of a greater circle when it [the arc] becomes an arc of a smaller circle, being the same arc and no other,[15] the [new] convexity generated [in it] belongs to no thing which was straight but not convex (for the more and the less does not exist as something to be interposed)[16] and (b) in the case of a flame there is no magnitude of it in which both heat and whiteness are not present,[17] so is the heat at an earlier time related to the heat at a later time. So, too, when a small sensible volume becomes great, the matter is extended not by adding to itself something else, but by virtue of the fact that it is potentially both. (Again, just as an arc of a circle does not take in something concave when it is drawn together into a smaller circle, but it is what existed before that was drawn together, and in the case of fire any part that one may take will be hot, so in the case of a whole it is the same matter that contracts or expands.)[18] So it is the same object that is at one time dense and at another rare,[19] and there is a single matter for these two. Now that which is dense is heavy, and that which is rare is light, for there are two [attributes] associated with each of these, that is, with the dense and the rare; for the heavy and the hard are thought to be dense, while their contraries (the light and the soft) are thought to be rare. However, in the case of lead and iron there is a discrepancy with respect to heaviness and hardness.[20]

From what has been said, then, it is evident that a void does not exist separately, whether without qualification[21] or in what is rare[22] or potentially,[23] unless one wishes to call "a void" any cause of locomotion, in which case the matter of what is heavy or light, qua such, would be a void;[24] for it is with respect to this contrariety that the dense and the rare can cause locomotion, while with respect to softness or hardness they can or cannot be affected and so be causes of alteration and not of locomotion.[25]

Concerning the void, then, how it exists and how it does not, let this be our account.

10

Next to what has been said comes the discussion of time. Concerning time, we would do well, by using the common[1] arguments also, to go over the *difficulties* (a) as to whether it is a being or a nonbeing and (b) as to what its nature is.[2]

That time is either altogether nonexistent, or that it exists but hardly or obscurely, might be suspected from the following: One part of it has come to be but no longer exists; the other part will be but does not yet exist; and it is of these two parts that infinite time, or any time one might take, is composed. But it is thought that what is composed of nonbeings cannot participate in *substance*.[3]

In addition, if any thing with parts is to exist, then, when it exists, all or some of its parts must exist. But, although time is divisible, some parts of it have been and the others will be, and no part of it exists. And as for a moment, it is no part of time; for a part measures the whole,[4] and the whole must be composed of the parts, but it is thought that time is not composed of moments.[5]

Again, it is not easy to see whether the moment which appears to divide the past and the future (1) always remains one and the same or (2) is always distinct.

(2) If it is always distinct, while no two distinct parts of time exist simultaneously unless one part contains while the other is contained (as the smaller interval of time is contained by the greater), and if a moment which does not exist but existed before must have been destroyed sometime, then two moments cannot exist simultaneously, but always the prior moment must have been destroyed. Now the prior moment cannot have been destroyed in itself[6] because it existed then. And it cannot have been destroyed in some later moment. For let us posit that moments, like points on a line, are not consecutive to each other; then if indeed it was not destroyed in a succeeding moment but in another,[7] it would have existed simultaneously with the infinitely many moments between itself and that other, and this is impossible.[8]

(1) Moreover, neither is it possible for the same moment to remain always the same; for no finite and divisible thing, whether continuous in one or in many dimensions, has just one limit, and the moment is a limit, and it is possible to cut off a finite time.[9] In addition, if to be simultaneous, but not prior or posterior, with respect to time is to be in the same thing, which in this case is the moment, and so if both the prior and the posterior[10] were to be in this moment,[11] things which happened ten thousand years ago would exist simultaneously with those happening today, and no one event would be either prior or posterior to another event.[12]

Let this, then, be the discussion of *difficulties* faced in connection with what belongs to time.

As to the whatness or the nature of time, it is as unclear from the accounts handed down to us as it is from the *difficulties* just discussed.

218*b*   Some say that time is the motion of the whole;[13] others say that it is the sphere itself.[14] But then a part of a revolution will be time, and it [i.e., that part] is certainly not a revolution; for what we have here taken is a part of a revolution, not a revolution. Moreover, if there were more than one heaven,[15] the motion of any one of them, like that of any other, would be time in a similar way, and so a plurality of times would exist simultaneously. As for those who said that time is the sphere of the whole, they thought so in view of the fact that all things are in time and also in the whole sphere; but this is too superficial [a doctrine] to require an examination of its impossible consequences.[16]

However, since time is thought to be most of all a sort of motion or of change, we should look into this. Now a change or motion of each thing exists only in the thing which is changing or wherever it happens to be moving or changing; but time exists alike both everywhere and with all things. Moreover, every change is faster or slower, but time is not; for the slow and the fast are defined in terms of time (the fast is that which moves much [distance] in a short [time], and the slow is that which moves a little [distance] in a long [time]), but time is not defined in terms of time, whether taken as being quantitative or as being qualitative.[17] Thus it is evident that time is not a motion; and it makes no difference at present whether we use the term "motion" or the term "change."[18]

11

On the other hand, time cannot exist without change; for when there is no change at all in our *thought* or when we do not notice any change, we do not think that time has elapsed, just like the legendary sleeping characters in Sardinia who, on awakening from a long sleep in the presence of heroes,[1] connect the earlier with the later moment into one moment, thus leaving out the time between the two moments because of their unconsciousness. Accordingly, just as there would be no intermediate time if the moment were one and the same, so people think that there is no intermediate time if no distinct moments are noticed. So if thinking that no time has elapsed happens to us when we specify no limits of a change at all but the soul appears to *rest* in something[2] which is one and indivisible, but we think that time has elapsed when sensation has occurred and limits of a change have been specified, evidently time does not exist without a motion or change.

It is evident, then, that neither is time a motion nor can it exist without a motion.

Since we are inquiring into the whatness of time, we should begin by considering how time belongs to a motion.[3] Now together with a motion we sense time also. For even if it is dark and we are not being affected through the body but some motion exists in the soul, we think without hesitation that along with that motion also time has elapsed; and further, when some time is thought to have elapsed, it appears that also some motion has occurred simultaneously. Thus time is either a motion or something belonging to a motion; and since it is not a motion,[4] it must be something belonging to a motion.

Since a thing in motion is moved from something to something else and every magnitude is continuous, a motion follows a magnitude;[5] for a motion is continuous because a magnitude is continuous, and time is continuous because a motion is continuous (for the time elapsed is al-

15 ways thought to be as much as the corresponding motion which took
place).[6] Now the prior or the posterior are attributes primarily of a
place, and in virtue of position. So since the prior and the posterior exist
in magnitudes, they must also exist in motions and be analogous to those
in magnitudes; and further, the prior and the posterior exist also in time
20 because time always follows a motion.[7] Now the prior and the posterior
exist in a motion whenever a motion exists,[8] but the essence of each of
them is distinct [from a motion] and is not a motion. Moreover, we also
know the time when we limit a motion by specifying in it a prior and a
posterior as its limits; and it is then that we say that time has elapsed,
25 that is, when we perceive the prior and the posterior in a motion. And
we limit it [the time] by believing that they are two distinct things and
that there is something else between them; for when we conceive the
extremes as being distinct from what is intermediate and the soul says
that there are two moments, the one prior and the other posterior, it is
then that we also say that this is time, for what is limited by moments
30 is thought to be time,[9] and let this be assumed. So when we perceive the
moment as being one, and not as prior and again as posterior in a motion, or as being the same thing, but as prior to something and as posterior to something else,[10] then no time is thought to have elapsed since
219*b* neither was there a motion. But when we perceive it now as prior and
later as posterior, then we say that time has elapsed. For time is just
this: The number of a motion with respect to the prior and the posterior.
So time is not a motion, but a motion has time qua the number of it.[11]
A sign of this is the following: We *judge* the greater and the less by a
5 number, and we *judge* a motion as being greater or less by time;[12] so
time is a sort of number.

Now since "a number" has two senses (for both that which is numbered or is numerable is a number, and also that by which[13] we number), time is that which is numbered[14] and not that by which we number
(that by which[13] we number is distinct from that which is numbered);
10 and just as a motion is always distinct, so is time.[15] But taken simultaneously every time is the same, for the moment whenever existing is
the same, though in essence it is distinct;[16] and, qua being prior and
posterior, it measures time.[17] The moment is in one way the same and
in another not the same; for, qua being now in one [subject] and now in
another, it is distinct (this is the essence of its being that moment), but
15 qua a being whenever it exists, it is the same.[18] For, as stated before,
and in our manner of saying, a motion follows a magnitude, and time
follows a motion. And a travelling object, by which we know the motion and both the prior and the posterior in it [the motion], follows a
point[19] in a similar way. And whatever this [20] may be (whether a point
20 or a stone or some other such thing), it is the same,[21] but in formula it is
distinct[22] (just as the sophists regard Coriscus in the Lyceum as being

distinct from Coriscus in the Agora); and it is distinct by being now in one place and now in another. A moment follows a body in locomotion just as time follows a motion, for it is by the body in locomotion that we

25 know the prior and the posterior in that motion;[23] and qua being numerable, the moment exists as prior or posterior.[24] So in these, too, when existing as a being, the moment is the same (for what is prior or posterior is the [same] body in motion),[25] but in essence it is distinct,[26] for it is qua numerable that the moment is prior and posterior. And it is this [27]

30 that is most knowable, for a motion too is known because of the body in motion; and a locomotion is known because of the body in locomotion, since it is the body in locomotion that is a *this* and not the motion. In one way, then, that which is called "a moment" is always the same, but in another it is not; for so it is in the case of the body in locomotion.

It is also evident that neither would a moment exist if time did not

220a exist, nor would time exist if a moment did not exist; for just as an object in locomotion and that locomotion are together, so the number[28] of an object in locomotion and the number of that locomotion are together. For the number of a locomotion is time, and a moment is like an object

5 in locomotion, as if a unit of a number.[29] Moreover, time is also continuous by means of a moment, and it is divisible with respect to a moment;[30] for this too follows from the corresponding locomotion and the object in that motion, since (a) the motion or locomotion is one with the object which is in locomotion, seeing that this [object] is one, not as a being when existing (for it might also stand still) but in formula,[31] and (b) the object in locomotion determines the prior and the posterior mo-

10 tion.[32] And an object in locomotion follows in a way a point; for a point both maintains the continuity and serves as a limit of a line, since it is the beginning of one and the end of another line. But if a point is so taken that it is used as two, a stop is necessary, if the same point is to be a beginning as well as an end. As for the moment, it is always distinct

15 because the body in locomotion is always in motion; hence time is a number not as in the case of the same point when this is both a beginning and an end,[33] but rather as the extremities of the same object,[34] and not as if these were parts, both because of what was said (for the intermediate point will be used as two, and so there will be rest) and because it is evident that neither is a moment a part of time nor is a division a

20 part of a motion, just as points are not parts of a line. However, two lines are parts of a line. Accordingly, qua being a limit, a moment is not time but an attribute [of it],[35] but qua numbering, it is a number; for the limits belong only to that of which they are the limits, but the number of [say] these horses, e. g., ten, belongs also elsewhere.

25 It is evident, then, that time is a number of motion with respect to the prior and the posterior and that it is also continuous (for it is of something which is continuous).

12

The smallest number, taken without qualification, is two.[1] But if the number is qualified,[2] in one sense there is a smallest, but in another there is not. For example, in the case of lines, the smallest number in
30   plurality is two or one;[3] but as a magnitude there is no smallest, for every line is always divisible.[4] So it is likewise with time; for, with respect to number, the smallest is one or two, but there is no smallest with respect to magnitude.

220*b*   It is also evident that we do not speak of time as being fast or slow, but we speak of it as being much or little and long or short. For qua continuous, it is long or short, but qua a number, it is much or little.[5]
5   But it is not fast or slow, just as no number by which we number things is fast or slow. Also, time everywhere is simultaneously the same; but time existing before is not the same[6] as time existing after, since a change, taken at present as one, is distinct from a change in the past and from one in the future.

Time as a number is not that by which we count[7] but that which is
10   counted, and, occurring before and after, it is always distinct, for the moments are distinct. The number of one hundred horses and of one hundred men is one and the same,[8] but the things of which it is the number are distinct: Horses are distinct from men. Also, just as a motion may be one and the same[8] again and again, so can time also, as a year or a spring or an autumn.

15   Not only do we measure a motion by time, but also time by a motion, because they limit each other; for an interval of time limits a motion by being the number of that motion, and a motion limits the time. And we say that the time taken is much or little by measuring by a motion just as we speak of a number by measuring by the numerable, as for example
20   by one horse in the case of the number of horses. For we know a plurality of horses by its number, and again, we know the number of horses itself by one horse.[9] And it is likewise with time and motion; for we measure a motion by time, and time by a motion.[10] And this happens
25   with good reason, for a motion follows a magnitude and time follows a motion, since they are all quantitative[11] and continuous and divisible; for a motion has these attributes because the corresponding magnitude is such-and-such a thing, and time has them because of the motion. And we measure both a magnitude by the corresponding motion, and the
30   motion by the magnitude; for we say that the road is of great distance if the journey is great, and the journey is great if the road is of great distance, and also that the time is much if the motion is, and the motion is much if the time is.[12]

221*a*   Since time is a measure of motion and of being moved,[13] it measures a given motion when some one motion is specified which will measure the whole motion (like a foot length which measures a given length, and this is done when some one magnitude is specified which will measure the whole [magnitude]). And for a motion to be in time is for both the motion and the being[14] of the motion[13] to be measurable by time (for that time will simultaneously measure both the motion and the being of that motion); and for a motion to be in time is just this, that its being be measurable. It is clear that for other things, too, to be in time is just this, that the being of each of them be measurable by time; for "to be in time" [for each thing] means one of the following two: (1) to exist when time exists, and (2) as we speak of some things, to be in a number, either (a) as a part or an *attribute* of a number, and in general, as something belonging to a number[15] or (b) in the sense that there is a number of the thing in question.[16]

Since time is a number, the moment and the prior and all such are in time just as the unit and the odd and the even are in numbers (for each of the latter is something belonging to a number, while each of the former to time), but things are in time as in a number.[16] If so, they are contained by time just as things in place are contained by place.[17] So it is also evident that to be in time is not to exist when time exists, just as to be in motion or in place is not to exist, respectively, when a motion or a place exists. For if to be in something were to be in it in this manner, all things would be in any chance thing, and so the heaven would be in a grain, for when the grain exists also the heaven exists. But this is an accident, while in the other case one thing necessarily follows another; so a thing in time is followed by time when the thing exists also, and a thing in motion is followed by a motion when the thing exists.

Since that which is in time is in a sense as in a number, corresponding to any thing which is in time, a greater time than that time may be taken. So all things in time are contained by time just like all other things which are in something, like the things in a place which are contained by a place. And a thing is somewhat affected by time, as in the usual saying that *time wastes things away,* and things grow old by time, and people forget through time, but they have not learned or become young or beautiful; for time in virtue of itself is a cause rather of destruction[18] since it is a number of motion, and what a motion does is to make a thing depart from what it is.[19]

It is evident, then, that eternal things, qua existing always, are not in time; for neither are they contained by time, nor is their existence measurable by time.[20] A sign of this is the fact that they are not affected at all by time, which indicates that they are not in time.

Since time is a measure of motion, it would also be, as an attribute,[21] a measure of rest, for every state of rest is in time. For, although a thing

10   in motion has necessarily moved, it does not follow that a thing in time moved also; for time is not a motion but a number of motion, and what is at rest may also be in a number of motion. However, not everything which is motionless may be at rest but only that which is deprived of motion but can by nature be moved, as it was stated earlier.[22]

15   To be in a number is to be a thing (a) of which there is a number and (b) whose existence is measurable by the number in which it is; and so if a thing is in time, it is measurable by time.[23] So time will measure both a thing in motion and a thing at rest, the one qua in motion and the other qua at rest; for it will measure the quantity of motion of the first and the quantity of rest of the other.[24] So a thing in motion will be mea-
20   surable qua a quantity[25] by time not without qualification, but insofar as its motion is a quantity. Thus no thing can be in time if it can be neither in motion nor at rest;[26] for to be in time is to be measurable by time, and time is a measure of motion as well as of rest.

It is evident, then, that not every nonbeing can be in time, as in the
25   case of things which cannot be otherwise, like the nonbeing of a diagonal of a square commensurate with the side.[27] In general, if time in virtue of itself is a measure of a motion, but a measure of the others[28] as an attribute, it is clear that the things whose existence is measurable by time must exist by being at rest or in motion. Accordingly things which are destructible and generable and, in general, things which at
30   one time exist and at another do not,[29] all of them must be in time; for there exists a greater time which will surpass their existence and the measure of their *substance.* Of objects which do not exist but are con-
222a   tained by time, some of them existed (e.g., Homer sometime existed) and others will exist (e.g., something in the future), depending on the direction in which time contains them, and if time contains them in both directions, then they both existed and will exist;[30] but if time does not contain them at all, then they neither existed nor exist nor will exist. Such are those nonbeings whose opposites[31] always exist. For example,
5   the diagonal of a square is always incommensurable with the side, and this[32] is not in time; accordingly a diagonal commensurate with the side does not exist in time, and so it always does not exist, seeing that it is the contrary of a thing which always exists. As for objects whose contraries are not eternal, it is possible for them to be and not to be, and generation and destruction of them is possible.

13

10   The [present] moment is a continuity of time, as it was stated,[1] for it makes the past and the future continuous; and it is a limit of time, for it

is the beginning of the one [the future] and the end of the other [the past]. But this is not evident as it is with the point, which persists.[2] The moment divides potentially, and, qua such, it is always distinct, but, qua connecting, it is always the same,[3] as in the case of mathematical lines. For, in thought, a point is not always one;[4] for if the parts [of a line] are divided, it [the point] is distinct, but qua one, the point is in every way the same.[5] So too with the moment: In one way, it is potentially a division of time; in another, it is the limit and[6] the unity of both [parts]. Both the division and the union are the same and with respect to the same, but in essence they are not the same.[7]

This is one way, then, in which the term "moment" [or "now"] is used, but in another, it means a moment which is near the moment in the first sense. We say "he will arrive now," meaning by this that he will arrive today; and we say "he arrived now," meaning that he came today.[8] But what is narrated in the *Iliad* did not take place now, nor did[9] the flood; for though the time from the present moment to these is continuous, their time is not near the present moment.

The expression "sometime" means a time definitely related to the moment taken in the first sense. For example, we say "Troy was captured sometime [ago]" and also "a flood will take place sometime [from now]"; for these [events] are determined in relation to the present moment. Thus there will be a certain quantity of time from now to the latter event, and there was a certain quantity of time from now to the former event; and if there is no time which is not sometime, every [interval of] time will be finite.[10] But will time come to an end? Certainly not, if indeed a motion always exists.[11] Is time then distinct or does the same time occur again and again? Clearly, as it is with motion, so it is with time. For if it is one and the same motion[12] that occurs at some time, then also the time will be one and the same, but if not, then not.

Since the present moment is both an end and a beginning of time, though not of the same time, but the end of what has passed and the beginning of the future, just as a circle has its convexity and its concavity in the same thing in some way, so is time always at a beginning and at an end;[13] and because of this, time is thought to be always distinct. For it is not of the same thing that the moment is both a beginning and an end, since if it were, it would be two opposites simultaneously and in the same respect.[14] And time will certainly not come to an end, for there is always a beginning of it.

The term "presently" signifies a part of future time which is near the present and indivisible moment, and "already" signifies a part of past time not far from that moment.[15] When will you walk? We say "presently", since we intend to do so in the near future, or we say "I already

walked". But we do not use the expression "Troy has already been captured" since the time of the event is too far from now. Also, "recently"
signifies a part of the past which is near the present moment. When did
you come?[16] We say "recently", if the time of this event is near the present moment. But we say "long ago", if a past event is far from now. A
thing is said to depart from its condition *suddenly* if it does so in a time
interval which is imperceptible because of its shortness; and every
change is by nature a departure from an existing condition.

All things which are generated or destroyed are so in time; and for this
reason some called time "the wisest of things", but Paron the Pythagorean, speaking more rightly, called it "the stupidest", in view of the fact
that we also forget in it.[17] It is clear then that time in virtue of itself
is a cause rather of destruction than of generation, as stated also earlier[18]
(for a change in virtue of itself is a departure from an existing condition),
but that it is accidentally a cause of generation and of being. An adequate sign of this is the fact that no thing is generated[19] without itself
being somehow in motion or acting, but a thing may be destroyed even
if it is not in motion. And it is this [change] most of all that is usually
said to be a destruction by time. However, it is not time that causes this
either, but this change happens to come to be in time.

We have stated, then, that time exists, what it is, the number of
senses of "moment", and what the terms "sometime", "recently", "already", "presently", "long ago", and "suddenly" mean.

14

With these distinctions thus laid down, it is evident that every change
or every thing in motion is in time; for the faster or slower exists with
respect to every change, since it appears to be so in every change. By
"the faster in motion" I mean that which, being in uniform motion and
over the same interval, changes into a subject before another does so,
for example, in locomotion, if both things move along the circumference
of a circle or both along a straight line, and similarly in the other cases.[1]
But what exists prior to another exists in time, for things are said to be
prior or posterior in virtue of their time interval from the present moment, which is the boundary of the past and the future; so since the
moments are in time, also the prior and the posterior will be in time, for
that in which the moments exist is also that in which the time intervals
between the moments exist. But the term "prior" with reference to the
past is used in a manner contrary to that with reference to the future;
for, with reference to the past, we call "prior" that which is further from
the present moment, and we call "posterior" that which is nearer, while

with reference to the future, we call "prior" that which is nearer to the present moment, and we call "posterior" that which is further. So since the prior is in time and every motion must have a prior, it is evident that every change and every motion is in time.

It is also worth inquiring how time is related to the soul and why time is thought to exist in everything, on the earth and on the sea and in the heaven. Is it not in view of the fact that it is an *attribute* or a possession of a motion, by being a number (of a motion), and the fact that all these things are movable? For all of them are in a place, and time is simultaneous with a motion, whether with respect to potentiality or with respect to *actuality*.[2]

One might also raise the problem of whether time would exist or not if no soul existed; for, if no one can exist to do the numbering, no thing can be numbered and so clearly no number can exist, for a number is that which has been numbered or that which can be numbered. So if nothing can do the numbering except a soul or the intellect of a soul, no time can exist without the existence of a soul,[3] unless it be that[4] which when existing, time exists, that is, if a motion can exist without a soul. As for the prior and the posterior, they exist in a motion; and they are time qua being numerable.[5]

One might also raise this question: Of what kind of motion is time the number? Is it of any kind? For things are generated and are destroyed and increase in time, and they also alter and travel in time. Accordingly, insofar as each of these [changes] is a motion, in that respect there is a number of each motion. On this account, it is of a continuous motion taken without qualification that there is a number, but not of a specific motion.[6] But, as it is, other things[7] may also be in motion, and there may be a number of each of those motions. Is there a distinct time for each of them, then, and will there be two equal times simultaneously, or is this not the case? Now there is one and the same time alike and simultaneously, though in species also those times which are not simultaneous are one and the same;[8] for if there were to exist dogs and also horses, seven in each case, their number would be the same. Likewise, the time of motions with simultaneous limits would be the same, although one motion might be fast and another not, or, one of them might be a locomotion and the other an alteration; yet their time would be the same, if indeed their number is equal and if they are also simultaneous, for example, in the case of an alteration and of a locomotion. And it is because of this that, although the motions may be distinct or separate,[9] their time is everywhere the same, seeing that the number of equal and simultaneous things is everywhere one and the same.

Since locomotions exist, and of these a circular locomotion also exists, and since the numerable is numbered by something which is of the

same kind (e.g., units by a unit, horses by a horse, etc.), in the same way
time is measured by some definite time. And it is measured as we said,
time by a motion and also a motion by time;[10] and this is so in view of
the fact that the quantity of both a motion and of a time interval is
measured by a motion definite in time. Accordingly, if of all things
under the same genus it is the primary that is their measure, a uniform
circular motion is a measure most of all since its number is most
known.[11] Neither an alteration nor an increase nor a generation can be
uniform, but a locomotion can.[12]

On account of this, it is thought that also time is the motion of the
sphere, for the other motions are measured by it and also time is measured by this motion. And because of this there arises also the common
saying that human affairs and all other things which have a natural
motion or generation or destruction are circles; and this is in view of
the fact that all these are *judged* by time and that they end and begin
as if according to some cycle, for also time itself is thought to be a
circle; and this again is thought to be so because it is of such locomotion
that time is the measure and is itself measured by such motion.[13] Thus,
to say that things which come into being are circles is to say that there
is a circle of time, this being so in view of the fact that time is measured
by a circular locomotion; for that which is measured appears to be
nothing else besides the measure, unless the whole be taken as a
plurality of measures.[14]

It is rightly said, too, that the number of sheep and that of dogs is the
same if they are equal; but they are neither the same ten nor the same
ten things, just as the equilateral and the scalene are not the same triangles although, being both triangles, they are the same figure; for
things are said to be the same if their differentiae do not differ, but not
so if their differentiae do differ.[15] For example, if the differentia of one
triangle differs from that of another, then the two triangles are distinct;
but as figures the two triangles come under one and the same differentia, and so they are not distinct figures. For one species of "a figure"
is "a circle", another is "a triangle", and of triangles, one species is "an
equilateral", another is "a scalene"; accordingly, also the latter [triangle]
is the same figure [as the former] for it too is a triangle, but it is not the
same triangle. So, too, the numbers mentioned are the same, for one of
them does not differ from the other by a differentia of "a number"; but
they are not the same ten, for the things of which "ten" is a predicate
differ: They are dogs in one case, but horses in the other.

Concerning time, then, both about time itself and whatever is pertinent to its inquiry,[16] let this be our discussion.

Book **E**

1

224*a*   Every thing that is changing does so either

(a) accidentally, as when we say that the musical is walking, when in fact what is walking is that of which musicality is an attribute;[1] or

25   (b) simply, i.e., when some part in it is changing, for we say that the body is being healed when in fact it is just the eye or the chest that is being healed, and these are parts of the whole body; or

(c) if it is in motion neither accidentally nor in the sense that only something in it is in motion, but by being primarily itself in motion,[2] and it is this that is essentially movable. Now one movable thing is distinguished from another in virtue of a distinct motion, as in the case

30   of the alterable,[3] and even within alteration the healable is distinct from that which can be heated.

It is likewise with the mover, for (a) it may move another accidentally,[4] or (b) it may do so in virtue of a part in it,[5] or (c) it may do so primarily and essentially; for example, it is the doctor who heals[6] [something], although it is the hand that strikes [something].

35   There are then (a) the primary mover and (b) that which is in motion and also (c) the time in which [a motion occurs], and besides these

224*b*   (d) that from which and (e) that to which [a motion proceeds]. For every motion proceeds from something and to something; and the primary object which is in motion and that from which it is moved and that to which it is moved are all distinct, as in the case of the wood and the hot and the cold which are, in the order given, that which is in motion, that to which the motion proceeds, and that from which the

5   motion proceeds.[7] Clearly, then, the motion is in the wood and not in the form; for what causes a motion or is moved is not the form[8] or the place or the so-much [a quantity], but there are a mover, that which is in motion, and that to which the thing in motion proceeds. (For a change is named after that to which a thing is moved rather

90

that that from which it is moved;[9] thus a destruction too is a change
to nonbeing, even if that which is being destroyed is changing from
being, and a generation is a change to being, even if from nonbeing.)

We have stated earlier what a motion is.[10] As to the forms and the
affections and the place to which things in motion are moved, these are
immovable,[11] like science and heat. However, one might raise the question of whether affections (like whiteness, which is an affection) are
motions,[12] for then there will be a change toward a motion. But perhaps
it is not whiteness that is a motion, but whitening.[13] And in these,[14] too,
a change may be (a) accidental or (b) in virtue of a part or of something
else or (c) primary and not in virtue of something else; for example,
that which is being whitened changes (1) to that which is being thought
accidentally (for to be thought is an accident of a color), (2) to a color
in view of the fact that the white is a part of a color, and (3) to Europe
in view of the fact that Athens is a part of Europe, but [it is changed]
to a white color essentially.

It has been made clear, then, how a thing, whether a mover or a thing
in motion, moves essentially or accidentally, or with respect to something else or primarily;[15] and it is also clear that a motion is not in the
form but in the thing in motion or in the movable when in *actuality*
[qua movable].[16]

Accidental change will be omitted from discussion, for it exists in all,
and always, and is a change for all things;[17] but nonaccidental change
does not exist in all, but only in contraries, in intermediates, and in contradictories.[18] We may be convinced of this by induction. Change proceeds also from an intermediate,[19] for this [the intermediate], being in
some sense an extreme, serves as a contrary relative to each of the two
contraries. On account of this, when an intermediate is related to a
contrary or a contrary to an intermediate, both are said to be contraries
in some sense; for example, the middle note is low relative to the high
but high relative to the low, and grey is white relative to black but black
relative to white.

Since every change is from something to something, as even the name
μεταβολή [= "change"] makes clear (for the word μετά indicates something after something else, and one of these comes before while the
other comes after), that which is changing would be limited to four
alternatives: either from a subject to a subject or from a subject to a
nonsubject or from a nonsubject to a subject or from a nonsubject to a
nonsubject; and by "a subject" I mean something signified by an affirmative term.[20] From what has been said, then, there must be only three
[kinds of] changes: (a) that from a subject to a subject,[21] (b) that from a

10   subject to a nonsubject,[22] and (c) that from a nonsubject to a subject; for there is no change from a nonsubject to a nonsubject because there is no opposition, whether between contraries or between contradictories.[23]

Now a change from a nonsubject to a subject with respect to contradiction[24] is a generation, and it is an unqualified[25] generation if the change is unqualified, but a qualified generation if the change is quali-

15   fied.[26] For example, a change from non-white to white is a qualified generation; but that from an unqualified not-being to a substance[27] is an unqualified generation, in virtue of which we say that a thing is generated in an unqualified and not in a qualified way.

A change from a subject to a nonsubject is a destruction, and it is an unqualified destruction if it is a change from a substance to not-being, but a qualified destruction if it is a change from a qualified being to the

20   opposed negative, as we said in the case of a generation.

Now if "nonbeing" has many meanings and there can be a motion neither of nonbeing according to composition or division[28] nor of potential nonbeing, which is the opposite of unqualified *actual* being [29] (for the not-white or not-good may nevertheless be accidentally in motion,

25   since the not-white might be a man,[30] but the unqualified not-*this* can in no way be in motion),[31] nonbeing can in no way be in motion;[32] and if this is so, then neither can a generation be a motion, for it is nonbeing that becomes [something].[33] For, however true it may be that something is generated with respect to an accident, it is still true to say that nonbeing belongs to that which is becoming [something] without quali-

30   fication. Likewise, nonbeing [34] cannot be at rest.[35] These difficulties, then, arise if nonbeing[34] is taken to be in motion; and, we may add, if every thing in motion is in a place, nonbeing would have to be somewhere, but it cannot be in a place. A destruction, too, cannot be a motion; for the contrary of a motion is a motion or rest, but a destruction is the contrary of a generation.

35   Since every motion is a kind of change, and there are three kinds of change as stated before,[36] and changes with respect to generation and

225b   destruction are not motions but are changes with respect to contradiction, only a change from a subject to a subject must be a motion. As for the subjects, they are contraries or intermediates; for a privation also is posited here as a contrary, and it is indicated by an affirmation, as in the

5   case of "naked", "toothless",[37] and "black". Hence, since the categories are distinguished as being of substance, quality, whereness, whenness, relation, quantity, acting, and being affected, there must be three [kinds of] motions, namely, those of quality, those of quantity, and those with respect to place.[38]

2

10 There is no motion with respect to a substance because no thing is contrary to a substance.[1] Nor is there a motion with respect to a relation; for, when one of the relatives is changing, the other may not be truly related to the first even if it is not changing,[2] and so their motion is accidental. Nor is there a motion of a thing which acts or is affected,

15 or of a thing in motion, or of a mover,[3] for there is no motion of a motion, no generation of a generation, and in general, no change of a change.

Now there may be a motion of a motion in two ways, either (1) when a motion is taken as a subject, as when a man [as a subject] is moved if he changes from light to dark (and in this sense, [we may ask] is a

20 motion, too, really heated or cooled or changing place or increasing or decreasing? This is impossible; for a change is not a subject.), or (2) when some other subject changes from one kind of change to another, as when a man changes from sickness to health.[4] But this too is not possible except accidentally, for this motion is a change from one kind to

25 another (and likewise with a generation and a destruction, except that the latter are changes into opposites in a certain way, while a motion is a change but not in a similar way).[5] Accordingly, a man will be changing from health to sickness and at the same time from this change to another change. So it is clear that if he becomes sick, he will have changed into some other kind of change (of course, he may also be rest-

30 ing), but not always into a chance change;[6] and this change, too, will be from something to something else. And so this opposite change will be that of becoming healthy.[7] But this [change] will be by accident; for example, in changing from recollection to forgetfulness, it is that to which these belong that changes now towards *knowledge* and now towards ignorance.[8]

Moreover, this will go on to infinity, if there is a change of a change or a generation of a generation; for if there is of the latter, so must there

35

226a be of the former.[9] For example, if an unqualified generation was being generated at some time, then also the thing in unqualified generation was being generated, and so it [that thing] was not yet a thing in unqualified generation but was in a qualified generation during this time; and again this, too, was something in the process of generation, and so it was not yet in the process of generation.[10] And since in an infinite

5 series there is no first, there will be no first [here] either, and thus no thing that succeeds it. Accordingly, none of them can be generated or be in motion or be changing.

Moreover, the same subject may have also a contrary motion and a coming to rest and a generation and a destruction. So when a thing in generation becomes a thing in generation, it is then being destroyed; for neither at the end of the process nor after the process is it a thing in generation, for what is [in the process of] being destroyed must exist.[11]

Again, there must be matter which underlies both that which is being generated and that which changes. What matter would this be which would become a motion or a generation in the manner in which a body or a soul changes with respect to quality?[12] And, in addition, into what will they be moving? For there must be something whose motion proceeds from something to something else, but this something is not a motion [as a subject] or a generation. And how can this be? For there is no learning of learning, and so no generation of a generation, and no specific generation of itself. Finally, since there are three kinds of motion [locomotion, alteration, increase or decrease], then the underlying nature, as well as that to which it proceeds, must be one of these; for example, a locomotion must be altering or moving locally.

In general, since a thing may be in motion in three ways,[13] either accidentally or in virtue of a part of it or in virtue of itself, a change may change only accidentally, as when he who is being healed is also running or learning.[14] However, we decided earlier to omit the discussion of accidental change.[15]

Since, then, there can be no motion of a substance or of a relation or of acting or of being affected, it remains that there can be a motion only with respect to quality or quantity or place, for there is a contrariety in each of these. Accordingly, let a motion with respect to quality be called "alteration", for this is the name commonly attached to this motion. By "a quality" I do not mean that which is in the *substance* of a thing (for a differentia, too, is called "a quality"),[16] but an affective quality in virtue of which a thing is said to be affected or to be incapable of being affected. As for a motion with respect to quantity, there is no general name for it, but "increase" and "decrease" are the names for the two kinds respectively: An increase is a motion toward a complete magnitude; a decrease is a motion away from a complete magnitude. Finally, a motion with respect to place has neither a general name nor a specific name for any of its kinds; so let "locomotion" be the general name, although this term in its main sense is applied only to things which do not by themselves stop when changing place and to things whose motion with respect to place is not caused by themselves.

A change within the same kind but with respect to the more and the less is an alteration; for a change from a contrary or to a contrary is a motion, whether unqualified or qualifiied,[17] and when toward the less,

5 it will be said to be a change to a contrary [of a quality], but when toward the more, it will be as if from a contrary to [the quality] itself. It makes no difference whether the change be qualified or unqualified,[17] except that the contraries in the first case must belong to the thing in a qualified way; as for "the more" or "the less", they apply to the thing which has or has not more or less of the contrary. From what has been said, then, it is clear that these are the only three motions that exist.

10 A thing is said to be motionless [or immovable] (a) if it cannot be moved at all, like a sound, which is [said to be] invisible; (b) if after much time a thing is moved with difficulty or its motion begins slowly, and in this case we say that it is hardly movable; (c) if a thing has a nature so as to be moved and can be moved, but it is not in motion when, where, and in the manner in which it is its nature to be in motion, and

15 of things called "motionless" only this is called "resting", for rest is the contrary of motion and so it would be the privation of motion in that which can be in motion.

It is evident from what has been said, then, what motion is, what rest is, how many changes there are, and what the kinds of motions are.

3

We shall next state what are togetherness, being apart, touching [or in
20 contact], intermediate [or between], succession, consecutiveness, and continuity, and to what kinds of things each of these by its nature belongs.[1]

Those things are said to be together in a place which are in one primary place;[2] and things are said to be apart if they are in distinct [primary places].[3] Things are said to touch if their boundaries are together.[4]

An intermediate is said to be that to which a changing thing by nature
25 first arrives before arriving at its extreme, if it changes by nature continuously. An intermediate exists as one among at least [5] three things. For whatever is an extreme is a contrary in a change, and a thing is moving continuously if it leaves no gap or [leaves] the smallest gap in the thing;[6] and we say "in the thing in which it moves", but not "during the time it moves", since nothing prevents a gap [in the thing] when,
30 for example, the highest note is sounded immediately after the lowest.[7] This is evident in changes with respect to place as well as in other kinds of changes. Since every change occurs between opposites, and these may be contraries or contradictories, and since there is nothing between contradictories,[8] it is evident that an intermediate must be between contraries.[9]

To be contrary in place is to be most distant along a straight line; for it is the shortest line that is limited [between two points], and a measure is that which is limited.[10] A thing is said to be in succession if, being after a principle, whether in position or nature or some other definite thing, there is no other thing in the same genus[11] [as itself] between itself and that which it succeeds.[12] For example, it is a line (or lines) that succeeds a line, a unit (or units) that succeeds a unit, and a house that succeeds a house (although nothing prevents something else [in another genus] from being between); for that which is in succession succeeds a certain thing and is posterior to it, e.g., it is not one that is posterior to two, nor the first day of the month which is posterior to the second,[13] but the other way around.

A thing which succeeds and also touches another is said to be consecutive to it. The continuous is a subdivision of the consecutive:[14] Things are said to be continuous if those of their limits which touch each other become one and the same, as the term "contained" signifies; but if these extremities are two, there can be no continuity. With this specification, it is evident that continuity belongs to a thing whose parts have become by nature one in virtue of the fact that their contact holds them together; and the manner of continuity which makes the parts one is also the manner in which the whole thing will be one, whether it be by being nailed together or by being glued together or by contact or by being grown along with each other.[15]

It is also evident that succession is first;[16] for that which touches must succeed, but not all that succeeds touches.[17] Hence succession exists in things which are prior in formula, as, for example, in numbers, in which there is no contact. And if there is continuity, there must be contact, but if there is contact, there need not be continuity;[18] for those extremities which touch and are together need not be one, but if they are one, they must also be together. Hence, a growing together is last in generation; for the extremities which are to grow together must [first] touch, but not all things that touch do grow together. But if things are not in contact, then clearly neither can they grow together. Accordingly, if, as some say,[19] there are points and units which exist separately, a unit can not be the same thing as a point; for contact may belong to the latter, but [only] succession to the former,[20] and something intermediate may be between points (for every line lies between points), but this is not necessary in the other case[21] (for there is nothing between two and a unit).

We have stated, then, what are togetherness,[22] being apart, touching, betweenness, succession, consecutiveness, and continuity and to what kinds of things each of these belongs.

35
227a

5

10

15

20

25

30

227b

4

There are many ways in which motions are said to be one, for "one" has many senses. Thus, (a) if they are motions with respect to the same form of predication, they are said to be generically one; for any loco-motion is generically one with any other locomotion, but an alteration is generically distinct from a locomotion;[1] (b) if they are generically one and also in an *indivisible* species,[2] they are said to be specifically one. For example, "color" has differentiae; so blackening is distinct from whitening, while with respect to a species every instance of whitening is the same[3] as every other instance of it, and every instance of blackening is the same as every other instance of it; and there are no differentiae to "whiteness". Hence any instance of whitening is specifically one with any other instance of whitening.[4] If, however, there are things which are genera and also species, it is clear that the corresponding motions will be specifically one but not in an unqualified way, as in the case of learn-ing, if "science" is a species of "belief", but a genus of each of the sciences.[5]

A problem might be raised, however, whether the motions are specifi-cally one if the same thing changes from the same to the same; for example, when a point[6] changes from A to B again and again. If they are specifically one, a circular motion will be the same as that along a straight line, and rolling will be the same as walking. But it was speci-fied that a motion is [specifically] distinct if that in which it occurs is specifically distinct, and, in this case, a circular line is distinct in species from a straight line.[7]

Generically and specifically, then, motions are one in the manner stated, but a motion is said to be simply one if it is one in *substance* and numerically one;[8] and what such a motion is will be clear from the distinctions that follow. Now there are three things which enter into what is said of a motion, namely, *that which, that in which,* and *that during which.* In saying "that which", I mean that there must be some-thing which is in motion, e.g., a man or gold;[9] and this must be moving in something, e.g., in a place or with respect to an affection;[10] and it must be in motion sometime, for every thing in motion is in time. Of these, to be generically or specifically one is to be one in *that in which* there is motion, and next, the motion must be in one time;[11] and to be simply one is to be one in all three. For *that in which* must be one and *indivisible,* e.g., one in species; and *that during which* must be one, that is, the time must be one and not intermittent;[12] and *that which* is in mo-tion must be one, but neither accidentally (like the light which is dark-

ening and Coriscus who is walking; Coriscus and the light are indeed
228a   one, but accidentally),[13] nor in virtue of something common (for two
men might be getting well during the same time from the same disease,
e.g., inflammation of the eye, yet this motion is not one [simply] but is
specifically one).[14]

In the case in which Socrates undergoes an alteration which is specifically the same but takes place now at one time and now at another, if
5   that which has been destroyed can become again numerically one, then
also this [alteration] will be one; otherwise, it will be the same [specifi-
cally] but not one.[15] There is another *difficulty* parallel to this,[16] namely,
whether health, and, in general, whether each habit or affection in a
body is one in *substance;* for the bodies which have them appear to be
10   in motion and in flux.[17] If a man's health in the morning is indeed the
same and one with his health now, why should it not also be numerically
one with his health after he recovers from sickness during an interval?
The same argument applies to both cases[18] (except for this difference:
if it is the same thing that is two, then it is numerically one in the case
of habits, for an *actuality* which is numerically one belongs to what is
15   numerically one; but if the habit is one, perhaps one might not think
that also the *actuality* need be one, for when one stops walking, the
walking no longer exists, but when he starts walking again, it exists).[19]
If, then, it is one and the same, one and the same thing might be destroyed and also exist many times.[20] These *difficulties,* however, lie out-
20   side of our present inquiry.[21]

Since every motion is continuous,[22] a motion which is simply one must
also be continuous (if indeed every motion is divisible); and if a motion
is continuous, it is one. For just as no chance thing is continuous with
any other chance thing,[23] so not every motion would become continuous
with every other motion, except for those whose extremities are one.
For, in the first place, some things have no extremities,[24] in the second,
25   other things do have extremities but they are distinct in kind and are
equivocally called "extremities";[25] for how would the extremity of a line
touch or become one with the extremity of walking? Accordingly, motions might be consecutive even if they are not the same, whether specifically or generically. For a man might fall sick immediately after running, but the two motions are not continuous; they are consecutive as in
30   a torch-race,[26] for the continuous was posited to be that whose ends are
one. Thus motions may be consecutive and in succession[27] in view of the
fact that time is continuous, but there may be continuity [in motions] in
228b   view of the motions [themselves], that is, when both extremities become
one. In view of this, it is necessary for a motion which is continuous and
simply one to be specifically the same, to be of one subject, and to occur
during one time. The motion must occur during one time in order that

there may be no interval of motionlessness between; for during such an interval there must be rest, and whenever there is rest between, there are many motions and not just one. Thus, if in a motion there is an interruption by a stop, there will be neither one motion nor a continuous motion; and a motion is [said to be] interrupted if there is an interval of time between [without motion]. And if not specifically one, there is not one motion, even if the time is not interrupted; for though the time is one, specifically there are distinct motions, for a motion which is one must also be specifically one, although a motion which is specifically one need not be simply one.[28] We have stated, then, the whatness of a motion which is simply one.

Again, a complete motion, too, is said to be one, whether it is with respect to a genus or to a species or to a *substance;* and this is like the other cases in which the complete and the whole come under unity.[29] But at times even an incomplete motion is called "one", but it must be continuous.[30]

Again, in a sense distinct from those mentioned, a motion is said to be one if it is regular. For in some sense an irregular motion is regarded as not one, but rather a regular motion is regarded as one, as in the case of a rectilinear motion; for an irregular motion is divisible.[31] The difference here, however, seems to be like that with respect to the more and the less.[32] Now regularity and irregularity exist in every [kind of] motion; for a thing might also alter regularly, and it might have a locomotion along a regular path, e.g., along a circle or a straight line, and it might increase or decrease in the same manner. Now irregularity may differ by being (a) in that [path] along which a thing is moving, for a motion cannot be regular if it is not along a regular magnitude (e.g., if it is along a broken line or a spiral or some other magnitude in which a random part does not [necessarily] fit on to another random part);[33] it may also differ by being (b) not in the place or in the time or in that toward which motion proceeds, but in the manner in which motion proceeds, for sometimes it is specified by fastness and slowness (for if the motion proceeds with the same speed, it is said to be regular [uniform], but if not, then irregular [nonuniform]). Consequently, neither are fastness and slowness species or differentiae of motion, seeing that they follow all motions which differ with respect to species;[34] nor again are heaviness and lightness, when a motion proceeds to the same thing, as when earth is related to earth or fire to fire.[35] Accordingly, although an irregular motion is one by being continuous, it is one to a lesser degree[36] [than a regular motion], as in the case of a locomotion along a broken line; and that which is to a lesser degree of something is always a blend which contains also the contrary.[37] So if every motion which is one may be regular or irregular, motions which are consecutive[38] but not the

5   same with respect to species would not be one or continuous; for how would a motion be regular if it is composed of an alteration and a loco-motion? The parts of a regular motion should fit one another.

5

Next, we must specify what kind of motion is contrary to a given mo-tion, and we must do likewise with *rest*. We must decide first whether
10   contrary motions are (a) [changes] from M and to M, e.g., from health and to health (like generation and destruction,[1] which are so regarded), or (b) from contraries, e.g., from health and from disease, or (c) to contraries, e.g., to health and to disease, or (d) from one contrary and to the other contrary, e.g., from health and to disease, or (e) from A to B and from B to A, where A and B are contraries, e.g., from health to
15   disease and from disease to health; for either one or more than one of these alternatives must be the case, as it is not possible to have opposi-tions in any other way.

Now (d) a change from a contrary to the other contrary is not a con-trary motion, for the two [changes] may be one and the same motion, e.g., the motion from health and the motion to disease.[2] However, to be one of these motions is not to be the other, just as to change from health
20   is not to change toward disease.[3]

Nor is (b) a change from one contrary a motion which is contrary to the change from the other contrary. For a motion from a contrary hap-pens to be a motion toward the other contrary as well as toward an intermediate[4] (we shall speak of this later).[5] Besides, the cause of con-trariety would seem to be in the change to a contrary rather than in the change from a contrary (for in the latter change there is a loss of a
25   contrary while in the former there is a gain)[6] and each change is named after that to which the thing changes rather than after that from which it changes,[7] e.g., healing takes its name from "health" and sickening from "sickness".

There remain, then, (c) changes to contraries and (e) a change from A to B and one from B to A, where A and B are contraries. Now it may happen that a change to a contrary is also a change from the other con-trary,[8] yet to be the former is not the same as to be the latter;[3] I mean,
30   for example, to be a change toward health is not the same as to be a change from disease and to be a change from health is not the same as to be a change toward disease. But since a change differs from a motion
229*b*   (for a motion is a change from a subject to a subject), motions which are contrary are changes from A to B and from B to A, where A and B are contraries, e.g., the change from health to disease is a motion contrary

to the change from disease to health.[9] From induction, too, it is clear what kinds [of motions] are contrary, for (1) falling sick[10] is thought to be contrary to becoming healthy, (2) being taught [is thought] to be contrary to being led into a mistake (not by oneself, for, as in *knowledge*, one may fall into a mistake by himself[11] as well as through another) since [in each case the two contrary changes proceed from contraries] to contraries, (3) a locomotion upwards [is thought] to be contrary to a locomotion downwards (for up and down are contrary with respect to length), (4) a locomotion to the right [is thought] to be contrary to a locomotion to the left (for right and left are contrary with respect to width), and (5) a locomotion forwards [is thought] to be contrary to a locomotion backwards (for forwards and backwards, too, are contrary).

As for (a), a change merely to a contrary, it is not a motion but [just] a change, e.g., becoming white but not from some thing.[12] And in those cases in which there is no contrary, it is the change from a thing that is contrary to the change toward the same thing.[13] Thus a generation is the contrary of a destruction, and losing is contrary to gaining; and these are changes, but not motions.

As for those contraries which have intermediates, a motion toward an intermediate should be posited as one toward a contrary, but only in a sense;[14] for the intermediate serves as a contrary in that motion, in whichever direction the change may proceed. For example, the motion from grey to white may be taken as if from black, the motion from white to grey as if to black, and the motion from black to grey as if the grey were white; for the intermediate, relative to each contrary, is stated in some sense as being the other contrary, as we said before.[15]

Two motions are contrary, then, in this manner: One is from A to B and the other from B to A, where A and B are contraries.

6

Since the contrary of a motion is thought to be not only a motion but also rest, these should be distinguished. For, in an unqualified sense, the contrary of a motion is another motion; but rest too is opposed [to a motion], for it is the privation [of a motion]. And there is a sense[1] in which a privation too is said to be a contrary, and to each kind of motion there is a corresponding kind of privation, e.g., to a motion with respect to place there is rest with respect to place. But this is a simplified way of stating the case, for is it the motion from or the motion toward a given place that is opposed to rest[2] at this place?

It is indeed clear that, since a motion requires two subjects,[3] *rest* at this place is opposed to the motion from this to the contrary place, while *rest* at the contrary place is opposed to the motion from that to this place. At the same time, these two[4] are contrary to each other; for it is absurd that contrary motions should exist but opposite states of rest should not.[5] So these exist in contraries; for example, (1) rest in health is opposed to rest in disease, and (2) it is also opposed to the motion from health to disease. For (2) it is unreasonable that it should be opposed to the motion from disease to health, since motion to that in which a thing is staying is rather a coming to be at rest there, at least insofar as this coming to be exists simultaneously with that motion, and it must be either this or the other motion;[6] and (1) certainly it is not rest in whiteness that is the contrary of rest in health.[7]

As for things which have no contraries, there exists in them a change from a thing which is opposed to a change toward the thing, e.g., a change from being is opposed to a change toward being, but opposite motions do not exist; and no *rest* exists in them, but changelessness may exist.[8] And if there were a subject underlying the change, changelessness of being would be contrary to changelessness of nonbeing;[9] but if nonbeing is not something, one might raise the problem of what is the contrary of changelessness of being and also whether this changelessness is a state of rest. But if it were a state of rest, then either not every state of rest would be contrary to a motion, or else generations and destructions would be motions.[10] So it is clear that, if these are not called "motions", this changelessness too should not be called "a state of rest"; but it is something similar to a state of rest and should be called just "changelessness";[11] and it is contrary either to no thing at all or to changelessness of not-being or to a destruction,[12] for a destruction is a change from being while a generation is a change to being.

One might raise the question of why in a change with respect to place there exist *rest* and motions according to nature as well as contrary to nature, but in other changes this is not so, e.g., in alteration it is not the case that one is according to nature while another is contrary to nature; for becoming healthy is no more according to nature or contrary to nature than falling sick is, becoming white no more according to nature or contrary to nature than becoming black. Similarly with increase and decrease, for neither are these contrary to each other in the sense that one of them is by nature and the other contrary to nature, nor is one increase contrary to another increase in that same sense.[13] And the same statement may be made concerning generations and destructions, for neither does a generation exist according to nature and a destruction contrary to nature (for old age exists according to nature),[14] nor do we observe one generation as being according to nature while another as being contrary to nature.

But if that which exists by force [15] exists contrary to nature, then also a destruction by force which is contrary to nature would be contrary to a destruction which is according to nature. So are there also some generations which occur by force and are not determined and whose contrary generations are according to nature, and also instances of increase and decrease by force, e.g., the rapid growth to maturity because of excessive indulgence and the rapid ripening of seeds even when not planted closely? And in the case of alterations, is it not in the same way? For some of them might be by force while others are natural, as in patients, some of whom get rid of their fever not on the day of crisis while others do so on the day of crisis, and so some alter contrary to nature while others alter according to nature. So there will be destructions which are contrary to each other but not to generations. And what will prevent this? For this is possible in a qualified way,[16] if it is also possible for one destruction to be pleasant and another painful. Thus one destruction may be contrary to another, not unqualifiedly, but insofar as the first is of this kind while the second is of that [the contrary] kind.

In general, then, contrary motions and states of rest exist in the manner already stated; for example, the one[17] up is contrary to the one down, for up and down are contraries of place. In locomotions by nature, that of fire is upwards while that of earth is downwards, and the locomotions of these two are contrary. In the case of fire, the locomotion upward is by nature while the one downward is contrary to nature; and its locomotion according to nature is contrary to that which is contrary to nature.[18] It is likewise with states of *rest*, for a state of *rest* up is contrary to a motion from up downwards: In the case of earth, its *rest* up exists contrary to nature, but its motion downwards according to nature; so a state of *rest* contrary to the nature of a thing is contrary to the motion according to the nature of the same thing, for its motion contrary to its nature is likewise contrary to it (for one of them will be according to nature, whether up or down, but the other contrary to nature).[19]

A problem that arises is whether there is a generation of every state of rest which is not eternal and whether this generation is a coming to a stop.[20] If yes, there would be a generation of that which *rests* contrary to its nature, e.g., of earth *resting* up; and so if earth were to be carried by force upwards it would be coming to a stop. But that which is coming to a stop is thought to be travelling always faster, while that which is carried by force is thought to be travelling in a contrary manner; and so the latter, though not coming to be at rest, would be at rest. Further, to come to a stop is thought either altogether to be travelling to one's own place or to occur simultaneously while travelling to one's own place.[21]

There is also the problem of whether a state of *rest* at a place is contrary to a motion from that place;[22] for when a thing is moving from

30   that place and is discarding something, it seems that it still has something left of what is being discarded.[23] So if it is rest itself that is contrary to the motion from that place to the contrary place, contraries will belong to something[24] at the same time. But does not the thing rest only in a qualified way, if something in it still remains? In general, then, part

231a   of the thing in motion is at the starting-point, and part, at the other contrary, to which it is changing.[25] And it is in view of this that what is contrary to a motion is a motion rather than rest.[26]

     Concerning motion and rest, then, we have stated how each is one and which is contrary to which.[27]

5   One might also raise the question concerning coming to a stop, whether to a motion there is an opposed state of rest even if it be contrary to nature. It would be absurd if this were not so, for a thing may *rest*, although by force, and there would be something in a noneternal state of rest without having become so. But it is clear that this is so, for just as a thing may be in motion contrary to nature, so it might rest con-

10   trary to nature. Since motion may belong to some things according to nature as well as contrary to nature, e.g., motion upwards belongs to fire according to nature but motion downwards belongs to it contrary to nature, is it the latter motion or earth's downward motion that is contrary to the former motion, seeing that earth's downward motion occurs according to nature? Clearly both are contrary to it, but not in

15   the same way; earth's downward motion is contrary to fire's upward motion as one natural motion is contrary to another natural motion, but fire's upward motion is contrary to its downward motion as a natural motion is contrary to a motion contrary to nature. It is likewise with states of *rest*. Perhaps a motion is opposed also to a state of rest, but in a qualified way.

Book Z

1

231a If continuity, contact, and succession are such as defined earlier[1] (that is, things are said to be continuous if their extremities are one, in contact if they are together, and in succession if there is no thing of the same kind between them), then no continuous thing can consist of in-

25 divisibles; for example, if a line is indeed continuous and a point is in-divisible,[2] then a line cannot consist of points. For (a) neither can the extremities of points be one, seeing that of an indivisible thing it is not the case that one part is an extremity while another is something else, (b) nor can the extremities be together, seeing that what has no parts has no extremities since an extremity is distinct from that of which it is the extremity.[3]

30 Moreover, if points were to form a continuum, it would be necessary for them to be either continuous with each other or in contact with each

231b other;[4] and the same remark applies to all other indivisibles.[5] Now points cannot be continuous because of what has just been said. As for their being in contact, when two things touch one another, either the whole of one touches the whole of the other, or a part of one touches a part of the other, or a part of one touches the whole of the other; but since the indivisible has no parts, indivisibles must touch each other as wholes.[6] But if it is a whole that touches a whole,[7] what results will not

5 be continuous; for that which is continuous has one part here and an-other there, and it may be divided into these, which are then distinct and separate in place.

Nor again can a point succeed a point or a moment succeed a moment in such a way that what results is a line consisting of points or time consisting of moments, respectively; for between two things in succes-sion there is no thing of the same kind, but there is always a line be-

10 tween points[8] and always time between moments. Again, the resulting thing would be divisible into indivisibles, if indeed each of these two [a line or time] is divisible into the parts of which it consists.[9] But no

continuous thing is divisible into things without parts. Nor can there be a thing of another genus between points or between moments;[10] for if there were, it is clear that it would be either indivisible or divisible, and if divisible, either into indivisibles or into things always divisible, but the latter would be continuous.[11]

It is also evident that every continuous thing is divisible into things which are always divisible; for if divisible into indivisibles, an indivisible will be touching an indivisible since the extremities of continuous things are one and are touching.

The same argument applies also to magnitudes and to time and to motions: either all are composed of indivisibles and are divisible into indivisibles, or none is. This is clear from what follows. If a magnitude is composed of indivisibles, the motion along this magnitude too will be composed of an equal number of motions each of which is indivisible; for example, if the magnitude ABC is composed of the indivisible magnitudes A, B, and C, the motion DEF of W along ABC will have as parts D, E, and F, each of which is indivisible.[12] So if something must be in motion when there is a motion and if there must be a motion when

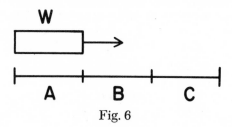

Fig. 6

something is in motion, then also the object-in-motion[13] will be composed of indivisibles. Now the object W has moved over A with the motion D, over B with the motion E, and likewise over C with the motion F. So if an object in motion from one place to another cannot be in the process of motion and at the same time have moved to the place to which it was moving (for example, if a man is walking to Thebes, he cannot be walking to Thebes and at the same time have gone to Thebes) and if W in virtue of its motion D was in the process of moving over A, which has no parts, then if it is later that W has gone or will have gone through A, that motion would be divisible; for when W was in the process of going, it was neither resting nor already gone but was between.[14] If, then, that which is walking is in the process of going and at the same time has gone when it is walking, it will have already walked and have moved to the place where it is in the process of moving. Thus, if an object is moving over all of ABC and its motion over it is composed of D, E, and F and if that object is not at all in the process of moving

over partless A but only has moved over it, then a motion will be composed not of motions but of impulses,[15] and the object will have moved
10   over something without being in the process of moving over it; for it
will have gone over A without being in the process of going over it. So
something will have completed a walk without being in the process of
walking, for it will have walked over A without being in the process of
walking over it. Accordingly, if every object must be either at rest or
in motion and if it is at rest over each of the parts of ABC, an object will
be continuously at rest and at the same time in motion; for, as we saw,
it will be in motion over the whole of ABC but at rest over any [partless]
15   part and so over the whole of ABC. Moreover, if the indivisible parts of
DEF are motions, then an object may be at rest although motion is present in it, but if they are not motions, then a motion may be composed
not of motions.[16]

Time too must be indivisible like a line and a motion, and it must be
20   composed of moments which are indivisible; for if each[17] [motion] is
divisible, then since an object with an equal speed will traverse the
smaller [line] in less time, time too will be continuous. And if the time
an object takes to travel A is divisible, then A too will be divisible.

2

Since every magnitude is divisible into magnitudes (for we have just
shown that no continuous thing is composed of *indivisible* parts and
25   every magnitude is continuous), a faster object must move (a) in an
equal time over a greater magnitude, (b) over an equal magnitude in
less time, and (c) over a greater magnitude in less time,[1] just as in the
definition of "faster" which is given by some thinkers.[2] Let A be faster
than B. Accordingly, since that which makes the change earlier is the
30   faster,[3] then in the time T_1T_4 taken by A to arrive at S_4 from S_1 the object B will not yet arrive at S_4 but will fall short of it; so in an equal time

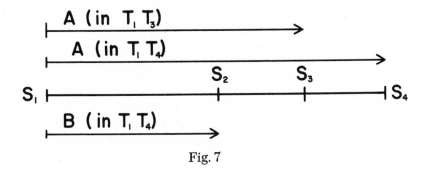

Fig. 7

the faster will traverse a greater magnitude. Moreover, the faster will traverse also some greater magnitude in less time. For in the time that A reaches S_4, let B, which is the slower, reach S_2. Then since A takes the whole of time T_1T_4 to arrive at S_4, to arrive at S_3 it will take a less time, say T_1T_3. Now the magnitude S_1S_4 traversed by A is greater than the magnitude S_1S_2, and the time, T_1T_3, is less than the whole of time T_1T_4;[4] so A traverses a greater magnitude [i.e., S_1S_3] in less time [i.e., in T_1T_3].

It is also evident from this that the faster will traverse an equal magnitude in less time than the slower. For since it traverses a greater magnitude in time less than that of the slower, and since it itself traverses a greater magnitude, say S_1S_3, in more time than it does a lesser magnitude, say S_1S_2, the time T_1T_3 it takes to traverse S_1S_3 is more than the time T_1T_2 it takes to traverse S_1S_2. And so if the time T_1T_3 is less than the time T_1T_4 taken by the slower to traverse S_1S_2, the time T_1T_2 will also be less than the time T_1T_4; for T_1T_2 is less than T_1T_3, and that which is less than the lesser of two things is also less than the greater of the two things.[5] Consequently, the faster will traverse an equal magnitude in less time. Moreover, since every object, say A, must move [along a given magnitude] either in an equal or in less or in more time [than another object], say B, and A is slower than B if it moves in more time, has a speed equal to that of B if it moves in an equal time, and neither has a speed equal to that of B nor is slower than B if it is faster than B, then if faster it would move neither in an equal nor in more time, and what is left is that it will move in less time; and so, if faster, it must also move over an equal magnitude in less time.

Since every motion is in time and in every interval of time it is possible for some object to be in motion, and since every object in motion may be moving faster or slower,[6] in every interval of time there can be a faster or a slower motion. This being so, it is also necessary that time be continuous. By "continuous" I mean that which is divisible into parts which are always divisible; for if continuity is assumed to be this, then time must be continuous. For since it has been shown that the faster will traverse an equal magnitude in less time, let A be the faster and B the slower, and let the slower traverse the magnitude S_1S_3 in time T_1T_3. Then it is clear that the faster will traverse this same magnitude in less time, and let this time be T_1T_2. Then again, since the faster traverses the whole of S_1S_3 in the time T_1T_2, in that time the slower will traverse a lesser magnitude, and let this be S_1S_2. And since B, the slower, traverses S_1S_2 in the time T_1T_2, the faster will traverse this magnitude in less time, and so once more the time T_1T_2 will have to be divided; and when this is divided, the magnitude S_1S_2 will also have to be divided and in the same ratio,[7] and if the magnitude, so the time will have to be

divided. And this will always be the case if we alternate from the faster
to the slower and from the slower to the faster and use the same demonstration, for the faster will be dividing the time, while the slower will
be dividing the length. Accordingly, if it is true that the alternation
always proceeds indefinitely and that whenever it does there is always a
division, it is evident that every interval of time is continuous. At the
same time this too is clear, that every magnitude is continuous, for the
divisions are the same and equal for both the time and the magnitude.

Again, it is also evident from the arguments ordinarily used that if
time is continuous, so is a magnitude, if indeed in half a given interval
of time an object traverses half the corresponding distance and, without
qualification, if in a less time it traverses a lesser magnitude; for the
divisions will be the same for both the time and the magnitude. And if
either one of these is infinite, so is the other; and the manner in which
either one of them is infinite is the same as that in which the other is
infinite.[8] For example, if the time is infinite with respect to extremities,[9]
the length too will be infinite with respect to extremities; if the time is
infinite with respect to division, the length too will be infinite with
respect to division; and if the time is infinite with respect to both, so will
the magnitude be.

It is in view of this that Zeno's argument is false in positing that it is
not possible to traverse an infinity of things or to touch each of an infinity of things in a finite time; for both length and time, and in general
everything continuous, are said to be infinite in two ways, either with
respect to division or with respect to their extremities. So, while it is not
possible in a finite time to touch things which are infinite with respect
to quantity,[10] it is possible to do so if they are infinite with respect to
division, for finite time itself is infinite in this latter sense. Accordingly,
it turns out that the infinite is traversed in an infinite and not in a finite
time and that things which are infinite are touched not by a finite time
but by an infinity of intervals of time.

Indeed, neither can an infinite magnitude be traversed in a finite
time nor a finite magnitude in an infinite time; but if the time is infinite,
the magnitude too will be infinite, and if the magnitude is infinite, so
will the time be. For let AM be a finite magnitude, T an infinite time,
and let a finite part T_1T_2 of T be taken. Now in this part of time an
object will traverse some [finite] magnitude, and let this be AB; and
this will either measure AM exactly or fall short of it or surpass it, for
it makes no difference which. For if in an equal time the object always
traverses a magnitude equal to AB,[11] then, since this [AB] measures
the whole [of AM], the time taken to traverse AM will be finite;[12] for
the divisions of the time taken will be equal in number as in the case
of the magnitude [AM]. Moreover, if an object does not traverse every

magnitude in an infinite time but if it is possible for it to traverse in a finite time some magnitude, say AB,[13] which will measure the whole magnitude, and the object traverses an equal magnitude in an equal time, then the time too will be finite.[14] That AB will not be traversed in an infinite time is evident if the time in both directions is taken as bounded; for if a part [of AB] is traversed in less time, this [time] must be bounded since one of the boundaries already exists.

If the length is taken as infinite but the time as finite, the demonstration will be the same.

It is evident from what has been said that neither a line nor a surface nor, in general, anything continuous can be *indivisible*, not only because of the arguments just given, but also in view of the fact that the *indivisible* will turn out to be divisible. For since in every interval of time the slower and the faster can exist and the faster traverses a greater length in an equal time, it [the faster] may traverse a length which is twice, or one and a half times, as great as that traversed by the slower, for this might be the ratio of their corresponding speeds. So let the faster traverse in the same time a magnitude which is one and a half times that which the slower traverses, and let the magnitude traversed by the faster be divided into the three *indivisible* parts AB, BC, and CD and that traversed by the slower into the two [*indivisible*] parts EF and FG.[15] Then the time T too will be divided into three *indivisible*[16] parts, for an equal magnitude is traversed in an equal time. Now let time T be divided into T_1T_2, T_2T_3, and T_3T_4. Again, since the slower has traversed EF and FG, the time T too will be *divided* into two [equal] parts. Thus the *indivisible* [i.e., T_2T_3] will be divided,[17] and that which has no parts [i.e., EF] will be traversed not in an *indivisible* time but in a greater time.[18] Thus it is evident that no continuous thing can be without parts.

3

The moment too (when the term "moment" is a predicate not of something else[1] but of something by itself and primary) must be indivisible, and as such it is present in every interval of time. For there is an extremity of the time past with no part of the future lying this side of it, and there is also an extremity of the future time with no part of the past lying on the other side of it;[2] and this is, as we said, a limit of both. And if in itself this [moment] is shown to be such and to be the same,[3] it will be evident at the same time that it is also indivisible.

Now the moment must be the same[4] extremity of both times; for if each were distinct, the one could not be in succession with the other because no continuous thing is composed of things without parts,[5] while if each were apart from the other, there would be time between them since a continuous thing is such that between two limits lies something

10   which is univocally named as that thing.[6] But if that which lies between is time, it will be divisible, for every interval of time has been shown to be divisible.[7] So the moment will be divisible;[8] and if the moment is divisible, some part of the past will be in the future and some part of the future in the past, for that at which it [i.e., the moment] might be

15   divided marks off the past from the future time.[9] At the same time the moment would be not something in itself but something in virtue of something else, for a division is not [of a moment] in itself.[10] In addition, part of the moment will be in the past and part of it in the future,[11] and it will not always be the same that is past or the same that is future; nor indeed will the moment be the same, for time is divisible in many

20   ways.[12] So if these attributes cannot belong to the moment, it must be the same moment that is in each of the two times. And if it is the same, it is evident that it is also indivisible; for if divisible, what will follow will be once more the same as before. From what has been said, then, it is clear that there is something in time which is indivisible, and this we call "a moment".

25   That no thing is in motion in a moment is evident from what follows. For if some thing is, the faster and the slower may be in motion in the same moment. So let M be that moment, and let the faster traverse the length AC in the moment M. Then, in the same moment, the slower will traverse a length less than AC, let us say the length AB. Now since the

30   slower has moved over AB in the whole moment M, the faster will move [over AB] in [a time] less than that moment. Hence, that moment will have been divided. But it is indivisible, as was shown. No thing, then, can be in motion in a moment.

Nor can anything be at rest in a moment. For a thing was said to be at rest if it can by nature be in motion but is not in motion when, where, and in the manner in which it can be in motion; so since no thing can by nature be in motion in a moment, it is clear that no thing can be [by nature] at rest in a moment either.

35   Again, if it is the same moment that belongs to both intervals of time[13]

234*b* and if a thing may be in motion during the whole of one of these intervals but at rest during the whole of the other and if when in motion during the whole of one interval the thing may be in motion during any part of that interval in which it can by nature be in motion and if likewise when at rest during the whole of an interval, then the same thing will turn out to be in motion and at rest at the same time; for it is the

5   same extremity which belongs to both intervals of time, that is, the same moment.[14]

Again, we speak of a thing as being at rest when both the thing and its parts are in a similar state[15] at some given moment and at a time prior to that moment. But in a moment there is nothing prior;[16] so a thing cannot rest [in a moment].

It follows, then, that a thing in motion must be moving in time, and a thing at rest must be resting in time.

4

10 Everything that is changing is of necessity divisible. For since every change is from something to something—and when a thing is in that to which it has changed, it is no longer changing,[1] while when in that from which it changes, neither itself nor any of its parts is changing (for if

15 both the thing and its parts are in a similar state, it is not changing)[2]— then the thing that is changing must be partly in that to which it is changing and partly in that from which it is changing (for it cannot be in both or in either of the two). By "that to which it is changing" I mean the first [state][3] with respect to that change, for example, the grey, not the black, if it is changing from the white, (for it is not necessary for

20 the changing thing to be at either of the extremes). Evidently, then, every thing that is changing must be divisible.[4]

Now a motion is divisible in two ways. In one way, it is divisible in time; in another, with respect to the motions of the parts of the moving thing, e.g., if the whole AC is in motion, also its parts AB and BC will be in motion. So let the motion of the part AB be M_1M_2 and that of the

25 part BC be M_2M_3; then the whole motion M_1M_3 will be that of AC, for the thing [AC] will be moving with this [M_1M_3] if indeed each of its parts is moving with its respective motion. But no thing moves with the motion of another; hence, the whole motion is the motion of the whole magnitude of the thing. Again, if every motion is a motion of something

30 and the whole motion M_1M_3 is neither that of either of the parts (for it is each of M_1M_2 and M_2M_3 that is the motion of each of the parts AB and BC respectively) nor that of anything else (for if a whole motion is that of a whole thing, then the parts of that motion will be of the parts of that thing respectively; and the parts of M_1M_3 are of the parts of AC and of no other thing, for, as we said, no motion which is one is of more than one thing), then the whole motion [M_1M_3] will be that of the magnitude

35 AC of the thing. Again, if the motion of the whole [AC] is some other than M_1M_3, let us say N_1N_3, the motion of each part may be subtracted

235a from it; and these motions [of the parts] are equal to M_1M_2 and M_2M_3 since the motion of one thing is just one. So if the whole motion N_1N_3 be divided into the motions of the parts, N_1N_3 will be equal to M_1M_3; but if there be a remainder, say the motion N_3N_4, this will be a motion of

5   no thing, for it cannot be the motion of the whole or of any of the parts
       (because the motion of one thing is just one) or of anything else, since a
       continuous motion is of that which is continuous. The argument is simi-
       lar if, by division, the motions of the parts are assumed to exceed the
       motion M_1M_3. So if these impossibilities result, the motion N_1N_3 must
       be equal to M_1M_3. This division of a motion, then, is a division accord-
10   ing to the motions of parts, and it must be the division of every thing
       that is divisible into parts.[5]

       Another division is that with respect to time; for, since every motion
       exists in time and every interval of time is divisible[6] and since the motion
       in less time is less, it is necessary for every motion to be divisible with
       respect to time. Since every thing in motion moves with respect to some-
15   thing[7] and for some time and the motion is of the entire thing, the divi-
       sions must be the same for (1) the time, (2) the motion, (3) the being-
       moved,[8] (4) the thing in motion, and (5) that with respect to which there
       is motion.[9] With respect to that in which there is motion, however, the
       divisions are not all alike; they are essential in the case of quantity but
       accidental in the case of quality.[10] For let the time in which a thing
20   moves be A and the motion be B. Then if the thing in all that time
       completes the whole motion, in half the time it completes less of that
       motion, and it completes still less than this if the time is divided again,
       and the division proceeds always in this manner. The time too is divided
       along with the motion in a similar way; for if the whole motion takes
       all of the time, half the motion will take half of the time, and less of this
       motion again will take less of this time.[11]

25   The division of being-moved, too, will take place in the same way.
       For let C be [the whole of] being-moved. Then with half the motion,
       the being-moved will be less than the whole [being-moved]; and with
       half of that half [motion], it will be less than that; and it will be in this
       way always. By exhibiting the being-moved with respect to each of the
30   two motions, let us say, M_1M_2 and M_2M_3, we may also argue that the
       whole being-moved will be that with respect to the whole motion. For
       if it were another [being-moved], there would be more being-moved
       with respect to the same motion, as in the case of a divisible motion,
       which was shown to be divisible into the motions of the parts [of the
       thing in motion];[12] for if each being-moved is considered with respect
       to each motion, the whole [being-moved] will be continuous.

35   Likewise, it may be shown that also a length is divisible and, in gen-
       eral, any state in which there is a change;[13] but in some cases the divi-
       sion is accidental, since what is divisible is the object which is changing;
       for when one of them is divided, all the others too will be divided.

235b   And as to their being finite or infinite, all of them will be alike finite
       and alike infinite. And it is most of all from the thing which is changing

that the attributes of being divided and of being infinite follow and belong also to the others, for divisibility and being infinite belong directly to the thing which is changing.[14] In the case of divisibility, this
5   was shown earlier;[15] as for being infinite, this will be made clear later on.[16]

5

Since every thing that is changing does so from something to something, that which has changed, when it has first changed,[1] must be in that to which it has changed. For that which is changing is being displaced from or is leaving that from which it is changing, and either
10   changing and leaving are the same,[2] or leaving follows from changing.[3] If leaving follows from changing, having left follows from having changed, for [in both cases] the relation of the first to the second is similar.[4]

Since one of the changes is with respect to contradiction,[5] when a
15   thing has changed from nonbeing to being, it has left nonbeing. Hence, it will be in being; for every object must either be or not be. It is evident, then, that in a change with respect to contradiction that which has changed will be in that to which it has changed. And if this is so in this [kind of change], it will be so also in the others;[6] for the case with one change is similar to those with the others.

Moreover, this becomes evident if we consider each [change] sepa-
20   rately, if indeed that which has changed must be somewhere or in some state.[7] For since the thing has left that from which it has changed and must be somewhere,[8] it will be either in this [to which it has changed] or in something else. If the thing which has changed to C is in something else, say in B, then again it is changing from B to C, for C cannot
25   be consecutive to B since a change is continuous;[9] and so the thing which has changed, when it has changed, turns out to be changing to that to which it has changed, which is impossible.[10] Hence that which has changed must be in that to which it has changed. It is evident, then, that also the thing which has been generated, when it has been generated, will exist[11] and that the thing which has been destroyed will not exist; for this has been universally stated for every [kind of] change
30   and, clearly, most of all for a change with respect to contradiction.[12] It is clear, then, that that which has changed, when it has changed first, exists in that to which it has changed.

Now that[13] in which the changed thing first[14] has changed must be *indivisible*, and by "first" I mean that it is not in virtue of some part of
35   it that it is such. For let AC[15] be divisible, and let it be divided at B. Now if the thing has changed [only] in AB or [only] in BC, it cannot

have first changed in AC. And if it were in the process of changing in
each (for in each it must either have changed or have been in the
process of changing), it would be in the process of changing also in the
whole.[16] But it was posited as having changed [in the whole]. The
argument is the same even if the thing is in the process of changing
in one part but has changed in the other, for then there will be something prior to what is first.[17] Thus that in which the thing has changed
cannot be divisible.[18] It is evident, then, that also that which has been
destroyed or has been generated did so in something *indivisible*.[19]

We speak of that in which a thing has first changed in two senses:
(a) as that in which a change has first been completed (for then it is true
to say that the thing has changed) and (b) as that in which the process
of a change first began. Now that which is called "first" at the end of a
change is a beginning[20] and exists;[21] for a change may be completed
and there is an end of a change, and this end was in fact shown to be
indivisible because it is a limit. As for what is called "first" at the
beginning of a change, it does not exist at all; for there is no beginning
of a change nor a first part of time in which a thing was in the process
of changing.[22] For let BC be a first part.[23] Now this is not indivisible,
for otherwise moments would turn out to be consecutive.[24] Moreover,
if the thing is at rest in all of the time AB[25] (for let it be posited as being
at rest [in AB]), it is also at rest[26] in B. So if BC is without parts,[27] the
thing will be at rest[25] and will have changed simultaneously; for it is
at rest[26] in B and has changed in C. Thus, since BC is not without parts,
it must be divisible and must have changed in any of its parts. For when
BC is divided, if the thing has not changed in either of the two parts,[28]
it has not changed in the whole; if it is changing in each of them, it is
changing in all of it;[29] and if it has changed in [just] one of the two
parts, it has not changed in the whole as in something first;[30] so it must
have changed in any part [of the whole]. Accordingly, it is evident that
there is no first [part] in which it has changed, for the divisions are
infinite.[31]

Neither of a changed thing is there a first [part] which has changed.
For of DF, let DE be the first which has changed (since every changing
thing has been shown to be divisible), and let T_1T_2 be the time in which
DE has changed. Then if DE has changed in the whole of that time,
in half that time a part less than DE will have changed,[32] and this part
will be prior to DE, and likewise a part of this part will also be prior,
and of this still another, and it will be so always. Thus of a changing
thing there will be no first at which the thing has changed. It is evident
from what has been said, then, that neither of the changing thing nor of
the time in which the change takes place is there a first [part] of a
change made.

As for that[33] which is changing or with respect to which the thing is changing, the situation is not similar. For we speak of three [elements] with respect to a change, namely, the thing which changes, that[34] in which it changes, and that to which it changes; for example, the man, the time, and paleness. Now the man and the time are certainly divisible;[35] but as for paleness, this is another matter, except that all these[36] are divisible accidentally; for what is divisible is that of which paleness or a quality is an attribute, although even in things which are said to be essentially and not accidentally divisible, as in magnitudes, there can be no first. For let AB be a magnitude, and let it have moved from B to C.[37] Then if BC is indivisible, a thing without parts will be consecutive to another thing without parts; but if it is divisible, there will be something prior to C into which the magnitude has changed,[38] and prior to this there will be still another in the same manner, and this will always be the case because the division[39] cannot be exhausted. Thus there can be no first to which the magnitude has changed. In a change of quantity,[40] the situation is similar; for this [change], too, proceeds continuously. It is evident, then, that only in motion with respect to quality can there be that which is essentially indivisible.[41]

6

Since every thing that is changing does so in time and it is said to be changing in time whether it is changing in a primary time or with respect to another time (for example, we say that it changed in a certain year if it changed in some day of that year),[1] if the thing is changing in a primary time, it must be changing in any part of that time. This is clear from the definition (for such was the meaning given to the term "primary"), but it is also evident from the following. Let AC be the primary time in which a thing is in motion, and let AC be divided at B (for every interval of time is divisible).[2] Now in the time AB either the thing is in motion or it is not, and in the time BC likewise. If in each of these two parts it is not in motion, then it will be resting in the whole, for it cannot be in motion [in the whole] if it is in motion in none of its parts. If it is in motion in only one of the two parts, then it cannot be in motion in AC as in a primary time, for its motion will be in virtue of a time other than AC.[3] Hence it must be in motion in any part of AC.

With this shown, it is evident that every thing which is in motion must have moved before. For if the thing has moved over the magnitude PQ in the primary time AC, then in half that time another thing which started simultaneously and with a like speed will have moved half that magnitude. And if that other thing with a like speed has moved a certain magnitude in an interval of time, the first thing too must have moved that same magnitude in the same interval of time, and so a thing in motion will have moved [some magnitude earlier].[4]

Again, in saying "having moved" we do so for all the time AC or for any part of it by taking an extremity of it, which is a moment (for it is this that does the limiting, and what is between moments is time); in other cases, too, we should be using the expression "having moved" in a similar manner. But the extremity of that which is half is a division. Thus a thing will have moved in half of the time, and, in general, in any part of it; for it is always the case that when a *division* is made, a time limited by moments simultaneously comes into existence. Accordingly, if every interval of time is divisible and what exists between moments is time, every thing in the process of change must have made an infinity of changes.[5]

Again, if that which is changing continuously, without having been destroyed or having ceased changing, must have been in the process of changing or must have changed in any element of time[6][during the change], since it cannot be in the process of changing in a moment, it must have changed at the end of each moment [of the time of change]. So if the moments are infinite, every thing in the process of change must have made an infinity of changes.

Not only is it necessary for that which is changing to have changed, but also it is necessary for that which has changed to have been changing before; for that which has changed from something to something else did so in time. For let a thing which has changed from A to B be at[7] a moment. Then it has not made the change at the moment at which it exists at A, for otherwise it would be at A and at B at the same time; for that which has changed, when it has changed, was shown earlier[8] not to be at that [from which it has changed]. And if it has made the change at another moment, there will be time between, for, as shown earlier,[9] moments are not consecutive. So since it has changed in an interval of time and every interval of time is divisible, in half that interval it must have made another change, and in half of that half it must have made still another change, and this is always so; hence the thing must have been in the process of changing earlier.[10]

Again, what has just been said is more evident in the case of magnitudes because a magnitude over which a thing is changing is continuous. For let a thing have changed from C to D. Then if CD is indivisible, one thing without parts will be consecutive to another thing without parts. Since this is impossible, what exists between C and D must be a magnitude and must be divisible into an infinite number of magnitudes; so the thing must have been changing earlier in each of these magnitudes. Hence every thing that has changed must have been in the process of changing previously; for the demonstration is the same also for what is not continuous, for example, in the case of contraries and of contra-dictories,[11] for in these we may take an interval of time in which the thing has changed and use the same argument once more.[12] So that which has changed[13] must have been [previously] in the process of changing, and that which is in the process of changing must have changed [previously]. And a process of change is preceded by some-thing which has changed; and if something has changed, there was an earlier process of change, and at no time can any one of these be the first which is taken.[14] The *reason* for this is the fact that no thing without parts can be consecutive to another thing without parts, for division can proceed infinitely, as in lines which are increasing or decreasing by division. So it is also evident that a thing which has become[15] must have been previously in the process of becoming and one that is in the process of becoming must have previously become (that is, in the case of things which are divisible and continuous), though not always that which the thing is coming to be, but sometimes something else, for example, some part of what is coming to be, like the foundation of a house;[16] and in the case of a thing which is in the process of being destroyed or has been destroyed, too, the situation is similar. For in a thing which is coming to be or is being destroyed and which is continuous there is immediately present something which is infinite. And the thing can neither be in the process of generation without something having been generated nor have been generated without previously being in the process of generation; and it is likewise in the case of the process of being destroyed or of having been destroyed, for the process of being destroyed is always preceded by [something] having been destroyed, and the latter is always preceded by a process of being destroyed. So it is evident that both that which has been generated must previously be in the process of generation and that which is in the process of gen-eration must previously have been generated, for every magnitude is always divisible, and so is every interval of time. Consequently, in what-ever [state of change][17] a thing may be, it cannot be in it as in something first.

7

Since everything in motion is moving in time and since in a longer interval of time a thing moves over a greater magnitude, in an infinite time no moving thing can move over [only] a finite [line],[1] that is, if the moving thing does not move always over the same [line] or a part of it[2] but moves over all of it in all the [infinite] time.

It is clear that if a thing were to move with an equal speed, it is necessary for it to move over a finite magnitude in a finite time; for if a part be taken which will measure the whole [line], the thing will have moved over the whole [line] in as many intervals of time as there are

30 parts. So since these parts are finite, both in magnitude individually and in number collectively,[3] the time too will be finite; for this time will be equal to the time taken to go through each part multiplied by the number of parts.[4]

Moreover, it makes no difference even if the thing were to move not

35 with an equal speed. For let AB be a finite interval along which the

238a thing has moved for an infinite time, and let this infinite time be CD. That one of two distinct parts [of AB] has been traversed before the other is clear from the fact that one was traversed in an earlier part of time and the other in a later part; for in a longer time another distinct

5 part was traversed,[5] and this is no less so whether the thing changed with or without an equal speed or whether the motion accelerated or decelerated or remained the same. Thus of the interval AB let AE be a part which will measure AB. Now this part was traversed in a [finite] interval of the infinite time, for it cannot have been traversed in the infinite time since it is the whole that was traversed in the infinite

10 time. If another part equal to AE be taken, it too must have been traversed in a finite time, since it is the whole that was traversed in the infinite time. And if we keep on taking parts in this manner, since no part of the infinite time will measure the infinite time (for the infinite cannot be composed of finite parts, whether equal or unequal, because

15 equal or unequal parts which are finite in number and in magnitude[6] will be exhausted when measured by some one unit, and so they will still be definite in magnitude) and since the finite interval [AB] is finitely measurable by AE, the interval AB would be traversed in a finite time.[7] It is likewise with coming to rest.[8] Hence one and the same thing cannot be always in the process of becoming or of being destroyed.[9]

20 The same argument may be used to show that it is not possible [for a body] to move or come to rest in a finite time over an infinite magnitude, whether with a uniform or a non-uniform speed. For if a part of time be taken which will measure the whole time, in that part some quantity of the magnitude will be traversed but not the whole magnitude (since the whole magnitude will be traversed by all of the time). And again, some other [quantity of the magnitude] will be traversed in

25 another equal part of the time, and similarly in each succeeding equal part of time, whether each magnitude traversed be equal or unequal to the first magnitude traversed, for it makes no difference as long as each part traversed is finite; for it is clear that when the time is exhausted, the magnitude traversed will not be exhausted (seeing that the traversed parts subtracted from the infinite magnitude are finite in extent as well

30   as in number). Hence the body will not traverse an infinite magnitude in a finite time; and it makes no difference whether the magnitude is infinite in one direction or in both, for the argument is the same.[10]

    Having demonstrated these facts, it is also evident through the same cause that no infinite magnitude can traverse a finite magnitude in a
35   finite time; for in a part of time only a part [of the infinite magnitude] will traverse it, and in each succeeding [equal] part likewise, and so in the whole time only a finite part will traverse it. And since, in a finite
238b   time, a finite magnitude cannot traverse an infinite magnitude, it is clear that neither can an infinite magnitude traverse a finite magnitude; for if the infinite magnitude can traverse the finite magnitude [in a finite time], the finite magnitude too can traverse the infinite magnitude [in a finite time], for it makes no difference which of the two magnitudes is
5   in motion since in both cases the finite would traverse[11] the infinite magnitude. For when the infinite magnitude A is in motion, a finite part of it, say CD, will traverse [the finite magnitude] B, then another finite part of it will do likewise, and still another, and it will be so always. So the result will be that the infinite magnitude A will have moved beyond the finite magnitude B at the same time as the finite magnitude B will have traversed[11] the infinite A; for perhaps no other
10   way is possible for the infinite magnitude to have moved beyond the finite magnitude than for the latter to have traversed[11] the infinite magnitude, whether by locomotion or by measuring.[12] So since this is impossible,[13] the infinite cannot traverse the finite magnitude.

    Moreover, nor can an infinite magnitude traverse an infinite magni-
15   tude in a finite time; for if it can, so can a finite [magnitude], for there exists a finite magnitude in an infinite magnitude.[14] Again, the demonstration will be the same if we consider it also from the point of view of time.[15]

    Since in a finite time, then, neither can a finite traverse an infinite magnitude, nor an infinite a finite, nor yet an infinite an infinite, it is
20   evident that a motion cannot be infinite in a finite time; for what difference does it make whether we posit a motion or a magnitude as being infinite?[16] If either of the two is infinite, so also must the other be; for every locomotion is in place.[17]

8

    Since every thing[1] to which motion or rest belongs by nature is either in motion or at rest when and where and in the manner in which it is its nature to be so, that which is coming to a stop must be in motion
25   when it is coming to a stop; for if it is not in motion, it will be resting,[2]

but that which is resting cannot be coming to a state of rest. This having been demonstrated, it is also evident that coming to a stop must take time; for a thing in motion moves in time, and that which is coming to a stop was shown to be in motion; so to come to a stop must take time.

30 Again, what we call "faster" or "slower" is in time, and in coming to a stop a thing may be faster or slower.[3]

Now if T is the primary time[4] in which a thing is coming to a stop, then the thing is necessarily coming to a stop in any part of T. For (a) if the thing is coming to a stop in neither of two parts into which T may be divided, it will not be coming to a stop in the whole T, and so that which is coming to a stop will not be coming to a stop, while (b) if the thing is coming to a stop in just one of the two parts, then the whole T will not be the primary time in which the thing is coming to a stop

35 (for it will be coming to a stop during T in virtue of something else [in virtue of a part of T], just as we argued earlier in the case of a thing in motion).[5]

239a Also, just as there is no first [time] in which a thing in motion is moving, so too there is no first [time] in which a thing which is coming to a stop is coming to a stop; for neither in the case of being in motion nor in that of coming to a stop is there a first [time].[6] For let AB be the first [time] in which a thing is coming to a stop. Now AB cannot be without parts, for there can be no motion in that which has no parts

5 because the thing will have partly moved [in part of that time], and that which is coming to a stop has been shown to be in motion. So if AB is divisible, the thing is coming to a stop in any one of the parts of AB, for this was shown earlier, namely, that a thing is coming to a stop in any part of that [i.e., the time] in which it is primarily coming to a stop. Accordingly, since that in which a thing is primarily in motion

10 is time, which is not *indivisible,* and since every [interval of] time is divisible into an infinite number of parts, there cannot be a first [time] in which the thing is [in the process of] coming to a stop.[7]

Nor again can there be a first time in which that which is resting has rested. For it cannot have rested in that which has no parts because there can be no motion in that which is *indivisible,* and in that in which there can be rest there can also be a motion;[8] for, as we have said, a thing is said to be resting at a time and in that [state][9] in which it can

15 by nature be in motion but is not in motion. And we also say that a thing is resting when it exists both now and at a previous moment in a similar [state],[9] as if *judged* not by something which is just one but by at least two,[10] and so that in which it is resting cannot be without parts; so since this can have parts, it will have to be an interval of time, and the thing will be resting in any of the parts of that interval (for this can

20 be shown in the same manner as that used in the previous cases).[11] Thus

there can be no first interval of time [in which the thing is resting]. The *reason* for this is the fact that everything at rest or in motion is in time and that there is no [interval of] time or magnitude or, in general, continuous thing that is first, for each of them is infinitely divisible into parts.

Since every thing in motion moves in time and changes from something to something,[12] if a thing during an interval of time is in motion in virtue of itself[13] and not in just a part of that interval, then it is impossible for the moving thing during that interval of time to be in a first state.[14] For to be at rest, for the thing as well as for each of its parts, is to be in the same state for some time, since we speak of being at rest in this manner, namely, when it can be truly said of the thing and its parts that they are in the same state at any two distinct moments [in some interval of time]. So if this is being at rest, then that which changes cannot as a whole be in a [fixed] state in a first interval of time; for every interval of time is divisible, and then it could be truly said that the thing and its parts would be in the same state now in one part of that interval and again in another part. For if it is not in this manner [that the thing is in the same state] but only at one moment, then the thing would be in the same state not for any interval of time but at a limit of an interval of time. However, although the thing is always fixed with respect to a state at a moment, nevertheless it is not resting; for a thing can be neither at rest nor in motion at a moment; so, on the one hand, it is true to say that at a moment a thing is not in motion and is in a [fixed] state, but, on the other, the thing cannot be at rest with respect to a state during an interval of time; otherwise, a thing in locomotion would turn out to be resting.

9

Zeno's argument is fallacious; for he says that if everything is either always at rest or always in motion when it exists over an equal part,[1] then, since that which is travelling exists always in a moment, the flying arrow is motionless.[2] But this is false, for time is not composed of moments (which are indivisible) just as no magnitude at all is composed of indivisibles.

Zeno's arguments concerning motion, which present difficulties for those who try to refute them, are four in number.

(a) The first states that there is no motion because the travelling object must arrive at the halfway point before reaching the end. We have gone through this in a preceding discussion.[3]

(b) The second, called "the argument of Achilles", asserts that the slower runner will never be overtaken by the fastest who pursues him, for the latter must first reach the point from which the former started, and in this way the slower runner must always be some distance ahead of the pursuer. This argument is the same as the one which depends on bisection, but it differs from it in that each additional magnitude taken is not a bisection. Now what follows from the argument [as given] is that the slower runner will never be overtaken, and the procedure here is the same as that in the argument which depends on bisection (for in both cases what follows is that the goal is not reached when a magnitude is divided in a certain manner, although in the latter case there is the added fact that, 'as the story goes, even the fastest runner will fail to catch the slowest runner); so the refutation must be the same in both cases. But the claim that the pursued runner who has a lead will never be overtaken is false; for although he will never be overtaken while he has the lead, nevertheless he will be overtaken if it is granted that he will traverse a certain finite distance.[4] These then are two of the arguments.

(c) The third argument, given at the start, states that a flying arrow is stationary. This results by granting that time is composed of moments; for if this is not granted, there will be no syllogism leading to that result.[5]

(d) The fourth is an argument concerning two rows with an equal number of bodies all of equal length, the rows extending from the opposite ends of the stadium to the midpoint and moving in opposite directions with the same speed; and the conclusion in this argument, so Zeno thinks, is that the half of an interval of time is equal to its double.[6] Here the fallacy lies in maintaining that an object with an equal speed takes an equal time to pass a moving body as to pass a stationary body of an equal length; and to maintain this is false.

For example, let $A_1A_2A_3A_4$ be a set of stationary bodies all of equal

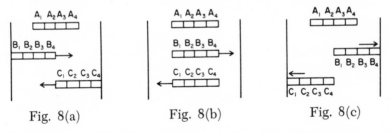

Fig. 8(a)   Fig. 8(b)   Fig. 8(c)

length, $B_1B_2B_3B_4$ another equal set of moving bodies starting on the right from the middle of the A's and having lengths equal to those of the A's, and $C_1C_2C_3C_4$ a third equal set with speed equal to and contrary to that of the B's, also of lengths equal to those of the A's and ending on the right with the end of the stadium [Fig. 8(a)]. Now as the B's and the C's pass one another, B_1 will be over C_4 at the same time as

C_1 will be over B_4 [Fig. 8(b)]. Thus, (1) C_1 will have passed[7] all the B's but only half the A's, and, as C_1 takes an equal time to go through each B as through each A [so says Zeno], its time in covering half the A's will be half that in covering all the B's.[8] Also, (2) during this same time the B's will have passed all the C's; for, since C_1 takes an equal time to pass each A as each B (so says Zeno), C_1 and B_1 will reach the contrary ends of the course at the same time because each of them takes an equal time to pass each A [Fig. 8(c)].[9] This then is the argument,[10] but it proceeds from something falsely maintained, as stated before.[11]

Nor are we facing an impossibility in the case of a change to a contradictory if, for example, in the case of a thing that is changing from not-white to white but is neither one nor the other,[12] one might be led to say that the thing is neither white nor not-white. For (a) if the thing is not wholly one or the other, nothing prevents us from calling it "white" or "not-white", since these terms are predicates of a thing not only when it is wholly one or wholly the other but also when it is in most of its parts or in its main parts one or the other, and (b) not to be in a thing is not the same as not to be in that thing wholly. It is likewise with being and not-being and the other pairs of contradictories; for the thing will necessarily be in one or the other of a pair of contradictories while changing, but never wholly in one or wholly in the other.[13]

Again, in the case of a [rotating] circle and a [rotating] sphere and, in general, of anything that moves within itself, one might say that each will also be resting, for each and its parts will be for some time in the same place and so it will be resting and moving at the same time. But in the first place, no part of the thing is in the same place for any given time, and in the second, even the whole thing is always changing to something else; for the circumference starting from A is not the same as that starting from B or C or some other point, except in the sense in which a musical man is a man by the fact that the musical is an attribute of the man.[14] Thus the circumference always changes to another which is distinct, and it is never at rest. The situation is similar in the case of a [rotating] sphere and the other things that move within themselves.

10

Having demonstrated the aforesaid, we now proceed to state that that which has no parts cannot be in motion except accidentally,[1] that is, by existing in a body or a magnitude[2] which is in motion, and it moves as the thing in the boat would move by the locomotion of the boat or as the part would move by the motion of the whole[3] (by "that which has no parts" I mean that which is indivisible with respect to quantity, for even the motions of the parts when taken with respect to

themselves are distinct from the motions of the parts when taken with
respect to the whole).[4] One might observe this difference especially in
the rotation of a sphere; for the parts near the center, those near the surface, and the sphere itself do not have the same speed,[5] and so there is
not just one motion.

As we have said, then, that which has no parts can be in motion in
the sense in which a man sitting in a boat is in motion when the boat
is travelling, but it cannot be essentially in motion. For let it be assumed
that it has changed from AB to BC, whether from one magnitude to
another or from one form to another or with respect to a contradiction;[6]
and let D be the primary time in which it has changed. Then during the
time[7] it is changing it must be either in AB or in BC or partly in one
and partly in the other; for, as shown earlier, everything that changes
does so in this manner. Now it cannot be partly in each of the two, for
then it would be divisible into parts. Nor again can it be in BC; for
then it will have completed the change, whereas it is assumed to be still
changing. So it can only be in AB while it is changing. But then it will
be resting, for, as shown earlier, to be in the same state during a given
time is to be resting. Hence that which has no parts cannot be in motion,
and in general, it cannot be changing; for a motion of it could have
been possible only in one way, namely, if time were composed of moments, since, then, in every moment it would have moved or have
changed in a way so as never to have been in the process of moving but
always in a state of having moved. That this is impossible, however, was
also shown earlier,[8] for neither is time composed of moments nor a line
of points nor a motion of [indivisible] impulses; and he who takes that
position does no other than posit a motion as composed of partless
things, as if he were to posit time as composed of moments and a
magnitude as composed of points.

Again, it is evident also from the following that neither a point nor
any other indivisible thing can be in motion. Whatever is in motion
cannot move over a magnitude greater than itself before having
moved over one equal to or less than itself. If this is so, then evidently
also a point will first have moved over a magnitude less than or equal
to itself. Since a point is indivisible, it cannot first move over a magnitude less than itself; so it will have to move over one which is equal to
itself. Then a line will be composed of points; for as the point keeps on
moving over one after another part equal to itself, it will measure the
whole line.[9] But if this is impossible, so is the motion of an indivisible
thing.

Again, if everything that moves does so in time but nothing moves in
a moment and every interval of time is divisible, there would be for
any moving thing a time less than the time required by that thing to
move over a part equal to itself (for to move over that part will take time

20 because every thing that moves takes time to do so, and it was shown before that every interval of time is divisible[10]). So if a point can move, there will be a time less than that in which the point has moved [over a part equal to itself]. But this is impossible since in a less time it would be necessary for it to have moved over a part which is smaller than itself, and then the indivisible would be divisible into something smaller than itself just as time is so divisible; for that which has no parts and is indivisible would move only in one way, namely, if it were possible for it to move in an *indivisible* moment, for the argument for a motion in a 25 moment is the same as that for a motion of something indivisible.

No change is infinite, for it was stated that every change, whether between contradictories or between contraries, is from something to something. Thus in a change with respect to a contradiction the two limits are the assertion and the denial, i.e., in generation it is a being and in 30 destruction it is a nonbeing. But in a change between contraries it is one or the other of the contraries, for these are the ends. So this is the case in every alteration, for alterations proceed from contraries; and it is likewise with increase and decrease, for in the case of increase the limit 241b is the complete magnitude of a thing according to the thing's *proper* nature, while in the case of decrease it is the departure from this. As for a locomotion, it is not limited in this manner, for not every locomotion exists between contraries. But since one meaning of "that which is in- 5 capable of being cut" is that which cannot be cut (for the term "incapable" has many senses[11]), that which is incapable of being cut in this sense cannot be [in the process of being] cut, and, in general, that which is incapable of being generated cannot be [in the process of being] generated, and that which is incapable of being changed cannot be [in the process of] changing into what it cannot be changed. Accordingly, if that which is in locomotion were to be changing into something, then it 10 would be possible for it to have changed. Thus its motion will not be infinite, and it will not be [in the process of] travelling an infinite distance, since it is impossible for it to traverse it. It is evident, then, that no change is infinite in this manner, namely, in the sense that it is not bounded by limits.[12]

However, whether one and the same change can be infinite in time 15 or not deserves inquiry.[13] For if the change is not one, perhaps nothing prevents it [from being infinite in time], for example, if a locomotion is followed by an alteration and this is followed by an increase and this by generation, and so on; for in this manner there will always be a motion in time, but it will not be just one motion because these do not form one motion.[14] Thus no one motion can be infinite in time, with one ex- 20 ception, namely, a circular locomotion.

Book H

1

241b
25

Every thing in motion is necessarily being moved by some thing. Now if it does not have the source of motion[2] in itself, it is evident that it is being moved by some other thing;[3] but if it has it in itself, let AC be that which is moved but not in the sense that some part of it [i.e., of AC] is moved.[4]

30

For one thing, the belief that AC is moved by itself because the whole of it is moved and is moved by nothing external is similar to the belief that DEF is moved by itself when DE moves EF and is itself in motion, because one does not perceive which is moved by which, whether DE by EF or EF by DE.[5] For another, a thing which is being

242a

moved by itself would never cease being in motion by virtue of the fact

---

Alternative Text

1

241b
35

Every thing in motion is necessarily being moved by some thing. For if it does not have the source of motion in itself, it is evident that it is being moved by some other thing (for what causes the motion is some other thing); but if it has it [the principle of motion] in itself, let AC be that which is being moved essentially and not in the sense that [only] some part of it is being moved.

40

For one thing, the belief that AC is moved by itself because the whole of it is moved and is moved by nothing external is similar to denying that DEF is moved by some [other] thing when DE moves EF and is itself moved, because it is not evident which [part] causes motion and

242a

which [part] is being moved. For another, that which is being moved that some other thing stops being in motion. So if a thing in motion ceases to be so by virtue of the fact that some other thing stops, then it is being moved by another thing. This having been made evident, every thing in motion is necessarily being moved by some thing.

5   To return, since AC is taken as being in motion, it must be divisible; for, as already shown, every thing in motion is divisible.[6] So let it be divided at B. Then when BC is resting, also AC must be resting; for if not, let it be in motion. Then while BC is resting, AB might be in motion, and then AC would not be in motion essentially.[7] But it was assumed

10   that it [i.e., AC] is in motion essentially and primarily. It is clear, then, that when BC is resting, also AC will be resting, and it is then that it [i.e., AC] ceases to be in motion. But if a thing stops or ceases to be in motion by the fact that something else rests, then it is being moved by another.[8]

It is evident, then, that every thing in motion is being moved by some

15   thing; for every thing in motion is divisible, and if a part of it is resting, then also the whole will be resting.[9]

Since every thing in motion is being moved by some thing, every thing whose motion is in place[10] must also be moved by another; and also the mover is being moved by another, that is, if it too is in motion,

---

35   not by something [else] need not cease being in motion by the fact that something else is resting, but if a thing is resting by the fact that something else has ceased being in motion, then that thing [when in motion] must be caused to be so by something [else]. If this is accepted, then every thing in motion is caused to be so by something.

To return, since AC is taken as being in motion, it must be divisible;

40   for every thing in motion is divisible. So let it be divded at B. Then when BC is not in motion, also AC is not in motion; for if it is, it is clear that AB would be in motion when BC is resting, and so it [i.e., AC] would not be in motion essentially and primarily. But it was assumed to be in motion essentially and primarily. Hence, if BC is not in motion, AC must be at rest. But it was agreed that that which is at rest while something else is not in motion is caused to be in motion by something. Thus every thing in motion must be caused to be so by something; for a thing in

45   motion will always be divisible, and if a part of it is not in motion, the whole too must be at rest.

50   Since every thing in motion is of necessity caused to be so by something, if a thing is caused to be in locomotion by another thing which is itself in motion and that other mover is itself caused to be moved by yet another which is itself in motion, and the latter by still another, and

and also that other mover is [likewise] being moved by another. Now
this does not go on to infinity but stops at some point, and there is something which is the first cause of being moved.[11] If this is not the case
but the process goes on to infinity, let A be moved by B, B by C, C by D,
and let this proceed in this manner infinitely. Then since that which
causes motion is itself in motion at the same time, it is clear that both
A and B will be in motion at the same time; for when B is in motion also
A is in motion, and when B is in motion also C is,[12] and when C, also D
is. Accordingly, the motion of A, B, C, and the rest will be simultaneous.
We may also consider each of these motions by itself; for even if each
of these things is moved by one of the others, nevertheless its motion is
numerically one and is not infinite with respect to its limits,[13] if indeed
every thing in motion proceeds from something to something, for the
motion is either numerically the same, or generically, or in species.

By "numerically the same motion" I mean one that starts from numerically the same limit and proceeds to numerically the same other
limit during the same numerical time, for example, from this whiteness,
which is one numerically, to that blackness [which is one numerically]
during this time, which is one numerically, for if during another time
[also], the motion is no longer numerically one but is one in species. A

---

this is so always, then this cannot proceed to infinity but there must be
something first which causes the motion. For let it not be so, and let
the process go on to infinity; and let A be moved by B, B by C, C by D,
and always each thing by another which is consecutive with it. Then
since by hypothesis the mover while causing motion is itself in motion,
the motion of the mover and that of the thing moved must occur simultaneously (for it is at the same time that the mover is causing the motion
and the thing moved is caused to be in motion). So it is evident that the
motions of A, B, C, and of each of the movers and of the things moved
will be simultaneous. Let each motion be considered, and let the motion
of A be P, that of B be Q, and that of C, D, etc., be R, S, etc.; for if
in every case each thing is moved by another, still the motion of each
may be taken as being numerically one, for every motion is from something to something else and is not infinite with respect to its extremities.
(By "numerically one" I mean a motion proceeding from something
which is numerically the same to something else also numerically the
same and occurring in a time which is numerically the same; for a
motion may be the same in genus or in species or numerically. And it
is (a) the same in genus if it is within the same category, as within
"substance" or within "quality", (b) the same in species if it proceeds

(Left margin line numbers: 20, 25, 30, 242b, 55, 60, 65, 242b 35)

5 motion is generically the same if it is in the same category of *substance* or genus; and it is the same in species if that from which it proceeds is the same in species and that to which it proceeds is the same in species— for example, the motion from whiteness to blackness or that from goodness to badness. These have been discussed also previously.[14]

To return, let the motion of A be E, that of B be F, that of C and D be
10 G and H, respectively, and let T be the time during which A is moved. If the motion of A is definite, so will its time be, and so T will not be infinite.[15] But A and B and each of the others were taken as being in motion at the same time. So it turns out that the motion EFGH,[16] which
15 is infinite, occurs in a definite time T; for the objects succeeding A, being infinite, were taken as being in motion during the [same] time in which A is in motion. So all are in motion during the same time. And whether the motion of A be taken as being equal to or greater than that of B, it makes no difference;[17] for in every case, an infinite motion will occur in a finite time, which is impossible.

20 It would thus seem that what we set out to show has been shown,[18] but it has not quite been shown, because nothing absurd follows; for in a finite time there may be an infinite motion, not the same motion, but one motion here and another there and so motions of many or of an

---

from that which is the same in species to that which is the same in species, as from white to black or from good to bad, if each of these has no further differentiae, and (c) the same numerically if it proceeds from that which is numerically one to that which is numerically one during
40 the same time, as from this white to that black or from this place to that place and at this particular time, for if at another time, it will be no longer a numerically one motion although it will be one in species. These distinctions were discussed previously.) Also, let the time in which A has performed its motions be taken, and let it be T. Then
45 since the motion of A is finite, the time too will be finite. Now since the movers and the things in motion are infinite, the entire motion of all of them, which is PQRS . . ., will also be infinite. For the motions of A and of B and of the others may be equal, or each of the motions of the others may be greater [than that of A or of B];[24] but whether equal or greater,
50 in both cases the whole motion will be infinite, for that which may be the case is here granted as being the case. Now since A and each of the others are simultaneously in motion, the whole motion will occur during the same time as the motion of A. But the motion of A occurs in a finite time; so there will be an infinite motion in a finite time, which is impossible.

infinite number of objects, and in this situation such indeed is the case.[19]
25   But if that which is moved primarily with respect to place and with a
corporeal motion must be in contact or continuous with the mover, as we
observe this happening in all cases, there will be of all of them [i.e., of
movers and things moved] something which is one[20] or is continuous.
So since this may be the case, let it be granted, and let the [resulting]
magnitude or the continuous thing be ABCD and its motion be EFGH.[16]
30   Whether it is finite or infinite makes no difference; for it will be in motion in the finite time T just the same, whether it is infinite or finite. Yet
each of the two alternatives is impossible.[21] So it is evident that the
series must stop somewhere and it will not proceed to infinity, and one
thing will not always be moved by another but there will be a first
243*a*   thing[22] which is moved. The fact that a hypothesis was introduced to
show this result, of course, makes no difference; for the positing of something which might be should not have resulted in anything absurd.[23]

2

The primary[1] mover, not as a final cause[2] but as a source of motion,[3]

It would thus seem that what we set out to show has been shown, but
55   it has not been demonstrated because nothing impossible has been
shown; for in a finite time an infinite motion may exist, not of a single
thing but of many of them.[25] And in the present problem this turns out
to be the case; for each of these things is moved with its own motion,
and there is nothing impossible when all of them are moved simultaneously. But if that which is first in causing motion with respect to place
60   and with a bodily motion must either be touching or be continuous
with that which is moved, as we observe in all cases, all the things
moved and the movers must be continuous with or touching one another, and so there must be some unity of all of them; and whether this
65   [unity] is finite or infinite makes no difference in the present case, for
in all cases the motion will be infinite when the things are infinite, if
indeed these [motions] may be equal or greater (for that which may be
the case is here taken as being the case). Consequently, if the totality
of ABCD . . . is infinite and is moved with the motion PQRS . . . and
70   in the time T, which is finite, it turns out that the finite[26] or the infinite
traverses an infinite [motion] in a finite time, which is impossible in
either case. So the series must come to a stop, and there must be a first
thing which is both a mover and in motion. The fact that it is from a

exists together with the thing which is being moved. I say "together" because there is nothing between the two, for this is common in every case of a thing in motion and its mover. Since the motions are three [in kind]—one with respect to place, another with respect to quality, and a third with respect to quantity—the things in motion too must be three [in kind]. Now a motion with respect to place is a locomotion, one with respect to quality is an alteration, and one with respect to quantity is an increase or decrease; we shall discuss first locomotion, for this is the primary[4] of [the kinds of] motions.

Every thing in locomotion is moved either by itself or by another thing. In the case of those things which are moved by themselves,[5] it is evident that the thing moved and the thing causing it to be moved are together; for it is in the things themselves that the primary mover exists, so there is nothing between them.

As for those things which are moved by other things, this must take place in four ways; for locomotions caused by other things are four in kind (pulling, pushing, carrying, and turning), since all other motions with respect to place are referred[6] to these [four]. Thus pushing along is a kind of pushing, namely, one in which the mover, in pushing the thing away from itself [i.e., from the mover], continues to do so behind it;

243a 30 hypothesis that the impossible follows here makes no difference; for the hypothesis which was taken is something which may be the case, and when that which may be the case is posited as being the case, nothing impossible should occur through it.

2

The primary mover, not as a final cause but as a source of motion, exists together with the thing which is being moved (by "together" here I mean that there is nothing between the two); for this is common to every thing which is being moved and the corresponding mover. Since there are three [kinds of] motions—one with respect to place, another with respect to quality, and the third with respect to quantity—the [kinds of] movers too must be three, namely, that which causes a loco-motion, that which causes an alteration, and that which causes an in-crease or decrease. And first we shall speak about a locomotion since this is the primary [kind of] motion.

Every thing in locomotion moves either by itself or by another thing. If by itself, it is evident that since the mover is in the thing itself, both pushing away, on the other hand, is a pushing in which the mover does not follow the thing which it causes to be in motion. As for throwing, this happens when the mover causes a thing to move from itself [i.e., from the mover] with a motion which is greater than the natural locomotion, and then the thing continues to travel as far as its motion holds. Again, pushing apart[7] and bringing together are, respectively, [kinds of] pushing away and pulling; for pushing apart is a [kind of] pushing away (for it is a pushing away either from itself or from another), whereas bringing together is a [kind of] pulling (for it is a pulling [a thing] toward itself or toward another). And such is the case with the species of these, e.g., packing and combing, for the one is a [species of] bringing together, the other a species of pushing apart. It is likewise with the other combinations and separations, for all will turn out to be [kinds of] pushing apart or bringing together, with the exception of those which take place in generation and destruction.[8] At the same time it is evident that there is no other genus of motion besides combination and separation; for all [the species of motions] are distributed within the ones mentioned. We may also add that inhaling is a [kind of] pulling and exhaling is a [kind of] pushing. It is likewise with spitting and all other motions occurring through the body by which something

243*b*

5

10

the mover and the thing moved are together and no thing exists between them.

A thing moved by another may do so in four ways, for [loco]motions by another may be four [in kind]—pushing, pulling, carrying, and turning; for all other motions with respect to place are referred to these. Thus, of pushing, one kind is pushing along; another, pushing away. When the mover does not leave the thing moved, this is pushing along; but when it stays behind, it is pushing away. In the case of carrying, it may take place in three [kinds of] motions. For that which is carried is moved not by itself but accidentally, since it is moved by being in that which is in motion or on that which is in motion; and that which carries it is moved either by being pushed or by being pulled or by being turned. So it is evident that carrying is a motion which may occur in three ways. As for pulling, which may be toward the thing causing it or toward another thing, it is a motion of that which pulls, and this [motion] is faster [than necessary to separate continuous things] and is not separated from the motion of the thing which is pulled; for pulling may be toward that which causes it or toward some other thing. And the other pullings, like inhaling and exhaling and spitting and the others which are corporeal, whether by giving out something or taking it in,

25

243*b* 21

25

15 is taken in or is given out, for some of them are pullings and the others are pushings away. The other motions with respect to place, too, should be referred [to the four genera], for they all come under them.

Again, of these four, carrying and turning are referred to pulling and pushing. Carrying may take place in three ways, for that which is
20 carried is moved accidentally in view of the fact that it is in or on a thing in motion, and that which carries it does so either by being pulled
244a or by being pushed or by being turned; and so carrying is common to all three. As for turning, it is a composite of pulling and pushing; for that which causes turning must be pulling one part of the thing and pushing another part since it forces one part away from itself and another part toward itself.[9]

5 Thus, if that which pushes and that which pulls are together, respectively, with that which is pushed and that which is pulled, it is evident that in locomotion there is nothing between that which is being moved and that which causes motion.

Moreover, this is evident also from the definitions; for pushing is a motion from the thing itself [which pushes] or from another to another, and pulling is a motion from another to the thing [which causes it] or
10 to another when the motion of that which pulls is faster than the motion

---

are the same in species and are referred to these, and so are packing and combing, for the one is a combination and the other is a separation. And indeed every motion with respect to place is a combination or a separa-
244a 16 tion. In the case of turning, it is a composite of pulling and pushing; for that which causes that motion pushes one part and pulls another. So it is evident that since that [part] which pushes and that which pulls are together, respectively, with that [part] which is pushed and that which is pulled, there is nothing between that which is being moved and that which causes the motion. This is clear also from what has
20 been said; for pushing is a motion from [the mover] itself or from another to another, while pulling is a motion from another to itself or to another. In addition, there is bringing together and there is pushing apart. As for throwing, this occurs when by means of an excessive pushing the motion resulting in the thing which travels is faster than its natural motion, and that motion [throwing] continues being so till it ceases to be excessive. It is evident, then, that the thing which is being moved and that which is causing the motion are together and that there
25 is nothing between them.

Nor is there anything between that which is altered and that which causes the alteration, and this is clear by induction; for in every case which would separate continuous things from each other, for it is in this way that one part is pulled along [with that which pulls]. It might be thought that pulling exists also in another way, for it is not in this way that wood pulls [i.e., attracts] fire. But it makes no difference whether that which pulls is in motion or at *rest* when it is pulling, for in the latter case its pulling is from where it is and in the former it is from where it was. Now a mover cannot cause a thing to be moved, whether it does so from itself to another or from another to itself, unless it is in contact with it; so it is evident that in locomotion there is nothing between the thing in motion and its mover.

Nor[10] is there anything between that which is being altered and that which is causing it to alter. This is clear by induction, for, in every case, the last thing which causes alteration is together with the [first] thing[11] which is being altered by the corresponding [mover], and these are affections coming under quality; for we say that a thing is being altered when it is being heated or being sweetened or getting dense or getting dry or getting white [etc.]. And this applies to inanimate and animate bodies alike and, in the case of animate things, to the parts without the power of sensation as well as to the powers of sensation themselves; for the latter are somewhat altered, since a sensation in

the last thing which causes the alteration and the first [part] which is being altered are together. For a thing with a quality is altered by being sensible, and bodies are sensible when they differ from each other with respect to such things as heaviness or lightness, hardness or softness, sound or the privation of it, whiteness or blackness, sweetness or bitterness, wetness or dryness, density or rarity, and whatever is between these. And likewise with respect to the others which come under the powers of sensation, like heat and cold and smoothness and roughness, since these are affections of quality which underlies them;[19] for sensible bodies differ with respect to these or with respect to the more and the less in each of these or by being affected by these (for animate bodies, inanimate bodies, and the inanimate parts of animate bodies are alike in becoming hot or cold or sweet or bitter or in being affected with respect to some of the other things previously mentioned). The powers of sensation themselves, too, are altered, for they are affected; for the *actuality* of each of them is a motion through the body and results when the [power of] sensation is affected by something. Now animate things are subject to all the alterations that inanimate things are subject to; but inanimate things are not subject to all the alterations that animate things are subject to, for they are not altered with respect to sensations actuality is a motion through the body, and during that [motion] the power of sensation is somewhat being affected. Thus an animate thing can be altered by every alteration by which an inanimate thing can, but an inanimate thing cannot be altered by every alteration by which an animate thing can;[12] for an inanimate thing cannot be altered with respect to a power of sensation, and further, an inanimate thing is not aware of being affected but an animate is aware.[13] Of course, nothing prevents an animate thing too from being unaware when the alteration takes place not with respect to the powers of sensation. Accordingly, if indeed the thing which is being altered is altered by a sensible,[14] it is evident that in every case the last thing which causes alteration is together with the first thing which is being altered. For example, the air is continuous with the thing [causing alteration], and the body [which is being affected] is continuous with air; and a color is continuous with light, and light with sight.[15] It is in the same way with hearing and smelling, for the primary mover[16] relative to that which is moved is air; and similarly with taste, for the flavor is together with the sense of taste. It is likewise with inanimate things and those without the power of sensation. So there can be nothing between that which is being altered and that which is causing alteration.

15

245*a*

5

10

---

and are not aware when they are altered. However, nothing prevents animate things also from being unaware of being altered when the alteration occurring in them is not with respect to sensation. Accordingly, if indeed the affections are sensible and an alteration takes place through them, at least this is evident—that the thing which is affected and the [corresponding] affection[20] are together and that there is nothing between them; for the air is continuous with the thing [causing alteration], while the body [which is being affected] is in contact with the air, and this is how the surface is related to light and the light to sight. And the sense of hearing and of smell are similarly related to the primary mover that moves them. In the same way, the sense of taste and the flavor are together. It is likewise with things which are inanimate or without the power of sensation..

20

25

In the case of that which is being increased and that which causes the increase the situation is similar; for an increase is a sort of an addition, and so that which is being increased and that which causes the increase are together. And it is likewise with decrease; for the cause of decrease is a sort of taking away.

It is evident, then, that there is nothing between the last thing causing motion and the first thing which is being moved.

245*b* 17

Nor again can there be anything between that which is being increased and that which is causing the increase; for the first thing that is causing the increase attaches itself to that which is being increased in such a way that the whole becomes one. Again, that which is causing decrease does so when some part is detached from that which is being decreased. So that which is causing increase or decrease is continuous [respectively with that which is being increased or decreased], and there is nothing between [two] things which are continuous [with each other].[17]

It is evident, then, that no intermediate exists between that which is being moved and the mover which is primary[18] or last in relation to the thing which is being moved.

15

245*b*

3

It will be seen from what follows that all things which are altered are altered by the sensibles and that alteration exists only in things which in virtue of themselves are said to be affected by the sensibles. For in other things one might come to the belief that alteration exists in shapes

5

3

We shall see from what follows that all things which are altered are altered by the sensibles and that there is alteration only of those things which are said to be essentially affected by these [sensibles]. For in other things one might come to the belief that an alteration exists in shapes and *forms* and possessions or in the processes of losing or of acquiring these, for alteration is thought to belong to these. However, it does not exist even in them, but these are generated[24] when some other things are altered; for they are being generated when the matter is becoming dense or rare or hot or cold, but they are not alterations. For we do not speak of the shape [of the statue] as being that from which that shape of the statue has come to be, nor of the shape of the pyramid or of the bed as being that from which it has come to be,[25] but it is derivatively that we call the one "brazen", the other "waxen", the third "wooden", and [in the case of an alteration] "altered"; for we call the bronze "wet" or "hot" or "hard", and not only so, but we also call the wet or the hot "bronze",[26] thus naming the matter in a manner similar to that of the affection. So since that [i.e., the subject] from which the *form* or the shape or the generated thing comes is not called

20

25

246*a* 21

and *forms* and habits[1] or the processes of acquiring or of losing these; yet alteration exists in none of these. For when the thing in the process of being shaped or arranged has been completed, we do not call it by the name of that out of which it is made (e.g., we do not call the statue "bronze", or the candle "wax", or the bed "wood", but we use derivative terms[2] and call them "brazen", "waxen", and "wooden", respectively). But when a thing has been affected or altered, we still call it by the [original] name; for we say that it is the bronze or the wax that is hot or hard, and not only so, but we also say that the wet or the hot is bronze, thus naming the matter in a manner similar[3] to that of the affection. So, if with respect to the shape or *form* the thing generated and in which the shape exists is not [so] named,[4] but with respect to the affections or the alterations it is [so] named, it is evident[5] that those generations cannot be alterations.

Again, it would also seem absurd to speak in such a manner and to say, for example, of a man or of a house or of any other thing that has been generated that it has been altered. But when a thing is being generated, perhaps there must be something which is being altered, for example, the matter may be condensing or becoming rarefied or becoming hot or cold; yet the things which are being generated are not

---

by an expression similar to that which applies to those things[27] which come from it, while that which is altered with respect to an affection is called by a similar form of expression,[28] it is evident that alterations exist only in sensibles.

Moreover, another absurdity would follow if this were not so; for it would be ridiculous to say that a man [when born] has been altered,[29] or in the case of a completed house that the process of completing a house, whether this be coping or roofing, is an alteration or that the house is being altered during the process of its coping or roofing. So clearly, the name "alteration" does not apply to things in the process of generation.

Nor is there an alteration in habits. For these are virtues and vices, and every virtue or vice is a relation, like health, which is a right proportion of the hot and the cold, either within the body itself or in relation to the surroundings; and in a similar way, physical beauty and strength are relations, for they are dispositions of that which is most conducive in relation to what is best (by "most conducive" I mean that which preserves and is disposed toward the nature [of the thing]). Accordingly, since virtues and vices are relations, and neither are they generations nor is there a generation or an alteration of them, it is evident

[only] altering, nor is their generation [just] an alteration.[6]

10   Further, neither the habits of the body nor those of the soul are alterations. For, of the habits, some are virtues and the others are vices, and
neither a virtue nor a vice is an alteration; but a virtue is a kind of
perfection[7] (for when each thing acquires its own virtue, it is then said
15   to be perfect; for a thing exists in the highest degree according to nature
when, to use an example, like a perfect circle, it has become a circle in
the highest sense and the best circle[8]), while a vice is the destruction of
or the departure from it [i.e., from that perfection]. Accordingly, just as
we do not call the completion of a house "an alteration" (for it is absurd
to say that the coping or the roofing with tiles is an alteration or that
20   the house is being altered when it is being coped or roofed but not that
246*b*   it is being completed), so it is in the case of virtues and vices and of
those who have them or are acquiring them; for some are perfections
while the others are departures, in which case none of them is an alteration.

Further, we also speak of virtues as coming under things which are
such that they are somehow related to something. For we take the vir-
5   tues of the body, such as health and good physical condition, to be mixtures and right proportions of hot and cold, in relation either to one

---

that "alteration" does not apply to what pertains to habits.[30]

Nor does it apply to what pertains to the virtues and the vices
of the soul. For a virtue is a kind of perfection[31] (for each thing is
perfect in the highest degree just when it reaches its *proper* virtue, and
30   most of all the one according to nature, just as a [individual] circle is
most of all according to nature when it is a circle in the highest de-
247*a* 20 gree),[32] while a vice is a destruction or a departure from this. So the
acquisition of a virtue or the loss of a vice comes to be when something
[else] has been altered, but neither the one nor the other is an alteration. That something [else] has been altered is clear. For a virtue is a
power either (a) of not being affected or (b) of being affected in a
certain manner, while a vice is a power either of being affected or of
being affected in a manner contrary to that of a virtue. And as a whole,
25   an ethical virtue is acquired through pleasures and pains, and the
pleasant here is either with respect to what is *actual* or through memory
or from what is expected; if with respect to what is *actual*, sensation is
the cause, while if through memory or through expectation, it is from
the one or from the other [i.e., remembering or expecting], respectively
(for the pleasant in the latter is either in remembering what has affected
us or in expecting what will affect us).

another or to the surroundings;[9] and it is likewise with physical beauty and strength and the other virtues and vices, for the being of each is such that it is somehow related to something, and that which has it is
10 well or badly disposed towards the *proper* affections[10] (and by "*proper* affections" I mean those by which it [i.e., the virtue or vice] is being generated or destroyed[11]). Thus, since neither the relations themselves are alterations, nor can any of them be altered or generated or, in general, change,[12] it is evident that neither a habit nor the losing or acquiring of a habit is an alteration; but perhaps when these are generated
15 or destroyed some other things must be altered, as is also the case with forms or *shapes*, as, for example, those which are present in things hot or cold or dry or wet or in things in which they happen to exist primarily.[13] For we say that a vice or a virtue has to do with those things by which the possessor of it is by nature altered; for a virtue makes one
20 be either unaffected or affected in a manner in which he ought to be, while a vice makes him be affected or unaffected in the contrary manner.
247a It is likewise with the habits of the soul, for the being of each of them, too, is such that it is somehow related to something; and the virtues [of the soul] are perfections, while the vices are departures. Again, a virtue is well disposed toward its *proper* affection, while a vice is badly

---

Further, in the *thinking* part of the soul, too, there is no alteration; for the scientific part in the highest sense is stated in relation to some-
30 thing. Clearly, the scientific part comes to be in us without our having moved with respect to any power but after something has been present;
247b 20 for we acquire universal *knowledge* by way of experience with particulars. *Actuality*, too, is not a generation, unless one is to say that also seeing and touching are generations; for *actuality* is such a thing as these are. As for the acquisition of *knowledge* when this first happens, there is neither a generation nor an alteration of it; for it is when the soul is coming to a rest and stays [at rest] that a man becomes a
25 *knower* and wise. So it is like one who does not become a scientist when he wakes up from sleep or ceases to be drunk or gets well from being sick, although during the earlier state in each of these he could not use or function according to *knowledge*, but when he is relieved of his restlessness and his *thinking* is settled down, the power of using his science, already there, is ready to function. It is a thing such as this that
30 takes place when *knowledge* first comes to be [in a person]; for it [i.e., *knowledge*] is a sort of rest or settled state from a state of restlessness.
248a 26 So it is with children; they cannot learn or *judge* with their powers of sensation as [well as] older people do, for there is much restlessness

disposed. Thus neither these [habits] nor the processes of losing or of
acquiring them could be alterations. And while they are being generated, the sensitive part of the soul is of necessity being altered, and it
is being altered by sensible objects. For every ethical virtue is about
bodily pleasures and pains, and these exist in *action* or in remembering
or in expecting; and in *action* they [pleasures and pains] occur by way
of sensation and so they are moved by some sensible objects,[14] while
in remembering and in expecting they come from sensation, for people
are pleased either by remembering what affected them or by expecting
what they will be affected by. Thus all such pleasures are produced by
sensible objects. Since along with pleasures and pains in a man virtues
and vices also arise (for these are concerned with pleasures and pains)
and since pleasures and pains are alterations of the sensible part of the
soul, it is evident that losing or acquiring them [virtues and vices] also
must take place when something else is being altered. Hence their
generation is accompanied by alteration, but they themselves are not
alterations.

247*b*   Moreover, neither are the habits of the thinking part of the soul alterations, nor is there a generation[15] of them. For one thing, we speak of
those [habits] of the *knowing* part very much more than of any of the
others as being among things which are somehow related to something.[16] Moreover, it is also evident that of these there is no generation;
for the potentially *knowing* becomes *knowing* not by having itself being moved at all but by the fact that something else existed;[17] for when
that which exists with respect to a part[18] comes into being, then it is
[only] in a sense[19] that one *knows* by the universal that which exists in
part.[18] Then again, there is no generation of the use or of the activity
[of something], unless one thinks that there is a generation also of seeing or of touching, and being in activity is similar to these.[20] As for the
acquisition of *knowledge,* when this first occurs, it is not a generation;
for we speak of *knowing* and of thinking wisely when *thought* has come
to a rest or to a stop, and there is no generation toward a state of rest,
for, as previously stated, there is no generation at all of any becoming.[21]

---

and motion in them. One settles down from restlessness or ceases to be
restless now by nature and now by other [causes];[33] but in both these
248*b* 26 cases something [else] happens to be altered, just as when one wakes
up or sobers up and is ready to function.

It is evident, then, that what pertains to alterations belongs to sensible
things and to the sensitive part of the soul, and it belongs to no other
things except by accident.

Again, just as we do not say that a man has become once more a scientist when from being drunk or asleep or sick he reverts to the contrary state (even if just before this [sober] state he could not use [his] science), so it is when at first he acquires the habit; for he comes to be thinking wisely and *knowing* when the soul has settled down from its natural restlessness. And on account of this, children can neither learn nor discriminate through sensation as adults do, for [in their soul] there is much restlessness and motion. And for some things the soul settles down and comes to a rest by nature itself, while for others it does so by other things,[22] but in both cases this occurs when certain things are altered in the body, as in the case of the use and the activity [of thought] when a man becomes sober or is awakened.[23]

From what has been said, then, it is evident that being altered and alteration occur in sensible things and in the sensitive part of the soul, and in no other things except accidentally.

4

One might raise the problem of whether every motion is comparable with every other motion or not.[1] If every motion is comparable with every other and if things in motion are said to be of like speed[2] when in equal times they move over an equal [amount],[3] then a circular may be equal to a straight,[4] and it may also be greater or less. Moreover, an alteration may be equal[5] to a locomotion, if in an equal time one thing has altered while another has moved with respect to place; and so an affection may be equal to a length.[6] But this is impossible. If so, then two things in motion are of equal speed[2] when in an equal time that over which the first has moved is equal to that over which the second has moved. Now an affection is not equal to a length.[7] Thus an alteration cannot be equal to or less than a locomotion; hence not all motions are comparable.

In the case of [one motion along] a circle and [another along] a straight line, what will the situation be? It would be absurd [to think] that the circular motion of one thing could not be similar to the rectilinear motion of another[8] but [to think] that the first must be immediately faster, or else slower, than the second, as in the case of one thing going downhill and another uphill. Moreover, if one were to say that a thing must immediately[9] move faster, or else slower, along the circular path than another along the straight, this makes no difference in the argument; for then a circular may [still] be greater, and [another] may be less than some straight, and so it [the circular] may also be equal [to some other straight]. For if in time T object P traverses the [circular] path B while object Q traverses the [straight] path C, then B will be greater than C;[10] for this was the meaning given to the term "faster".[11] Then again, if in less time a thing traverses an equal distance, it is faster.[11] So there will be a part of T in which P traverses a part of the circular path which is equal [to C], while Q traverses C in the whole of time T.[12] Then if these are comparable, what has just been stated follows, namely, that the straight will be equal to the circular.[13] But these [i.e., the straight and the circular] are not comparable; so neither are the motions.

Then all things which are not named equivocally are comparable.[14] For example, why is it that the pencil and the wine and the highest musical note are not comparable with respect to the term "sharper"? They are not comparable in view of the fact that that term is equivocally predicable of them. But the highest note is comparable with the note next to it[15] since the term "sharp" has the same meaning when applied to each. Is it the case, then, that the term "fast" does not have the same meaning when applied to the one and to the other [the circular motion and the rectilinear motion]? If so, then the two meanings are much further apart when the term is applied to an alteration and to a locomotion.[16]

In the first place, it is not [even] true to say that things are comparable if the term is not equivocally predicable of them. For the term "much" has the same meaning when predicated of water and of air, and these are not comparable; or if this term does not have the same meaning, at least the term "double" has the same meaning when predicated of them[17] (for it means the ratio of two to one), but they are [still] not comparable [with respect to this term]. Yet here, too, the same argument applies, for it is as in the case of the term "much", which is equivocal. Thus there are some terms whose formulae too are equivocal, like the term "much", whose formula is "an equal amount and still more", in which "an equal amount" has distinct meanings to begin with,[18] and also the term "equal" is likewise equivocal.[19] And the term "one", too, if predicated if any chance things, is immediately equivocal; and if so, so is the term "two", for if oneness were indeed a single nature, why is it that in some cases the things [of which "one" is a predicate] are comparable while in other cases they are not comparable?[20]

Is it not the case that we have incomparability when the primary subjects in which the attributes are present are distinct? Thus a horse and a dog are comparable, if a question arises as to which is whiter, for the primary subject [in which whiteness is present] is the same in both, and this is a surface; and they are likewise comparable with respect to their magnitude.[21] But water and voice are not comparable [with respect to clearness],[22] for the attribute[23] in question is present in a dis-

25   tinct [primary] subject. Or else it is clear that a man may in a way make
them [the attributes] all one, but he must say that each of them exists
249*a*   in a distinct subject; and the same thing may be equal and also sweet
and white, but each of these will exist in a distinct subject.[24] Moreover,
it is not any chance subject that can receive a given attribute, but a
given attribute can be received by just one primary subject.[25]

    Should comparable things, then, besides not being equivocal, possess
5   no differentiae, whether in themselves or in the subjects to which they
belong? For example, in the case of "color", which has subdivisions,
what I mean is this: In being more or less colored, but not with respect
to some given color, things are not comparable qua just having color;
but they are comparable with respect to [for example] being white.

    In the case of motion, too, it is likewise: Things are of like speed if
they are equal and have moved such-and-such an amount in an equal
10   time.[26] Then if one part of the thing has altered while another part[27] has
travelled during the same time, is the alteration equal to, or of like speed
as, the locomotion? This would be absurd, and the *reason* for this is the
fact that "motion" has species.[28] But then, if things are of equal speed
when in an equal time they travel over equal lengths, a rectilinear will
be equal to a circular.[29] What, then, will the *reason* be?[30] Will it be the
fact that the genus here is "locomotion" or the fact that it is "line"?
15   (Time here makes no difference, for it is *indivisible* in species.) Is it that
both of them differ in species? For if that over which a locomotion proceeds has species, "locomotion" too will have species.[31] Moreover, there
is also that by which [a locomotion takes place]; for example, a locomotion by feet is walking, while by wings it is flying. But this makes no
difference, for locomotion in this way is distinct [only] in mode,[32] and
so things are of equal speed if they move over the same[33] magnitude in
20   an equal time; and if that which is the same[34] does not differ in species,
neither does it differ in motion. Thus we should inquire what the
differentiae of "motion" are.[35]

    Indeed, this argument indicates that the genus is not something which
is [just] one, but that in it there are many latent [species].[36] And as for
equivocations, some of them are far apart and some have some similar-
25   ity, while others are close to each other either in genus or by analogy,
so the latter are not thought to be equivocations although they are.[37]

    When, then, is one species [of motion] distinct from another? Is it
when the same [thing] is in distinct [subjects] or when distinct
[things] are in distinct [subjects]?[38] And what will the definition be?[39]
Or by what are we to *judge* that the white and[40] the sweet are the same
or that they are distinct? Is it in view of the fact that they appear distinct
in distinct [subjects]? Or is it in view of the fact that they are not the
same at all?[41]

30   As for alterations, how will one have a speed equal to that of another?

If to recover one's health is to be altered, and one man may be cured quickly and another slowly, while others may be cured simultaneously, then some alterations may be of equal speeds, for they take place in equal times. But what is that which has been altered? For the term "equal" does not apply here, but just as in quantity there is equality, so here there is similarity.[42] However, let things be of equal speed if they undergo the same change in equal times.[43] Then should we compare the subjects which underlie the affection or [just] the affections? In the example under consideration in which it is the same[44] health, we may say that one [alteration] is neither more nor less than the other but that the two are similar. But if the affections are distinct,[45] as in becoming white and recovering one's health (which are alterations), insofar as they give rise to [different] species of alteration, there is no sameness or equality or likeness here, and so there is not [just] one alteration, just as in the case of locomotions.[46] So we should find out how many species of "alteration" there are and how many of "locomotion". If, then, things which are in motion (that is, in motion essentially and not accidentally) differ in species, their motions too will differ in species; if they differ in genus, so will their motions; and if numerically, so will their motions. But then, if the alterations are to be of equal speed, should we attend to the affections to see whether they are the same or similar or to the things which are being altered and see, for example, whether so-much of one has become white and so-much of the other? Should we not rather attend to both and regard the alterations as the same or distinct in affection, if [the subjects are] the same,[47] and equal or unequal, if they are unequal?[48]

Our inquiry into generations and destructions, too, should be the same. How can generations be of equal speed? They will be of equal speed if in equal times the things [generated] are the same[49] and *indivisible* [in species], for example, if they are men and not [just] animals; but one [of the two generations] may be *faster* than the other if in equal times the things are *distinct*;[50] for here we do not have two things in which this *otherness* is like a dissimilarity.[51] And if the *substance* [of what is generated] is a number, then one number may be greater and the other less but both [must be] of the same kind,[52] but no common name exists for these,[53] and each of these[54] is like the "more" in a greater or an excessive affection, or like the "greater" in a quantity.

5

Since in every case a mover[1] is moving something and in something and as far as something (by "in something" I mean in time, and by "as far as something" I mean [for example] that the length [traversed] is so-much of a quantity; for it is always the case that when a mover is causing a motion it has at the same time also caused a motion,[2] so that there will be so-much of a quantity over which something has moved and so-much of time in which it did so), then if A is the mover, B the thing in motion, S the length over which motion has occurred, and T the time taken, (1) in time T a force equal to that of A will cause a thing which is half of B to move over length 2S, and (2) it will cause it to move over length S in half the time of T; for thus there will be a proportion.[3] And (3) if the force of A causes B to move over the length S in time T, it also causes B to move over half of S in half the time of of T, and (4) a force equal to half of A causes a thing equal to half of B to move over a length S in time T. For example, let E = A/2 and F = B/2; then the strengths are similarly and proportionately related to the weights, so in equal times they will cause motion over equal lengths.

But (5) if E causes F to move over length S in time T, it does not follow that in time T it will cause 2F to move over S/2. Thus, if A can cause B to move over a distance S in time T, then half of A, which is E, may not cause B to move, either for a part of time T over a part of S or over a part X of S so related that X:S::E:A. For it may happen that E will not cause B to move at all; for if a given strength causes a quantity of motion, half that strength may not cause any quantity of motion, or it may not cause a motion in any given time (for if the total strength of the shiphaulers is indeed divisible into their number and the distance over which they caused the motion, one of them might cause the ship to move).[4] It is because of this that Zeno's statement is false when he says that any part of the millet causes a sound;[5] for nothing prevents a part from failing in any interval of time to move the air which is moved when the whole bushel of wheat falls. Indeed, when by itself, it will not move even such a part [of the air] as it would when it acts as a part of the whole, for in the whole it does not exist except potentially. On the other hand, (6) if one force moves one weight and another moves another over a given distance S in a given time T, then the forces when combined will also move the combined weights over an equal distance S in an equal time T, for here a proportion does apply.

Is the situation similar in the case of an alteration and an increase? For there is (a) that which causes an increase, (b) that which is being increased, (c) so-much time taken, and (d) one thing causing some quantity of increase while another is being increased by that quantity. Similarly, there is that which causes an alteration, that which is being altered, a quantity[6] of alteration with respect to more or less, and a quantity of time taken, twice as much [alteration] taking twice the time while in twice the time twice as much [alteration] taking place, and half the alteration taking half the time or in half the time half the alteration taking place, or in equal time twice as much.[7] But if that which causes an alteration or increase does so-much of it in so-much time, it does not follow that half of it will (a) cause it [i.e., the same alteration or increase] in twice the time or will (b) cause half of it in an equal time, but it may happen that it will cause no alteration or no increase at all, as in the case of weights.[8]

Book Ⓗ

1

250*b* Was motion ever generated without having existed before, and is it being destroyed in such a way that nothing will be in motion, or neither was it generated nor is it being destroyed, but it always existed and it will always exist, being (a) everlasting and (b) without the possibility
15 of ceasing in what exists and (c) as if a sort of life belonging to things which are formed by nature?[1]

All thinkers who say something about nature declare that motion exists because they posit an ordered universe; and all of them speculate about generation and destruction, and this speculation is not possible if motion does not exist.[2] Now those who say that there is an infinity of universes, some of them in the process of generation and others in the
20 process of destruction, declare that motion always exists (for the generation and destruction of the universes must take place with motion);[3] but those who say that there is just one universe, whether existing always or not, make assumptions also concerning motion as reason requires. If, however, it is possible that at some time no thing be in motion, this must happen in two ways: either (a) as Anaxagoras declares
25 (for he says that all things were together and at rest for an infinite interval of time but that *Intelligence* caused motion in things and separated them) or (b) as Empedocles does (according to whom things are now in motion and now at rest, in motion when *Friendship* is causing the *Many* to become *One* or when *Strife* is causing the *Many* from the *One*, but at rest during the time intervals which separate these processes), when he speaks thus:

30   Once more do they achieve plurality
        From scattered oneness, and thus far they come
        To being, with no permanent existence;
251*a*   And in so far as they continuously
        Never cease interchanging, just so far
        Their cycle is unmovable forever.[4]

148

For we must take him to be saying: "but since the motions alternate from one kind to the other". So we must examine these alternatives and see what the situation is, for the truth will be of use not only to the investigation of nature but also to the *inquiry* into the first principle.[5]

Let us begin with what we laid down earlier in the *Discourses on Nature*.[6] We have stated that motion is the actuality of the movable qua movable. So the things capable of having each kind of motion must exist.[7] And even apart from the definition of motion, everyone would agree that, for each kind of motion, it is the object capable of that motion which has that motion (for example, what is being altered is the alterable, and what travels is that which can change with respect to place), so that there must be a burnable object before there is a process of being burned, and an object which can burn another object, before a process of burning another object. Certainly, these [objects] too must either (a) have been generated at some particular time, before which they did not exist, or (b) be eternal.

Now if each kind of movable object was generated, then before its kind of motion there must have occurred some other change or motion by which the object, capable of being moved or able of causing motion, was generated.[8] But if such objects always preexisted without motion, this appears to be in itself unreasonable, and it must appear even more unreasonable as we consider the matter further.[9] For if, when there exist things which can be moved and things which can cause motion, at one time there is a first thing that causes motion and also one that is being moved, but at another [i.e., prior] time there is no such thing but there is only rest, then this[10] must have changed before;[11] for there must have been some cause of rest, since rest is the privation of motion. Thus there would be a change before the first change. For some things cause motion in one way only, while others can cause contrary motions; for example, fire burns but does not cool, but it is thought that there is just one science[12] of contraries. Even in things of the former type[13] there appears to be some similarity; for cold causes heat if it changes direction somehow or departs,[14] just as a scientist voluntarily commits an error when he uses his science in the contrary manner. Things, then, which have the potentiality of acting or of being acted upon, or else of causing motion or of being moved, have it not in every way but [only] when they are disposed in a certain way and approach one another. Thus it is when there is an approach[15] of two things that one of them causes a motion and the other is moved, and when disposed to act in a certain way[16] that the one can cause motion and the other can be moved. Accordingly, if motion did not always exist, it is clear that no two things would be so disposed as to have the potentiality of being moved and of

10

15

20

25

30

251b

5

causing motion, respectively, but it is necessary for [at least] one of them to change; for in things which are related[17] this must take place; for example, if A is double of B now but was not double of B before, then at least one of them, if not both, must have changed. Hence, prior to the first change there would be another change.

Moreover, how can there be a before and an after if time does not exist? Or, how can time exist if motion does not exist? So if time is a number of motion or a sort of motion,[18] then if indeed time always exists, motion too must be eternal.[19]

Now all thinkers, with one exception, appear to agree concerning time, for they say that time is ungenerable. And it is at least because of this that Democritus shows that it is impossible for all things to have been generated, for he considers time to be ungenerable. Plato alone says that time was generated; for he says that both time and the heaven came into existence simultaneously[20] (the heaven was generated, according to him). So if it is impossible for time to exist or to be conceived without moments and a moment is a sort of middle serving both as a beginning and an end, the beginning of future time but the end of past time, then time must always exist; for the extremity of any last part of an interval of time that may be taken will have to be in some[21] one of the moments, since nothing of time is present to us except a moment. Thus, since the moment is both a beginning and an end, there must always be time on both sides of it. And if there is [always] time, it is evident that there must [always] be motion too, if indeed time is an *attribute* of motion.

The same may be said concerning the indestructibility of motion. For just as in positing the generation of a first motion it was shown that a change prior to that motion existed, so in positing a last motion [it can be shown that a change later than that motion will exist]; for that which ceases to be in motion does not at the same time cease to be movable (for example, that which ceases being burned[22] does not at the same time cease being burnable, since a thing may be burnable without being in the process of being burned) and that which stops causing a motion does not at the same time [necessarily] stop being able to cause a motion. And when the destructive destroys something, it [the destructive] too will have to be destroyed,[23] and that which will destroy this will also have to be destroyed later; for a destruction too is a kind of change. So if the consequences are impossible,[24] it is clear that motion is eternal and does not at one time exist and at another cease to exist; and indeed, the manner in which these thinkers speak seems rather that of fiction.

Similar remarks apply also to the statement that such is the case by nature and that this should be regarded as a principle; and this would

seem to be the statement of Empedocles, who says that to rule and
cause motion alternately, at one time by *Friendship* and at another by
Strife, is something which belongs to things of necessity and that things
10   are at rest during the intervals separating these states. Perhaps also
those who posit one principle, like Anaxagoras, would speak in the
same manner.[25] Yet none of the things formed by nature or according to
nature is disorderly, for nature is a cause of order in each thing;[26] and
the relation of the infinite to the infinite has no formula,[27] while every
order is a formula. Nor indeed is it the work of nature that things should
15   be at rest for an infinite time, then in motion at some later time, with no
more difference in the latter time than in the former and no order of
any sort. For a thing by nature is either disposed in a simple way and
not in one way at one time but in another at another time (for example,
by nature fire travels up, and it is not the case that at one time it travels
up but at another it does not), or it has a pattern if it is not simple.[28]
20   Hence, it would be better to say that things are at rest and in motion
alternately, as Empedocles or any other thinker who may have spoken
in this manner does, for there is order in such a state of affairs.[28] Yet
even he who asserts this should not only state it but also state its cause,
and he should neither avoid positing something nor posit an unreason-
25   able axiom but should use an induction or a demonstration;[29] for these
hypotheses are not causes, nor is the essence of *Friendship* or of *Strife*
to be these, but the essence of *Friendship* is to unite and that of *Strife* is
to separate.[30] And if he says that each of these [i.e., *Friendship* or *Strife*]
acts on some things only, he should mention those things for each case,[31]
as in the case of men (in whom there is something which brings them
30   together, and this is friendship, while enemies avoid each other); but
he assumes this to be the case in the whole universe, for [according to
him] it appears to be so in some cases. Also, some argument is needed
to show that each of the two principles rules alternately for an equal
interval of time.[32]

It is not a right belief to regard universally as an adequate principle
the following, that it is always so or it always happens to be so, which is
35   what Democritus does in referring the causes of nature to this, that
252*b*   things were happening in the same way before. He does not think that
one should seek a principle of that which is or happens always, and he
is right in some cases but not in all cases; for the triangle too has its
angles equal to two right angles always, yet there is some other cause
5   of this eternality, although of principles which are eternal there are no
other causes.[33]

Let these be our remarks concerning the fact that there was no time
when motion did not exist and that there will be no time when motion
will not exist.

2

Arguments which are contrary to our position are not difficult to refute. From an examination of arguments such as the following it might seem most likely that motion may at one time exist though it did not exist at all prior to that time:

(1) No change is eternal; for every change proceeds by nature from something to something; so every change has as its limits the contraries within which it takes place and no thing can be in motion to infinity.[1]

(2) We observe that a thing which is not in motion and has no motion within itself may be set in motion; for example, lifeless things which are neither partly nor wholly in motion but are at rest may sometimes be in motion, but they should be either always in motion or always at rest, if indeed motion cannot be generated from its nonexistence.[2]

(3) Most of all, this seems to be evident in living things. For, although at one time there is no motion at all in us but we are still, nevertheless, we are in motion at another time; and sometimes what begins that motion comes to be in us from ourselves even if no outside thing causes any motion in us. Now nothing like this occurs in lifeless things but always some other external thing causes them to be in motion, but we say that it is the animal itself that causes itself to be in motion. Hence, if sometimes an animal is entirely at rest, a motion might come to be in a motionless object from itself and not from outside. If this, then, can occur in an animal, what prevents the same thing from occurring also all over the universe? For if this occurs in a small universe, it can occur also in a great universe; and if it can occur in a universe, it can occur also in the infinite, if indeed the whole infinite can be in motion and at rest.[3]

Now the first of these three arguments is rightly maintained, namely, that no motion which is the same and numerically one and proceeds to an opposite is eternal. For this is perhaps necessarily so, if indeed a motion of an object which is the same and [numerically] one is not always the same and [numerically] one. What I mean, for example, is this: There may be a problem of whether a note from a string which is [numerically] one is one and the same or is always distinct, assuming the string to be in a similar state and to be in motion in a similar way. But whatever the case may be, nothing prevents some motion from being the same by being continuous and eternal. This will become clearer from later arguments.[4]

As for the argument that a thing may be in motion although it was not in motion before, there is nothing absurd in it, whether that which causes the motion is external or not. However, how this can come about

5 is a matter of inquiry,[5] that is, how the same thing can be caused to be now in motion and now not in motion by another thing which can cause motion; for he who introduces this argument does no more than raise the question of why some things are not always at rest and others are not always in motion.

The third argument, that in living things motion comes to be in them although not existing in them before, would seem to be the most *diffi-*
10 *cult* [to refute]; for it seems that a thing which is at one time resting is at a later time walking, although nothing external has caused the motion. But this is false. For we observe that there is some natural part of the animal which is always in motion[6] and that the cause of its motion is not the animal itself but perhaps its environment. We do say that the animal causes itself to be in motion, not every [kind of] motion, how-
15 ever, but a motion with respect to place. So nothing prevents many motions in the body from being caused by the surroundings (or rather, perhaps this is necessary), some of these causing *thought* or desire to move and the latter causing in turn the whole animal to move; and such thing happens in sleep, for although [in animals] there is no motion
20 caused by any power of sensation, nevertheless, there is some kind of motion, and animals wake up. These too, however, will be made evident from our later discussions.[7]

3

The starting-point of our inquiry will be the very same as that which concerns itself with the *difficulty* already mentioned, namely, why it is that some things are in motion at one time but at rest at another.[1]

Now the alternatives must be either (1) all [things] are always at
25 rest,[2] or (2) all things are always in motion, or (3) some things are in motion and others are at rest; and in the last alternative, either (a) the things in motion are always in motion and those at rest are [always] at rest, or (b) all [things] are by nature alike disposed so as to be in motion and at rest,[3] or (c) the remaining and third alternative: it may be that some things are always immovable, others are always in motion, and
30 still others admit of both.[4] This last alternative should be discussed, for it contains the solution to all the problems raised and it is the conclusion of our *inquiry*.

To think that all things are at rest and to seek an argument for this without regard to sensation[5] is a weakness of *thought* and is a dispute about a whole and not a part;[6] and it is an attack not only on the
253b physicist but also on all sciences, so to speak, and all opinions because all of these use motion.[7] Moreover, just as objections concerning principles

in discussions on mathematics are not directed against the mathematician (and the situation is similar in other sciences), so in the present case the position stated is not directed against the physicist; for [in physics] it is a hypothesis that nature is a principle of motion.[8]

To say also that all things are in motion is nearly as false, but it is less damaging to our *inquiry*. For, although in our discussions on physics nature was posited as a principle of rest as well as of motion,[9] still motion is a physical fact;[10] and further, some thinkers[11] even maintain, not that some things are in motion and others are at rest, but that all things are always in motion but our power of sensation fails to notice this.

Now even if these thinkers do not specify what kind of motion they mean or whether they mean all kinds, still it is not difficult to reply to them; for neither can a thing be increasing continuously, nor can it be decreasing so, but there is also an intermediate state.[12] Their statement is like that about the stone which is worn away by drops of water or which is split by plants growing through it. For if a certain amount of the stone was pushed away or removed by the drops, this does not mean that half that amount was previously taken away in half the time; but as in the case of hauling a ship,[13] here too, so-many drops cause so-much to be removed, but no time may exist in which a part of those drops cause a corresponding part of the stone to be removed. Each part that was removed is divisible into many parts, but none of these was set in motion separately: All of them were moved together. It is evident, then, that sometimes the whole may be removed, but that from the infinite divisibility of what is removed it does not follow that something is removed during any interval of time.

It is likewise with an alteration, regardless of its kind; for if the object which is altering is infinitely divisible into parts, it is not the case that because of this the alteration too is [always] so divisible; for an alteration often takes place all at once, as in the case of freezing.[14] Again, when one becomes sick, time must elapse in which he will become healthy, and he will not change in a limit [i.e., a moment] of time;[15] and he must change to health and to nothing else. Hence, to say that he will be altering continuously is to disagree with what is quite evident. For an alteration proceeds to a contrary; and a stone becomes neither harder nor softer.[16] And as for a locomotion, it would be strange if we failed to notice a stone when it falls down and stays on the ground. Further, earth and each of the other [elements] necessarily stay in their *proper* places, and it is by force that they are moved away from these; so if indeed some of them are in their *proper* places, then also with respect to place not all things can [always][17] be in motion.

From these and other such arguments, then, one might be convinced that it is impossible for all things to be either always in motion or always at rest.

Moreover, neither can some of them be always at rest, others always in motion, and none of them sometimes at rest and sometimes in motion. We must say that this is impossible also in this case, as we did in the previous cases (for we observe the changes previously stated[18] occurring in the same things), and, in addition, that he who maintains this position is attacking what is evident. For there will be neither an increase[19] nor a motion by force, if no thing which is first at rest afterwards moves contrary to nature.[20] Indeed, this position does away with generation and destruction.[21] And also a motion is thought by almost all to be a sort of generation or destruction;[22] for that to which a thing is changing is that which is being generated[23] or that in which[24] the thing comes to be, and that from which it is changing is that which is being destroyed or that from which it goes away. So it is clear that there are things which are sometimes in motion and sometimes at rest.

As for the claim that all things are sometimes at rest and sometimes in motion, it must directly face the arguments already given.[25] From what is now laid down, our starting-point must again be the same as that made previously. So either (1) all things are at rest, or (2) all are in motion, or (3) some things are at rest and the others are in motion. And if some are at rest and the others are in motion, then either (3a) all of them must be sometimes at rest and sometimes in motion, or (3b) some of them must be always at rest, some always in motion, and the remaining sometimes at rest and sometimes in motion.

We have stated previously that not all things can be at rest,[26] but let us speak again about it now. Even if it is true, as some say,[27] that being is infinite and immovable, still it does not appear to be so at all according to sensation but many things appear to be in motion.[28] Now if false opinion exists or, in general, if opinion exists, then also motion exists;[29] and it is likewise if there exists imagination or thinking that things are sometimes in one way and sometimes in another; for imagination and opinion are thought to be motions of some sort. So to be concerned with this alternative and to seek a reason for things which we know better rather than for things which need a reason is to *judge* badly what is better and what is worse; what we should be convinced of and what, not; and what is a principle and what is not.[30]

Similarly, it is impossible for all things to be [always] in motion or for some to be always in motion and the others to be always at rest; for a conviction of one alternative is sufficient against the others since we observe some things to be sometimes in motion and sometimes at rest.[31] It is evident, then, that for all things to be continuously at rest or continuously in motion is as impossible as for some of them to be always in motion and the others always at rest.

It remains, then, to investigate whether (a) all things are such as to be now in motion and now at rest or (b) some of them exist in this manner, but of the remaining some are always at rest while the others are always in motion; and it is the second alternative which we must show.

4

Of the things that cause motion or are moved,[1] some cause motion or are moved accidentally and others essentially; for example, a thing causes a motion or is in motion accidentally (a) by belonging to a mover or to a thing in motion or (b) with respect to a part, but essentially if it does not belong to a mover or to a thing in motion or if it is not [just] a part [of the thing] that causes a motion or is in motion.[2]

Of things which are essentially in motion,[3] some are moved by themselves and some are moved by others, and some are moved by nature but others by force or contrary to nature.[4] For (1) that which is moved by itself is moved by [its] nature, as in the case of each animal. (For an animal is moved by itself; and we say that things whose principle of motion[5] is in themselves are moved by nature; and so it is by [its] nature that the whole animal moves itself, while the body[6] can be moved both by nature and contrary to nature, for there is a difference both in the kinds of motions which a body may chance to have and the kind(s) of element(s) of which it may consist.) And (2) of things which are moved by others, some are in motion by nature while others are in motion contrary to nature (for example, it is contrary to nature that things made of earth are moved up and that fire is moved down). And, we may add, the parts of animals are often moved contrary to nature, depending on their position and the manner of their motion.[7]

Now the fact that a thing is moved by another is most evident in cases in which the motion is contrary to nature, and this is because it is clear that [in such motion] the thing is moved by another thing.[8] Next to things whose motions are contrary to nature there are those (of the things which are in motion by nature) which cause themselves to be in motion, e.g., animals, for in these what is unclear is not the fact that they are moved by something[9] but how to distinguish in them that which causes motion and that which is moved;[10] for it seems that in animals, as in ships and things which are composed not by nature,[11] that which causes motion and that which is moved are divided,[12] and likewise for every thing which causes itself to be in motion.

The greatest *difficulty*, however, lies in the remaining part of the
35   last division; for of things moved by others, some were posited by us as
being in motion contrary to nature, and opposed to these there remain
255*a*   those which are in motion by nature. The latter are those (e.g., light
and heavy objects) which would cause the following *difficulty:* By what
are they moved? For each of these is moved to its opposite place by
force and to its *proper* place by nature (the light moves up; the heavy
5   moves down), but that by which it is moved is not quite so evident as
it is in a thing which is moved contrary to nature.[13] To say that it is
moved by itself is impossible; for this [i.e., to be moved by itself] is an
attribute of living things and is proper to them, and, besides, the thing
would also be capable of standing still. I mean, for example, that if the
thing itself is the cause of its walking, it will also be the cause of its not
10   walking; so if it were up to fire itself to go up, clearly it would also be
up to fire itself to go down.[14] It is also unreasonable that such a thing
should be causing only one motion[15] in itself, if indeed it is causing
itself to be moved. Again, how can something which is continuous and
has a natural unity[16] cause itself to be moved? For insofar as a thing
is one and continuous but not in contact, it is incapable of being acted
upon [by itself]; but insofar as a separation has been made, one [part]
15   can by nature act and the other, be acted upon.[17] So none of these
things causes itself to be moved (for each has a uniform nature[16]), nor
does anything else which is continuous, but in each case the mover must
be divided from that which is moved, as in the case of lifeless things
when observed to be moved by living things. But these[18] too happen to
20   be moved always by something; and this would be evident if the causes
are distinguished.[19]
The above-mentioned [distinctions] may be made also in the case
of the movers, for it is contrary to nature that some of them can cause
motion, as in the case of a lever, which can cause the heavy to be moved
not by nature, but others can do so by nature, like the *actually* hot,
which can move the potentially hot;[20] and similarly with other such
25   cases. And that which is potentially of a certain quality or of a certain
quantity or in a certain place, when it has such a principle[21] in itself,
is in a like manner movable by nature and not accidentally (for the same
thing may have both a quality and a quantity, but the one belongs to
the other accidentally[22] and not in virtue of itself). Thus it is by force
that fire and earth are moved by something when they are moved
30   contrary to their nature,[23] but by nature when they exist potentially on
their way to their *actuality*.[24]
Now "potentially" has many senses; and this is the *reason* why it is
not evident by what movers these objects are moved, e.g., upwards in
the case of fire and downwards in the case of earth. The learner [for

example] is potentially a scientist in a manner distinct from that of a man who already has the science but is not investigating.[25] Now whenever that which can act and that which can be acted upon are together, then the potential always comes to be in *actuality*. Thus the learner, from being potentially something, [first] comes to be potentially something else,[26] for he who has the science but is not investigating is in a certain way potentially a scientist, but not in the way in which he was prior to learning the science; but when he has the power and nothing is preventing [him from investigating],[27] he is in activity and he investigates; otherwise, he would be in a contradictory disposition or in ignorance.

The situation is similar in physical objects; for the cold is potentially hot, but, after changing, it is fire, and if nothing is preventing or obstructing it, it [actually] burns [another object]. And it is likewise with the heavy and the light, for the light is generated from the heavy, as air from water; for water is potentially[28] air first, and when it is already air, it is at once in activity, unless something prevents it. Now the *actuality* of the light is to be at a certain place, which is up, and it is prevented from being there when it is in a contrary place (and the situation is similar with a quantity or a quality).

However, we may still raise this question: Why are light and heavy things moved to their respective places? The *reason* is this: It is the nature of each to be at a certain place, and to be light or to be heavy is to be just this, specifically, to be up in the case of the light or to be down in the case of the heavy. So a thing is potentially light or heavy in many ways, as already stated. For when the object is water, it is potentially light but in a certain way,[29] and when [it becomes] air, it still exists potentially, since it may not be up if obstructed, but when that which obstructs it from going up is removed, then air is in activity and always moves upwards. Similarly, an object with a quality changes so as to be in activity, for a man who has just become a scientist immediately begins investigating, unless something prevents him; and [an object which has gained] a quantity is extended, unless something prevents it. As for him who moves that which supports or prevents the object (as in the case of one who pulls away the supporting pillar or removes the stone which holds the skin below the water), in one sense he moves the object but in another sense he does not; for he moves it accidentally, as in the case of a rebounding ball which was moved not by the wall[30] but by the thrower. It is clear, then, that none of those objects causes itself to be moved; but each of them has a principle of motion, not of causing motion or of acting, but of being acted upon.

Now if all things in motion are moved either (a) by nature or (b) contrary to nature or by force and if things which are moved by force or

contrary to nature are moved by something or by things other than
themselves and if also things which are in motion by nature are moved
35   by something, both those which are moved by themselves and those
256a   which are not so moved (e.g., light and heavy objects, for either they
come to be such by that which generates them or acts on them or they
are moved by that which removes the obstructing or preventing object),
then all things in motion would have to be moved by something.

5

Now this may take place in two ways: Either it is not through[1] itself
5   that the mover moves [the object] but through some other thing by
which the mover is moved, or it moves the object through itself; and it
[the mover] moves either by being next to the last [object moved] or
through a number of [intermediate] things, as in the case of a stick
which moves the stone but is moved by the hand, which is itself moved
by the man, who is not moved by anything else. Now we say that both
10   the last mover[2] and the first mover cause motion, but that the first does
so to a higher degree; for the first moves the last but the last does not
move the first, and[3] without the first the last will not cause motion but
without the last the first may do so, as in the case of the stick, which will
not move the object unless the man causes it to do so. So if in every case
a thing in motion must be moved by a second thing, which either is
15   moved by a third or is not, and if by a third then there must be a first
mover which is not moved by anything else, while if not by a third
then the second itself is such [a first mover] and no other mover is
necessary (for it is impossible that a mover which is itself moved by
another proceed to infinity since in this infinity there will be no first
mover); if, to repeat, every thing in motion is moved by another thing
20   and the first mover is also moved but not by another thing, then the first
mover must be moved by itself.[4]
We may arrive at this very same conclusion also in another way.
Every mover moves something, and it moves it with something [as with
an instrument], either with itself or with something else; e.g., a man
moves something either with himself or with a stick, and the wind has
25   knocked down something either with itself or with a stone which it
dislodged. Now it is impossible for a mover to cause a motion [in an
object] unless it causes a motion with itself as with an instrument; but
if it is with itself that a mover moves [the object], then no other thing
is necessary with which to move [that object], whereas if it is with
something else that the mover moves [that object], then there will be
a [first] thing which it moves not with something else but with itself,

or else there will be an infinite series.[5] Accordingly, if a thing causes something to be in motion, the series must stop and not proceed to infinity; for if a stick causes a motion by being itself moved by the hand, it is the hand that moves the stick, and if it is something else that moves this [i.e., the hand], then some other thing is the mover of this. Thus, whenever that which causes a motion with something, say A, is someting else, say B, there must be a prior mover[6] which causes a motion with itself. Accordingly, if this [prior mover] is in motion but there is no other mover[7] which moves it, then it must move itself. So, according to this argument, too, either·a thing in motion is moved directly by a thing that moves itself, or it is so moved that through intermediate steps we come to such a mover.

If in addition to the above we examine the matter in still another way, the result will be the following.[8] Now if everything in motion is moved by a thing in motion, then either (1) this [motion] belongs to the thing [i.e., the mover] by accident, so that it [the mover] causes a motion while in motion though not because it is always in motion, or (2) it belongs [to the thing, i.e., to the mover] not in this way but essentially.

First, if (1) it belongs by accident, the thing[9] is in motion but not of necessity; and if this is so, then it may be that at some time no thing is in motion, for an accident exists but not of necessity and so it may not exist. Now if we were to posit that which is possible [as being actually the case], nothing impossible should result, although perhaps something false might. But to posit the nonexistence of [all] motion is to posit the impossible, for it was shown earlier[10] that motion always exists of necessity.[11]

And this result, we may add, is reasonable.[12] For there are three things: that which is in motion, that which moves another, and that with which this [the mover] moves another. Now that which is in motion must be moved [by another], but it is not necessary for it to move another,[13] whereas that with which the mover moves must both be moved and also move another, for it changes [along with the thing it moves] at the same time[14] and at the same [surface of contact] (and this is clear in things which move others with respect to place, for they must be in contact with each other to a certain extent); but as for the mover which causes a motion in such a way as to be not that with which it moves another, it is [of necessity] immovable. Now since we observe the extreme, that is, that which can be moved by another but has no principle of motion [on another][15] and also that which is moved by itself and not by another, it is reasonable, not to say necessary, that there should exist a third which causes a motion but is immovable.[16] And in this respect Anaxagoras speaks rightly when he says that *Intelligence* cannot be affected and is unblended, seeing that he posits it [i.e., *Intelligence*] as the source of motion [on others]; for only when it is immovable would it cause motion in others, and only when it is unblended would it be the ruler [of other things].[17]

Second, if (2) that which causes a motion is moved of necessity[18] and not by accident, so that if not moved it would cause no motion, then
30   the mover qua moved is moved either (a) with the same kind of motion [which it causes] or (b) with another kind. I mean, for example, that either that which is heating is itself being heated and that which causes healing is itself being healed and that which is carrying another is itself being carried, or that which causes healing is being carried and that which carries another is being increased, etc.

257*a*   But evidently these are impossible. For (a) in speaking of a motion one must specify an *indivisible* [species], so that if someone, for example, is teaching a geometrical theorem, he himself will be learning the same theorem,[19] and if he is throwing something, he himself will be thrown in the same manner. Or if this is not the way, then (b) the mover will be moved with a motion from another genus; for example, that
5   which carries another will be increased, and that which causes an increase in this carrier will be altered by another, and that which causes this alteration will be moved by another with some other motion. But this must stop, for the [kinds of] motions are finite.[20] And if one says that the motions repeat themselves and that that which causes the above-mentioned alteration is being carried, this amounts to the same thing as if one had said that that which carries another is being carried
10   or that he who teaches another is being taught; for clearly every thing in motion is moved also by a mover prior to its own immediate mover, and even more so by every such prior mover.[21] However, this is impossible; for the consequence is that the teacher will be learning [the same things], but as a learner he cannot have the knowledge [yet to be learned] while as a teacher he must have it.[22]

15   Moreover, a more unreasonable consequence is that every thing that can move another will be movable, if indeed every thing in motion is moved by a thing in motion. For that which can move another will be movable,[23] which would be like saying that whatever can heal or is healing another can also be healed and whatever can build something can also be built, whether (a) directly or (b) through intermediate steps (that is, if whatever can cause a motion can also be moved by another,
20   but by a motion other than that which it directly causes, e.g., if that which can cause health can learn; but such steps backward lead ultimately to a motion of the same kind, as we stated before). Of the two alternatives, one is impossible while the other is fictitious;[24] for it is absurd that [for example] that which has the potentiality of causing an
25   alteration must have the potentiality of being increased. So it is not

necessary that a thing in motion be always moved by another which is itself in motion, but there will be a stop. Hence, either the thing which is first in motion will be moved by another thing which is at rest, or it will cause itself to be in motion. Moreover, if there were any need of inquiring whether the mover which is the cause and principle of motion is that which causes itself to be moved or that whose motion is caused by another, all should posit the former; for that which is a cause in virtue of itself is always prior to that which is a cause but in virtue of something else.[25]

We must make a fresh start, then, and consider this question: If there is something which causes itself to be moved, how does it do it and in what way? Now every thing in motion is divisible into things which are always divisible; for it has been shown earlier in our general discussions *Concerning Nature* that every thing which is essentially in motion is continuous.[26] Now it is impossible for that which moves itself to move itself in its entirety;[27] for if so, being one and *indivisible* in kind, it would both (a) be caused to have and (b) cause the same locomotion, or it would both have and cause the same alteration [etc.], and so at the same time a man would be both teaching and in the process of being taught [the same things], and he would be both restoring and in the process of being restored to the same health.[28] Moreover, it was specified that it is the movable that is moved, and this [i.e., the movable] is that which is potentially in motion, and not in actuality; and it is the potentially existing which proceeds to actuality. Now a motion is an incomplete actuality of the movable. But that which causes a motion is already in *actuality*; for example, what causes something to be hot is the [already] hot, and what gives birth to another is that which [already] has a form. If so, then the same thing and with respect to the same thing will at the same time be both hot and not hot; and it is likewise in each of the others, in which the mover [and the moved] share the same name. Accordingly, in that which is causing itself to be moved there is that which is causing the motion and that which is being moved.[29]

It is evident from the following that what causes itself to be moved cannot be such that each of its two parts is moved by the other.

First, if each of the two parts is moving the other, there can be no first mover at all,[30] for that which is prior is a cause of motion to a higher degree than that which succeeds it, and it will cause more motion than the succeeding;[31] for, as already shown,[32] a thing can cause a motion in two ways, either when it is moved by another and is itself in motion or when it is moved by itself, and that which is further from the thing moved is nearer to the source [of motion] than that which is intermediate.[33] Second, it is not necessary for the mover to be moved, unless it be by itself; so the second part [of a self-mover] may cause a reciprocal motion [in the first part], but by accident. So if one part may be taken as not causing a motion, then one of the parts will be in motion but the other will be a motionless[34] mover.[35] Third, there is no necessity for the mover to be moved reciprocally; but if it is necessary for motion to be eternal, then what causes motion must be either something motionless[34]

25 or something whose motion is caused by itself.[36] Fourth, a mover would be moved with the same motion as the one it causes, and so that which is causing heat would be in the process of being heated. Moreover, no thing which moves itself primarily has one or more parts each of which moves itself. For if the whole is moved by itself, either it will be moved

30 by some part of it or the whole of it will be moved by the whole. Now if [it is moved] by virtue of the fact that a part of it is moved by itself, that part would be the primary mover which moves itself, for if separated, it would move itself but would no longer move the whole. But if the whole is moved by the whole, it would be by accident that each of the parts is moved by itself. So if [the parts do] not necessarily [move

258a themselves], they may be taken as being in motion not caused by themselves. Consequently, one part of the whole will cause motion but be motionless[34] while the other part will be moved; for only in this way is it possible for something to be self-moved. Fifth, if indeed the whole moves itself, one part of it will cause motion and the other will be

5 moved. Thus [the whole] AB will be moved both by itself and by A. But since that which causes motion may either be moved by another or be motionless[34] and that which is moved may either move another or move no other thing, that which causes itself to be moved must be composed of (a) that which is motionless[34] but causes motion and (b) that which is moved [by another] but does not necessarily cause motion, though it may or it may not do so.

Thus, let A be that which causes motion but is motionless,[34] B be that

10 which is in motion caused by A and which causes motion in C, and C be in motion caused by B but causing no motion in another thing (even if C is reached through many intermediates, let it be reached here through just one). The entire ABC, then, will cause itself to be moved. But if C is removed, AB will cause itself to be moved, with A causing

15 the motion and B being in motion, but C will neither cause itself to be moved nor will it be moved at all.[37] Moreover, also BC without A will not cause itself to be moved; for B causes motion [in another] by being moved by another and not by any part of itself. So only AB will cause itself to be moved. Hence, that which causes itself to be moved must have that which causes motion but which is motionless[34] and also that

20 which is in motion but does not necessarily cause motion in another, and either the two must be touching each other or one of them must be

touching the other.[38] Now if the mover is continuous (as for that which is in motion, it must be continuous), it is clear that the entire thing moves itself not in virtue of the fact that a part of it is such that it moves itself,[39] but it is the whole which moves itself, and it is both in motion and caus-

25 ing motion in virtue of the fact that one part of it causes motion and the other is in motion. Neither the whole causes motion nor the whole is being moved,[40] but only A causes motion and only B is being moved (and C is not moved by A, for this would be impossible).

If one removes some part of A, assuming the mover which is motion-less[34] to be continuous, or some part of B which is in motion, a *difficulty*

30 arises as to whether the remaining part of A, or of B, will cause motion, or be moved, respectively. For if it will, then AB would be in motion caused by itself, but not primarily; for after the removal of that part,

258b what remains of AB will still move itself. However, nothing prevents each of the two parts, or just the part in motion, from being potentially divisible though actually undivided and from not having the same power if it is divided; and so, nothing prevents self-motion from existing primarily within things which are potentially divisible.[41]

5 From what has been said, then, it is evident that the first mover is motionless;[34] for (a) whether the thing which is in motion but is moved by something leads immediately to that which is first and motionless [34] or (b) whether it leads to a thing which moves itself and stops itself, in both cases the result is that in all things which are in motion the first mover is motionless.[34]

6

10 Since motion must always exist without interruption,[1] there exists necessarily something first which causes motion,[2] and this may be one or many; and a first mover must be immovable. The problem of whether each immovable mover is eternal is not relevant to the present argu-ment; but the fact that there must exist something which is immovable

15 and exempt from all external change, both unqualified and accidental,[3] and which can move another, is clear from the following considerations.

If one wishes, let it be possible for some things to exist sometime and then not to exist, but without being in the process of generation or destruction;[4] for, if any thing without parts exists at one time and does not exist at another, perhaps it is necessary for it to be at one time and

20 not at another without being in the process of changing.[5] And let also this be possible, namely, that some principles which are immovable but can cause motion be now existing and now not existing.[6] Still, not all of them [i.e., the principles] can be so;[7] for clearly there is something that

causes things which move themselves to be at one time and not to be
25   at another.[8] For although every thing that moves itself must have a
magnitude,[9] that is, if no thing without parts can be moved, still from
what has been said this is not necessary for a mover.[10]

Now no one of the things which are immovable but not alway existing can be the cause of [all] the things that are continuously[11] being generated and destroyed, nor yet can any of those which always move certain things while others [always] move others. For neither each of them
30   nor all of them can be the cause of a process which exists always and
is continuous,[12] for that process is eternal and exists of necessity whereas
all those [movers] are infinite and do not exist at the same time. So it
259a   is clear that, even if (a) countless times some principles which are immovable movers and many of those which move themselves are being
destroyed while others are coming into being and (b) one immovable
mover moves one thing while another moves another,[13] nevertheless,
there is something which contains and exists apart from each of them   \
5   and which is the cause of the existence of some of them and the nonexistence of the others and also of the continuous change; and this is a
cause[14] of these [movers], while these are the causes of the motion in
other things. So if motion is indeed eternal, the primary mover too will
be eternal, if it is just one; but if there are many [primary movers],
there will be many eternal [movers]. We should regard them to be one
rather than many, or finite rather than infinite; for if the consequences
10   are the same, we should always posit a finite number [of causes], since
in things existing by nature what is finite and better should exist to a
higher degree, if this is possible. It is sufficient even if it [i.e., the mover]
is just one, which, being first among the immovable [movers] and also
eternal, would be the principle of motion in all the rest.[15]

It is evident also from the following that there must be some one
15   mover which is eternal. Now we have shown that there must always be
a motion, and if always, it must also be continuous;[16] for also that which
exists always may also be continuous, but what is in succession is not
[necessarily] continuous. Further, if [a motion is] continuous, it is one.
And it is one if both the mover is one and the thing in motion is one; for
if now one thing causes it to move and now another, the whole motion
20   will be not continuous but in succession.

One might be led to the belief that there exists a first immovable
mover, both from the arguments just given and by attending to the
principles[17] of movers. Evidently there are some things which are
sometimes moved but sometimes at rest, and because of this it was made
clear that neither all things are moved or all are at rest, nor that some of
25   them are always at rest and the others are always moved; for this is
shown by those things which have the double potentiality of being

sometimes moved and sometimes at rest.[18] So since such things are clear to all and since we also wish to show the nature of each of the other two (namely, that there are things which are always immovable and also others which are always in motion), having proceeded in this direction and posited that (a) every thing in motion is moved by something which is either immovable or in motion and (b) a thing in motion is always moved either by itself or by another, we arrived at the position that of things in motion there is a first; and this is (a) a self-mover if [only] things in motion are considered but (b) immovable if all are considered.[19] And evidently we do observe such things which move themselves, for example, living things or the genus of animals. Indeed, these [e.g., animals] even helped create the opinion[20] that in a thing a motion which did not exist at all [before] may arise, because we observe this happening in them; for it seems that at one time they are without motion but later they are moved.

This must be granted, then, that such things do cause in themselves one [kind of] motion,[21] but that they do not cause it independently;[22] for the cause is not from them, but there are other natural motions which animals have but not through themselves, such as increase,[23] decrease, and respiration, and each animal has these motions while it is at rest and is not being moved by itself. The cause of these [motions] is the surrounding objects [e.g., air] and many things which enter the animal, such as food in some [motions]; for while this is being digested, it sleeps, and when the food is distributed, the animal wakes up and moves itself, but the first source [of these motions] comes from the outside. On account of this, animals are not moved by themselves continuously; for what causes the motion is something else, which is itself in motion and is changing in relation to each thing that can move itself.

Now in all these the first mover and the cause of that which moves itself is [also] moved by itself, but accidentally, for it is the body that changes its place;[24] and so what is in the body also moves itself as if by a lever.[25] From these arguments one may be convinced that if there is an immovable mover that is itself in motion but accidentally, then that mover cannot cause a continuous motion.[26] So if indeed a motion[26] must exist continuously, then there should be some first mover which cannot be moved even accidentally, if, as we have said, there is to be in things an unceasing and everlasting motion and if being[27] itself is to rest [always] in itself and be in the same [state];[28] for if the principle stays [always] the same, then the whole too must stay the same[29] and be continuous in its relation to the principle.[30] Now to be moved accidentally by itself is not the same as to be moved accidentally by another; for to be moved by another belongs also to some principles[31] in the heavens, those which have many locomotions, whereas the former be-

longs only to destructible things. Further, if there is something which is
eternally of this kind, causing something to be moved but being itself
immovable and eternal, then the first thing that is moved by it must
also be eternal. This is clear also from the fact that there would otherwise be no generation or destruction or change in the other things unless
there were something which would cause motion while being in motion.
For the immovable [mover] will always cause one and the same motion
and in the same manner inasmuch as it itself in no way changes in relation to the thing moved; and as for that which is moved by something
whose motion is directly caused by the immovable [mover], because
of the fact that it[32] is related to things [which it moves] now in one
way and now in another, it is a cause but not of the same motion. And
so, because of the fact that it is in contrary places or forms [at different
times], it imparts motion to each thing in contrary ways and so makes
it be [for example] now at rest and now in motion. From what has been
said, then, the problem which was first raised[33]—why it is that not all
things are in motion or at rest or why some are not always in motion and
the others not always at rest, but some of them are now in motion and
now at rest—has now become evident, for the cause of it is now clear: It
is the fact that some things are moved by an eternal immovable mover,
and so they are always changing;[34] others are moved by an object in
motion, which [object] is changing, and so they too must change;[35] and
as for the immovable [mover], as already stated, inasmuch as it remains
[always] simple and in the same manner and in the same [state], it
causes [always] one and a simple motion.[36]

7

These will be even more evident by proceeding from another starting-
point: We should consider (a) whether a continuous[1] motion can exist
or not, and if it can, what that motion is, and (b) which of the motions
is primary; for it is clear that if indeed a motion must always exist and
if some one motion is primary and continuous,[1] then it is this motion that
the first mover causes, and this motion must be one and the same as
well as continuous[1] and primary.

Of the three [kinds of] motions, namely, one with respect to magnitude, another with respect to affection, and a third with respect to place
(which we call "locomotion"), it is the last one which must be primary.[2]

For one thing, there can be no increase[3] without a previous alteration,
since that which is increased is in a sense increased by what is like and
in a sense by what is unlike, like food, which is said to be contrary to a
contrary. Now whatever is added becomes like that to which it is added;

260b so a change to that contrary must be an alteration.[4] Moreover, if a thing
is being altered, there must be something which causes the alteration
and, for example, causes that which is potentially hot to become *actually* hot. It is clear, then, that the mover is not similarly related [to
what is moved] but is at one time nearer and at another further from
that which is being altered. But these [changes] cannot take place
5 without a locomotion. So if it is necessary for a motion to exist always,
it is also necessary for a locomotion to exist as the primary of [all] motions, and this [locomotion] must be the primary of [all kinds of] locomotions, if [of locomotions] there is a primary and a secondary.

Further, condensation and rarefaction are principles of all changing
affections; for heaviness and lightness, softness and hardness, hotness
10 and coldness—all these are thought to be kinds of density or thinness.
Now condensations and rarefactions are, respectively, coming closer and
going further, and in virtue of these it is said that substances are generated and destroyed. But if things are coming closer or are going further,
they must be changing with respect to place.[5] Moreover, even the magnitude of that which is increasing or decreasing is changing with respect to place.[6]

15 Again, that locomotions are primary is evident if the situation is examined from still another point of view. Now as in other things, so also
in motions the term "primary" is used in many senses. A thing is said to
be prior to other things (a) if the others cannot exist without its existence
but it can exist without theirs, (b) if it is prior in time to them, (c) if it
20 is prior to them with respect to substance.[7] So since a motion must exist
continuously—and it does so when it is either continuous or in succession,[8] but it exists continuously to a higher degree if it is continuous[9]—
and since it is better if a motion is continuous than if it exists in succession (and we always believe that what is better exists [actually] in nature, if this is possible) and since a continuous motion is possible (this
25 will be shown later but is assumed now)[10] and such motion can be no
other than a locomotion, then it is necessary for the primary motion to
be a locomotion. For there is no necessity for an object in locomotion to
be increasing [or decreasing] or to be in the process of generation or
destruction, but none of these [changes] can exist if there is no continuous motion, which is caused by the primary mover.

Again, locomotion must be primary in time; for in eternal things
30 this is the only kind of motion possible.[11] In the case of any individual
thing which has a generation, however, a locomotion is of necessity the
latest of all [the kinds of] motions; for after being generated, that thing
first alters and increases, and its motion can be a locomotion when the
261a thing is already complete.[12] Yet prior to this individual there must exist
in locomotion another individual which is not in generation and is also

the cause of the generation of that individual, as in the case of that which begets in relation to that which is begotten,[13] although a generation might seem to be the first of motions because of the fact that, as far as the generated thing is concerned, it is a generation that belongs to it first.[14] So for any individual which is generated, the case is as stated; yet prior to the generated individual there must exist another individual which is in motion[15] and is not in the process of being generated,[16] and likewise there must be still another prior to the latter [etc.]. So since a generation cannot be primary (for otherwise all things in motion would be destructible), it is clear that none of the succeeding motions is prior [to locomotion]; and by "succeeding" I mean increase, then alteration and decrease and also destruction, for all these are posterior to generation, and so if generation is not prior to locomotion, neither are any of the other changes prior to it.[17]

In general, that which is being generated appears to be incomplete and on its way to a principle;[18] hence, that which is posterior in generation appears to be prior by nature.[19] And [of all kinds of changes] locomotions are the last which belong to things in generation. And so some living things, e.g., plants and many genera of animals, exist entirely without [loco]motion because of organic deficiency, but others have it when they are completed. Hence, if locomotions belong to a higher degree to living things which received more of nature, then these motions would also be prior to the others with respect to *substance*;[20] and it would be so both because of this and because of the fact that a thing in motion departs least from its *substance* if it is in locomotion rather than in any other [kind of] motion. For it is with respect to this [motion] alone that the thing does not change in its being, whereas as it alters, it changes in quality, and as it increases or decreases, it changes in quantity.[21] But clearest is the fact that that which moves itself causes this motion (i.e., locomotion) above all; and indeed we say that it is this [a self-mover] that is the principle of things in motion and of movers and that among things in motion it is the self-mover which is first.[22]

From the above discussion, then, it is evident that a locomotion is the primary of [the kinds of] motions. We shall now show which of the locomotions this is; and by the same *inquiry*, that which is now and was previously assumed,[23] namely, that it is possible for some motion to be both continuous and eternal, will at the same time be evident.

From the following it is evident that none of the other motions can be continuous. All the other motions or changes proceed from opposites to opposites, for example, in a generation and a destruction the limits are being and non-being; in an alteration they are the contrary affections; in an increase and decrease they are either greatness and smallness of magnitude or completeness and incompleteness of magnitude; and

261b changes to contraries are contrary. As for a thing which does not always have a given motion but existed previously, it must have been at rest.[24] It is evident, then, that a thing which is changing[25] will come to a rest in a contrary. The situation with changes is similar; for a generation

5 and a destruction, whether taken in an unqualified way or as a particular [generation] in relation to the corresponding [destruction], are opposed. So if a thing cannot be changing in opposite directions at the same time, a change will not be continuous but there will be time between changes. It makes no difference whether contradictory changes are contrary or not, as long as they cannot be present in the same thing

10 at the same time, for the argument is not affected. Nor does it make a difference if it is not necessary for the thing to be at rest in the contradictory state or if change is not contrary to rest (for a nonbeing is perhaps not at rest,[26] and a destruction is a change to a nonbeing), as long as there is a time interval between, for in this way the change will not be

15 continuous; and it is not [just] a contrariety which is useful in the previous cases, but the impossibility of belonging to the same thing at the same time. Nor need one be disturbed by the fact that a thing is contrary to more than one thing, like a motion which is contrary both to a standstill and to the contrary motion, as long as he notices (a) the fact that it is in different senses that a motion is opposed to rest[27] and to the

20 contrary motion, like the equal or the right measure in relation to that which exceeds and that which is exceeded[28] and (b) the fact that contrary motions or changes cannot belong to a thing at the same time. Moreover, in the case of a generation or a destruction it would even seem utterly absurd if a thing must be destroyed immediately after generation without lasting for an interval of time; and from these

25 changes one might be convinced as regards the other changes, for it is natural for all of them to be similar in this respect.[29]

8

We shall now proceed to set forth the fact that it is possible for a motion, which is one and continuous, to be infinite, and the fact that this motion is circular.

Now everything in locomotion is moved with a motion which is either

30 circular or rectilinear or a blend of the two; so if one of the first two kinds of motion is not continuous,[1] neither can the composite of the two be.[2] It is clear that a thing in locomotion along a finite straight line cannot proceed continuously, for it must turn back;[3] and that which turns back along a straight line has contrary motions, for an upward

35 locomotion is contrary to a downward locomotion, a forward locomotion

is contrary to a backward one, and that to the left is contrary to that to
the right, and this is so since the corresponding places are pairs of contraries. Previously we have defined a motion as being one and continuous if it is of one thing and during one time and without difference in
kind.[4] For there are three things here[5]—(a) that which is in motion, e.g.,
a man or a divine being;[6] (b) the whenness of the motion, i.e., the [in-
dividual] time; and (c) that in which [i.e., the category], and this is
either a place or an affection or a form[7] or a magnitude. Now contraries
differ in species[8] and are not one; and the differentiae of place are those
which have just been stated. A sign that the motion from A to B is contrary to that from B to A is the fact that, if occurring simultaneously,
they stop or cancel each other.[9] And it is likewise with motions along a
circle, e.g., that from A going toward B is contrary to that from A go-

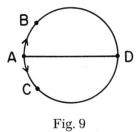

Fig. 9

ing the other way toward C, for these too stop even if they are continuous, and there is no return, and this is because contraries destroy or
obstruct each other;[10] but a lateral motion is not contrary to an upward
motion.[11] That a rectilinear motion cannot be continuous is most evident
from the fact that the object must stop before turning back. This is so
not only in the case of a rectilinear motion, but also if the object were to
go around a circle. (For to have a circular locomotion and to go around
a circle are not the same: In the first case, the motion is connected; in
the second, the object must come to the starting point but then turn
back.)[12]

One may be convinced that the object must come to a stop not only
from sensation[13] but also from argument.[14] We may begin as follows:
When there are three things, a beginning, a middle,[15] and an end, the
middle is in relation to each of the other two; and though it is one
numerically, it is two in formula.[16] Further, potential existence is distinct from *actual* existence.[17] Hence any point between the ends of a
straight line is potentially a middle; but it is not [a middle] in *actuality*
unless one divides the line,[18] and the object in motion stops there and
then begins its motion again, in which case the middle becomes [*actually*] both a beginning and an end, the beginning of the later line

262*a*

5

10

15

20

25

[after division] and the end of the first line. For example, this would be the case if P, which travels [from A], stops at B and then again starts travelling to C. But when travelling continuously [from A] to C, it has neither arrived at B nor departed[19] from B; but it is there only at a moment and not in any interval of time, unless it be in the sense in which the moment as a division is in the whole of the time [taken to traverse AC].[20] If one were to posit that P has arrived at B and also has departed from it, then P, while travelling, must stop, for P cannot have simultaneously[21] arrived at B and departed from it; it will do so, then, at distinct cuts[22] of time, and so there will be a time interval between these [moments] and P will be resting at B, and similarly with all other points since the same argument applies to all. But if the travelling object P is to use the intermediate point B both as an end and as a beginning, then it must stop, because it will be using it as two, as if it were to think of it [as two] also. However, it is from A, which is the beginning, that P departs, and it is at C that it has arrived, that is, when it has ended and stopped. So it is this that should be used against a *difficulty* that arises,[23] which is as follows.

If line L is equal to line M and P travels continuously from one end [of L] to C and if P is at B while at the same time Q, having started from

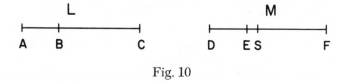

Fig. 10

one end of M also with a uniform speed and equal to that of P, is travelling toward F, then Q will arrive at F before P arrives at C; for that which started earlier and ends must arrive earlier, since P does not arrive at B and depart from it at the same time but is delayed (for if it arrives there and departs at the same time, it will not be delayed; but it must stop there).

We should not posit, however, that when P has arrived at B, then Q, which started from one end of M, is simultaneously [in the process of] travelling [toward F]; for if there is an arrival of P at B, there will also be a departure [from B] which is not simultaneous [with the arrival], but P is at B in a *division* of time and not for an interval of time. Accordingly, we cannot truly speak in the above manner concerning a continuous motion.[24]

But we must truly speak in that manner if the thing in motion turns back. For if R, in travelling upward to H, were to turn back at H, it would use H both as an end and as a starting-point and would thus use one point as two;[25] and so it would be necessary for it to stop there and not both arrive at H and depart from H simultaneously, since otherwise it would both be and not be there at the same moment.[26] And we should not use the former refutation; for one cannot [truly] say that R is at H

30   in a *division* of time and that it has neither arrived there nor departed from there, since it must reach the end [i.e., the goal] *actually* and not potentially. Accordingly, [in the previous case] the object exists poten-tially at a midpoint [i.e., P at B], but in the present case it exists *actually*

263a   [at H], and viewed from below, H is an end, but from above [i.e., from H], it is a starting-point; and so it [i.e., H] is related to the [two] mo-tions in the same way.[27] So that which is to turn back when travelling along a straight line must [first] stop. Hence a motion along a straight line cannot be eternally continuous.[28]

5   We should reply in the same way (a) to those who bring up Zeno's argument[29] and claim that if always half of the [remaining] dis-tance must be traversed, there will be infinite halves, and it is impossible to traverse the infinite,[30] or (b) to those who raise the same argument in another way and claim that if a motion were to exist, the first half [of the distance] would have to be counted, and this would be the case for each previous half, so in traversing the whole [distance] an infinite

10   number would have to be counted, and this is something which people agree to be impossible.

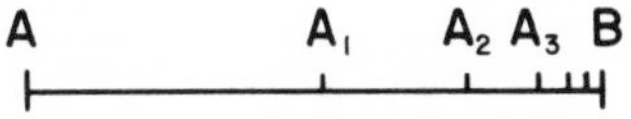

A   A₁   A₂ A₃ B   A A₃ A₂   A₁   B

Fig. 11(a) 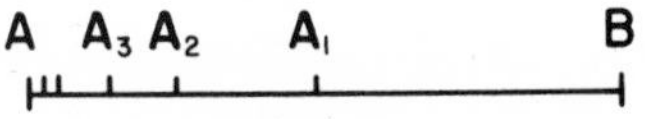   Fig. 11(b)

Now in our first discussion concerning motion we have solved the problem through the fact that time has in itself an infinite number of parts; for there is nothing absurd if in an infinite time one traverses an

15   infinite number of parts since the infinite exists alike in length and in time.[31] But although this solution is adequate for him who raises the problem (for he raises the problem of whether it is possible to traverse an infinity of things in a finite time), it is not adequate regarding the fact itself and the truth;[32] for if, leaving out of account the length and the

20   question of whether it is possible to traverse an infinity of things in a finite time, one raises these questions concerning time itself (for time has an infinite number of divisions[33]), this solution will not be adequate, but what must be presented is the truth which was stated just previously. For if one divides the continuous into two halves, he uses one point as

25   two since he regards the same point both as a starting-point and as an end. Now both he who counts and he who divides into halves do like-wise.[34] But in dividing in this manner, neither the line nor the motion

will be continuous; for a continuous motion is of something continuous, and in that which is continuous an infinite number of halves do exist, but potentially and not in actuality. And if he were to make these [halves] actual, he would not be making something continuous but would be stopping (something which evidently happens to one who is counting the halves); for it would be necessary for him to count one point as two since one [point] would be the end of one of the halves and the other would be the starting-point of the other half (that is, if he were to count the continuous not as one but as two halves).[35] Thus, if one asks us whether it is possible or not to traverse an infinite number of things in time or in length, our answer to him must be: In one way it is, in another way it is not. If these things be considered as existing actually, it is not possible, but if potentially, then it is possible; for he who is in motion continuously traverses the infinite not in an unqualified way but accidentally,[36] in view of the fact that the line is an infinity of halves in an accidental way while its *substance* or its being is something else.[37]

It will also be clear that if we do not posit a cut[22] in time, which [cut] divides the earlier from the later time, as belonging to the thing [only] in its later state, then the same thing would both exist and not exist simultaneously, and it would also not exist when it has been generated.[38] Now a cut [i.e., a moment] is common to both [times], i.e., it belongs to the earlier as well as to the later time, and it is the same and numerically one, but it is not one in formula,[39] for it is the end of the earlier but the beginning of the later time. But it belongs always to the thing in its later affection.[40] Let ABC[41] be the time, P be the thing, and P be white in [time] A, but not-white in [time] C. Then it would be white and not-white at [moment] B; for it would be true to say that it is white at any moment of A if it were white in all this time [i.e., in A], and [likewise true] to say that it is not-white in C, and B is in both [A and C]. We must not grant, then, that P is white in all A but must delete its last moment, which is B. The moment B, then, belongs to the later state of the thing;[42] and whether P was becoming not-white or was being destroyed as white in all of A, it is at B that it came to be in its later state or was destroyed [as white], respectively.[43] So it is true to say that it is at B (a) that the thing is first generated and is not-white and so is not white or (b) that it is first destroyed [as white] and is not-white; otherwise, it would be necessary for it to be simultaneously both white and not-white, and in general, both a being and not a being.[44]

Now if that which exists without having existed previously was necessarily becoming a being [previously] and if it was not a being while in the process of becoming, then an interval of time cannot be divided into *indivisible* intervals of time. For if P was becoming white in time

A and has simultaneously become [white] and exists [as white] at an-
30   other *indivisible* time B which is consecutive with A and if it was not
white while becoming white in A but is white in B, then there must be a
264*a*   becoming of the thing between [A and B] and so [there must be] a
time during which it was in the process of becoming.[45] Now the same
argument does not apply also to those who say that no *indivisible* time
exists, but for them the thing has become and is white at the last cut of
the time during which [time] it was in the process of becoming; and
this [cut] does not at all have a cut consecutive or in succession with it,
whereas *indivisible* intervals of time would have to be in succession.[46]
5   So it is evident that if the thing was becoming white in the whole of
time A, the sum of that at which[47] the thing [first] became white and
the time during which it was becoming white is not greater than all the
time during which it was becoming white.

By these and other such arguments, which are *proper* to the subject,
one might be convinced [of what has been said]. And if, from the
following, one examines the matter logically,[48] the result would again
10   seem to be the same.

Now every thing in continuous locomotion which has arrived somewhere, provided that it was not deflected by anything, was previously
travelling to that place. For example, if it has arrived at B, then it was
previously travelling toward B, and not [only] when it was near B, but
immediately when it started travelling; for why should it be [travelling
toward B] at a later moment rather than at an earlier one? It is likewise
with the other kinds of motions. So let P, which is travelling from A
15   toward C, turn back immediately after reaching C and arrive at A,
[making the whole trip] in one continuous motion.[49] Then, when travelling from A in the direction of C, it will also be travelling toward A
during the [part of the] motion from C to A; so it will have contrary
motions at the same time, for motions along a straight line in contrary
directions are contrary.[50] At the same time, it will also be travelling
20   from that at which it is not.[51] So if these are impossible, the object must
stop at C.[52] Its motion, then, will not be one, for a motion interrupted
by a stop is not one.

Again, this is also evident from what follows, and more universally
for every kind of motion. If every thing in motion is moved with one
of the motions specified earlier[53] or rests with the corresponding opposite state of rest (for we have shown that besides these [motions] no
25   other exists), then that which[54] has a given motion (I mean one which
is distinct in species, and not one which is a part of a whole [motion])
but does not have it always must have previously been at rest with
the corresponding opposite state of rest, for the privation of a motion
is rest. Thus, if rectilinear motions [in opposite directions] are contrary

and no thing can have contrary motions at the same time, then a thing
30 travelling from A toward C would not at the same time be travelling
from C toward A; and so since the thing [when in motion from C to A]
cannot have both [contrary] motions at the same time but will have
this motion [C to A], prior to this motion it must have rested at C, for
this rest was shown to be opposite to the motion from C.[55] So it is clear
264b from these statements that the motion is not continuous.[56]

Again, the following argument is even more special than the preceding. Now a thing [in alteration] is destroyed as not-white and becomes
white simultaneously. So if the alteration [of the thing from not-white]
to white and from white [to not-white] is continuous and [the thing]
5 does not *rest* [as white] for some time, then there will be simultaneously
a destruction of the not-white, a generation of the white, and a generation of the not-white; for the time of all three will be the same.[57]

Again, motion need not be continuous if time is, but it may be in
succession. How could a pair of contraries, e.g., whiteness and blackness, have the same extremity?[58]

A circular motion, on the other hand, may be one and continuous,
10 since nothing impossible follows; for, with the same forward direction,[59]
the object in motion from A will be moving at the same time toward A,
since that at which it is to arrive is also that toward which it is moving,
and without having contrary or contradictory motions at the same
time.[60] For not every motion to A is contrary or contradictory to a
motion from A; but motions to and from A are contrary if they are
15 along a straight line (for in such a line the ends are contrary with respect
to place, as in a motion along the diameter, whose ends are furthest
apart), and they are contradictory if they are along the same line.[61] So
nothing prevents this [moving] object from being in motion continuously without pausing for an interval of time; for a circular motion is
from A to A, a rectilinear motion is from A to something else, and a
20 circular motion is never within the same limits, whereas a rectilinear
motion is repeatedly within the same limits [i.e., ends].[62] Accordingly,
a motion which occurs within limits which are [always] distinct may
proceed continuously, but one which occurs repeatedly within the same
[two contradictory] limits cannot; otherwise, the object would have
contradictory motions at the same time. So neither along a semicircular
25 arc nor along any other arc[63] can an object be in motion continuously,
for it is necessary for it to proceed within the same limits and have
contrary changes,[64] since the beginning of one motion is not connected
with the end of the preceding.[65] But in a motion along a circle the
connection takes place, and only this [motion] is complete.[66]
30 It is also evident from this distinction that the other [kinds of] motions
too cannot be continuous; for in each of them the motion proceeds

repeatedly within the same limits, e.g., in an alteration it is between the same limits,[67] in a quantity it is between the same magnitudes, and in a generation and a destruction, likewise. Nor does it make any difference whether the stages within the limits are posited as being few or many, or whether some are added or removed, for in either case the object in motion will still go through them repeatedly.

It is clear from these statements, then, that the natural philosophers who say that all things are always in motion do not speak well; for the motion of each of those things must be some one of those mentioned, and an alteration, most of all according to them, since they say that things are always in flux and decay and, moreover, that both generations and destructions are alterations.[68] But the above argument concerning all motions states universally that an object cannot be in motion continuously with any of the motions except with a circular motion, and so it cannot alter or increase continuously.

Let this be our account, then, of the fact that no change can be infinite or take place continuously[69] except a circular locomotion.

9

It will now be made clear that of the locomotions the circular is the primary.[1]

As we stated previously, every locomotion is either circular or rectilinear or a blend of these two, and the first two must be prior to the last since the last consists of those two.[2] Also, the circular locomotion is prior to the rectilinear since it is simpler and more complete.[3] For an object cannot have an infinite rectilinear motion since infinity in this manner does not exist;[4] and even if it existed, no object would go through it, for what is impossible cannot come to be, and it is impossible to traverse the infinite.[5] But in the case of a locomotion along a straight line, if it turns back it is composite and becomes two motions,[6] but if not, it is incomplete and destructible.[7] Now what is complete is prior in nature and in formula and in time to what is incomplete,[8] and that which is indestructible is likewise prior to that which is destructible. Again, a motion which can be eternal is prior to one which cannot be eternal.[9] And a circular locomotion can be eternal, whereas of the rest neither a locomotion nor any other motion can be eternal; for there must be a stop in each of these, and if a stop, then the motion is destroyed.

It is also reasonable that a circular locomotion should be one and continuous[10] but that a rectilinear should not. For a rectilinear [locomotion] has a definite beginning and an end and a middle,[11] and it has all that an object in motion requires so it can start from one place and end at another (for everything rests at the limits [of its motion], whether at the starting-point or at the end); but in a circular [locomotion] these are indefinite, for why should one[12] rather than another be a limit on a circular line? For each is alike a beginning and an intermediate and an end, and so the object [in locomotion] is always at the beginning and at the end and it is never there.[13] And so a rotating sphere is in motion in one sense, and at rest in another (for it is occupying the same place).[14] The *reason* for this is the fact that all [three] belong to the center, for it is both a beginning[15] and a middle of the magnitude,[16] and it is also an end.[17] So because of the fact that it [i.e., the center] is outside of the circumference,[18] there is no position at which the travelling object will rest by having completed traversing a distance, for it always travels around the middle and not toward an extreme,[19] but because of the fact that it [i.e., the center] *rests,* in one sense the whole [object] always rests and in another it is always continuously in motion.[20]

It also happens that each of two things implies the other; for both (a) in view of the fact that a circular locomotion is a measure of motions, it is necessary for it to be primary (for it is by what is primary that all the others are measured), and (b) because it is primary, it is the measure of all others.[21] Moreover, a circular motion is also the only one which can be uniform; for objects with rectilinear locomotion travel nonuniformly from the starting-point and toward the end since the farther they are from the state of rest the faster they travel,[22] and only a circular locomotion has by nature neither a starting-point nor an end but is exempt in this respect.[23]

That a locomotion is the primary of motions is confirmed by all those who have said something about motion, for they assign the principles of motion to things which cause this kind of motion.[24] For a combination and a separation are motions with respect to place, and it is in this manner that *Friendship* and *Strife* cause motion in things, *Strife* causing them to separate and *Friendship,* to combine.[25] Anaxagoras, too, says that *Intelligence,* which was the first to cause motion, separated things.[26] Similarly, those who mention no such cause[24] say that things are in motion because of the void;[27] for they, too, say that the motion of nature[28] is a motion with respect to place, since a motion through the void is a locomotion, as if a motion in place.[29] And they think that none of the other motions belongs to the primary objects but that they belong to the composites of these; for they say that increase and decrease and alterations in things occur by combination and separation of *indivisible* bodies.[30] Those who describe generations and destructions as resulting through density and rarity speak in the same manner, for they arrange these [*indivisible bodies*] by combination and separation.[31] To these

we may add those who posit the soul as the cause of motion; for they say that things which move themselves are the source of the motion in
266a   things and that animals and all things with a soul cause in themselves a motion with respect to place.[32] And we do say (a) that a thing is moved in the main sense only when it has a motion with respect to place and (b) that if it rests in the same place but happens to be increasing or
5   decreasing or altering, it is moved in a qualified way but not in an unqualified way.[33]

We have given an account, then, of (a) the fact that motion always existed and will always exist throughout all time, (b) what is the principle of eternal motion, (c) which is the primary motion, (d) which is the only motion that can be eternal, and (e) the fact that the primary mover is immovable.

10

10   Let us now discuss the fact that the primary mover must have no parts and no magnitude, after having first determined some prior facts in connection with it.

One of these is the fact that nothing which is finite can cause a motion for an infinite time. Now there are three things, the mover, the object in motion, and the time during which the motion occurs; and
15   either all of these are infinite, or all are finite, or [only] some (i.e., one or two) are finite. Let A be the mover, B the object in motion,[1] and T the infinite time. Now let A_1 [a part of A] move B_1, which is a part of B. Then the time taken to do this is not equal to T, for it takes more time to move a greater object.[2] Hence, the time T_1 taken [for A_1 to move B_1] is not infinite.[3] Now by adding to A_1 [equal parts from A], I shall
20   use up all A, and by doing likewise to B_1, I shall use up all B; but I shall not use up the time T by always subtracting a part which is equal [to T_1],[4] for T is infinite. So the entire A will move the whole of B in a finite part of T. Consequently, no object can be given an infinite motion by that which is finite.[5] Evidently, then, nothing which is finite can cause a motion for an infinite time.[6]

25   In general, it will be made clear from what follows that it is not possible for an infinite power[7] to be in a finite magnitude. Let a greater power be that which always effects an equal result in less time, for example, as in heating or in sweetening or in throwing or, in general, in causing a motion. If so, then that which can be affected must also be
30   affected by that which is finite but has infinite power, and more by this than by another,[8] for an infinite power is greater [than a finite power]. But this cannot take place in an interval of time. For if T be the time

in which an infinite power has heated or pushed something and S be
that [time] in which a finite [power] did so, then when I increase the
latter power by adding to it repeatedly one finite power after another,
I shall eventually reach a finite [power] which will cause the motion
[the heating or pushing] performed in time T [by the infinite power];
for by always adding to a finite [quantity an equal quantity] I shall
eventually exceed any finite [quantity], and likewise by always subtracting [an equal quantity] I shall eventually arrive at one which is
less [than any given finite quantity]. But then, a finite power [will be
reached which] in an equal time will cause the motion caused by the
infinite power, and this is impossible.[9] Consequently, no thing which is
finite [in magnitude] can have an infinite power.

Moreover, nor can a finite [power] be in an infinite [magnitude]. In
fact, though in a smaller magnitude [of one kind of body] there may be
a greater power [than in a greater magnitude of another kind], still a
greater power will be in some greater [magnitude of the second kind].

Let AZ be an infinite [magnitude]. Now [a finite magnitude] AB has
a certain power which, let us say, will move M [over a certain interval]
in time T. If I take a magnitude twice as great as AB, this will move M
in half the time T (for let this be the proportion), and so it will move
M in $T/2$. Now if I continue increasing the magnitude in a similar way,[10]
I shall never exhaust AZ, but the time required for the increasing magnitude to move M will eventually be less than any given time. So the
power [in AZ] will be infinite, for it will surpass any finite power.[10]
But for a given finite power the time taken [to move M] must also be
finite; for if power P_1 moves M in time T_1, a greater power P_2 will move
M in a lesser but a definite time T_2 in inverse proportion [that is,
$P_1:P_2 :: T_2:T_1$]. And like a plurality and a magnitude, a force is infinite if
it exceeds every definite force.[11]

This result may also be shown in this way, namely, by taking a power,
which is generically the same[12] as that in the infinite magnitude but
which is in a finite magnitude, and then measuring by it the finite power
which is [assumed to be] in the infinite [magnitude].[13]

It is clear from the above arguments, then, that neither can an infinite
power be in a finite magnitude, nor a finite power in an infinite magnitude.

At this point, it is well to discuss first a problem concerning objects in
locomotion. If every thing in motion but not moved by itself is caused
to be moved by another, how is it that some of them, like things
thrown,[14] are continuously in motion when the mover is not touching
them? If the mover moves at the same time something else also, e.g., air,
and if it is this [air] which causes the motion[15] while being in motion,
it is likewise impossible for this [air] to be in motion when the first

mover neither touches it nor causes it to be in motion, so all of them
should be simultaneously in motion, or they should all cease simultaneously when the first mover ceases[16] even if, like a stone,[17] it [the
first mover] makes that which it causes to be moved to act like a mover.

We must then say this, that the first mover causes air or water or
some other such object, which by nature can move another and be
moved by another,[18] to be like a mover. But this object does not simultaneously cease being a mover and an object moved.[19] It ceases simultaneously being moved[19] when the mover ceases causing it to be
moved,[20] but it may still be a mover; and in view of this, it may cause
some other consecutive object to be moved (and the same may be said
of this other object). But an object begins to cease [being a mover]
when the power to cause motion which is transmitted to the consecutive
object is lessened; and the object finally ceases [being a mover] when
the preceding mover transmits to it no power to cause motion but only
causes it to be in motion.[21] These[22] must cease simultaneously, i.e., the
one being a mover and the other being in motion, and so must the whole
motion.[23] Now this [kind of] motion occurs in things which may sometimes be in motion and sometimes at rest, and the motion is not
continuous[24] though it appears to be so; for it is a motion of objects
which are either in succession or in contact, since there is not [just]
one mover but the objects are consecutive with each other.[25] And in
view of this, such motion, which some call "circular displacement",[26]
takes place also in air and in water. Now the problem raised cannot be
solved in a way other than that just stated.[27] In a circular displacement
all objects are movers and in motion at the same time, and so they cease
at the same time. But it appears that there is [just] one object continuously in motion. If so, by what is it moved? Certainly, not by itself.[28]

Since in things there must exist a continuous motion,[29] which is one,[30]
this one motion must be of some magnitude (for that which has no
magnitude cannot be in motion) which is also one and is moved by one
[mover]; otherwise, there will be not a continuous motion but a number
of consecutive and divided motions. As for the mover that causes the
motion, if one, either it is a mover in motion or it is immovable. If in
motion, then it will have to be following along[31] and be changing[32]
and also be moved by another object;[33] so this series will stop and end
with a motion caused by something immovable. Now the latter of
necessity does not change[34] along with the object moved, but it will
always have the power to cause motion (for to cause motion in this
way occurs without effort); and this motion alone, or more than any
other, is regular,[35] since the mover does not change at all.[36] And if
the motion is to be similar, the object in motion, too, should not be
changing in relation to it [the mover].[37] Now this [the mover] must be

either in the middle or at the circumference [of the sphere],[38] for these are the principles [of the sphere].[39] But things whose motions are fastest are nearest the mover, and such [i.e., fastest] is the motion of the circumference;[40] so the mover is there.[41]

A problem arises, namely, whether it is possible for a thing in motion to cause motion continuously,[42] but not like that which pushes again and again and so does something continuously by doing successively; for either the thing itself pushes or pulls or does both, or else this is passed on from one thing to another, as it was stated earlier in the case of things thrown,[43] in which the air or the water causes motion in the sense that it is one part after another that is moved. In either case, it cannot be one motion; it is a number of consecutive motions. So the only continuous motion is that which the immovable mover causes; for, being in a similar state, that mover will be similarly disposed towards the object moved and be continuously so.[44]

With these things settled, it is evident that the first and immovable mover cannot have a magnitude. For if it has a magnitude, this must be either finite or infinite. Now it was shown earlier in our discussions on nature that no infinite magnitude can exist [actually];[45] and it was just shown that a finite [magnitude] cannot have an infinite power[46] and that an object cannot be moved by a finite [magnitude] for an infinite time.[47] But the prime mover causes eternal motion and for an infinite time. Hence, it is evident that He [the prime mover] is indivisible and without parts and has no magnitude at all.[48]

Commentaries

Commentaries

The references given in the Commentaries and in the Glossary are to the standard pages (sections) and lines according to Bekker's edition of Aristotle's works (Berlin, 1831). In particular, pages 184a10–267b26 cover the whole of the *Physics,* and these pages (and lines) appear as such in the margins of the translation. The Bekker pages covering each of Aristotle's works are as follows:

Categories: 1a1–15b33.
Nature of Propositions (De Interpretatione): 16a1–24b9.
Prior Analytics: 24a10–70b38.
Posterior Analytics: 71a1–100b17.
Topics: 100a18–164b19.
Sophistical Refutations: 164a20–184b8.
Physics: 184a10–267b26.
On the Heavens: 268a1–313b23.
On Generation and Destruction: 314a1–338b19.
Meteorology: 338a20–390b22.
On the Universe, To Alexander: 391a1–401b29.
On the Soul: 402a1–435b25.
On Sensation and Sensibles: 436a1–449a31.
On Memory and Recollection: 449b1–453b11.
On Sleep and Wakefulness: 453b11–458a32.
On Dreams: 458a33–462b11.
On Divination from Dreams: 462b12–464b18.
On Longevity and Shortness of Life: 464b19–467b9.
On Youth, Old Age, Life, and Death: 467b10–470b5.
On Respiration: 470b6–480b30.
On Breath: 481a1–486b4.
A Treatise On Animals: 486a5–638b37.
On Parts of Animals: 639a1–697b30.
On Motion of Animals: 698a1–704b3.
On Locomotion of Animals: 704a4–714b23.
On Generation of Animals: 715a1–789b20.

On Colors: 791a1–799b20.
On Objects of Hearing: 800a1–804b39.
Physiognomy: 805a1–814b9.
On Plants: 815a10–830b4.
On Reported Marvels: 830a5–847b10.
Mechanics: 847a11–858b31.
Problems: 859a1–967b27.
On Indivisible Lines: 968a1–972b33.
Positions and Names of Winds: 973a1–b25.
On Xenophanes, Zeno, and Gorgias: 974a1–980b21.
Metaphysics: 980a21–1093b29.
Nichomachean Ethics: 1094a1–1181b23.
Great Ethics: 1181a24–1213b30.
Eudemean Ethics: 1214a1–1249b25.
On Virtues and Vices: 1249a26–1251b37.
Politics: 1252a1–1342b34.
Household Management: 1343a1–1353b27.
Rhetoric: 1354a1–1420b4.
Rhetoric for Alexander: 1420a5–1447b7.
Poetics: 1447a8–1462b18.

Book A

1

1. Are the terms "understanding" and *"knowing"* synonymous? For Thomas Aquinas, understanding is of definitions, *knowing,* of demonstrations; but Aristotle uses *"knowledge"* for both (71b9–17), though sometimes he restricts this term to what is demonstrated and uses "intellect" for what is not demonstrated (100b5–17). Both *knowledge* and intellect are of what is necessarily true; but there are also causes which are true for the most part, and Aristotle does not seem to restrict the term "understanding" either to necessary truth or to truth for the most part (194b18–20, 981a24–30, 983a25–6), so perhaps "understanding" is wider.

2. In Book A, it is the constituent principles of changing objects that are considered.

3. At first, we know a thing as a sort of a whole without analysis, or as something by its accidents, such as a man by his shape or his walk, and not by his nature as a rational animal, which would be scientific knowing or knowing without qualification.

4. The usual translation of καθόλου is "universal", which means this: by nature predicable of many. At times Aristotle uses the term in a different but allied meaning (24a18, 73b26–4a3, 87b32, etc.). Perhaps

here it is used as a contraction of καθ' ὅλου, which means this: said of a whole, or, taken in its entirety; and this meaning is suggested by the examples that follow immediately and the discussion leading to the principles, which are matter, form, and privation. The awareness of a whole precedes its analysis, and so we use "triangle" before "three-sided plane figure"; and the child, unaware of the distinctions but vaguely aware of some similarity, calls all women "mama" as if using this term universally for some whole or for all women.

In a sense, even things which are named universally are qua such analyzable into parts. For example, every object called "a man" is analyzable into its principles, called "body" and "soul"; and likewise, every thing called "a body" is analyzable into what are called "matter" and "form", or, if the body changes, into subject, form, and privation. In a sense, then, a universal too is analyzable into parts. The position of the Rev. J. Owens is somewhat similar to mine.

5. They distinguish their father from other men and their mother from other women.

2

1. From what follows, it seems that "principle" here signifies a primary underlying subject, that is, one not further analyzable into another subject.

2. That is, the whole universe as a subject is one (984a27–b4, 986b18–31).

3. Anaximenes and Diogenes (984a5–7).

4. Thales (983b20–4a3).

5. The *Hot* and the *Cold,* or *Fire* and *Earth,* or the *Odd* and the *Even* for some Pythagoreans may be instances of two principles (984b1–8, 188a19–26).

6. For example, Empedocles (984a8–9).

7. For Democritus, the matter of the indivisible atoms is one in kind (i.e., completely solid with no qualitative difference), but these atoms are infinite in number and form, for there is an infinite variety of order, shape, and position in them (203a19–23, 303a3–8, 314a21–4, 1042b11–5). Anaxagoras, too, posits as principles an infinity of homogeneous elements, such as flesh and bone and the rest (187a22–6, 203a19–28, 314a17–20).

8. If "or even contrary" refers to the position of Democritus, then these contraries are the *Solid* and the *Void,* or *Being* and *Nonbeing,* or else they are the contraries of position, shape, and order, in which case the term "principle" applies to attributes as well as to subjects (188a19–25). But if the phrase refers to someone else, it may be Alcmaion, who posited an indefinite number of contraries as principles (986a27–b2).

9. An inquiry into the principles of all things rather than of all changing things would be a more general inquiry of course; and for most predecessors such inquiry was limited to material causes, also

called "elements", and so coincided somehow with the principles of all changing things.

10. That is, this is not an inquiry about nature, if nature as a principle of motion is posited to exist. An inquiry into the existence or nonexistence of nature is more general and belongs to a science presupposed by physics, and such is first philosophy (1026a27–32, 1064b9–14).

11. For example, universal mathematics is common to geometry and arithmetic; and arithmetic or geometry is presupposed, respectively, by harmonics or optics (78b34–9a6), for arithmetic and geometry investigate the causes, while harmonics and optics assume them. As for the principles of geometry, they are the concern either of universal mathematics or of first philosophy (1061b17–27).

12. In a sense, a principle is relative, for it is of something other than a principle, e.g., the form of a statue is a principle not of itself but of the statue; so, if a principle exists, also something else exists, and hence at least two things exist. Thus, contrary to Parmenides, being cannot be just one and also a principle.

13. Perhaps this is the belief that a thing both is and is not, or that it has both contraries (185b19–25, 1005b23–5).

14. The belief that being is just one man is obviously false.

15. These thinkers will be considered in Section 3.

16. Examples of things existing by nature are animals, their parts, simple bodies, etc., all of which have physical matter and form (192b8–23, 1015a6–7).

17. Though motion is a common and not a proper sensible, its existence, nevertheless, is sufficiently clear through our senses (425a13–7a16).

18. Whatever this refutation may have been, it uses only accepted principles of geometry, including the axioms of universal mathematics (concerning equality, inequality, etc.) and those of logic. Heath, *History of Greek Mathematics,* Vol.. 1, pp. 183–200, and Ross, *Aristotle's Physics,* pp. 463–466 (Oxford, 1936).

19. By inscribing an equilateral triangle (or a square) in a circle, then a regular hexagon, then a regular dodecagon, and continuing in this manner, Antiphon may have concluded that there will be a last polygon whose sides will coincide with the circumference of the circle. But this conclusion assumes that the continuum is not infinitely divisible, while a principle in geometry assumes that the continuum is infinitely divisible. To refute Antiphon, then, one must not start like a geometer by accepting the infinite divisibility of the continuum; he must go to another science and refute Antiphon by showing (as Aristotle does in 202b30–208a23) that the continuum is infinitely divisible. Heath, *History of Greek Mathematics,* Vol. 1, pp. 221–3, and Ross, *Aristotle's Physics,* pp. 466–7.

20. The statement "all things are one" has in it the terms "things" (or "beings") and "one". So the senses of both "being" and "one" should

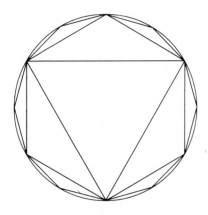

Fig. 12

be investigated. The term "being" is considered first; the term "one" is considered later (185b5).

21. Since things may be together and still be distinguishable, like the color and the surface of a ball, they may be many in at least one sense of "many".

22. If substances do exist, then all things cannot be, say, qualities; if substances do not exist, then (let us say) qualities cannot exist in something else, for if they did, not all things would be *just* qualities, and further, qualities do not exist by themselves anyway.

23. Aristotle has often been criticized when he refutes other thinkers by using his own definitions of terms used by those thinkers. However, if we remember that, before refuting others, he enumerates the senses in which a term has been used (as he does here with "being" and "one") or that the definition he introduces is very close in meaning to the intended meaning of the term used by most thinkers or by the thinker who is refuted, then such criticism loses most of its force. Aristotle has listed the various senses of "infinite" in 204a3–7; so the question here is How did Melissus speak of the "infinite", if not in any of the senses listed?

24. A man is infinitely divisible not qua a man but qua a magnitude; if a magnitude which is white is infinitely divisible, each part of such division will also be white, but whiteness is not divisible in the same sense. While one magnitude may be twice another, one whiteness cannot be twice another. Thus, if a man is a substance or is white and also has quantity, he can be infinite only qua a quantity.

25. 204a3–7, 207a7–8.

26. If being is a magnitude, then it is a quantity, and so it is two, a substance and a quantity; and if it is infinite, since the infinite exists in a quantity, a quantity also has to exist, and being will again be at least two.

27. 1015b16–7a6.

28. He is referring to Melissus and Parmenides, who posit *One* as the principle. An alternative to "totality" is "universe".

29. The two terms "vintage" and "wine" have the same meaning, so their definition (or definiens) will be the same.

30. Even if the totality is one by continuity, still it has many parts and so it is many in some sense, namely, potentially many. Besides, if separate, it is a substance, and as it is contiuous, it is also a quantity; so it is at least two.

31. Perhaps he has in mind the distinction between actuality and potentiality and also that between essence and accident. A whole is actually one; but it is potentially many, that is, it can be actually many after division. Thus, what is one may be many, but in a different sense, namely, potentially. Further, a whole is one, and since it contains the part, to say that the whole and the part are two is to count the same part twice. One might as well say that Socrates is ten by mentioning (counting) him ten times. But ten is an attribute of counting, not of Socrates, and so it is accidental to Socrates. Other such difficulties may be added.

If the whole is not continuous, one may inquire as to the cause of its unity, as in the unity of the number five, or in a whole whose parts are not necessarily quantities, like a colored ball, which has a color, a surface, weight, etc.

32. An alternative to "undivided" is "indivisible". Anyway, if each part is undivided (or indivisible) from the whole, a problem arises as to how the parts are divided (or divisible) from each other.

33. If indivisible, the totality cannot be a quantity (of which divisibility is an attribute) and hence not infinite, but Melissus says it is infinite; nor can it be limited, as Parmenides says, for what is limited is a quantity (like a sphere) and hence divisible, and a distinction between the limit and that which is limited may also be made. Nor can it be a quality, for this exists in a substance, and then two things distinct in formula will exist.

34. An alternative to "is" is "may be". The verb is omitted in the Greek. In a finite line, the limit is a point, which is indivisible; in a plane figure, it is a line (or curve), which is itself divisible, although in a qualified way, since actually only a body is divisible without qualification. So for both Melissus and Permenides, being will be many if it is infinite or limited.

35. If both A and non-A are predicates of the same thing, then, as in the case of Heraclitus, here too, the *One* will be one as well as not-one or not one (1005b23–32). An alternative to "not even one" is "nothing".

36. The term "such-and-such" refers to a quality, and "so-much" to a quantity. The point here is this: It is evident that a quality is not the same in formula as a quantity; e.g., redness is not five.

37. That is, one in one sense but many in another sense; for example, Socrates and his wisdom are one numerically, for there is one substance, but they are many in definition.

38. If a thing is called "one" in one sense but "many" in another, these terms are not necessarily opposites. For example, Socrates is one substance, but he is wise, white, etc., and this indicates that he has many attributes or that he is many but not many substances.

3

1. The term "statement" here applies to premises as well as to what these thinkers offer as syllogisms.

2. Whether he is referring to a premise or to an argument is not clear. According to Simplicius, he is referring to "Only the *One* exists", and from this it follows that there exists no motion or plurality or the like.

3. Evidently, from "every A is B" it does not follow that "no non-A is B"; for a dog is not a man, yet it is mortal. Thus, if that which is generated has a beginning, that which always exists (the heavens or the *One*) may still have a spatial though not a temporal beginning (the center or outer surface of heaven) and not be infinite (167b13–7, 168b35–40, 181a27–9, 325a2–16, 974a2–18, 986b16–27).

4. The full argument is not given. One guess may be this: In arguing for the eternity and the infinity of the *One* or of heaven, Melissus uses the hypothesis that every thing other than the *One* has a beginning, but he does not include time as a thing with a beginning. If he did so, then two things would exist, the *One* and time.

According to Thomas Aquinas, Melissus restricts the meaning of "beginning" to that of a magnitude, as in the case of the beginning of a road or the beginning of a sphere (the center or the surface). But one may speak of the beginning of time and of generation; and though a form may be finite, there is no generation of it and so no beginning of the generation of it, or else, the form comes into existence at a moment, which has no beginning since it is indivisible (1033b3–8).

5. For Aristotle, an alteration may be instantaneous, as in freezing, and so without a temporal beginning; for a beginning is of a thing which has also a middle (and an end), but a moment is not such a thing (253b23–6).

6. If Melissus regards the *One* as infinite, should it not then have parts? If so, like the water (in a glass) whose parts may be in motion, so may the parts of the infinite.

7. For Aristotle, there is just one formula for prime matter (1029a21–6), and this seems to indicate that he posits just one kind of matter, if "kind" be the right term to use.

8. Thales posits just *Water;* Anaximenes and Diogenes, just *Air;* Hippasus and Heraclitus, just *Fire* (983b20–4a8).

9. "Being" signifies a substance or a quantity, etc., and also what is actual or what is potential, etc. (1017a7–b9).

10. If for Parmenides "being" has just one meaning, this for Aristotle does not seem to contradict the plurality of things of which "being" is a

predicate; so (a) *Being* need not be one by continuity or in number, and (b) if numerically many, one may distinguish in each of those beings that which is received (form) and that which receives (matter or subject). Parmenides himself allows this distinction, for in saying that *Being* is limited, he distinguishes a limit from that which is limited (986b18–21, 1074a31–6). Perhaps Aristotle uses "white" rather than "being" in order to make his point clearer by analogy.

11. The term "*just* being" signifies a thing by itself which is not dependent upon or is not present in something else. For example, a virtue is an attribute and cannot exist by itself, for it is in a man; but a man is not an attribute of anything, he is a substance or a full being, so to say. The contrast here is one between qualified and unqualified being. For Parmenides, if only *just* being exists, there will not even be a contrast, for no qualified being would exist, so anything that one might conceive of as different or distinct from being would not exist or would be nonbeing; and further, differences within being are totally excluded.

12. If "being" has only one meaning and if it signifies an attribute, then since an attribute by definition exists in something else, say in X, then X, being something (a substance) which has an attribute, cannot be a being since "being" is limited only to an attribute. So X is nonbeing, for (according to Parmenides) what is not a being is a nonbeing. But X is nonbeing, and X has the attribute signified by "being"; and this is saying that nonbeing has being, which is a contradiction.

13. If *just* being is not an attribute, but if something else, say B, is an attribute of it, since only *just* being exists, the attribute would not be *just* being and would consequently be nonbeing (for if it were a being but not a *just* being, then "being" would have two meanings, a *just* being and an attribute). So we would have, *just* being is B, B is nonbeing, hence *just* being is nonbeing, a contradiction. Hence, *just* being will have no attribute at all, and predicating something else of it will be false.

14. To be a whole and to be a part are distinct, while "*just* being" has one meaning. An alternative translation: "for each of its two parts would have a distinct existence [or essence]". If for Parmenides the *One* is finite or limited (986b18–21), since the finite is divisible qua a magnitude, and the limit and that of which it is the limit are distinct, the *One* would turn out to be many.

15. Apparently, the argument assumes the truth of "man is an animal" and "man is two-footed". Parmenides will have to deny this if "being" for him is to have one meaning; for "man" and "animal" are distinct in meaning, and, as before, *just* being would be nonbeing. The previous argument assumes that a magnitude is divisible; the present argument assumes the indivisibility of ultimate predicates as qualities.

16. That is, a man need not be sitting.

17. Of course, a man is a substance; so we should discard the alternative that animality and two-footedness, and their combination, are attri-

butes. The definition of a man as a two-footed animal may have been popularly used, and Aristotle uses it often to illustrate a point. This is not his definition.

18. Perhaps he is referring to the man who will be composed of animal and of two-footedness, or else to the *One* of Parmenides.

19. Perhaps the meaning is this: If animality and two-footedness are not attributes but are truly said of a man and thus each is a *just* being, then, since the ultimate parts of a definition are indefinable and thus indivisible, a man (and likewise the universe or the *One*) will be composed of indivisibles. If so, the *One* will be divisible into indivisibles, contrary to what Parmenides believes.

20. Perhaps he is referring to the material principle which is posited by most as a not-being and is used to generate the plurality of things. For Plato, this is the *Great* and the *Small* (192a6–8); for Democritus, it is the *Void* (985b4–10, 1009a25–30); for others, it is an analogous principle.

21. Whether this is Zeno's argument which denies motion (239b5–29) or some other is not stated. Plato posited indivisible lines (992a20–2) and indivisible planes *(Timaeus)*. See also Ross' *Aristotle's Physics*, pp. 479–81.

22. For example, if only white things exist, let us say A_1, A_2, ... A_n, then it is true to say that A_1 is not-A_2 or that it is not-black; and to say this is not to say "A_1 is not" in an unqualified sense, for A_1 exists.

23. Perhaps the meaning is this: If *just* being is unique and nothing else exists, then he who knows *just* being cannot learn anything else, for there is nothing else to learn; for no statement of the form "A is B" will be true, since if A is *just* being, B will not exist and so will not be a predicate of A. For example, "five is odd" will be false, for five will exist but oddness will not.

4

1. These are the thinkers who posit change.

2. Fire or air or water; but earth is excluded because its parts are great (988b22–9a12).

3. See also 328b33–5 and 332a20–2. A principle between air and water is posited by other thinkers (203a16–8, 205a25–8, 303b9–13, 332a20–2, 989a12–5) not explicitly mentioned in Aristotle's extant works.

4. Perhaps Anaximenes has used these principles.

5. Plato generates all other things from two principles: the *One* as form and the *Great* and *Small* as matter (987b18–22).

6. This is the same as the *One*, from which the many are generated by segregation. In view of this, these thinkers say that the *Blend* is both one and many.

7. This is Empedocles, according to whom *Friendship* and *Strife* alternate as movers, the first uniting things and the second separating them (985a2–b4).

8. For Anaxagoras, the *Blend* existed first, then *Intelligence* as a mover began to put order into things (984b15–9, 989a30–b21).

9. Anaxagoras (984a11–6).

10. Empedocles posits *Earth, Fire, Air,* and *Water* (984a8–11).

11. Those who posit only one principle (for example, *Air*), generating all other things from it, regard generation as only alteration, for the *substance* of all things is that one principle, which is ungenerable and indestructible; and alteration would be caused by, say, *Density* and *Rarity* or whatever the other principles (contraries or forms, but less substantial than the material principle) might be (187a12–20, 314a6–16). But in the case of those who posit more than one element, there appear two distinctions which give rise to a difference between generation and alteration. Thus generation would be a combination or a separation of the principles, while alteration would be, for example, just a change in order or position of the principles in the blend. For example, the terms "form" and "from" have the same letters, which are principles, and a change from one to the other would be an alteration (315b6–19).

12. Referring to Anaxagoras and those who posit more than one material principle.

13. By definition, understanding is knowing through the causes; if so, scientific knowledge of something whose parts or principles are infinite in kind would be impossible.

14. This seems to have been the position of Anaxagoras and perhaps of others who did not posit indivisible atoms or magnitudes.

15. In line 187b13, perhaps ἔτι δ'εἰ should be ἔτι δέ.

16. This would be a material part, like a bone.

17. The argument, perhaps dialectical, seems to be that if, for Anaxagoras and others, the parts of a thing can be of any size, whether small or large, so can the thing; but if the things themselves cannot be of any size (a man two inches tall does not exist, nor an apple one mile long), neither can the parts be of any size. Of course, one might argue, if it is true that a man two inches tall does not exist, there is still the problem of whether such a man can or cannot exist.

18. This is the so-called "Postulate of Archimedes", wrongly credited to him, perhaps first announced by Eudoxus and often mentioned by Aristotle.

19. The argument aims to disprove the statement of Anaxagoras that in any given body all homogeneous things are present. It assumes that a homogeneous thing (a body) is separable, that it has a smallest part as shown earlier, and that a magnitude m, however small, will exhaust any finite magnitude M (Postulate of Archimedes). Thus, if m_1, m_2, m_3, ... are parts of flesh taken away from M, and $m_1 > m_2 > m_3 > ... > m$, then the series m_1, m_2, m_3, ... must stop, and what remains in M will not be flesh; otherwise the amount of flesh in M will exceed M.

20. The word οὐ (= "not") is missing and should be inserted; otherwise the text contradicts the position of Anaxagoras.

21. A color or a straight line or a virtue or any attribute does not exist by itself; each of these is in an underlying subject (e.g., a virtue is in a man) or is a predicate of it.

22. According to Anaxagoras, *Intelligence* sought to separate things from the *Blend.* Yet not all things can be separated, for attributes are inseparable; and besides, if according to Anaxagoras all things are to be found in any given body, then no separation of any one element in a body can take place at all.

23. This somehow refers to the last part of the preceding Commentary, namely, that according to Anaxagoras no body, however small, would be such as to be pure bone or pure flesh, etc., and so *Intelligence* cannot have made a separation of any homogeneous thing from the rest.

24. The view of Anaxagoras may have been that a homogeneous body comes to be only from parts like itself. Yet mud may be said to consist of parts each like the whole, and it may also be formed from earth and water, which are distinct. Further, a house comes from bricks, or bricks from a house, by combination or separation, which are locomotions; but water is generated from air when the latter is destroyed, and this change is not just a locomotion, but a change of *substance.*

25. That is, if things are adequately explained (189a14–7).

5

1. For Parmenides, *Being* is one according to formula or definition. However, according to sensation or phenomena, but in an inferior sense, there are two principles: the *Hot* and the *Cold,* or *Fire* and *Earth,* and he regards the first as being like *Being* and the second as being like *Nonbeing* (318b6–7, 330b13–5, 984b1–4, 986b27–7a2).

2. Also called "the *Full*" (985b5, 1009a28).

3. He says "in a sense", for these thinkers are not quite clear or definite about the nature of these contraries—about whether, for example, they are substances or forms or attributes or movers or what not; and they use different kinds of contraries rather than the general term "contraries".

4. These are the irreducible contraries. The term "contrary" has many senses. Thus, a white marble is contrary to a black marble, but "contrary" here is a predicate of a *composite,* e.g., of the white marble, which is composed of whiteness and marble (as a subject). So, if also whiteness and blackness happen to have something in common, say color, then these too would be *composites,* and if what is common (i.e., color) is abstracted, what remains (if these are not composites) would be the primary contraries (1018a25–35, 1055a3–b29, 1057b4–11).

5. For example, a body is acted upon by certain things, e.g., by a body, not by a color or a thought; and when we say that a body is acted upon by the white, we mean that whiteness does not contribute to that action but just happens to be an attribute of the body which does the

acting. Similarly, that which comes to be white *must* first be non-white, and it *may* also be musical; but musicality does not contribute to its coming to be white.

6. A number is nonwhite, and so is a point, and a thought; for to be nonwhite is not to be white, and that which is not a body is not white. So the white is generated only from some nonwhite things, from bodies which are colored but are not white (or, from what is not-white, for the not-white is a certain color or colored body).

7. The term "unmusical" signifies the contrary of the musical, just as the black is the contrary of the white.

8. That into which the white is destroyed may be musical; but this is an accident, for while the nonwhite into which the white is destroyed must be not-white (of some color other than white), it need not be musical.

9. That which is harmonious or inharmonious is not simple but a composite of notes. The inharmonious here is the contrary of the harmonious.

10. That which is opposed here is not any contradictory but the contrary of the harmonious; for a number too is not harmonious, but it is a contradictory of the harmonious and not the contrary of it.

11. By "shapelessness" he means that which can have a shape but does not have it; so it is the contrary of shape, or something between shape and that contrary, as, for example, the scattered materials before they are made into a house.

12. See discussion of this in 1057a18–b34.

13. Perhaps prior in formula (or definition) or in existence is meant. What is prior in existence is nearer to a principle, as in the case of hydrogen, which is prior in existence to water, since the latter cannot exist without hydrogen, but not conversely. Also, the more universal is prior in formula, e.g., oneness and plurality are prior in formula to sameness and otherness, respectively, for the latter are defined in terms of the former, but not conversely.

14. The hot, the cold, the moist, and the dry are closer to sensation than the odd, the even, strife, and friendship. What is more known according to sensation is opposed to what is more known in formula as the particular is to the universal. Sensation is of the individual or particular, but to *know* a thing by formula is to *know* it by universals gained by abstraction, and this is knowledge of the thing in terms of its elements.

15. They are distinct insofar as they are particular and different contraries; for example, for some thinkers these are the *Hot* and the *Cold*, for others they are the *Odd* and the *Even*. They are the same insofar as they are all contraries; or, they are the same by analogy, for example, *Fire* : *Earth* :: *Hot* : *Cold,* and *Odd* : *Even* :: *Friendship* : *Strife.*

16. The prior or more universal or more known by nature is better, the posterior or less universal or more known to us (nearer to sensation) is worse.

17. These are Plato's material principles (987b20–2).

18. These are posited by Leucippus and Democritus (985b4–10).

6

1. Contraries go in pairs, like black and white, odd and even.

2. 184a10–4, 994a1–b31.

3. Does he mean a physical substance? If so, there is contrariety with respect to substance (form and privation), with respect to quality (e.g., black and white), with respect to place (e.g., up and down), and with respect to magnitude; for a physical substance (a body) may change in any of these ways. Again, it seems that within a category there is more than one contrariety: Within quantity there is oddness and evenness in numbers, straightness and curvature in lines, and these two contrarieties are not reducible to one; and within quality there is whiteness and blackness, coldness and hotness, and these two are not reducible to one. Within a genus which is subject to differentiation, however, there is one contrariety.

4. If he is referring to the principles as contraries, these for Empedocles are *Friendship* and *Strife,* and for Anaxagoras they are the infinite contrarieties mentioned in 187a25–6. But if he is referring to the elements, these are the four elements for Empedocles *(Earth, Water, Air, Fire),* and for Anaxagoras they are the homogeneous elements. He may be referring to both the principles and the elements.

5. For example, whiteness and blackness are prior to a white body and a black body (1018a25–35).

6. As in the examples that follow, the white (body) is generated from the black (body), but a principle must persist. There is a sense in which the principles in a change are always three: In a statement one must always mention three elements, the two contraries and the subject. Thus, although the particular contraries and the particular subject may vary, nevertheless two contraries and a subject are always required.

7. Those who posit the *Dense* and the *Rare* as principles must posit also a subject which is to be dense or rare.

8. This is the *Blend* of Empedocles or the four elements acted on by *Friendship* and *Strife.*

9. He may be referring to the four elements of Empedocles or to the infinite homogeneous elements of Anaxagoras.

10. An alternative translation may be, "for among things, we observe no contraries (or no contrary) as being the *substance* of any thing". In either case, if a primary contrary is not a substance or the *substance* of a thing, then it must be in a subject which is a substance.

11. A subject is prior in existence to a predicate; for example, if sickness exists, an animal must exist, but not conversely. A principle must be prior in existence to that of which it is a principle.

12. And if so, a contrary cannot be a substance and must be a predi-

cate, and as a predicate it must exist in a substance and be posterior in existence to it (3b24–7).

13. If a substance were composed of nonsubstances, each of these would be more of a principle than, and so prior in existence to, a substance. Further, a nonsubstance can have no separate existence. In what would it then exist? Certainly not in a substance, which is assumed as posterior in existence.

14. Perhaps the statement that all thinkers posit contraries as principles (188a19).

15. Perhaps the argument that contraries exist in substances and that substances are prior in existence to contraries and are not composed of contraries.

16. Thales posits *Water* (983b20–1); Hippasus and Heraclitus posit *Fire* (984a7–8).

17. Fire is hot and dry, air is hot and moist, water is cold and moist, and earth is cold and dry (230b3–5). Hence, the third principle as a subject should have none of these contraries (coldness is contrary to heat, wetness to dryness).

18. 187a16–7.

19. That is, the *One* as subject and as the third principle present in a change.

20. Perhaps he includes Plato, who posits the *One* as form and perhaps as a mover but the *Great* and *Small* as the material principle.

21. That is, two contraries and a material principle as a subject.

22. Whether "they" refers to the two contrarieties or to the two intermediate natures just hinted, is not clear.

23. An alternative to "can generate" is "can be generated".

24. There is some difficulty in getting the meaning of this paragraph. If the principles in a change are sought, then in any one change there is a subject and two contraries (from which and to which, as extremes, change takes place). If the principles of any change are sought, the contraries in an unqualified generation become form and privation, and in a qualified generation they are contraries of place or of quantity or of quality. Each specific change within each of these categories, of course, has just one contrariety and one primary subject, though the kinds of specific contrarieties of all changes are many; for a genus has just one proper contrariety. For example, "whiteness" and "blackness" are the contrary species of "color", and the subject is a surface of a physical body. The term "contrary", of course, has many senses, and there is a primary contrariety, as stated in 1018a25–35.

25. 1018a25–35, 1055a3–b29.

7

1. This, of course, is the scientific way of proceeding.

2. For linguistic propriety, the expressions, "to become", "to come to be", and "to be generated" will have the same meaning.

3. An alternative to "by speaking either of simple or of composite

things" is "by using either simple or composite terms". He is using "simple" and "composite" in a special sense and for the sake of clarity, for in a change he wishes to distinguish the subject, the contrary (or intermediate), and the two combined. Thus, "simple" will apply either to the subject or to the contrary, while "composite" will apply to the two combined into one thing.

4. That is, the not-musical man and the musical man are composites.

5. What persists, of course, is the subject. In the case of unqualified generation, as when a man dies or when water becomes a gas, there is still a subject that underlies the change, and in ultimate cases this is prime matter.

6. For example, while in the process of generation, the unmusical man is numerically one thing, and he may be called either "a man" or "unmusical"; but while these two terms apply to (or denote, as we say) numerically one object, their meaning (or connotation, as we say) is not the same.

7. An alternative to "kind" is "form", used in a wide or loose sense.

8. The subject persists.

9. That is, if it is the musical which is becoming unmusical, then the musical does not persist, and if the unmusical is becoming musical, then the unmusical does not persist.

10. That is, the unmusical man as a whole does not persist, although one part of it, the man, does.

11. Perhaps because "bronze" has two senses: (a) the matter without the form, and (b) the matter with the form which, unless nameable, is irregular; and when bronze is used in the latter sense, it is like saying that the musical man comes to be from the unmusical man, as stated later.

12. For example, a man becomes sick, and here we have a generation not of a substance but of a quality, which is an instance of a qualified generation; and the man underlies this generation and persists even at the end of it.

13. Of course, "substance" has many senses, and here he may be using the term in a limited sense to what has a form by nature, e.g., to a man or to a tree or the like, thus excluding works of art and also earth and the other elements and perhaps even parts of animals which elsewhere he calls "potencies" but which, being loose unities or separate or separable, are unqualified beings and not attributes (1040b5-10, 1043b21-3).

14. This subject may be prime matter.

15. The seed as an example seems to be a subject with the privation of form and not a subject that remains throughout, and perhaps he is using "subject" in this sense here. In the previous Commentary we assumed a subject to be that which remains throughout the change.

16. He seems to be using "subject" here as that which remains, without the privation in it.

17. Either the subject and the two contraries are meant or the sub-

ject, the form, and its privation; and both qualified and unqualified generations are included.

18. This would be the formula or definition of the thing as the result of generation, and the thing qua such a result would be a unity of (a) subject and of (b) one contrary (form or its privation).

19. The subject remains one; and in numbering, it is the subjects that are numbered and not their attributes. Thus, we regard Socrates as one, whether sick or healthy, at home or in the marketplace, etc. But though one, a thing in a change has now one contrary (form) and now the other (privation), and it must be known as such in this manner.

20. Perhaps he means this: The principles are two, if we regard the contraries as *composite,* e.g., healthy Socrates, sick Socrates; but they are three if these contraries are broken down, namely, Socrates, health, sickness (1018a31-5). Of course, if *composites,* the contraries are not principles in an unqualified sense.

21. If we speak of them as contraries, then they are *composite* contraries, as indicated in the previous Commentary; but if they are meant not as *composite,* then something else, the subject, is missing or required. Thus, in positing the subject as a principle, we make it possible for the contraries (not as *composite*) to act on something, since they cannot act on each other.

22. Namely, the problem of the possibility of contraries acting on each other.

23. In healthy Socrates, for example, we must distinguish between (a) Socrates without including his health and (b) his health; each will not be defined in the same way.

24. The term "unmusical" here signifies the attribute without the subject, and the same applies to "unshaped". Alternatives to these are "unmusicality" and "unshapedness" or "shapelessness". Each of the two corresponding Greek terms has two meanings; one of them includes the subject but the other does not.

25. Is this underlying nature prime matter, as St. Thomas Aquinas says? If the principles of every change are sought, then even if that nature is posited as prime matter in substantial changes, must it also be prime matter in qualified changes (alteration, locomotion, etc.)? If Socrates gets well from being sick, Socrates is the subject, and he is a substance and not prime matter. Thus, it seems that the subject may be prime matter, and it may also be a substance; so since it is not a definite nature, it is known by analogy thus, healthy Socrates: Socrates :: water : prime matter. Of course, prime matter as such is unknowable (1036a8-9).

26. 1028b33–9a34.

8

1. This may be a simple or a qualified generation.

2. We may use the analogies, being : not-being :: doctor : not-doctor, being X : being not-X :: healthy doctor : not-healthy doctor.

Just as a doctor changes from healthy to not healthy, yet still remains a doctor, so an unqualified or separate being may change from some qualified being to the privation of that qualified being, yet still remain an unqualified being. But if it is qua doctor that he changes, then he must become a not-doctor, and likewise a man qua man changes by becoming not-man (he dies). Yet even here there is something which persists, an underlying subject, the matter which is a part of a man (not the living flesh, for this is matter of a living man), perhaps the molecules or the atoms which existed also before death.

3. For example, this would be nothing, or pure nonbeing, like an odd four which is an attribute of any subject and which never exists.

4. For example, this would be not-health in a man, when he is not healthy or is sick; and not-health or sickness is an attribute of the man.

5. If an animal is generated from an animal, then (a) either the second is numerically distinct from the first, as when the parents or the mother give birth to a baby, or (b) the same animal, while remaining an animal, changes with respect to an attribute, as when the same man becomes not-healthy from healthy or vice versa.

The generation of a dog from a horse is introduced hypothetically for the sake of making the point clear, not that Aristotle believes in its possibility. Here, since both before and after generation the subject remains an animal, it does not change qua animal; but it does change with respect to species, though the genus remains the same. It is as if a scalene triangle were to change to an isoscles triangle when two of its unequal sides become equal.

6. That is, it must not be an animal but something else, say the egg or fertilized egg or something of this sort; and so there must be a subject which is to change from non-animal to animal.

7. Perhaps he means that if being is to be generated, it will be so not from any kind of nonbeing, or else not from unqualified nonbeing or pure nonbeing or nothingness, but from qualified being or from something which is not the being that is generated, as when the not-white becomes white.

8. To say "it will do so not from being, nor from nonbeing" is not necessarily to deny "everything either is or is not"; for the being and the nonbeing here meant are both unqualified, but there is also qualified being and qualified nonbeing..

Let A = unqualified being, B = unqualified nonbeing, C = qualified being, D = qualified nonbeing, and let these be the only alternatives. Then one may deny both A and B without violating the principle of excluded middle, for there are still others, C and D.

9. Perhaps 1045b27–1051a33.

9

1. The Platonists in particular, as indicated in 192a6–8; and non-being for them is the *Great* and *Small* or the *(Indefinite) Dyad* (1088b 28–9a6).

2. For Parmenides, since "being" has only one meaning, if being is generated, it is so either from being or from nonbeing. The Platonists assumed the correctness of this statement; but while Parmenides rejected both alternatives (i.e., generation from being or nonbeing), they accepted the second alternative by positing nonbeing (see previous Commentary) as somehow existing.

3. Perhaps the meaning is this: For these thinkers what exists is only being and nonbeing, so if nonbeing is to be with or become something, this will be being; thus, the underlying nature cannot be with or become sometimes now a form and sometimes the privation of that form, e.g., a body for these thinkers cannot become sometimes white and sometimes black.

4. To call a body "not-white" is to deny not the existence of the body but that of whiteness in that body, and so the body is a nonbeing with respect to the attribute whiteness, that is, whiteness as such does not exist in the body.

5. Matter, as underlying both the form and the privation, and also as persisting throughout a change, is nearer to being a substance than the contraries which in the change now exist and now do not and which when existing are just attributes in a subject or substance.

6. For Aristotle, "great" would signify a subject (a quantity) with the attribute greatness (a relation to some other quantity), and so the great would be a *composite* of a subject and an attribute, and "nonbeing" as a predicate of the great would be either the nonexistence of just the greatness in the subject or the nonexistence of the subject itself. For Plato, on the other hand, the *Great* and the *Small* are simple underlying subjects (if two), or one subject (if one), or matter (or nonbeing), with no form or attribute in them at all (*Timaeus* 50).

7. Aristotle uses form and privation as two opposites in a change, and matter as the underlying subject; the Platonists use *One* as form, and the *Great* and *Small* as the subject.

8. This is the privation, which is neglected in a change.

9. Matter is never separate by itself; it is always with a contrary or an intermediate.

10. Aristotle is using Plato's language here (*Timaeus*, 50).

11. He may be referring to the prime form, which is God; or to the perpetuation of any one form, which in perpetuating its kind is somewhat divine, or to just a form, which is divine relative to the corresponding privation.

12. This is matter, which strives after a form.

13. Perhaps the meaning is this: If the principles are just two, whether two contraries or privation and form (188a19–26), then the desire of any one of them to be the other is a desire to destroy itself. What if one desires to be with the other? But contraries cannot exist together. What if the principles are just matter and form? Then matter would not be potentially now with a form and now with the privation of it.

14. That is, it is not the attribute of femininity that desires the male, nor the attribute of ugliness that desires beauty, but the other part of each corresponding *composite*, that is, of subject with femininity or subject with ugliness; it is just the subject.

15. Perhaps by "that" he means the contrary as an attribute, for if this is not in the subject after the change, it does not exist at all. But of the *composite* something will exist after the change, the material part as a subject.

16. That is, potentiality without any privation or form, and this would be prime matter.

17. For example, if a black becomes a white body, then the *composite* black body is destroyed in the sense that that *composite* body no longer exists. Now what does not exist at all after the change is the blackness (a privation), but the other part of the *composite*, the body, does exist, and with whiteness. If instead of the body we consider prime matter as the underlying subject, then this subject is altogether indestructable and ungenerable (while a body, on the other hand, e.g., water, is in a sense a *composite*, and as such it is destructible and generable).

18. If that which is just potentiality were to be generated, it would be so from a subject (some other prime matter) and would have a privation or a form, and so it would be a *composite* and not just a subject. But it is prime matter to begin with, and not a *composite*, and so it cannot come to be itself from itself.

19. If it is destroyed, it will become itself, so to say, and so what results after destruction is prime matter, which is identical to that existing prior to the destruction.

20. Perhaps he is referring to any form as actuality, or else to the prime mover or movers, and these are discussed in the *Metaphysics*.

21. These are treated generically in Book B, which follows, and specifically in other special sciences which come under *Physics*, such as *Generation and Destruction, On the Soul, On Plants*, and the like.

Book B

1

1. Aristotle takes the expression "by nature" in the way it was ordinarily applied, and by analysis of the objects to which it applies and those to which it does not, he proceeds to make distinctions and arrive at the principles and so give the expression "by nature" a clear and definite meaning.

2. Both the principle of causing motion or of rest and that of being caused to move or to rest are included here. The distinction will be made later (193a9–b21). When the stone goes down, is the moving principle in the stone itself or not? If not (and this is the position of St.

Thomas Aquinas), what is it that acts or presses on the wood when the stone rests (or presses) on it? Similarly, what is the moving cause when fire heats water?

3. I am not sure of the distinction between the Greek terms for "standstill" (στάσις) and "rest" (ἠρεμία); elsewhere he uses "rest" as the contrary of "motion".

4. For example, fire goes up (locomotion); animals and plants grow (increase); cold water can be heated and a man can get sick (alteration).

5. Such a thing has physical matter but is a product of art; and its ultimate genus qua a work of art might be "artistic object".

6. We call an object "a chair", and the form of the chair qua chair was produced not by the materials of it but by something external, by art, which is in the artist. The chair can be in motion and also at rest, yet it is not in virtue of its form as a chair that it can be so, but in virtue of its being a physical object with physical matter and physical form (the form of wood or of iron).

7. When a man falls, also his finger falls, but this falls in virtue of its being a part of the man and not primarily. It is like coffee which is in the cup primarily but in the room secondarily (209a31–b2).

8. That which causes health in a sick man is the art in a doctor, who in general is not the man who is healed. So the moving cause of health is outside, although it may by accident be in the man who is healed, if he is a doctor. Similarly, a stone may be in motion upwards, but this accidentally, as when thrown up.

9. He means that the moving principle may or may not be in the man who is healed, not that art can exist by itself apart from the artist.

10. And this is always so in such cases (1034a9–b19).

11. For example, at times it happens that he who heals is the same one as he who is being healed.

12. These are the kinds of substances mentioned at the start of this section; they are *composites* of physical form and physical matter, which are natures (193a9–b21).

13. Are the expressions "by nature" and "according to nature" synonymous? At the start of this section he uses the first for physical substances, and here he uses the second to include also the essential attributes of substances. But then he uses the first also for such attributes, as in the rise of fire.

14. An alternative to "and" is "or". See previous Commentary.

15. Perhaps he has in mind Parmenides and those who deny motion and so the principles of motion, which are natures.

16. Universal knowledge is impossible without the corresponding concepts, and one gets these from sensation and then by abstraction.

17. Does "first" here mean proximate or ultimate? From what follows, the wood and bronze are given as proximate and air and fire and the others are posited by other thinkers as ultimate, but in both cases the subject persists in the change, though proximate subjects do not per-

sist eternally. He probably allows for both (as long as the subject persists in a given change), and he states this explicitly in 1015a7–10.

18. Nature for these thinkers is regarded as an ultimate and so eternal constituent. For example, the nature of all things for Thales is water.

19. For Empedocles they are *Air*, *Fire*, *Water* and *Earth*.

20. The *shape* or form is known through the formula.

21. Perhaps "that" here signifies the artistic form, which is also called "art"; for it is this that is put into the raw material by art (as it exists in the soul, being knowledge of how to produce a work of art), and the result is a work of art, a composite of matter and form. Perhaps the Greek term for "art" had at least three meanings: that which exists in the soul, the form in the work of art, and the work of art itself as a *composite*.

22. Here "art" means that which exists in the soul.

23. Perhaps by "artistic" he means produced in accordance with the rules of art.

24. Perhaps "in virtue of nature" parallels "in virtue of art", and "natural" parallels "artistic"; and just as with (a) art in the soul as a moving cause and (b) the corresponding artistic process, we have (c) a work of art into which art as form has been put, so with (a) nature (a form) as a moving cause and (b) the corresponding natural process, we have (c) an object by nature into which nature as form has come to be.

25. As existing in the soul.

26. As the artistic form in the work of art, or else as the work of art itself. Perhaps "art" here parallels "*composites* by nature" in what follows.

27. That is, nature as form.

28. It may be distinguished though not actually separated; but its formula may be given, just as a surface may be defined even if it cannot exist apart from a body.

29. A composite thing receives its name from its form rather than from its matter. We call an object "a statue", whether made of bronze or wood, and this naming comes from the form alone; but we do not call an object "a statue" if that form is absent, whether that object is of bronze or of wood.

30. Perhaps the meaning is this: If it is from art as a form in the soul that art is produced as a form in a work of art, then it is from the the form of a man that a form comes to be in a man who is generated; and, in the opinion of some, what is generated in a generation by nature is said to be nature, so from the above argument this is a form.

31. Perhaps the argument is this: Just as art as form in the soul is the moving cause of the form in a bed, so the form of a man is the moving cause of the form in the child generated; and since the moving cause as actuality is better than and prior to matter which is potentiality (1051a4–33), nature as a principle of motion should be form rather than matter.

32. The term "doctoring" receives its name from the moving cause, the doctor or his art of doctoring, and it causes health, a qualified generation (change of quality). But nature as unqualified generation is a process which receives its name not from the beginning or material cause like the seed or sperm, but from the end of that process; and this end is the final cause or the form, like the form of a tree or of a man when born. So "nature" which signifies a process is derived from "nature" which signifies a form. So, dialectically, nature should be form rather than matter.

33. Privation is the absence of *form* in that which can have a *form,* and there is no genus common to a form and its privation, for as primary differentiae they do not include the genus. But since they are related as extremes or as principles in a change, or as that from which and that to which (as primary principles) change takes place, the term "form" is used as if a genus of both, but strictly speaking it is used in two senses.

34. There is a privation of form, if "form" signifies a substantial form, like the soul of a man, but this privation is not a contrariety: It is, as he says, a contradiction, or an opposition. Thus a man comes from the contradictory not-man, and not-man is not the contrary of a man. Of course, there is an underlying subject in this change (224b26–9).

2

1. The problem is this: The mathematician studies surfaces and solids and lengths and points; but, since these exist in physical bodies, should they not be studied by the physicist?

2. Astronomy was regarded as a part of mathematics, yet its subject is physical (989b32–3, 1073b3–8). So is astronomy a part of mathematics or of physics or of both, or is it a distinct science?

3. In a way, physics is like mathematics: There is universal physics, concerned with general problems of motion, which in Aristotle's works is called "Physics", and there are parts of physics concerned with less general problems, e.g., such parts as *On the Heavens, Generation and Destruction, On Plants,* and the like. Now the Sun and the Moon are particular physical objects. So should the part of physics which is concerned with them study also their shapes, which are mathematical?

4. Surfaces, solids, and the like do exist in physical bodies which have principles of motion (physical matter and form); but this fact does not enter into or contribute to the investigation of these quantities qua such quantities. A circle qua a circle has the same properties whether it is bronze, wooden, or in some other physical material. Thus quantities are separable in thought, that is, they may be investigated without reference to the things in which they exist; and such investigation deals with the discovery of universal truths about quantities without reference to the substances in which they exist.

5. The term "objects" refers to physical bodies (subjects) as well as to their properties qua physical.

6. Both physical and mathematical objects are alike in this respect:

They can be investigated universally without reference to their individual attributes qua individual; for science in the primary sense is universal knowledge. Also those who posit the Ideas separate the objects of their investigation; but this separation is also one of existence and from motion, for the Ideas are posited as immovable objects existing apart from the individuals. Moreover, while the mathematical objects qua such cannot be in motion, as one may gather from their definition (mathematicians speak metaphorically when they mention motion; for example, instead of saying "a parabola is a curve generated by a moving point such that, etc.", one should say "a parabola is a curve such that, etc."), some of the physical objects may be in motion, e.g., animals and simple bodies. And in the definition of some physical objects, e.g., snubness and the like, the subject which can be in motion must appear (of course, not all objects of physics are essentially in motion, for a color and a place are not essentially in motion). Evidently the objects of physics are on the whole less separable (in thought and from motion) than those of mathematics; yet the Ideas as objects of physics are posited as immovable.

7. That is, the lines investigated by mathematicians can exist only in physical bodies; however, they are investigated not with respect to how or where they exist, but with respect to their whatness and the properties which follow from their definition.

8. The path of a light ray, for example, proceeds (according to Aristotle) along a straight line, but this is like saying that a straight line is predicated of or exists in the path of a light ray, and this mathematical line is investigated as an attribute of the light ray, which is physical. Take this relation of the two away and what remains, the line itself or the light ray itself (not as related to the line), is no longer an object within optics; for the first is in mathematics, the second in physics.

The equality of the angle of incidence of a light ray falling on a smooth surface to the angle of reflection is a principle in optics, obtained by induction, but what follows from this is through mathematics. Thus let m = angle of incidence, and n = angle of reflection. To prove: p = q. The proof proceeds as follows: In mathematics, let M = N; then P = Q, for complements of equal angles are equal. But M and N

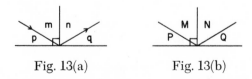

Fig. 13(a)   Fig. 13(b)

are predicated of m and n, respectively; hence, the equality P = Q is predicated of the equality p = q, where p and q are the complementary angles and are attributes of the path of a light ray. What causes the equality p = q in that path? Evidently, the equality P = Q, which is itself ultimately caused by principles in mathematics. We conclude, then, that the cause of p = q is to be found in mathematics (78b32–9a10).

In *Mechanics* (847a24–8) Aristotle speaks in general about combined objects, as in the case of the linear path of a light ray, when he says that the manner of treatment is through mathematics, but the object is known through physics; and the proper principles are known by the composite science.

9. Of course, if both senses of "nature" signify a principle of motion or of change, one of acting and the other of being acted upon, while form and privation too are principles in a change, and acting and being acted upon are relatives and simultaneous, then if physics is to be a science of the movable qua movable, both matter and form are required and therefore should be investigated.

10. For a discussion of this, see 983b6–4a18, 993a15–24, 1014b35–5a3, and 1078b19–21.

11. If the artist should understand both matter and form to some extent and if art imitates nature, then the science of nature should be about both matter and form to some extent. This dialectical argument proceeds from what is more known and clear to us to what is by its nature more known and clear to us, that is, to what is scientific (71b33–2a5, 184a16–b14).

12. Perhaps this is another argument favoring the inclusion of form and matter under physics. If both the final cause and whatever is needed for it should be included under one science (and the final cause in a change is often a form, as that of a man or of a house when each of these is generated), then since matter is necessary in the generation of a man and materials in that of a house, both matter and form should be the concern of physics. Since form and final cause are sometimes numerically the same, this may also be an argument for including final cause in physics.

The moving cause as form is not explicitly mentioned, though it is needed in, say, the generation of a man or of a house. Is it included under "whatever is needed"? Perhaps not, for it does not add to the argument when the final cause as form is mentioned. If the mover is mentioned as a form, then the necessity of including matter may be introduced.

13. A lost work. One interpretation of "two senses" is, the form of the object generated (e.g., the form of a chair) and the (pleasurable) use of the object or the man for whom the object is produced; for there is a proximate final cause, and an ultimate, and possibly intermediate ones. One man manufactures paper, which has a form qua paper; another uses it to make a book, which also has a form; a third reads the book.

14. The art of using directs the art of producing, for the use is a final cause relative to whatever is necessary for it. For example, if living comfortably is the purpose, the building of a house is necessary, and if this, then building the parts of the house in a certain way is also necessary.

15. Is this always so? We might mix liquids or juices of fruits in certain proportions according to art to produce certain drinks.

16. Just as the productive arts, which make the matter [materials], are for the sake of the using arts, so in physics matter is for the sake of form. But while there may be a hierarchy of productive arts, which produce the matter, in natural things matter is already there.

17. The form of a saw is not just the shape, for such a shape in wood will not make cutting possible. Hard material is required, such as steel, so the kind of matter cannot be neglected.

18. It is not necessary to know the ultimate material or final or formal or moving causes to understand or to produce something. The producer of chairs from wood need not know the molecular or atomic structure of wood. The proximate moving cause of Socrates is his father or parents, the Sun is a distant moving cause, and the prime mover is the most distant mover.

19. Such forms are the movers of the spheres (1069a18–1076a4).

3

1. Does the term "first" signify a proximate cause or an ultimate cause or either or both? Lines 194b24–6 and 195b21–5 indicate a proximate, and from lines 184a10–4 an added analysis into principles and elements is required. For example, without an analysis of an artist into a man and the art in him, the art as a proximate cause cannot be stated. But should the analysis be complete? According to lines 194b9–13 a complete analysis is not necessary for the physicist to understand the causes, for perhaps such analysis would require him to be a philosopher and a biologist and a scientist of other subjects; so the proximate cause is perhaps sufficient, e.g., one may stop with the father as a moving cause and not go to the Sun and to the prime mover, and he may stop with the art in a sculptor without the necessity of understanding the causes of a man.

2. These may be definitions or properties.

3. A material part in the thing.

4. Of bronze statues it is bronze; of this bronze statue it is this bronze; of a statue in general one may state the genus of the various materials that may be used. If any genus of bronze is given, this may be not a proximate but a distant cause, more or less.

5. Plato used this term (see *Glossary*).

6. If by "formula of the essence" he means what is in the thing, this would be the form, or what we might call the "structure", like the soul of a man; but if he means what is in the mind as signifying what is in the thing, then this is the *knowledge* of that form.

7. In the formula of the ratio 2:1 the term "number" appears. Of course, this term signifies a cause, or better, a part of the cause, but not the proper or proximate cause. Does "formula" here mean the form in the thing or what is in the mind?

8. For example, this may be a force (in the modern sense) which slows down a motion to a stop.

9. Here, too, the proximate cause is indicated. One may go on and say that happiness is the cause, but this is a distant cause and not proper. Besides, if the distant cause were used always for men, then "happiness" would always be the answer, simple enough but not specific. However, one may set a given end as the final cause in a given context and proceed to discover the means for it.

10. If A is done for the sake of B, B for the sake of C, and C is the end, then B is the proximate end of A, but C is the ultimate end of A, that is, A is done ultimately for the sake of C.

11. A principle is also a cause (1013a16-7).

12. How can the same thing be the cause of contraries? By "the same" he means the same numerically or as a subject, though different with respect to an accident, e.g., the pilot's presence or absence. But it is in virtue of his presence on the one hand and his absence on the other as causes that safety and capsizing, respectively, are the effects.

13. By "hypotheses" he may mean the premises; if not, then probably the first unproved premises. If the premises cannot be proved, they are first or ultimate material causes, so to speak; if proved, they are proximate.

14. The hypotheses are, in a manner of speaking, the materials from which a conclusion is proved or formed.

15. By *"that of which"* he means the two constituents in the *composite* thing, matter and form, or material and formal cause.

16. Referring to the syllables, manufactured articles, bodies, etc., each of which is a *composite*.

17. Evidently, the so-called "material cause" or "matter" is not restricted to physical or sensible matter; for neither the letters of the syllable need be such, nor the elements or the genus of a definition, nor the so-called "intelligible matter" in quantity (1036a9-12, b35, 1045a33-5).

18. That would be the other constituent in each *composite,* and this is the form or essence. For example, the order of the letters in the case of a syllable, the shape in the case of a manufactured article, etc.

19. Perhaps by "whole" here he does not mean the *composite* (matter and form), like the whole bronze statue, but that (the wholeness as a form, so to speak) which makes the thing a whole (a *composite*), and this is the form or the cause of unity (1023b29-36). The form itself may be a kind of whole with parts, as in the case of a man's soul, which has parts.

20. The term "end" is wide enough to include both the good and the apparent good (the latter may be evil or bad, yet it exists and must be considered).

21. Perhaps the prior in existence is meant (which could be prior also in other ways, as in definition or in time), but whether the example given (an artist is prior in existence to a doctor) exemplifies this priority

or no example of it is given here is not clear. If A is the moving cause of B, and B of C, then A is prior to B as a moving cause. For example, let A = art of building, B = builder, C = house (195b21–5). Perhaps this is the priority meant, or this more than the other; for in this the causes themselves in the things are considered, while in the other, the genus and species are considered, and these are related to knowledge.

But again, perhaps any priority is meant.

22. By "includes" he probably means the kind of inclusion which relates the genus and the species. For example, "the artist" includes "the doctor", and "a number" includes "two"; thus, the genus includes the species.

23. The moving cause of a statue (universally taken) must be a sculptor, and it may or may not be Polyclitus; so Polyclitus is an accidental moving cause of a statue. For a certain statue (by Polyclitus), however, Polyclitus is not an accidental moving cause (195b25–7).

24. By "includes" here perhaps he means *has*, whether as an accident or as any predicate. For example, "Polyclitus" is an accidental predicate of the sculptor, and "man" and "animal" are also predicates of the sculptor.

25. That is, if the white or the musical were to be called "a cause" of the statue rather than Polyclitus, for they are more remote than Polyclitus as moving accidental causes (1014a4–6). Perhaps also the white is more remote than the musical, for the latter is an accident of a man, but the former of any body.

26. By *"proper"* he means essential causes, which in 195a5 he calls "nonaccidental"; and these are contrasted with accidental causes.

27. That is, the builder who is to build it.

28. This is not prime matter but materials, which may be used for some purpose. For example, we may say that a brickmaker manufactures bricks, thus specifying the moving cause and the products, and we may use the more general terms "productive artist" and "materials produced", the latter being a genus of "bricks".

29. In other words, causes as potential or as actual may be stated of individuals or by species or by genus. For example, we may say *"potential builders* must consider the overhead cost of *houses to be built."*

30. The combination need not be of just two terms.

31. If by "particular" he means an individual, like Socrates, then a genus may be any essential predicate in the same category, including "man"; if not, then "particular" may be a predicate of an individual as well as of a species, in which case "genus" would have its usual restricted meaning and would not be applicable to a species.

32. The simultaneity of cause and effect is discussed in 95a22–b12 and 98a35–9b8.

33. By "ultimate" here he does not mean the most distant or most generic, but rather the proximate or nearest or most precise, or, as we would say, the necessary and sufficient condition. For example, the cause of the fall of a white round bronze ball is the fact that it has a

greater density than the medium has. The whiteness and roundness and bronzeness of the material do not contribute.

4

1. The inquiry into the way in which luck and *chance* are causes or into whether luck is the same as or distinct from *chance,* is an inquiry into their attributes; but an inquiry into their whatness is an inquiry into their essence or their wholeness.

2. The inquiry into the existence of à thing is prior, for a science is not concerned with nonbeing (71b25–6).

3. Probably Democritus and Leucippus are included (252a32–b2, 641b15–23, 789b2–5).

4. 334a1–7.

5. 198b27–32.

6. Probably Democritus is included.

7. Instead of coining a new term, Aristotle often uses the same term now generically and now specifically. He uses αὐτόματον in this way to mean sometimes *chance* and sometimes chance. The meanings of *"chance"* and "chance" are given in the *Glossary.*

5

1. For example, every man eventually dies, and for Aristotle the Sun always and of necessity rises every day; but in going to the store to buy oil, a man buys it not always but most of the time, for sometimes the grocer is out of stock.

2. Luck (or *chance*) is a cause of a certain kind yet to be discussed, but what comes to be by luck is an effect of a certain kind. So we have the proportion, cause : effect :: luck (or *chance*) : thing coming to be by luck (or *chance*). Luck or *chance* will be specified later as being a moving cause (198a2–3).

3. Since there are things which happen most of the time but not always, it is in those cases in which they do not happen in the usual manner that luck or *chance* exists. Usually, a baby is born with five fingers, and it is by chance that it is born with six fingers; and usually a man gets to his office as scheduled, but sometimes the car breaks down.

4. The argument is dialectical. Things which happen in a certain way occasionally are said by people to happen by luck, and when people speak of things as happening by luck, such things happen occasionally. So luck exists in events.

5. For example, building is for the sake of a house or its form, exercise for the sake of health, earning money for the sake of use; but activities which are ends in themselves, such as listening to music, enjoying a spectacle, etc., are not for the sake of something else.

6. Those according to *choice* require *thought,* but those by nature,

such as the generation from a sperm to an animal or from a seed to a tree, do not require *thought*. Thus, if to these two kinds are added also the activities which are ends in themselves, the use of the term "for the sake of" or "final cause" is wide enough to include all activities caused by a moving cause, whether this cause be conscious or without consciousness; and that term should not be taken in any narrow anthropomorphic sense. Perhaps the term "tendency toward" or some other such term is more suitable for generations in which no *thought* is present; for we are more inclined to use such expressions as "the seed tends to become a tree" or "under favorable conditions it usually becomes a tree". Evidently, a bad choice of English terms can easily lead to a misunderstanding of the meaning intended by Aristotle.

7. These are things that come to be by accident; for example, the house was built by a musician, a man recovered a debt though he did not go to the agora for that purpose, and a two-headed calf was born.

8. Aristotle himself would use the term "chance", but perhaps he is using the term in common usage here when he says "we do say".

9. Whether by "essential being" here he means any simple thing in any category (1017a22–7) or a thing which is a necessary unity of two things, like an odd five or a diagonal of a square incommensurable with the side, is not clear. If he wishes to indicate a similarity, perhaps the latter is intended. For example, just as the cause-effect connection between the builder and the house is essential, so the subject-attribute connection between nine and squareness (or oddness) is essential; and the same applies to the accidental connections musician-house and man-six-fingered, respectively.

10. The man may be musical, five feet tall, a poker player, etc., but it is in virtue of the art of building and not in virtue of any of these that the man built the house. We might add that just as we speak of an essential cause either of an individual or universally, so we may speak of chance causes or of effects by chance either of an individual or universally (195b13–4, 25–7).

11. Literally, "by chance" means by a moving cause which is accidental; for "chance" means an accidental moving cause, and its two species are "*chance*" and "luck". We use "*chance*" here because "chance" would make "luck" redundant.

12. 197a36–b37.

13. Perhaps he is referring to the money owed him by someone.

14. By "a cause" he means final cause, not a moving cause; and by "present in him" he probably means present by nature in him, as against something done by *thought* or *choice*.

15. Here, the intention of going there (to collect contributions) is luck; and this is a *chosen* but an accidental moving cause of the effect, of getting the money.

16. By "the same thing" he means a thing by *choice* or *thought*, whether done actually or would be done if one knew, and whether intentionally or by luck. For example, collecting the debt is done inten-

tionally if the man goes there for that purpose, but by luck if he goes there for another purpose; and in both cases the moving cause is a cause that *chooses.*

17. It is indefinite, since it can be any of an indefinite number of distinct things or causes; and it is not revealed to us since we cannot know or predict that which is not definite. For example, we can definitely say that the cause of a house is a builder, universally taken, but we cannot know the various accidents of a builder.

18. For example, for any given individual effect luck as a cause is in a sense definite and can be known; the cause of getting the money, in the example mentioned, is the intention of going there to collect contributions.

19. Luck is qualified, since for each individual effect it is an individual cause, whether known or not, as in *this house* built by *that musician.* But it is not an unqualified cause like the builder in the case of a house built, for the latter cause (the builder) needs no qualification; it is a necessary cause or a cause for the most part.

20. A reason is a universal statement of things existing necessarily or for the most part. For example, "any two even (whole) numbers are commensurable with respect to some (whole) number: the number two," and "men are unable to beget children at age 80", which is true for the most part.

21. The meaning is not spelled out. Perhaps it is this: Assuming that a purge of a sick man is occasionally the cause of health, and so an accidental cause, the purge itself may have been caused somehow by the wind, which was itself caused by the Sun. Thus, the purge, the wind, and the Sun are all accidental causes, given in the order of nearness relative to the effect.

22. By definition, luck is not frequent, and so one cannot be certain when it will present itself.

23. That is, in a generation there is the mover, that which is moved, that from which it is moved, and that to which it is moved; so luck and *chance* in a generation are the moving causes.

6

1. Luck may be good or bad. If the goodness is considerable, luck is said to be good fortune; if the badness is considerable, it is said to be misfortune. Luck in general is limited to events where *action* is involved.

2. He says "seems", for although good fortune usually benefits a man, it may also harm him if he does not use the result of it virtuously. Happiness is not possible without virtue, and the result of good fortune is therefore instrumental.

3. Virtue and vice are involved in *choice* and *action;* and children, not yet mature enough to make *choice,* cannot be happy or unhappy except by analogy. This, of course, does not deny them pleasures and

pains. As we would say, they have not yet attained the state of responsibility and knowledge of what is good and bad.

4. Referring to inanimate things, brutes, children, etc.

5. For example, when there is *action* on the part of the cause but the effect by chance is an inanimate object, then we have the case in point. A man enjoys putting certain valuable glasses in order but accidentally breaks one of them; then the effect on that glass is caused by a bad luck, the man, for it is a bad effect.

6. By definition, chance is an accidental cause. Perhaps the term "chance cause" is a better English idiom than the term "chance".

7. Apparently, both effects are good, the safety of the horse and the ready position of the tripod; so chance in both cases is good. The story of each of the two examples is not given, but one may easily create a story.

8. Since in an event there is both a cause and an effect, *choice* may or may not belong to the cause or to the effect, and the effect may or may not be good; so there are eight kinds of events or cause-effect combinations with respect to *choice,* goodness, or their negation. Others may be added if the indicated dichotomy is made, namely, into causes which may or may not be outside the thing affected.

9. The term αὐτόματον (= "chance") is perhaps derived from μάτην (= "in vain"); so just as we use "in vain" when the intended effect occasionally fails, so we use "chance" when the expected effect occasionally fails.

10. Of course, things occurring in vain are only a part of those occurring by chance; but he connects "chance" etymologically to "in vain" in order to indicate that events by chance occur infrequently just as events in vain do. An alternative to "chance" here is "*chance*"; and in either case, what is indicated is the infrequency just mentioned.

11. Perhaps the meaning is this: Art or *thought* as an accidental cause is outside the thing affected, but nature is inside. Monstrosity is generated by *chance,* which is a cause in, let us say, the sperm, and monstrosity is not the usual effect. But, one may say, the cause of a thing generated without a sperm is not in the matter, but outside, and this may be the heat of the Sun or some such thing, although once that heat is inside, it may be viewed as a chance cause.

12. Under "chance" the species "*chance*" may also be included.

13. In 1026b27–21 he states that occurrence for the most part is the cause of accidental occurrence. Thus accidental occurrence is a privation of the occurrence for the most part. But in a definition, the privation of a thing is posterior to that thing; so accidental occurrence is posterior in definition to occurrence for the most part. But it is also posterior in existence; for the infrequent occurs by subtraction, so to speak. An accidental cause-effect connection cannot exist unless the contrary of it exists. By nature men turn grey by the age of 70, and it is by accident that this does not happen; and by art an artist produces a work of

art, though occasionally he fails. So if nature did not exist, neither would its contrary. Can nature exist if accident does not? If not impeded, a given nature always acts in the same way; and things existing by nature (e.g., men) are necessarily destructible.

14. The term "heavens" has many senses (278b11–21), and, from what follows, its meaning here does not take in the whole universe. Perhaps at least the part around us, where all kinds of changes take place, is excluded. He seems to be answering the view stated in lines 196a24–35.

7

1. 194b23–5a3.

2. The whatness as form or essence, and without physical matter, is necessarily immovable (1067b9–11).

3. If attribute A belongs to subject S in mathematics, the ultimate *why* is the definition. For example, the equality of the angles to two right angles belongs to a right triangle in virtue of its definition, or better, in virtue of a part of its definition, i.e., its being a three-sided plane figure (73b32–9). A physical object, too, has a whatness in the sense of a cause as form.

4. Since a physical object may change, one may ask for the cause of a change in the sense of a moving cause.

5. This cause is taken in a generic sense. In inanimate objects we often call it "a tendency", that is, objects with a given definite nature have a definite tendency of a kind. Dense objects tend towards the center of the Earth, seeds of a given kind tend to become trees of a given kind, and so on; or, in Aristotle's manner of speaking, things will get there unless impeded, e.g., rocks will fall unless prevented, seeds under certain conditions will become trees, unless something interferes.

6. He means the proximate. Does this include matter and form or the *whole* man? But it is the form he has in mind, and the *composite* causes motion in virtue of the form. So perhaps he is thinking of the forms of *composites* which can be moved. God and art, too, are movers, but they do not come under the study of physics; and while God is separate, art is inseparable from man.

7. The final cause of a sperm (of a man) is the form it is to attain, and the mover is the form of the father; so the mover, the final cause, and the form are of the same kind. They are all forms, and they differ in the way they are viewed or in what it is to be each. A mover is a source from which change begins, a final cause is that toward which a thing in generation proceeds, and a form is that in virtue of which a thing exists and has unity. He says "often", for at times this is not the case. The final cause of a man is not a form but happiness; the mover of the form of a statue is the corresponding art, as knowledge in the soul, and the mover of certain lower animals is (according to Aristotle) sometimes the heat of the Sun (743a35–6).

8. These are the movers of the spheres, and they are pure forms and immovable. By "a movable mover", then, he means a natural substance, a *composite*, like a man.

9. He means a principle of being moved, and this principle is matter.

10. Perhaps he is considering disciplines whose objects are separate or separable substances. If so, mathematics is not included, for quantities are inseparable and are not substances. Separate and immovable objects (the movers of the spheres) will come under first philosophy (*Metaphysics*, 980a21–1093b29); this which change only with respect to place (the heavenly objects), under a second discipline (268a1–298a20); and destructible objects, under a third (298a24–338b19, and others).

Where does astronomy fit in? But astronomy investigates only certain mathematical attributes of movable but indestructible objects; there are also other attributes, and non-mathematical ones too. Perhaps the science indicated is *On the Heavens*, Books A and B, while the third science starts with *On the Heavens*, Books Γ and Δ, and proceeds to *On Generation and Destruction* and other subordinate sciences.

How does *Physics* fit in, then? Perhaps the *Physics* is like universal mathematics, for it seems to consider the universal and prior attributes of the others, which would be parts of physics, so to speak (74a17–25, 189b30–2, 1026a25–7, 1064b8–9).

11. Perhaps the final cause is included in the whatness, for this is the end of the subject in generation.

12. This seems to indicate a final cause, for it signifies a process to something.

13. But neither nature as a form and a mover can be moved, nor can art which has no matter, although both must be with matter. Perhaps by "a principle that causes physical motion" he means a separate substance, like God or a man.

14. The semicolon after "all" is inserted purposely, even if there is no punctuation in the Greek text as it stands.

15. By "from that" he probably means from the moving cause.

16. Perhaps he has in mind the fact that if the mover acts, the effect does not necessarily come to be, for something might prevent it.

17. By "that" he means the material cause. The premises are matter for the conclusion; if a man comes to be, then a sperm pre-existed; if a house is to be built, then there must be materials for it. See 199b34–200b8.

18. The proximate final cause is indicated. Thus, a man's tongue and hands are so-and-so constructed in a particular way because they can best serve a particular part of his form or end.

19. Much has been left unsaid in this highly concentrated paragraph, which is therefore highly subject to interpretation. The translation and commentaries given have been dictated by consistency in thought.

8

1. There are alternative meanings: (a) why nature exists as a final cause, as that for the sake of which something takes place, and (b) why nature acts for the sake of something. In the Greek the verb ("exists" or "acts" or whatever is intended) is omitted. Literally, the translation is "why nature of causes for the sake of something." Lines beginning from 198b16 suggest the second alternative. Perhaps both are included in this sense: Nature acts for the sake of some nature. Thus nature acts as a moving cause, and it does so for the sake of something which is or may be nature, as in the case of a man who begets a man or a seed which through a moving cause within it grows into something having the form of a tree. Of course, in men, final cause also goes beyond nature—it is a certain activity, happiness.

2. This problem amounts to our present problem of determinism vs. free will.

3. Empedocles.

4. Anaxagoras.

5. The expression "for the sake of something" is wider; the term "better" is more restricted, for example, to men.

6. In the first case, the end result (growth of corn) is good; in the second, the spoiling is bad. So it would seem that nature does not act for the best but by necessity and that the end result, whether good or bad, is a coincidence.

7. Perhaps "whenever" here means at any time or place.

8. That is, not fitfully composed as if generated for the sake of something.

9. Empedocles, fr. 61.

10. Evidently, the doctrine of evolution in some form was introduced and became a topic of discussion among Greek thinkers.

11. By definition, chance causes or effects by chance are infrequent; but rain in the winter (resulting in growth), non-rain in the summer (tending not to spoil the wheat) and also heat, sharp teeth in front, broad molars at the sides—all these come to be for the most part and not infrequently. So by definition these things do not come to be by chance.

12. That is, they would admit that such things exist by nature, according to the way the expression "by nature" is used here: coming to be by a given cause in a definite way unless prevented by chance, and this results in that which comes to be for the most part.

One might object. What right has Aristotle to assign his own meanings to terms and then use them to refute other thinkers? However, if we note the fact that (a) other thinkers did not take the trouble to use the terms consistently or with a definite meaning and that (b) Aristotle gave each term a definite meaning and one that is closest to common usage, then the objection loses its force. For, if the thinker criticized is dead or not present, how can one speak scientifically or criticize him scientifically if not in this manner?

13. In our way of saying it, perhaps this amounts to saying that cer-

tain things of a given definite nature proceed to a given definite end unless prevented, or tend to a given definite end. For example, dense objects tend toward the center of the Earth, water tends to evaporate when heated, an acorn tends to become an oak, and man begets man.

14. For example, when the seed starts to germinate, it may be obstructed by something outside, e.g., by a rock above it or by being eaten. Thus its disposition to reach an end through a series of ordered stages may never be actualized.

15. That is, if it does something, then it follows that it has the power to do this, this power being in its nature.

16. The main difference would be that while art is an outside moving cause of the thing, nature is in the thing.

17. Each stage is a preparation or a precondition for the next: In the case of a house, the order would be foundation, walls, etc., roof; in the case of a tree, roots, trunk, branches, leaves, and fruit.

18. For example if an external cause obstructs nature or prevents it from actualizing its disposition, then art steps in to remove that cause and/or assist the weakened nature.

19. When art imitates nature, then again there is a one-to-one correspondence, so to speak, between the stages in the natural process leading to an end and those in the case of art.

20. In the direction of living things of lower order.

21. Final cause.

22. In things generated by art and nature, an error in the nature of the mover or in the source of motion would lead to an end result which is not the end intended. Of course, a failure may occur also when another cause intervenes during the process, for example, when the right medicine is given or when the seed is perfect but other accidental causes intervene during the process and cause a failure.

23. Perhaps Empedocles said that animals came from animals all at once, so Aristotle raises an objection and supports it even by a quotation from Empedocles himself.

24. Of course, whether this be a combination of olive and vine or some other combination makes no difference, as long as *some* accidental combination is posited as having come into being.

25. If one denies that from a given seed (e.g., a corn seed) the corresponding plant (a corn plant) comes into being either always or for the most part, then it would follow that, for example, from a corn seed any chance thing might grow and that a corn plant would grow only by chance. But this contradicts the facts. A corn plant came into being in a definite way from a definite seed (in species), and so it came into being by nature, and to say a corn seed or a corn plant has a nature implies that it has a definite power of acting in a certain way.

26. Men are not born from cows or pigs or horses, etc.

27. From the sperm of a man only a man is generated (unless it be a monstrosity, which happens occasionally), but not a dog or a horse, etc.

28. He came for some other reason, and this other reason is accidental to paying the ransom; but he would have come to pay the ransom,

had he known. Thus, his coming for that other reason, or his intention to do so, is luck or an accidental moving cause of the effect (paying the ransom). Perhaps he is referring to Anniceris of Cyrene, who, having gone to Aegina for some other reason (an accidental), paid the ransom for Plato who was in prison there.

29. 196b23–7.

30. One might question this. But he who deliberates does not yet know, and the artist knows. Thus the artist already has the art and proceeds by habit. If he deliberates or judges in the course of producing a work of art, this is accidental to the art. For example, he is given $100,000 to create a work of art worth so much. Connecting this amount with the magnitude of the work of art may require some calculation or thinking, but such connection is not a part of art but is accidental to it.

31. The implication is that final cause in art does exist.

32. If a doctor heals a patient, the moving cause (art) is not in the patient who is moved (healed); but if he heals himself, both the mover and the thing moved exist in the same subject. In a thing by nature, such as a seed, both nature as a mover and nature as that which is moved are in the same subject, the seed; and the seed in this respect resembles the doctor who heals himself. Likewise, a stone which is up has a principle of causing itself to be down, and it moves down unless prevented (1049b8–10).

9

1. An alternative to "simply" is "without qualification". Is the necessary either hypothetical or simple, but not both? Or better, what are the definitions of simple and hypothetical necessity? Apparently, from what follows, the concern is primarily with necessity in things which exist or come to be by nature, and necessity in art and in mathematics is introduced for comparison and contrast and to make things clearer.

Necessity in nature for Aristotle is not the kind which nowadays may be termed "materialistic determinism"; it is rather a hypothetical necessity. Let the proposition "If P exists or is to be, then Q must exist or will have to be" be true, in which P is posited as the hypothesis. In things by nature, such a hypothesis may or may not exist, for such things are destructible. Then Q is said to be hypothetically necessary, that is, it exists or will exist if the hypothesis P exists or will exist. Q may be prior in time to P, as in the things which necessarily precede the birth of a baby. So P, which is the hypothesis, is posited as a final cause in things by nature; and Q is then said to be hypothetically necessary, that is, necessary if P is.

In art, the wall and the saw as examples of hypotheses are similar in kind, for they too are things generated, and they are more evident to us than the examples in nature; but the hypotheses in mathematics are not so similar, though even here there is a parallelism. If an oak tree exists, an acorn must have existed from which it developed; but if an acorn existed, its development into an oak tree is not necessary, and if it did not exist, such development into a tree would be impossible. In mathematics, if the principles are posited, the conclusion follows; but if the conclusion as a statement is true, it is not necessary for the principles to be such as posited (for a true conclusion may follow also from false premises), and if it is false, the principles (some or all) must be denied.

Returning to the question at the start, we may ask "What are the definitions of simple and hypothetical necessity?" If the simple necessary is that which exists necessarily without any restriction, then this is eternal (what exists necessarily is eternal, and conversely, 338a1–2), like the prime mover and the circular motion of the outer heaven and generation (for Aristotle), and lines 338a14–5 and 1139b23–4 seem to indicate this though lines 639b23–5 and 1072b11–3 do not, and what is scientifically known would be included, for this too is necessary. However, there is a distinction here. It is the prime mover that causes the circular motion, and not conversely; and in science, it is the principles that cause the conclusion, and not conversely. In a sense, then, the conclusion, even if necessarily true, follows from the principles which are posited as hypotheses, though not hypotheses in the same sense as that of a posited final cause in nature. Thus though not sure of Aristotle's exact definitions of the kinds of necessity, we can say that knowledge of the distinctions is the next best thing, for definitions are introduced after the distinctions have been made.

2. That is, if the wall is to be (of a certain kind), then certain materials or material causes are necessary.

3. The hypothesis is the final cause—the function of a saw, to cut certain things in such-and-such a way.

4. Perhaps he means that the final cause is stated in the formula or definition of the saw.

5. For example, if the final cause is a house to be built, then one starts to reason as to what is necessary and what must be done to build the house.

6. If the final cause is to exist, not only matter but also motions may be necessary, as in the making of a saw.

7. In what sense of the term "cause"? For one thing, it is the starting-point of reasoning to what is necessary, and a starting-point (or principle) is also a cause (1003b22–4).

8. The operation of sawing may be defined in terms of the function alone, or it may include also the other causes, the matter being one of them.

Book Γ

1

1. An alternative to "or" is "and".

2. Why discuss motion first, if change is more universal than motion

(for motion is limited to locomotion, alteration, increase, and decrease, while change extends also to generation and destruction, 224b35–5b9)? Is it because there is motion in every change, so that nothing would be added by a discussion of change? According to St. Thomas Aquinas, Aristotle is using "motion" in a wider sense here, in the same sense as that of "change".

3. By "what follows" he means the infinite, place, void, and time, and perhaps the kinds of motion, that which causes motion, and that which is caused to move.

4. As discussed later (202b30–8a23), the infinite exists potentially, and it does so primarily in magnitudes or in what is continuous. As a magnitude is divided into parts, a number of parts arises, and as division of a magnitude may proceed without an end (infinitely), a number of parts may likewise increase without an end (infinitely); so an infinite number follows an infinite division of a magnitude.

5. This is not Aristotle's definition of the continuous (227a10–7, 231a22), although it follows from the definition (231a21–2a22).

6. That which is in motion (any motion) must be a body, and this must be in a place, and while in motion it must take time, and if there is a motion, there must be that which causes the motion and that which is caused to be in motion.

7. As he will show later, the void will be excluded since it does not exist (213a12–7b28).

8. This is the scientific way of proceeding.

9. The prime mover (God) and the other movers of the spheres are just actualities (no potentiality in them); but a form which exists with matter (for example, a soul) is also an actuality, though not separate, and it may be said to be a qualified actuality.

10. A man who is sick is potentially healthy, and when he gets well, he is actually healthy. Thus a subject may at one time have the potentiality of having an attribute, and at another time it may actually have that attribute. In another sense, some subjects (e.g., a man) have both a potentiality (matter) and an actuality (soul, which is form).

11. The discussion of relatives here is similar to that in 1020b26–1b11, but less complete (perhaps because what is needed here is just the relation of the mover to the moved). A relative, it may be added, is posterior in definition and in existence to that of which it is a predicate, for the unequal is a number, and that which causes a motion is, let us say, a man or art.

12. A motion does not exist by itself and is not a substance; it belongs to something, to a body. Moreover, since it exists with respect to some category and no two categories signify a common nature, the term "motion", like the term "being", is analogous. For example, an alteration is a change with respect to quality, a locomotion is a change with respect to place.

13. Each motion occurs with respect to just one category, and within this category it proceeds from *something* definite to *something else*

which is definite, a *form* or a privation; but the motion within this category is not a definite or static actuality but an incomplete actuality. If a body stays white, we have a definite actuality or form, whiteness; but if there is a motion from one color to another, we have no definite actuality or *form*, so this actuality is indefinite or incomplete.

14. Since a definition is in terms of elements, each of these must be more abstract or universal than the thing defined. In the case of "motion", then, such are the terms "actuality" and "potentiality". To define a motion as a passage of some sort is (as St. Thomas Aquinas points out) circular, for a passage is a species of motion. The definition given, we may add, is analogous, just as "motion" is.

Again, that which causes a motion may or may not be in motion, but a motion must be in that which is caused to be moved. In the definition, then, we have "the potentially existing", and specifically, "the alterable", "generable", and the like, and so in the definition of a motion the actuality is said to be in that which is acted upon or is moved. Of course, if the mover is physical (a physical body or substance), it too is movable.

15. Of course, we might use "motion with respect to quantity" or "quantitative motion".

16. It is a physical body or substance. An immaterial object, such as God or art in the soul, is excluded.

17. 258b10–267b26.

18. The actuality of bronze qua bronze is not a motion; for example, in the case of a bronze statue, its actuality is the form of the statue, and the statue need not be in motion. The notion "bronze" does not signify a motion but something static; but the potentiality of bronze to be moved by something else indicates a possible motion.

19. The underlying subject here is to be taken without sickness or health. If Socrates is in the Agora at one time and at home at another, there is something common to the two occasions, namely, Socrates as a subject, without reference to the place in which he may be.

20. By "the same" he means not numerically the same but the same in formula or definition.

2

1. Plato used such terms *(Timaeus, Sophist)*.

2. Six is other than three, and it is unequal to three, but it need not be in motion; and the nonexistent, whether Socrates when dead or a commensurate diagonal, does not move either.

3. A motion may be from or to the equal as well as from or to the unequal, and likewise for that which is the same and that which is distinct, and that which is being and that which is nonbeing.

4. A motion has some similarity to what is indefinite but is not identical with it, and so its definition is not that of the indefinite.

5. In the columns of opposites, one indicates possession and the other privation; and the latter were considered as indefinite, e.g., the in-

finite, the invisible, motion, plurality, and others like these are indefinite.

6. That is, a motion is neither just an actuality nor just a potentiality.

7. In a manner of speaking, a motion is a mixture of potentiality and actuality. When the object in motion is considered at a moment (which is not time), it is definite, e.g., grey if the motion is from black to white, but it is not of any definite color throughout the motion; and a motion is an event, an *actuality*, but no ultimate species of a category can describe it.

8. 201a10–1.

9. This is saying that every action by a body has a reaction to that body, without any reference to the quantity of the action and the reaction. However, not every action has a reaction, for there is no reaction to the prime mover since he is immovable. The action indicated here is of a movable mover.

10. The mover too may be in motion, but qua movable and not qua a mover. In an unqualified way, then, a motion is of a movable (object), but not of the mover; for some movers, i.e., immovable movers, cannot be in motion.

11. Not all manuscripts include "or a *so-much*", and perhaps correctly so; for a mover is either a *composite* (a *this*) or a form (e.g., God or some form).

12. A moving cause.

3

1. Perhaps he is referring to the familiar problem of whether a motion is in the mover or in the movable or in both (201a25–7) or the (less likely) problem of whether a motion exists apart from things (200b32–3).

2. The actuality of the mover and the moved is not distinct numerically although it is distinct in formula, as the example of the interval from A to B indicates later on. Both actualities must exist simultaneously, and they are inseparable parts of a whole. A mover does not cause a motion if that motion is not in the movable, and the movable is not in motion unless it is being caused by the mover. We have a case of a relation which is impossible without the two things which are related.

3. In the first case, the interval is viewed from A in the upward direction to B; in the second, in the downward direction from B to A. It is in a way like the two vectors $\overrightarrow{AB}$ and $\overrightarrow{BA}$ which, though equal in magnitude, have opposite directions. Likewise, the two *actualities* of the mover and of the moved are numerically one, but the definition of the *actuality* of the mover differs from that of the moved.

4. The third alternative (both *actualities* being in the mover) is omitted, perhaps (1) because it is somewhat similar to alternative (a), and so there would be a repetition of arguments, or (2) because it has been stated that a motion is in the movable, and this would either

exclude that alternative or else allow the mover to be movable and thus call for another mover, in which case we would be back to the same problem of the mover and the movable.

5. The distinction between that which acts and that which is affected still stands, and arbitrary usage of names will not destroy that distinction.

6. That is, the argument which applies to that which is acting and that which is being affected applies also to the mover and the moved.

7. If every mover is moved, then any given mover in motion will need to have another mover causing it to be in motion, and this will lead to an infinite regress of movers, which is impossible (994a1–7). Moreover, it will be shown later that not every mover can cause self-motion (256a4–8b9).

8. An object in motion without something causing it to be moved is ruled out, for every motion is assumed to be caused by something.

9. In particular, the *actuality* of the mover will not be in the mover, but the *actuality* of a thing is in that thing itself, or else the mover will not be causing a motion.

10. A thing may accidentally have two motions at the same time, as when a man becomes sick and also thin or pale; but to have two motions always and at the same time is impossible. Besides, how can two motions always proceed to the same end, e.g., to the same sickness?

11. If the two motions (acting, and being acted upon) are one *actuality*, whether they are one in essence or inseparably one and so in one subject, then if one of the two motions is in a subject, so is the other.

Since in the argument it is assumed that the two motions are in the object which is being moved or affected, perhaps it is more proper to assign teaching and learning to the learner rather than to the teacher. However, both alternatives are still unreasonable.

12. The *actuality* of A includes the fact that it is upon B, and the *actuality* of B includes the fact that it is so by A, so the two *actualities* (if we are to call them "two") are like aspects of one *actuality*, differing in that they are viewed from different directions. It is like three in relation to six, the first being the half and the second being the double. So the *actuality* of both is numerically one, like the half-double relation.

13. To be (or the essence of) that which acts is not to be that which is acted upon, just as to be half of something is not to be the double of something.

14. In a statue, its *actuality* is the shape and its potentiality is the material (e.g., the bronze). Yet the statue is one thing, and the shape and the material cannot exist apart but exist as inseparable principles of the statue. It is likewise with that which acts and that which is acted upon qua such.

15. That is, numerically the same and not the same in essence.

16. The formula (or definition) of clothing is the same as that of garment, so the terms "clothing" and "garment" are synonyms.

17. 202a18–20.

18. For example, the definition (which states the essence) of a triangle and a trilateral is the same: "a three-sided plane figure". And if two things have the same definition, they have the same essential attributes, and if they have the same essential attributes, they have the same definition.

19. He may mean that teaching and learning are the same numerically; or else, like the term "distance", the terms "teaching" and "learning" are used dialectically to signify the same relation of that which teaches and that which learns, without reference to the direction from the one or from the other.

20. By "the main sense" he means the sense of the term "teaching" (and likewise for "learning"), which includes the direction from that which teaches to that which learns.

21. The motion is numerically the same, even if two aspects or principles are included in it (that which moves another and that which is moved by another).

22. Here A is that which acts or causes a motion, and B is that which is affected or caused to be in motion.

23. For example, alteration has species, and one should define alteration (in general) in generic terms, but each species of alteration in specific terms.

4

1. As indicated in 200b15–21, after a discussion of motion, certain attributes of motion will be considered, the infinite being one of them. Of course, the infinite belongs also to magnitudes and to time and to number.

2. The term "infinite" has many senses, one being the contradictory of the finite and another a sort of contrary of the finite (204a2–7); and the use of "perhaps" indicates a dialectical stage of the usage of the term. Since a point or an affection is not a quantity and therefore cannot be finite, neither can it be infinite, if "infinite" signifies the contrary of finite.

3. As stated in the *Posterior Analytics* (89b23–35), in considering a thing, we should first establish its existence and its whatness.

4. By "a principle" here he probably means a substance of some kind, as opposed to an attribute which, by existing in another thing, is not a principle.

5. That is, a material substance, so to speak, but neither a substance as form, nor an attribute.

6. 213b22–5, 985b23–6a23.

7. 209b33–210a2, 987a29–8a14.

8. Probably the infinity of things in kind as well as in number is meant, or else the Pythagoreans may not have been explicit.

9. Whether the Greek for "and apart" (χωρίς) is a corruption or a Pythagorean expression or Aristotle's abbreviation is not known. Per-

haps Aristotle is citing an example used by the Pythagoreans to support their doctrine of the *Even* or the *Infinite* as the principle from which the infinitude of things arises.

Fig. 1 shows that if consecutive gnomons, each of them an odd number, are placed around the one, which is indivisible, the result is always the same, a square, for $1 + 3 + 5 + \ldots + (2n - 1) = n.^2$

Various interpretations have been put forward for the second case (see Ross, *Aristotle's Physics,* pp. 542–5). (1) Milhaud, Burnet, and Heath suggest gnomons around two, which is even, as in Fig. 2(a), in which $2 + 4 + 6 + \ldots + 2n = n(n + 1)$; and as the ratio $n : (n + 1)$ of the sides of the resulting rectangle always varies as n varies, so the form of the rectangle varies. If by "apart" Aristotle means neglecting the unit around which gnomons are placed, we have Fig. 2(b), in which what results is $n^2 - 1$ or $(n - 1)(n + 1)$, a rectangular number, not a square, and with the ratio $(n - 1) : (n + 1)$ of its sides always varying.

Whatever the interpretation, the main point is that what is even or divisible or unlimited gives rise to a plurality or infinitude of things, but that which is indivisible or that which limits causes oneness or uniqueness.

10. Perhaps because in things there may be an indefinite increase as well as an indefinite decrease.

11. That nature would be not a substance like *Water* (Thales) or *Air* (Diogenes, 983b20–4a7) or something intermediate (303a10–2, 989a12–5), but an attribute; and for both Anaxagoras and Democritus, it would be a continuum or a quantity of substances resulting by contact.

12. This is the moving principle, *Intelligence.*

13. These are indivisible particles or atoms.

14. Just as Thales posits *Water,* so Democritus posits common body as the material principle. This body would be something solid, without any of the other sensible qualities like heat or cold or sweetness or the like; and so the indivisible atoms of Democritus (and Newton seems to follow him here in a sense) are the same with respect to the kind of matter, but they differ in size and shape (1042b11–5).

15. The reasons that follow are, of course, dialectical.

16. What exists in vain happens sometimes, and so it is posterior in existence and in definition to what exists for the most part or necessarily; but a principle is prior in existence and in definition, and the infinite, being a principle, does not exist in vain.

17. If the infinite has no principle or beginning, it is itself a principle; a sphere, on the other hand, has a beginning or a principle, and this is its surface which limits it. The argument seems dialectical.

18. What are generated or destroyed are *composites* of principles, not the principles themselves; and besides, since the infinite is inexhaustible and not finite, neither can it be finally generated nor can it be finally destroyed.

19. What contains is a principle, like the surface of a sphere or the

form of a thing; what rules is a principle, for this is a moving cause, and causes are principles; what is eternal is a principle, for the eternal is the cause of the temporal. These and others like these may be used as dialectical arguments.

20. Criticism of these beliefs will be given in 208a5–23.

21. It is assumed in this sophistical argument that, if a thing is destroyed, nothing remains of it after its destruction, and so an infinite supply is needed for the endless generation of new things.

22. The argument seems to rest (a) on the assumption that what appears to be or is thought to be the case actually is the case, an assumption used also to deny the principle of contradiction (1009a6–16), and (b) on the Pythagorean assumption that what is outside of heaven is infinite.

23. The existence of a void, into which a body may enter, is assumed here.

24. If a place is that in which a body can be, then an infinite place is that in which an infinite body can be; but if no infinite body exists, and no such body can be generated from what is finite, then by definition no infinite place can exist. Thus, if an infinite body can exist in an infinite place, such a body must exist.

25. What is eternal is necessary, and conversely (337b35–8a2); and one of the meanings of "it may be" is "it is necessary that it be" (25a37–9).

26. For example, equality is an essential attribute of quantity, not that every quantity is equal to any quantity, but that equality can exist only in the genus of quantity; in other words, what is equal must be a quantity.

27. By using "infinity", Aristotle may be referring to Plato's *Great* and *Small* or to the *Even* of the Pythagoreans or to some other principle, none of which is in any genus or category; as for an infinite plurality, this is not necessarily in a given category, for a plurality must be numerable in order to be a number (1020a8–9, 1057a2–4).

28. Of course, qua sensible, such a body must be considered by the physicist. Further, if such a body does not exist, neither does an infinite mathematical solid exist, for a solid (i.e., volume) is an attribute of a physical body.

29. Just as redness is neither curved nor straight, as it is not a line to which one of the two belongs (but the contradictories "not curved" and "not straight" are predicates of redness), so "infinite" in this sense applies to what is not a quantity and signifies that contradictory of finite which is not the privation of finite.

30. Another way of saying (b) is this: You can start going through it, since its nature admits this, but you will never finish going through all of it.

31. An example of an infinite with respect to addition is an ever increasing number; one with respect to division, when one starts with the straight line AB, bisects it at A_1, then bisects A_1B at A_2, then A_2B

at A_3, and so on indefinitely; and an infinite with respect to both, when in the line AB just considered, in addition to its division, one takes the sum $AA_1 + A_1A_2 + A_2A_3 + \ldots$ without reaching an end but gets closer and closer to the length AB, or one begins to number the parts AA_1, A_1A_2, A_2A_3, etc.

5

1. That is, if its nature is such that it is not an attribute of something else but is a separate substance like air or a man.

2. He has in mind Plato and the Pythagoreans, who posited an infinite as a principle separate from sensible things.

3. A magnitude is an attribute of, let us say, a body; it is not itself a substance. Likewise, a numerable plurality is a number, but also a number of something, say of men or horses, and so such plurality is not a substance.

4. If a substance is divisible, it is qua a magnitude and not qua a substance. There is no such thing as half of a man qua a substance.

5. This is the first sense in 204a3–4, in which the infinite is the contradictory and not the contrary of the finite.

6. Neither Plato nor the Pythagoreans consider the infinite as indivisible in the first sense; and they posit it as a substance.

7. This is: as something in sense 2(a) in 204a4–6.

8. He means an element as matter, for this is how Plato regarded it, calling it also "the *Dyad*" or "the *Great* and *Small*", and this is how the Pythagoreans regarded it, calling it also "the *Even*".

9. If it is an attribute, and an attribute of something, but not of a number or of a magnitude (to which it is usually regarded as belonging), then of what?

10. If it is an attribute of a number, and an attribute is posterior in existence to its subject (whiteness cannot exist without a body, but a body can exist without whiteness), then the infinite cannot be an element and a principle; thus the *Even* of the Pythagoreans as an attribute would belong to a plurality or to a magnitude and would therefore not be a material element or a principle, and the same applies to Plato's *Great* and *Small*.

11. An alternative to "substance" is "*substance*".

12. He now considers the infinite as a substance and a principle but with parts; and each part in this case would have to be infinite, for if something else, then this would be a principle and not the infinite to begin with. Does he mean by "a thing in *actuality*" just a form or matter or a *composite* of form and matter? Perhaps his argument is directed against Plato and the Pythagoreans, who may not have been clear about it. If it is just matter or just form, then, as divisible and a principle, both the infinite and to be infinite would seem to be the same (1043b1–4).

13. Is it because qua divisible it would be a quantity or because an *actuality* or a *substance* is indivisible or because "infinitely divisible"

would give rise to two senses of "infinite" (one as a principle and another as an attribute) or because of something else?

14. If the infinite is a substance like air and so divisible, then like air it too would have quantity; but air, though an element, is not pure matter like the *Even* or the *Great* and *Small*. Is this the argument?

15. Whether he means a substance in the sense of just matter or not is not clear. Then again, the Pythagoreans were probably vague about it, for they used the *Even* like just matter, and at the same time they gave it the attribute of divisibility, thus making it a sort of quantity.

16. Whether he is referring to Plato's Mathematical Objects and the Ideas or to the mathematical objects which are abstracted from sensible objects and are intelligible or to both is not clear.

17. Perhaps by "logically" he means from premises which are dialectical or arise from definitions and other such considerations and not from those within a specific field. This contrasts with "from the point of view of physics" taken up next, in which factual premises from physics are used.

18. That which is sensible or thinkable and has magnitude must have a surface, and its definition must include a surface. Also, to be numerable is to have a number by which a thing can be mathematically known; and a number is finite by definition and therefore can be actually traversed; but the infinite cannot be traversed, so a number cannot be infinite.

19. These are the material elements, such as air, fire, water, and earth, and these are assumed to have such elementary sensible attributes as heat, cold, etc.

20. He assumes "infinite" to mean a magnitude in the direction of increase without an end. So if, for example, the element which has heat as its contrary were infinite in magnitude, then, regardless of the ratio of heat to cold with respect to their power, it would destroy the contrary (coldness) of the other element, and so also that element itself. It is assumed that any two elements have at least one contrariety, whether heat and cold, moist and dry, or some other, so that the infinite element would destroy in turn each of the finite elements.

21. If all elements were infinite, it would follow from the definition of the infinite given here that all would occupy the same space, and this is impossible. Aristotle is not considering partial infinites, such as the space in each octant in a Cartesian System.

22. For example, air, fire, earth, and water, if these are regarded as the simple elements.

23. Such an infinite body would have none of the contraries which might cause any destruction.

24. Perhaps his meaning is this: If all things become fire, they will stay so, and further change is impossible; but changes are occurring.

25. The place of a body is the surface of the medium which coincides with the surface of the body; and a part of that body, whatever its place relative to the whole body, is by definition in the same place as the place of the whole body (212a20–1).

26. There is no more reason for that body to be travelling in one direction rather than in another (not to speak of the fact that there would not even be such a thing as a motion in some direction if the body were infinite, although for the sake of argument Aristotle seems to grant that there is); and the same applies to *resting* at one place rather than at another.

27. Perhaps here, too, the term "infinite place" is assumed to have meaning for the sake of argument; for a place is an inner surface of a containing body, and an infinite body cannot be contained by such a surface.

28. The word "it" here seems to refer to the infinite body.

29. Again, if no place exists to contain an infinite body, neither locomotion nor rest with respect to place can exist for that body, or even for any of its parts.

30. There is no more reason for an infinite body to move in one direction rather than in another or to be *resting* in one place rather than in another. But to be moving in all directions is evidently impossible; and to be *resting* everywhere is also impossible, if it is assumed that one or more places exist in each of which the body or a part of it may *rest*. Besides, as St. Thomas Aquinas points out, if always moving, *rest* will be impossible, and if always *resting*, motion will be impossible; but this cannot be, for nature is a principle of both motion and rest, and nature would be destroyed.

31. Literally, it should be "of unlikes", and whether these unlikes are wholes or parts is left out; and it should be "parts" if the universe is considered as one or as having unity, but loosely so, and "wholes" if it is considered as a plurality of wholes. Of course, what follows suggests unlike wholes.

32. The assumption seems to be this: Things tend to be with their kind; so if two things are different, then by nature their places are different.

33. In fact, only one part might be infinite, while the others would be in this part, as already considered in 204b19–22.

34. 204b13–9.

35. By *"One"* and *"Infinite"* here he is referring to a material principle posited by the natural philosophers.

36. Anaximenes and Diogenes posited *Air;* Thales posited *Water;* others, something between (303b10–3, 983b20–4a7, 989a12–5).

37. Fire is up, earth is down. The others have an indefinite place, and having no obvious contrariety, they are less likely to destroy anything.

38. Each part [or whole] is an element if it is homogeneous [always divisible into the same kind] or if it consists of the same kind of indivisible elements (1014a26–b15). The elements are not infinite in kind; for the places are finite (208b12–4) and for each place there corresponds one kind of body. Besides, if the elements are infinite in kind, knowledge of things having so many material elements will be impossible; and, in general, knowledge of the material elements of the universe will be im-

possible. Aristotle denies an infinitude of elements in kind (993a30–1b31).

39. Since a place is defined as the primary inner boundary of a containing body and such a boundary is finite, the body contained will be finite too.

40. If the place (primary inner boundary) is greater than the body contained, there will be a void between that place and the surface of the body; but a void will be shown not to exist (213a12–7b28).

41. If the body is larger than the place (if this phrase have any meaning at all), then part of some body (this body will be furthest away from the center of the universe) will be outside of every place, so to speak, or in no place at all.

42. Observation shows that stones are held up in air by force and that when let go they fall.

43. It is heavy, and the nature of what is heavy is to be at the Center.

44. Perhaps the contradiction, by implication, is this: Some parts are observed to be moving, whereas they should be at *rest*.

45. That is, neither the infinite body nor either of its halves can be either up or down or in any place.

46. An alternative to "how will one divide it", perhaps less probable, is "how will one make any distinctions", that is, how can one truly say that this place is the center, this is up, this is to the left, etc.? All parts, if "all" is the appropriate word, are alike.

Further, if we accept "how will one divide it" as the alternative, there seems to be a difficulty in getting equals or unequals. For one begins dividing by contact with the surface, and the infinite has no surface; besides, one may divide a body by a plane into equals or unequals, but a division of an infinite body by a plane into unequals, or even equals, does not seem to make sense.

47. The distinctions of up, down, and the rest do not exist in the case of an infinite body; for no outer limits exist, and there is no one point that is the center more than any other.

48. Relative to us, what is above our head is up, what is below is down, what is ahead of us is in front, etc.; but we may assume any position, e.g., standing, lying flat, etc.

49. That is, the whole universe.

50. Perhaps "place" is related to "somewhere" as a genus to a species. Thus the definition of a place applies equally to up, down, etc., as long as "the primary inner boundary of that which contains" is given. But in "somewhere" one must specify that the body is up or down or in this or in that place. Now what is in place, generically taken, must also be in a specified place, for the genus does not exist apart from all the species or the individuals, just as an animal must be a horse or a man or this horse, etc. Hence, from the text that follows, just as a quantity, generically taken, must be either three feet long or two units or the like, so that which is in a place must be either up or down, etc. To say that the infinite body is in a place, then, is to say that it is either up or down, etc.,

and to say any of these for an infinite body is either false or meaningless.

51. By definition, place is the inner boundary of a containing body.

6

1. Impossiblities follow not only if an actual infinite is assumed existing, but also if the infinite is denied altogether, that is, in every sense. Of course, the contradictory of actual existence is not actual non-existence, for there is also potential existence in some way between; so the impossibilities mentioned can be avoided by a definition of the infinite which uses potentiality.

2. A beginning or end of time would deny the eternity of motion and other beliefs assumed true; if a magnitude is not infinitely divisible, an important mathematical axiom and many consequent theorems will be false; and the denial of an infinite number appears false and limits the axioms of arithmetic.

3. For example, one may keep on adding one part after another to a line, thus increasing it indefinitely; or one may keep on taking away one part after another from a line by, let us say, bisecting it indefinitely.

4. 204a8–6a8.

5. 968a1–972b33, 992a20–2.

6. The potentially infinite cannot become an actual infinite.

7. If half of a line is taken away and if this is repeated indefinitely, what is taken away may still exist, but, in the case of men, they come and go (are born and die).

8. By the "same" he does not mean the same in essence, but numerically the same in some sense; for example, if line AB is bisected at A_1, then A_1B at A_2, A_2B at A_3, and so on without end, there arises at the same time a corresponding addition of the parts taken to the left, that is,

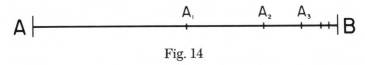

Fig. 14

the sum $AA_1 + A_1A_2 + A_2A_3 + \ldots$, which increases indefinitely and approaches the line AB without ever reaching it or surpassing it.

9. In the preceding Commentary the ratio was ½, but it can be shown mathematically that any ratio between 0 and 1 will result in a sum which approaches the line. For let $0 < r < 1$, and let p be the length of the line. Then after the first part on the left is taken away, the remainder is $p - pr$, or $p(1 - r)$; after the second part is taken away, the remainder is $p(1 - r)^2$; after the n-th part, it is $p(1 - r)^n$. But $p(1 - r)^n$ approaches 0 as n increases indefinitely. Hence, the sum on the left approaches but does not exceed p.

10. This is now known as the *Axiom of Archimedes,* but it was known

before him. Aristotle knew it, and either Eudoxus or someone else introduced it into mathematics as an axiom.

11. Perhaps he is referring to the infinite as it exists in a finite magnitude, the one under discussion; for the infinite in men, who come and go, or in time, which comes and goes, though potentially existing, is not limited in this manner.

12. Just as the games exist actually one after the other, but one is completed and another comes and it is not numerically one game that actually exists, so do divisions, or what is added or subtracted or is left after each division.

13. Perhaps what exists in virtue of itself here is the given finite magnitude, not as a substance but as a definite quantity, and the infinite is something which exists potentially or is coming to be but *within this magnitude*, as if an attribute of it, and as something potential it is like matter.

An alternative to "and, unlike that which is limited, it exists not in virtue of itself" is "and it exists not by itself, like that which is limited". In other words, the infinite is not something separate like a man or a table, but it is like matter which is limited by a form, for matter qua matter cannot exist by itself.

14. The corresponding infinite by addition, too, exists potentially and like matter, for it keeps on going by addition, and, like matter, it does so within a finite magnitude.

15. We might add that the infinite cannot surpass the magnitude of the universe, for nothing can exceed the universe in magnitude (207b15–21).

16. Shown in 204a8–6a8.

17. The *Great* and the *Small* (203a15–6), as matter (987b20–1).

18. In his later theory, Plato regards the Ideas as Numbers, each with units. Thus, whether we consider the *One* (the principle as form) as the smallest Number, or any unit in any Number, or any unit in a Mathematical Number, still there will be something smallest; and since Plato stops the Numbers with Ten, there is a maximum Number (991b9–31, 1084a12–5). The *Great* and *Small*, then, is useless in making possible an infinite in the direction of increase or decrease.

19. What is similar in both Figures is the fact that there is always something beyond that may be taken. In both Figures, if one reaches A_2 from A_1, there is yet A_2A_3 to be covered. But while in line A_1B the part A_2A_3 is always distinct from any preceding part, the corresponding part A_2A_3 in the ring will be taken many times as one goes around the ring many times. By "the main sense", then, he means that what is yet to be taken has not been taken before and so is distinct from any of the previous parts already taken.

20. By "this" he means something beyond yet to be taken, whether it has been taken before or not.

21. The part A_2A_3 in the ring is distinct from the preceeding part A_1A_2, and similarly for any two parts in succession.

22. It is implied here that that part has not yet been taken; or else this implication is included in the phrase "with respect to taking a quantity".

23. 1023b26–7.

24. There are also other meanings of the term "whole" (1023b26–4a10).

25. Perhaps "complete" is wider in meaning or is used with a greater number of meanings than "whole". For example, for Aristotle, God is complete (or perfect) but not a whole, for He has no parts (1021b12–2a3, 1023b26–4a10).

26. Perhaps τὸ ἄπειρον ὅλον should be ἄπειρον τὸ ὅλον, and this is confirmed by 167b13–4, 181a27–9, 185a32–3, 254a24–5; so we translate accordingly. As it stands, the translation would be "for the latter says that the infinite is a whole".

27. The expression *"to tie a string to a string"* seems to be an idiom or a metaphor or a proverb and is intended to indicate attributes which are common to things in virtue of their similarity. Aristotle denies that the infinite has such similarity to the whole.

28. Matter is that which is potentially this or that, and qua potentially something, it is in the process of coming to be something; and an infinite quantity is one that is in the process of becoming or of tending to something although never getting there. So the infinite is like matter in a sense.

29. It is the complete magnitude, which has the infinite as matter, that is a whole and finite; and to say that the infinite is a whole is in a sense like saying that the white, which is a man, is a whole, for here too the white is an attribute and in a sense a part of the man and is not by itself a whole (substance).

So the infinite is only matter of the completeness of a magnitude, that is, only matter within a complete magnitude and not the whole magnitude. We start with a whole magnitude, and the infinite is in that magnitude, like the infinite bisection of it.

30. Like matter (1036a8–9), the infinite is unknowable in itself; for how can we definitely know what an infinite quantity is while it is still in the process of becoming?

31. For Plato, the *Infinite* is the *Great* and *Small*, and this is posited as the material principle; and it is so posited that, although indefinite, it is given a limit only when it receives the *One*, which is the principle of all forms or the principle as form (987b18–22). So Plato, too, considers the *Infite* as matter and as a part of each Idea and each sensible thing, and he does not regard the *Infinite* as containing the Ideas or the sensible things.

7

1. If the infinite could surpass every magnitude, it would contain every magnitude (even the largest or the magnitude of the universe, in

which case the universe would not even be the largest) and would not be contained by any magnitude. But like matter, it is contained, for what contains is a form; and the infinite in the direction of smallness in magnitude is in the direction of what is contained and not in the direction of what contains.

2. This is the unit, which is indivisible and a measure in a number, and it is a principle or beginning of number but not a number.

3. A problem seems to arise: If three men is a number and a number is one thing, then three men is one thing and not just a plurality. Three men, then, seems to be a very loose unity; for each man, being a substance, is a unity in the proper sense. One may say that measurability is the cause of unity in three men, for the measure is one man; but measurability here seems to be a weak cause for unity. It is not like a line three feet long, for the unity here is caused by the continuity between two successive lengths each one foot long.

In calling "two" and "three" derivative terms, perhaps he wishes to emphasize the plurality of the unities in the number two or the number three, and not the unity (if there is a unity) of each number; and the expression "a number is many ones" seems to indicate this.

4. Since a magnitude is divisible into magnitudes, division of a magnitude has no end. And as such division may proceed without end, the resulting number of magnitudes may also increase without end (that is, infinitely); and such a number exists potentially, since it never stops so as to be definite and actual.

5. The number increases simultaneously with each bisection of a magnitude.

6. But the magnitudes resulting from bisection exist simultaneously, while the parts of time or of motion come and go. Thus, as motion continues indefinitely, one day comes and another goes.

7. The size of the universe, then, can be neither exceeded nor expanded; and it is finite.

8. Motion takes place in or along a magnitude, and time is an attribute and is defined in terms of motion. So magnitude comes first, then motion, then time. For example, let A move over B in time T. Since A is infinitely divisible, there will be infinite parts of A each with a motion and so an infinity of partial motions, and since B is infinitely divisible, there will be an infinite divisibility of motions of A along B; and each of the latter infinite motions along B will take some time, and so the time taken for A to move along B is infinitely divisible. Thus the infinite in magnitude is prior to that in motion, and that in motion is prior to that in time (217b29–220a26, 231a21–5b5).

9. Theorems in Greek mathematics were concerned with definite mathematical objects, and when the infinite was used, it was as a potential and not as an actual infinite, as in the theorem that the prime numbers are infinite; for here the proof rests upon the denial of a greatest prime, and the denial of an actuality is not necessarily another actuality. Thus, just as numbers are potentially infinite, so are prime numbers.

10. Of course, the phrase "as far as they wish" is true as long as the distance does not exceed the diameter of the universe. The theorems concerning magnitudes, then, will be true only for any existing or potential magnitudes and not for all hypothetical ones, and their universality is likewise limited; so a statement such as "the angles of an equilateral triangle, of sides greater than the diameter of the universe, are equal" will be false, since such a triangle does not have even a potential existence. Anyway, the mathematician need not worry about such limitations (for this is the task of the physicist), as long as magnitudes exist which make universal theorems about them possible. Perhaps the term "universal" should be defined so as to include the limitation indicated.

11. The infinite is the privation of the completeness of a magnitude, and, as something incomplete and a part, it is like matter.

12. It exists in the continuous, which in turn exists in sensible bodies; and just as sensible bodies are neither actually infinite nor as great as one may wish, so the existence of the potential infinite will be subject to the corresponding limitations.

An alternative to "the subject in virtue of which it exists" is "the subject which exists by itself", that is, the separate subject in which the infinite exists.

13. Plato uses the *Infinite* (*Great* and *Small*) as matter; the Pythagoreans use it (the *Even*) likewise, etc.

8

1. Errors may be committed either by positing false premises or by concluding falsely from premises. Perhaps by "not necessary" he means that the conclusions do not follow, and by "true replies", that there is falsity in the premises they use.

2. This answers the second argument for the existence of an actual infinite (203b18–20). In generation or destruction there is a subject or matter which remains the same; hence, while one thing is being generated, another is being destroyed, the matter remaining the same, and so an infinite source of matter is not necessary.

3. In this argument (203b20–2), the premise that every body touches another is false. A body may or may not touch another, so touching another body is an accident and not a necessary attribute of a body. A body, on the other hand, is of necessity limited by its own shape, and the limit (i.e., the shape) of a body is in that body and is not related to some other body. Aristotle's reply, then, is that the universe has a limit, its shape, and that there is nothing outside of it touching that limit.

4. Perhaps by "excess and deficiency" he means a state of affairs in which things are or are thought to be bigger or smaller or, in general, different from what they actually are. Of course, things are what they are, and if they are thought to be different, such thought is false. Thus thoughts of actual infinity or of an infinite body or infinite universe are

false; or, in general, a thought is accidental to the thing, that is, it may or may not signify the thing as it actually exists. This answers the argument in lines 203b22–30.

5. Just as a motion comes and goes, so does time, since the latter is an attribute of a motion; and a motion is not *actually* infinite, for as one part comes, another is destroyed. This answers the argument in lines 203b16–7.

6. This answers the argument in lines 203b17–8. If one keeps on cutting a magnitude continually, no final magnitude is reached, and so no magnitude which is actually infinite in smallness is reached; and if a magnitude is increased through thought, then likewise no actual magnitude which is infinitely large is reached, and thinking about a magnitude does not affect the magnitude anyway.

Book Δ

1

1. These beliefs, though pointing to the existence of a place, are not altogether true; for only bodies are in a place, while things which are not bodies are not in a place or are accidentally in a place. God is not in a place; and a thought is in a place only accidentally, for it is in a body, and it is this that is in a place in the proper sense.

2. Locomotion is most common since in every kind of motion there is a locomotion. Perhaps the term κυριωτάτη, translated as "most independent", means that every other motion or change depends on a locomotion. Hence, locomotion is prior in existence to the other changes (243a10–1, 260a26–1a26, 1072b8–9, 1073a12).

3. He says "place or space", for at this stage the problem of whether a place is a boundary or an interval between boundaries is not settled.

4. Different places seem to have different powers; for example, the place called "down" seems to attract earth or what is heavy, but not fire or what is light. This is a dialectical argument.

5. Only bodies are in a place. Mathematical objects are not bodies and so have no physical matter or weight; they are just attributes of bodies or substances. Hence, they are not in a place, in the proper sense. But lines and surfaces and solids have parts, and these have relative position, and relative to us they are thought in some position; so relative to us, they and their parts have relative position accidentally (as attributes) and in a weaker sense than bodies do, for the latter at least are in a place.

6. That is, each mathematical object has no nature of being up or down or to the left or somewhere in general, although we may think of it as having a place.

7. The *Gap* here seems to be posited (by Hesiod, 984b27–31) as something like a space or a place.

8. That is, prior in existence to all other things, or first in existence. For Aristotle, of course, a place is only an attribute, and so it does not have such priority.

9. That which exists actually must come under one of the categories; and if it exists in some other way, e.g., as something potentially, it must be a principle or a cause. The arguments against the belief in the existence of a place which follow are dialectical.

10. He means primarily in the same thing, for two men may both be in a room, but secondarily so, since each is primarily in a different part of the room. That two bodies cannot be (fully) in the same place primarily is taken as a fact or a principle.

11. For they, too, are somewhere, and they, too, are replaced when the body is replaced.

12. While the mass of a body might be considered as distinct from the interval (which may be taken as a space or a void) which it occupies, a point cannot be taken as distinct from an interval, for there is no interval for it. This argument seems to assume a place as being a sort of space or an interval or a void.

13. By "having such a nature" he means that a place has magnitude but is not a body, as he indicates in what follows. Since a place is not a body, it is neither a corporeal element nor composed of corporeal elements; and since neither the elements of incorporeal things nor the composites of such elements have magnitude, while a place does have magnitude, it follows that a place cannot be incorporeal, whether an incorporeal element or an incorporeal composite.

Apparently, here the intelligible and the incorporeal are identified, or else the incorporeal comes under the intelligible, and the argument has more force if what is intelligible excludes mathematical magnitudes. Such intelligibles would then be such things as genus, differentia, thoughts, etc.

14. In considering whether a place is a cause (or a principle), Aristotle goes beyond the categories, for not every cause comes under a category; matter does not come under a category.

A place cannot be a cause as matter, for it is not a corporeal or an incorporeal element. It cannot be a cause as the form of a thing, for the thing is always with its own form though it may change from one place to another. It cannot be a moving cause, for contact is necessary to move something, whereas a place is not a body and so cannot touch anything; and to say that the place of earth causes it to come down is to admit action at a distance, which for Aristotle is impossible. And it cannot be a final cause; for a man, for example, would have two final causes, both his happiness and his place (which is ridiculous). Other arguments might be added.

15. An infinite regress is impossible; consequently, the belief that a

place exists and that everything is in a place leads to something impossible.

16. Perhaps he means that there is no place which is void or empty, that is, without a body, and so place and body are coextensive.

17. The difficulty arises from the fact that since it is only bodies that can move, a place must be motionless, and so if the dimensions of a body are the same as those of its place, the growth of a body would imply that its place too grows and so moves.

2

1. What is contrasted here is a predicate which is proper as against one which is not proper.

2. The meanings of "proper place" and "common place" and "to contain primarily" are still to be worked out in full.

3. An alternative to "or" is "and".

4. Such removal cannot be actually performed, so perhaps a removal in thought is meant; or, the removal is posited as a hypothesis, for the sake of the argument.

5. Plato seems to use "receptacle", "space", and "matter" synonymously.

6. Perhaps it is in the *Unpublished Doctrines,* or the formal doctrines of his thought, where Plato considers the *Great* and the *Small* as the material cause of things (987b18–22, 988a8–14).

7. The investigation of matter and form comes under first philosophy, and this is the most difficult science (982a4–25).

8. For example, heat and hardness and other such attributes would be possessions.

9. Like a vessel, which remains one and the same, a place can contain now one body and now another, and so it is not any of them.

10. That is, of the thing it contains.

11. In other words, when we speak of a thing as being in a place, we speak of it in relation to some other thing; so a place is not something in the thing itself but is outside of it, whether it be something in itself or in something else. From what follows, a place is in a containing body.

12. Plato spoke first of Forms or Ideas as generated from the *One* as form and the *Great* and *Small* as matter; later he said that Forms are Numbers. So if the *Great* and *Small* (or matter or the receptacle or space or place) is what receives the *One,* then the *One* as form is in the *Great* and *Small* or in place as matter; and in general, since the Ideas have *Great* and *Small* or a place in them, they are in place in some sense.

13. If a thing, while remaining itself, always has its matter and its form, how can it travel to its matter or to its form if either of these were a place to travel to? That towards which a thing travels must be outside of it; so a place is not in the form or in the matter of the thing but is outside of the thing.

14. To be carried to a place, whether up or down, the place or up or down must be outside of the thing.

15. If a place is in the thing itself, whether in its form or its matter, and if it is also assumed that a thing is going to a place which may vary and to which it has not yet arrived, then a thing would be in that place at the time of arrival, and so the thing's form or matter (which is also a place) would also be in that place; and the latter place would be distinct from the thing's matter or form, which is also a place. Hence a place (as form or matter) would be in another place.

16. Will the destruction be of the form or of the matter of the thing? The argument still rests on the assumption that the place of a thing is either the form or the matter of that thing. It is also assumed that if air becomes water, the air's place is destroyed, since the water generated does not have that place.

Now if the place of the air is its matter and the matter of both the air and the water which is generated from the air is the same (since the matter is not destroyed during a generation), then the place of the air will not be destroyed, contrary to the common opinion that the place of the water generated is distinct from that of the air destroyed. But if the place of the air is its form, perhaps the argument is or might be this: Since the form of the air is destroyed and the form here is its place, the place of the air is destroyed; but this cannot be, for the place of the air after its destruction will remain the same since it will be the place of some other body.

3

1. The senses of the "in" are considered also in 1023a8–25.

2. Perhaps a material part is meant.

3. In an analogous sense, this seems like (2), for the genus is divided in a sense into the various species and cannot exist apart from the species.

4. In an analogous sense, this seems like (1), for a definition as an expression has parts, and these are like material parts.

5. Health is a certain proportion (a kind of form) of the hot and the cold (139b20–1, 145b7–11).

6. The term "form" here is used in a wide sense; it is not restricted to just substantial form. Health, in the example given, is such a form.

7. The Greek word for "in" here is idiomatic; in English, perhaps "depend on" or some other such expression is more proper. The relation is between that which is moved or effected and the moving cause.

8. As in the previous Commentary, here too the Greek word for "in" is idiomatic; in English, perhaps "is determined by" or "is a means to" or some other such expression is more proper. The relation seems to be that between the means and the end or between that which desires or is done or is required and that which is desired or for the sake of which something is done or which dictates what is required.

9. An alternative to "most important" is "most proper" or "main". This is the sense to be discussed in connection with place.

10. Anaxagoras spoke of a thing (the *Infinite*) as being in itself (205b1–5). Perhaps others did so.

11. For example, in calling a man "sick" when just his eye is diseased, we take sickness to be not in the whole body or the whole man but in something else, the eye, which is only a part of him or of his body.

12. Just as the man is called "sick" when sickness is only in the eye, so he is called "white" or "scientist" when whiteness or science is in just a part of him; for whiteness is not in the whole man but in the surface of his skin, and in the same way science (e.g., mathematics) is in his reasoning power. Thus he (qua his sickness in the eye) is in himself (qua the eye), but the sickness and the eye are distinct parts.

13. He is considering the jar in itself and not with respect to its having parts, and likewise for the wine. And when each is so considered and the wine is in the jar and the two are the only two parts of the whole (which consists of the jar and the wine), then each of them is in the whole in sense (1). Of course, if each is considered as actually one, then the wine is in the jar in the primary sense (8), but he is not considering this sense here.

14. He is addressed in this manner in virtue of something else, that is, in virtue of a part.

15. That is, in virtue of the fact that each part is in the whole.

16. Whiteness is in a surface primarily and not in virtue of something else (1022a14–36).

17. The surface is a physical quantity, whiteness is a color and a quality, and the surface is related to whiteness as a subject to an attribute or to a form (in the wide sense). Thus if "A is in itself" is to be true, "A" and "itself" must not have the same meaning.

18. By "inductively" he is referring to the list of the eight senses in which "in" has been used; and by "thing" he means a thing as a whole or in its entirety, without reference to its parts, and this becomes evident from the examples that follow.

19. Perhaps the meaning is this: Whatever may be the sense in which "A is in B" is true, A and B must be distinct in essence or definition, and so "A is in A" cannot be true if A has just one meaning.

20. An alternative phrase to "what it is to be each" is "the essence of each"; the two phrases have the same meaning.

21. That is, distinct in essence, and hence in definition, for a definition is a statement of the essence (101b39).

22. In a thermos bottle full of coffee, the coffee is in the bottle primarily (that is, the boundary of the coffee touches the inner boundary of the bottle), and the bottle is in the surrounding air primarily (that is, the outer surface of the bottle touches the inner surface of the surrounding air). But the inner boundary of the bottle, which is the place for the coffee, is in the bottle as an attribute of it and not in the sense that the

bottle is the place for that boundary; for the bottle is a substance and not a place, and to say that the coffee is in the bottle is to say that it is in the bottle's place in the sense indicated (the bottle's inner boundary and the coffee's outer boundary coincide).

Thus, if one truly says "A is in B, B is in C, C is in D, etc., to infinity", he is using "in" equivocally; and it is possible to say so truly, for, using "in" alternately in senses (3) and (4), one may truly say that "man" is in "animal", "animal" is in "man", "man" is in "animal", etc., to infinity. Zeno, then, has not shown a process to infinity by using a univocal meaning of "in".

23. For example, while the inner boundary of the containing vessel, which has wine, is in the vessel in the sense that it is an attribute of the vessel, that boundary, also called "the place in which the wine is", is no part of the wine contained, and so it is neither the form nor the matter of the wine.

4

1. The four attributes of a place which follow are dialectical, admitted by most thinkers. Any definition of a place, then, should, among other things, somehow contain these attributes if it is not (a) to be too general or (b) to avoid what people have in mind when they are discussing or thinking of what goes by the name of "place". The same method is used in establishing the whatness or definition of the soul (402b16–3a2).

2. In other words, the dimensions of a primary place coincide with those of the body contained.

3. For example, the inner boundary of a cup, while remaining one and the same, may contain now coffee, now tea, now water, etc. By "separable from it" he does not mean that it is separable in such a way as not to contain anything.

4. Perhaps the other directions (right, left, front, behind) are not as generally admitted as up and down, and so for dialectical purposes only up and down are assumed.

5. Up and down are the contraries, the intermediates are mixtures of up and down, or else they are up and down in a relative way (the place of water is up relative to that of earth, down relative to that of air or fire). Aristotle often gives only the two contraries, leaving the others to be supplied by the reader.

6. It appears that "motion with respect to place" here is used like a genus with "locomotion" and "increase or decrease" as species. If so, then a locomotion may be a motion with respect to place but not with respect to quantity, as when a body moves up or down; and an increase or decrease may be a motion with respect to quantity (for if a body increases, its primary place changes) but not with respect to just place, as when a fish in the water grows. Of course, a body may have both a locomotion and an increase (or decrease) at the same time.

7. This would be a body which is in motion, and such a body is one (like one man) and is not a part of another body (like a hand).

8. When detached, a hand or a nail can be in motion, as when it falls upon release.

9. In general, only composites of form and physical matter, which are substances, may be in motion essentially; things in the other categories cannot be in motion essentially (1067b9–11), but they may be accidentally, that is, as attributes or principles existing in a body.

10. Literally, the English term for ἔσχατον is "last", which may lead to ambiguity; so we use "the innermost part". An alternative is "the innermost boundary". In this example, this is the air's inner surface, which coincides with the surface of the body T.

11. It is in the air just as the inner surface of a tomato can is in the tomato can, and in general, as an attribute is in a subject.

12. According to the second requirement (211a1–2), the magnitude of T is equal to that of the place in which it is.

13. This is a material part, like a finger in a hand or the heart in an animal's body.

14. Here, unlike a finger, which is a part of a hand, that which contains and that which is contained are not parts of one thing but are actually two things; and their relation is that of touching and not of being continuous.

15. This part is a part of the containing body, not of the contained body; and it is a part as an attribute.

16. Since the relation of a part to a whole is distinct from that of one thing to another thing, the distinction between the motion of a part and that of a whole is necessary; and "with" is used in the first case, but "in" in the second.

17. Sight is a part of the eye as the form is a part of the *composite*, while a hand is a part of the body as a material part; but both sight and the hand are parts, though in a distinct sense (1023b12–25). Perhaps a better example than that of the eye could have been used, for the eye itself is a part of something else. For example, the shape of a statue is such a part of the statue.

18. The water and the vessel are two distinct things, so neither is a part of the other or of the two taken as if one.

19. The term *"shape"* here is restricted to the surface of the body contained, like the surface of a statue.

20. This is the matter of the body contained, like the wine without its shape or the bronze of a statue without the shape of the statue.

21. What is meant is not the matter, but something like space or void as if occupied by matter or by the contained body. The term "interval" here is used dialectically, not necessarily signifying something which exists.

22. This is what we earlier called "the innermost parts" or "the innermost boundaries", which belong to (or are parts of) the containing body and not to what is contained.

23. These are (1), (2), and (3).

24. In a sense, the *shape* of a body contains the body; and one may be misled in believing that a place is the *shape* of a body. Again, that *shape* coincides with the inner surface of the surrounding body which touches the contained body, and the two touching surfaces are distinct; but the *shape* of the body cannot be its place since by requirement (1) the body's place is no part of that body.

25. If that which contains remains the same while that which is contained comes and goes, that in which the contained thing exists seems to be the space or interval within the inner surface of the container, as if a sort of void or space within, for example, a can which contains soup.

26. Aristotle holds that that which contains (primarily) is the inner surface of the containing body, for no empty space or void exists within that surface. (This will be considered in detail when the void is discussed.)

27. Manuscripts differ in details as to the text. If the text in line 211b20, by transferring the comma, were πεφυκὸς καὶ μένον, ἐν τῷ αὐτῷ ἄπειροι ἄν ἦσαν τόποι and if the interval is assumed stationary as a whole within the container just as the contained body is stationary as a whole in the container even if the container may be in motion relative to an outside object, then, in view of the text that follows, the following consistent argument results.

Let also an interval which is distinct from the body contained exist in any container, and let us assume a number of concentric spherical surfaces A_1, A_2, A_3, etc.—A_1 contained by A_2, A_2 by A_3, etc.—and also a body within A_1 and between the interval of any two spherical surfaces in succession, as between A_2 and A_3. Then since A_2 contains its contents (the body between A_1 and A_2 and also A_1) and also has an interval I_2, while A_1 contains a body and also an interval I_1, I_1 and part of I_2 will be together; and using the same argument, I_1 will coincide with a part of I_2, a part of I_3, etc. So if each I is regarded as being a place, there will be many places in the same place (let this place be I_1). Thus a place may be in another place, and many places may be together. In addition, if A_1 moves, its interval I_1 (which is considered as being a place) will also move to another interval (or place).

The water mentioned in the vessel may be regarded as a set of concentric containers; and the argument is similar.

28. Perhaps the argument, which is Aristotle's position, is as follows.

Consider a spherical shell A of some thickness as being full of water W, A being surrounded by a body B. Let the inner surface of A be P_1 (this is a place for Aristotle, and it is an attribute of A). Now P_1 touches the surface of W, and W is said to be in place P_1, or else in A but in virtue of being in P_1 or in virtue of touching P_1. Also, any part W_1 of W is also said to be in A, but in virtue of W, which is a whole.

If A moves to some other place (if it becomes surrounded by another body C), then W is still in A; and any part W_1 of W, whether in motion or at rest relative to the other parts of W, is also in A, for a part is not a unity and has only potential existence and is therefore in a place in virtue of the whole (W_1 is in A in virtue of W). If W remains in A, then the parts of W, if in motion relative to each other, replace each other in A, regardless of whether A is at rest or in motion, and they are in A in virtue of being parts of W. Now A itself may be in motion, but this is another matter.

The translation "for the air . . . heaven", of lines 211b27–9, is literal, but there is some difficulty in meaning. Perhaps there is some corruption in the Greek. The expression "part of a place" is meaningless or strange, for if a place is an inner boundary, a part of that place would be a part of that boundary; but how can a part of that which is contained have as its place only a part of that boundary? We may offer one interpretation, though others are possible, depending on Aristotle's direction of thought. The sphere A may be moving from one place to another, but not what that sphere contains; but A may always be in B, if B has A and other bodies as parts, even if A is moving relative to those parts. B itself may be in C, but ultimately there is a final place, the inner boundary of the outermost heaven (which may be the outermost shell of the whole universe). Thus, in one sense, all other bodies exist in that outermost heaven or in a place, and they do not move relative to that place but only relative to themselves or to other subordinate places. Further, a place, not being a body, is immovable.

29. By "that" he means the matter or the subject which, remaining the same in itself, takes on now one attribute and now another, e.g., water, qua a subject, becomes now hot and now cold.

30. The thing here is considered without reference to its being white or black, hard or soft; and as such, it is viewed as being at rest, so to speak, and continuous.

31. These are the two parts of requirement (1) for a place. In the case of matter, we do not speak of it as *containing* an attribute or a form; and while a body and its place are separable and may exist apart from each other, the *composite* of matter and an attribute cannot exist apart from each other in that sense.

32. This is alternative (4) in 211b8–9.

33. The body contained appears to occupy such an interval, if "occupy" be the right word.

34. Since air seems to be incorporeal, as if a void, an empty can seems to contain a void.

35. In saying "the vessel is a place", perhaps he is using "place" to signify the vessel as a body along with its inner surface; for what can move essentially must be a body, and a place as a surface moves accidentally, in virtue of being an attribute of a body. We, too, use the term in this sense, for "in a house" and "in a place" suggest that "house" and "place" come under the same genus, signifying a body of some kind.

In saying "a place is an immovable vessel", he seems to be using both "place" and "vessel" for the inner surface alone, without including the body, for a surface is immovable, and it is this that he now wishes to consider. So each of the terms "place" and "vessel" has two senses, a body with an inner surface so as to contain something and also that inner surface itself.

36. The boat uses the river (a moving body of water) as a vessel (a moving body with an inner surface) rather than as a place (the surface itself as something motionless).

37. By "whole river" he seems to mean the motionless river basin which touches the moving body of water, and this is a surface. So he will now use "place" to signify a certain surface which contains something, and any surface qua surface is immovable.

38. By "that" he means the body which has the surface to be called "place".

39. The Center of the heaven would be the inner boundary of the spherical shell D, and this boundary would be (theoretically) in contact with the whole contained earth E; and the last [inner surface] of the rotating part of heaven would be the inner surface of the outer shell A (see figure), and fire is just within that surface. If by "Center" here he means the center of the universe, which is a point, then this too is within the inner surface of D. See Comm. 44 below.

40. He says "most of all", for one thing may be more up than another, like the region B relative to that of C in the Figure. Perhaps "principally" suggests that the inner surface of A is the starting-point, a principle, so to say, upon which depends any other sense of "up" when used as a relative, as when we say that B is up relative to C.

41. The inner surface of D stays (theoretically) the same; it is stationary so to say, neither rotating nor increasing outwards or inwards.

42. The inner surface of region A remains in the same condition; for, although A and its inner surface rotate around the center of E, that surface taken as whole is always equidistant from the center of the universe.

43. This is the inner surface of D.

44. This is the center of E. Of course, "down" has two senses in English also. It means (a) a certain place, which is an inner surface of a containing body, and it also means (b) in a certain place, which is an attribute of a contained body, as when we say that E is down, that is, within the inner surface of D.

45. That part is region B, and this is the fiery body by nature, and it is up in the sense of being immediately within the inner surface of A, just as E is within the surface of D.

46. This is the inner surface of shell A, and it is called "up" just as the inner surface of D is called "down", each of the two being a place as defined in 212a20–1.

47. In calling a place "a surface", he is using "place" to accord with the definition he has given, and this was one sense in which the term was dialectically used; but in calling it "something like a vessel and something which contains", he uses it as a *composite* of (a) a containing body and (b) its inner surface which touches the contained body, and this was another sense of "place", as when we say that a glass is a place for water.

48. The inner boundary of a containing body coincides with the shape of the contained body, if the latter is contained primarily, as in the case of a can full of water.

5

1. Two possibilities arise: (a) The water forms the outer shell of the universe; (b) the water is the whole universe. Perhaps he means the first alternative. An alternative to "its parts" is "some parts".

2. If the outer shell of the universe were just water, the universe as a whole would not be in motion because it would not be in a place (as defined).

3. A circular motion of the outer shell of the universe is possible; and so parts of that shell, surrounded by other parts, have a relative place and so can be in motion.

4. There is no up or down for such parts; for up would be the inner surface of the shell made of water, and if all the water is assumed to be in that shell, the parts would not be moved down (as defined). Parts other than water, however, might move up or down, depending on their relative density.

5. A part is not actually one, and so it has no place; but it has a place potentially, in virtue of the whole of which it is part, and its place is said to be the same as that of the whole.

6. Of course, if separated, they are no longer parts but wholes and unities, existing in actuality, and as such they may be *actually* in place.

7. Perhaps by "locomotion" he means a motion in which the dimensions of the body in motion remain unchanged. If also the dimensions change, then the body has a complex motion, so to say. Of course, a body changes place whether in a locomotion or in a motion with respect to magnitude.

8. Decrease is omitted; perhaps it is understood. Aristotle often leaves statements incomplete if what is left out is obvious.

9. Only bodies are in place essentially, except the universe (since no body can contain it).

10. Perhaps he means those parts which are contained or can be contained by other parts or bodies.

11. A material part can be essentially in a place, if separated; but an attribute or a form can never be so, for it can never be a body, and only bodies can be in a place. The heaven is in a place accidentally in the sense that the parts of it, such as the planets, are in a place.

12. Perhaps the heaven revolving about the center is one by contact only. If so, its parts may be of two kinds: wholes in contact, like the stars, and parts of such wholes. A star, then, is called "a part" (but in a loose sense of the term "part") if the revolving heaven is regarded as many and not a whole (for "a whole" has many senses).

13. Perhaps he uses "in" in sense (1) here (210a15–6); and perhaps "heaven" here is synonymous with "universe" (278b11–21).

14. Perhaps there is a problem as to whether the immovable movers are in the universe, and if so, in what sense of "in".

15. Since only a body can be essentially in motion and so essentially at rest and a boundary is not a body, a boundary is essentially immovable, though it may be accidentally (as an attribute) in motion or at rest.

16. Perhaps "ether" here is synonymous with "fire", or else he abbreviates or speaks dialectically; but the meaning is clear.

17. These are listed in 209a4–29. Problems (c) and (d) are not considered; for their solution is sufficiently evident from what has been said.

18. If a place is the first inner boundary of a containing body, then when the contained body grows (essentially), it is the containing body that changes essentially and not its inner boundary. Of course, this boundary too changes or grows, but accidentally (as an attribute of the container) and not essentially.

19. If a place is the first inner boundary of a containing body, then no such boundary can contain just a point; so a point cannot be in a primary place.

20. The place of a body is *in* the container and not coextensive with the body contained; so it is not necessary for two bodies (i.e., the contained body and its place) to be coextensive. By "coextensive" we mean (a) that every part of the contained body coincides with a part of that place and (b) that a place is not just a boundary but also the interval within it.

21. There are two alternative meanings of "a bodily interval": (1) a space which comes under the genus "body" and (2) a space which is not a body but in which a body exists, so that the body and its space coincide or are coextensive. Perhaps the second alternative is meant, for the first part of problem (a) takes care of the first alternative.

22. What the place (as defined) of a containing body contains is just the contained body, and no additional thing such as an interval.

23. A place is not in place but in the container (using "in" in sense (5), 210a20–1); and it is in the container as an attribute, like heat in hot water or a surface in a body or a form (in a wide sense) in a subject in general. Thus a place is not in a place essentially; only a body is essentially in a place.

24. What is dialectically taken as true of a place, in lines 211a4–6, is here shown to be reasonable.

25. The terms "in contact" and "alike in kind" apply both to things which are generically one and to those which are specifically one. Thus things in contact may also be continuous, and things which are alike may also be one in species. This becomes evident from what follows.

26. For example, one part of a bone does not affect another part of it, for the whole bone acts or functions as one.

27. For example, a book is just in contact but not continuous with the table on which it rests; and the book acts on the table, while the table is acted upon by the book.

In the case of the four elements, earth, water, air, and fire, taken in this order, any two of them which are in succession have an attribute in common (330a30–b5), for their respective sensible attributes are as follows:

earth:	water:	air:	fire:
dry, cold	cold, wet	wet, hot	hot, dry

For example, water and air are both wet. The assumption seems to be, the more things are alike (have something in common), the closer they are. What about earth and fire, which are furthest apart and yet both are dry?

28. For example, if one splashes water in a tub, the scattered particles of water finally join the original body of water, and the unity of water is restored and remains so. Similarly, if a part of earth is lifted in air and then released, it joins by nature its own kind (earth). In each case, if no force is applied, the detached parts of each kind of body come together and stay together as parts of a whole, and hence they are in one place.

29. The expression "as if" indicates an analogy, though not a strong one. Thus, part : whole :: matter : form (or composite of matter and form) :: water : air, for air is closer to form than water is. Just as a part is contained by the whole and matter is contained by form, so is water contained (using "contained" analogously) by air. Water, then, is contained by air (is in air, using "in" as in a place) as if it were a part of a whole (*composite* of air and water).

30. When water becomes air, this is a change from the imperfect to the perfect, a generation, so to say, from matter to a *composite* of matter and form, like the seed becoming a tree; but when air becomes water, it is the opposite, a destruction, so to say.

31. 317a32–9b5.

32. Perhaps the meaning is this: If both water and air are in a sense water, and the first is actually water but potentially air while air is water with the actuality or form of air, then the first (water) is to the second (air) in some manner (analogically) as a part to a whole.

33. They are in contact in the sense that the contained, which is water and like matter so to say, is in the container, which is air and is like a form or a whole. But if one of them, whether air or water, becomes the other, then we have water, or we have air; and if no force prevents, the resulting unity of the two is a natural one and not a unity just by contact; and in that case the resulting body has just one place (by nature) since it is one body.

6

1. Perhaps "void" should be distinguished from "a void", the latter signifying the interval as such, whether it contains a body or not, and the

former being an adjective signifying the interval without a body in it.

2. An alternative to "a void" is "void".

3. By "the same thing" he means numerically the same; thus "George Washington" and "the first President of the United States" signify numerically the same man—the first by his name, the second by a certain title of position. A void, then, may be void of anything or full of something or a place for something.

4. An essence is signified by a definition. In this case, the definition of that which is void, that which is full, and that which is a place would have to be different, even if referring to numerically the same thing, a void. All three have "that" as if their genus, and the expressions "which is void", "which is full", and "which is a place" are like adjectives or predicates qualifying "that". Thus the differences in the definitions would be differences in these qualifications, while "that" would signify what is common (a void), like a genus.

5. The word "them" may refer to the problems concerning a void; or else, if the Greek is slightly corrupt, it should be "it", referring to the void.

6. He is also mentioned in 309a19–21, 470b30–1a2, 976b19–22.

7. Apparently, wineskins into which air has been blown.

8. Otherwise stated, a void taken in itself is an interval, and the meaning of "a void" does not include any body in it, regardless of whether a void has a body or not.

9. The word "that" refers to a void when filled with air.

10. The contradiction is only apparent, for he is saying that that in which air exists or into which it enters is a void.

11. Perhaps he means the total universe, which is a plurality of bodies.

12. For Democritus, void exists between the indivisible atoms.

13. He is referring to the Pythagorean doctrine (213b22–7).

14. Leucippus, Democritus, and Empedocles are among these (325a23–b7).

15. The smallest volume or space of some substance could receive the substance in the greatest volume, if the latter were divided into parts each equal to that of the smallest and each part could be compressed into it.

16. If five volume-units of matter taken separately could be compressed into a volume-unit, then a three-volume-unit and a two-volume unit of that matter could.

17. 325a2–16.

18. That is, the skins which formerly held the wine.

19. Either the wine is compressed into its own interstices (tiny void intervals) or into those of the skins or both.

20. Perhaps the argument is this: When food is taken, no apparent increase in volume is observed, though the body increases in weight. So food occupies previously existing void.

21. 938b24–9a9.

22. Since, for the Pythagoreans, all things are composed of or are numbers, numbers are prior to all other things. But a number is composed of units, each of which is indivisible but with a magnitude. Hence units, and so numbers, must be somehow demarcated, and this is done by the void (1080b16–21, 30–3).

7

1. These are the existence and the non-existence of a void.

2. In a discussion concerning the existence of a thing, the meaning of the term signifying the thing must be posited before the existence or nonexistence of the thing is considered (1006a18–22).

3. If the formula of a void is "that in which there is nothing heavy or light", then a point would be a void; but if "a place" replaces "that" in the formula (it has already been granted earlier that a void is a sort of place), then a point cannot be a void since it is not a place (as already defined).

4. It appears that he gives this as the first meaning of "a void" using the common opinions which preceded.

5. Of course, there is the problem of whether a sound or a color can exist without body, for if it is an attribute of a body, the problem disappears. Anyway, Aristotle answers the question by referring it to the meaning of "a void" already given.

6. Perhaps "that" assumes that it is a place.

7. This formula omits "tangible", so it appears to be more universal. Are the terms "a *this*" and "a corporeal substance" synonymous? From what follows, perhaps "a corporeal substance" does not mean just matter without form (one meaning of "substance" is matter, 1029a1–27). Perhaps a composite is meant, like a man or any body which has unity in some way or other.

8. Plato seems to take this view (209b11–6), for space and matter and place for him seem to be the same, a receptacle so to speak, and a void seems to be the same.

9. The matter of a statue is in (or with) the statue, regardless of where the statue is.

10. 211b29–2a2.

11. This would be a place (as Aristotle defined it) with a bodiless interval between, shown to lead to difficulties (211b14–29).

12. Such thinkers use "void" and "place" in the same sense, so the existence of the one implies that of the other.

13. This would be a change in quality alone, like changing a color or getting sick, but not increasing or decreasing or moving from one place to another, for it is the latter motions which *seem* to need a void.

14. This would be a change in place without the necessity of a void, as in rotating water in a glass.

15. This is a case of bodies making way for each other simultaneously, without the need of a void; it is a change in place without the need of a void.

16. This is a case of increase, because a body alters or changes its *substance* (or nature or form). Evidently, no body is taken in to cause such increase.

17. This is the argument for the existence of a void, 213b18–20. Aristotle gives the results of his refutation; the detailed steps are not given.

18. An alternative to "no one" is "not any".

19. A body increases primarily if every part of it increases, and it increases secondarily if some but not all parts increase (321a2–3).

If the food taken into the body occupies the voids in the body, then no part of the body increases primarily, and this appears contrary to observation; or else the whole body does not increase, for the food taken in goes into the voids, and yet increase of the body as a whole is assumed.

20. Perhaps the argument is this: If some part of the body has increased primarily, it did not increase by the food taken in, for this filled the void. So that part increased, but not by a body.

21. Perhaps the argument is this: If, in the last Commentary, the part which increased did so by a body, but not by the food taken in, then two bodies must have been in that part prior to its increase.

22. Perhaps the argument is this: If each part of the body increased by the food taken in and this food occupied the voids, then the whole body was a void; for if not, the part which was not a void but was full could not have taken in any food, and so it could not have increased, contrary to the assumption that each part of the body increased.

23. Perhaps the argument is this: If the vessel can hold as much water when empty as when full of ashes, then (a) if the water goes into the voids, the whole volume of ashes will be a void, and (b) if part of the volume of ashes is not a void, that part will have to absorb an equal volume of water, and so two bodies will be in the same place.

8

1. This would mean, for example, that the cause of the going up of fire is in the fire itself, for the place of fire is up.

2. Whether those who regarded the void as a cause of motion meant it as a moving cause or just as something necessary but not sufficient is not clear. In either case, if the void is a cause, both fire and earth should alike travel toward it; but they do not. What is more, they consistently travel in contrary directions; in addition, earth travels down, and this place has, if at all, less void than the place up. Thus a void does not appear to be a cause or the cause.

3. 211a29–b1.

4. We translated literally from Bekker, but there are variants in dif-

ferent texts and much remains unsaid in the arguments, which seem difficult to unravel.

5. If a void surrounds a body, then since the void is homogeneous or uniform or possesses no differentiae, the body will either move in all directions, which is impossible, or remain at rest, not supported by sensation.

6. Posterior in existence as well as in definition. If a motion by nature does not exist, the distinction indicated "by nature" and "contrary to nature" disappears; but this is not supported by observation, for, usually, heavy things go down and fire goes up.

7. This may mean either (a) things by nature differ from those contrary to nature, or (b) there are different things whose motion by nature differs. Both alternatives make sense.

8. Aristotle does not indicate here whether or not these thinkers included a moving cause.

9. The air pushed gathers behind the thing pushed and so pushes the thing forward; so the thing, probably heavy, such as a stone, travels faster when thrown downward than when released. Thus the pushing air gives additional speed to the speed with which the thing would travel naturally if released.

10. There can be no replacement, for a void is not a body to replace or be replaced by something; and unlike air, which as a body pushes the thrown body and adds to its natural speed, a void cannot do this since it is not a body. So since observation confirms a faster downward motion of a thrown body, the argument does not favor the existence of a void.

11. As an example, a stationary body of spherical shape has no natural tendency to move horizontally, but if it is suddenly pushed, it will roll on even after it is pushed, for the air behind it or the body itself acts as a mover (266b27–7a12). But in the absence of air or of any other medium, it should stop, for the void is not a body to act as a mover after the spherical body has been pushed.

12. Some premises are needed for this argument. Two alternatives are given for the body. (a) If the body rests, perhaps this is in view of the absence of a medium behind it which might be pushing it; (b) if the body is assumed in motion for any interval of time after the mover stops moving it, then it should always be travelling in the same way (unless obstructed), which perhaps means with the same velocity and direction, for the void has no differentia to change its manner of travelling (214b31–5a1). This amounts to Newton's first law, the law of inertia.

13. Of course, this would be impossible. It is not stated whether the body is initially travelling or not; but perhaps it makes no difference. One might answer that cohesion of the parts would prevent the body from travelling in all directions. Perhaps by "void" he means a place without a body in it, for in an infinite void there can be no place and so neither motion nor rest. Earth, it may be added, should travel up where there is void; but it does not.

14. An alternative to "weight or" is "weight and", and one text omits this expression. Perhaps the expression should not be omitted, for "weight" indicates a body by nature going down, "body" includes a body which by nature goes up, and "same" indicates other things being equal (216a14–5), although what those things are is not specified. It may be that the dimensions are assumed similar but the weight (or pull upwards) the same or that the dimensions are the same but the density or lightness is not. Thus the common belief that Aristotle posits the velocity of a body as proportional to its weight may be erroneous. Of course, no units of measurement are given, and the premise, perhaps dialectical, is still questionable.

15. A body can travel faster either upward or downward. If the body has an excess of density, like iron, its motion is assumed to be downwards; if it has an excess of lightness, like fire, then it is assumed to be upwards.

16. Three attributes of a medium that might retard the motion of a moving body are mentioned: density (or specific gravity), a motion opposed to the motion of the body, and viscosity.

17. Though the assumption (the intervals C and E are proportional to the resistances of B and D) is dialectical, one may still question the validity of this kind of proportion.

18. In the Greek, the corresponding phrase should be traslated into "twice as thin"; but we use "half as viscous" for the sake of consistency in the translated terminology.

19. The two quantities of a ratio must be of the same kind, but "nothing" does not signify a quantity, whether a number or a magnitude.

20. Both the excess and that which is exceeded, of course, must be quantities, and zero (or nothing) is not a quantity.

21. For Aristotle, a line is not composed of points (231a21–9) and hence is not measurable by a point; and so a point and a line, not being objects of the same kind, cannot be compared or have a ratio.

22. Comparing a void to something full (or a body) is like comparing zero (or nothing) to a quantity.

23. The ratio of two motions is somehow (whether inversely or in some other way) related to that of the two media through which the object moves. But since there is no ratio of a void to a medium (which is a body), neither can there be a ratio of the two motions.

24. The medium which is least viscous is still a body and not a void. We use "least viscous" rather than "thinnest" for the sake of consistency in terminology.

25. By "it" he means the distance through the void.

26. More specifically, the body L is thinner or less viscous than air. We are using "viscosity", but the corresponding Greek term signifies thinness. So the meaning is this: The ratio in thinness of L to D is equal to the ratio E:H. For example, if E:H = 3:1, then L is three times as thin as D, or D is three times as thick as L. The magnitude of L is assumed to be equal to that of D or of Z.

27. That is, A is posited as traversing the magnitude of Z (of the void) in time H.

28. By "full" here he means the body L.

29. That is, corresponding to D (or air), there exists a body, which is given as L here, such that D is as much more viscous or resistant than L as the ratio E:H.

30. An alternative translation is "if the shapes are similar in other ways". See Comm. 14 of this Section.

31. Whether "the magnitudes" refers to the preponderance in weight or lightness, which may be the density or the pull (either upwards or downwards) or to something else is not specified. See Comm. 14 of this Section.

32. The preponderance in density acts more effectively in dividing the medium, and so a body travels with a greater speed. But if no medium is present, no division takes place and there is nothing to overcome in order to travel, so nothing will cause a difference in speed. This suggests that bodies will travel with the same speed in the void (or in vacuum, as taken nowadays). For Aristotle, observation did not support this, for instruments to create what we call "near-vacuum" did not exist.

33. 211b9–29.

34. That is, difficulties arise even if the void is examined without reference to motion.

35. For example, water would travel by nature up if it is down where earth by nature is, but down if it is where air by nature is.

36. For example, it may travel horizontally.

37. If it is not a body, it cannot displace or be displaced by something; so it is not something which exists in something else, but something in which something else is.

38. That is, the magnitude or volume of the cube, whether separable in existence from the cube or not, is distinct in essence or definition from the affections of the cube.

39. An alternative to "volume" is "mass" or "matter".

40. Perhaps this is the void which is posited as being always with the cube, not the stationary void in which the cube happens to be as it changes from one place to another.

41. Perhaps by "itself" he means the void which is always with the cube. Thus, the void which is always with the cube is equal to the stationary void in which the cube is.

42. Perhaps by "the body of the cube" he means the mass or matter of the cube; for this would always be with the void which is always with the cube, and one could not give a good reason for distinguishing the void from that matter with which it is supposed to be.

43. Perhaps by "two such things" he means the two voids, the stationary and the one which is always with the cube, or, one of the voids and the matter, or else, the magnitude of the stationary void and that in the cube. If one distinguishes the mass of the cube from the void which

is always with that mass, then one may make another such distinction in the mass itself, etc.

44. Perhaps by "this" he means the void or space or volume which is always with the cube, not the stationary void.

45. According to Bekker's text, the translation should be "So, if it makes no difference at all where this is"; and if so, perhaps "this" refers to the cube or to its volume or to its own void.

46. That is, nor would the water seem to exist for the fishes, if these were made of iron. The analogy is, we are to air as iron fishes are to water.

47. Though air does not seem by means of sight to exist to us, yet by touch it does, for blowing winds do affect our touch. Lines 216b17–20 enclosed by parentheses are omitted by Greek commentators, and perhaps they do not belong here.

9

1. An alternative to "pulsate" is "expand".

2. These arguments for the existence of a void may be (a) those given by the upholders of a void or (b) just common arguments or (c) arguments articulated by Aristotle himself for the sake of attacking the existence of a void effectively.

If no rare or dense things exist, everything is full; so a thing surrounded by what is full would have nowhere to move to, and argument (a) sounds reasonable. If no rare or dense things exist, perhaps a pulsating universe requires an assumption, the existence of generation or destruction. For example, as water is becoming air (and air is full), it pushes out the surroundings and so the universe increases in volume, and as air becomes water, the universe decreases in volume, and so it pulsates, as Xuthus said. Perhaps most of the physical philosophers denied a pulsating universe.

If the universe does not pulsate but generation and destruction exists, then argument (c) follows; and the things changing need not be just water and air, for many things can be changing while the volume of the universe remains the same. If ΣV_i are the volumes of the various things, then $\frac{d}{dt} [\Sigma V_i] = 0$ will assure a constant volume at any moment.

If these thinkers deny the above arguments, then a void must exist. For they would deny argument (a) because a motion exists; they would deny a pulsating universe and so argument (b); and they would deny argument (c) perhaps because of its improbability. So a void for them must exist.

3. 211b18–29.

4. In this sense, a void would be present in every part of the object, though there is a problem as to how such a situation could exist, if it could exist at all. Perhaps these thinkers would say that the void is diffused throughout the object, or something of this sort.

5. Void in things makes them rare, rare things are light, light things go up; hence, void in things makes them go up. But they spoke of the void as being the cause of motion in general.

6. Perhaps the argument is not spelled out. If the void is not a body, and only bodies travel, how can the void in bodies travel? And will it travel through a void or place (without a body)? If the void in a body causes it to travel up, and the body travels up through the void outside of it, then this void would be travelling up too, and through another void, etc.

7. If it is not the void in an object that causes it to go down, what is it? Perhaps it is the absence of a void, but they did not say this; and one could just as well have said that it is the presence of (full) body that causes things to move (down), and the absence of (full) body, to move up. Again, why should things with an excess of void travel up rather than down?

8. But this argument assumes the existence of a void as separate, and the hypothesis rests on a void diffused throughout and not as something separate.

9. 217a8–10.

10. It is not explicitly stated whether this locomotion is of the whole universe as a unit, without a change of the relative places of the parts, or of some part of the universe, like a shell of it with its parts going around, or of parts of the universe in some way or other.

11. This is evident by observation.

12. It exists as potentiality, and it is a principle in physical bodies.

13. It is the same matter that can be at one time with heat and at another with coldness, at one time of a certain volume and at another otherwise (whether larger or smaller), and at one time red but at another white; and the same matter can receive more than one contrariety.

14. In other words, if B is a body with M as its matter and H_1 as its heat and if B becomes hotter later with H_2 as its heat, then it is the same M which exists potentially in B that leaves H_1 and takes on H_2, and no other [hot] matter or no separate hotness is introduced into B to make it hotter than before. If C makes B hotter, it is not the hotness (as numerically the same) that enters B, but C is a moving cause in making B hotter than before.

15. An alternative to "being the same arc and no other" is "whether it is the same or a distinct arc"; and if so, perhaps the problem indicated is whether one wishes to regard the new arc as being the same as the original arc or not. It is numerically the same but different in definition.

16. The additional amount of convexity in the new arc was not introduced from some arc or line other than the original and added to the original, but the original arc was changed from being less convex to being more convex. Thus there was an underlying matter, so to speak (we say "so to speak", for quantities are essentially immovable, though accidentally movable, that is, as a physical body moves, so may its quantity but accidentally), and this matter was the line (or curve, in

modern terms), but without reference to its differentia (curvature or straightness).

17. Heat and whiteness are not substances introduced to the flame from the outside; they are attributes which are inseparable from the flame, and they can become more or less in the flame without any substance or attribute added to the flame from the outside.

18. In other words, the size of a body is an attribute like the heat or color of a body or like the curvature or straightness of a line (or a curve, in modern terms), and its change in magnitude is similar to the change of those other attributes. Hence, no void enters into or exits from the body when its volume increases or decreases.

The Greek text in lines 217b12–6 seems to say just about the same as lines 217b2–10. Some texts do not contain this part. Whether it was intended to replace or be replaced by lines 217b2–10 is not known.

19. Rareness, in this case, is an attribute of a body but not something in which a void is present.

20. Lead is heavier but softer than iron, and by "heavier" we today mean with a greater specific gravity.

21. By "without qualification" he probably means separately.

22. By "what is rare" perhaps he means something in which void exists in a sort of diffused manner, so that any part of the rare thing would have some void.

23. By "potentially" perhaps he means a void which can exist or be brought about by some cause.

24. Thus a heavy body goes down, so one might call the matter of that body "void"; and similarly with a light body which goes up, like fire.

25. In other words, lightness and heaviness in bodies are causes of upward and downward locomotions respectively, while their softness and hardness are causes of their yielding or not yielding to pressure respectively; and although the dense usually go down and are hard while the rare go up and are soft, some exceptions exist, as in wood relative to water and iron relative to lead.

10

1. An alternative to "common" is "popular". These may be arguments which Aristotle used in his dialogues or before general audiences.

2. Aristotle's usual procedure is to show the existence of a thing before proceeding to its nature or definition, for a nonbeing has neither a nature nor a definition (it may have a formula, like the formula of a circle with two centers, which circle cannot exist). Besides, it is easier to observe the existence of a thing than to state its definition, as in the case of a man or a tree.

3. If time is considered as composed of parts which do not exist, then time itself does not exist and so has no nature or *substance*.

4. This is only one sense of "part" (1023b15–7), and just as a point

is not a part of a line (in this sense), so a moment is not a part of time. The argument here is dialectical.

5. If a moment is not a part of time, as already indicated, and if the parts of time are in the past or future, then time does not exist.

6. We use "in itself" rather than "during itself", for "during" indicates divisible time and a moment is indivisible. So the moment cannot be destroyed in itself, for otherwise it will be and not be simultaneously.

7. If moments are not consecutive, then they cannot succeed each other.

8. If moment M_1 was destroyed in moment M_5, then it still existed prior to M_5; but to exist in this way is to exist simultaneously with the moments which are between M_1 and M_5, and this is impossible.

9. Time is like a straight line, and the limits of an interval of time are distinct like the ends of a straight line.

10. The terms "prior" and "posterior" mean earlier and later in time respectively.

11. The prior and posterior would be in this moment if the moment is assumed to be numerically one and the same.

12. Events in the same moment would be simultaneous, and so even if we call one "prior" and another "posterior", they would really not be so.

13. Plato seems to have taken this position in *Timaeus* 39.

14. Perhaps some Pythagoreans.

15. Perhaps some thinkers believed in the existence of more than one heaven (276a18–7b29, 1074a31–8).

16. From the truth of the proposition "A is in B" and "A is in C", it does not follow that B and C have the same nature or definition; and besides, "in" is equivocally or analogously used in "A is in time" and "A is in the sphere", and not with a single meaning.

17. Time is defined as a kind of a number (219b1–2), and as such it is a quantity. In what sense is it a quality? Of course, the unit of time is not time as a number but some nature connected with motion, and a motion is not a quantity nor defined in terms of time.

18. The term "change" is wider than "motion", but any essential change requires a motion; and of motions locomotion is prior to all others and is usually used to define time.

11

1. For the story, see Ross's *Aristotle's Physics*, p. 597.

2. This is a moment, which is numerically one and indivisible.

3. Literally, it should be "what of a motion time is", that is, time is what part or attribute of a motion? Of course, he is thinking of time as being somehow an attribute of a motion; and as an attribute, it must be in some category, and this is the next problem.

4. Already shown in 218b18–20.

5. A magnitude can exist without motion, but not conversely; and

"follows" here indicates that magnitudes are prior in existence to motions.

6. Perhaps the parenthetical statement, in view of "is always thought to be", is dialectical. There is a sense in which time is as much as the corresponding motion, but another sense in which it is not. Time, unlike a motion, is neither slow nor fast; and if time is a number of a sort, a motion too would have to be a number in order to be comparable.

If time is a (whole) number, as defined later (219b1–2), it is not continuous; so to be continuous, the term "time" has to be taken in another sense. Perhaps it is like the foot which, though it may be taken as a unit to measure a magnitude numerically in units, is continuous as a magnitude or as a subject.

7. If a body moves from A to M along a straight line, the parts of AM have relative position and one part is prior to another if it is nearer to A, which is taken as a principle (1018b9–9a14). The parts of the motion from A to M, too, are related by being prior or posterior, and part M_1 of a motion is prior to part M_2 if the magnitude over which the motion M_1 has occurred is prior to that over which M_2 has occurred. But "prior" as applied to M_1 is not the same as but is analogous in meaning to "prior" as applied to the corresponding magnitude. In time, too, there is priority and posteriority of the parts and also of the moments, but also in an analogous sense. Hence priority and posteriority in the primary sense exist in place or in magnitudes; then follow priority and posteriority in motion; and finally, in time.

8. The expression ὃ ποτε ὄν seems to be technical, and "whenever a motion exists" may not be the accurate translation, if one exists. Perhaps the prior and posterior in a motion as a subject are necessary distinctions, not to be identified with the motion itself, just as being in the Lyceum or in the agora or in some other place is necessary for Coriscus as a subject (219b18–21), not to be identified with Coriscus in definition.

9. The moments as limits are included in time.

10. For example, this is the same moment, but it is viewed as the end of the preceding time but as the beginning of the time that follows.

11. It is still a problem what that number is or how it is determined, for a unit of time is needed. Further, is time the number of the motion of anything whatever that is in motion? If so, many times would exist simultaneously. If time is to be unique, then, perhaps it must be an attribute of some principal or primary motion to which the other motions are somehow related, or else an attribute universally applicable to motions.

12. The terms "greater" and "less" as used here apply only to numbers, if two motions are compared with respect to their times, but they may apply to motions qua continuous also, if the motions are compared by their numbers. For example, five feet is greater than two feet qua numbers, and line AB is greater than line CD qua a magnitude, if AB is five feet long and CD is two feet long. Perhaps the argument is dialectical.

13. By "that by which we number", as in the case of five apples, does

he mean the unit, which in this case is one apple, or the concept "five"? Perhaps he means the concept "five".

14. If so, then time is not in us, although the intellect must specify the unit of time before expressing a given time interval (which is continuous) as a number (223a16–29).

15. For example, just as the motion from A to B is distinct from the motion from B to C, in the sense that one motion comes before or after the other, so it is in time, like the month of January and that of March.

16. Perhaps he means, for example, that the time from 8 A.M. to 9 A.M. on a certain day is the same everywhere and for every motion, for the moment at, say, 8:31 A.M. is the same everywhere. But the moment 8:31 A.M. is numerically distinct from that at 8:32 A.M.

17. Perhaps the moment measures time in this sense: If 12:00 noon is taken as the principle or starting-point, then the moment at 1 P.M. specifies one unit of time (1 hour) elapsed, 2 P.M. specifies two such units, etc.

18. For example, the moment at 2 P.M. is distinct from that at 4 P.M., for the formulas which specify the two moments show a difference; but they are the same in this sense: They are both moments. It is like Socrates who moved from A to B; for "Socrates at A" and "Socrates at B" differ, but it is the same Socrates as a subject, whether at A or at B or at any other position. Thus, A and B are to Socrates as the priority and posteriority are to the moment.

19. Perhaps he means a travelling point which changes position but remains the same point.

20. Perhaps by "this" he means that which travels.

21. It is the same thing that travels, like Socrates who walks from A to B.

22. For example, since to be at A is distinct from to be at B, it follows that Socrates at A is distinct from Socrates at B.

23. Two useful proportions would be (a) body : motion :: moment : time and (b) body at A : body at B :: moment at 2 P.M. : moment at 4 P.M.

24. Time as a number of motion arises when the moment assumes different states of posteriority, for example, the same moment at 1 P.M., at 2 P.M., etc.

25. The body which is the same is taken here without reference to its distinct states of priority.

26. The moment is distinct qua being now prior and now posterior.

27. Perhaps "this" refers to the moment, for, as indicated in Comm. 23 previously, the moment is analogous to the body in motion. It seems, then, that priority and posteriority are to the moment as attributes to a subject. However, a subject need not be a substance; for a line is a subject relative to its curvature but is not a substance.

28. Perhaps that number is the set of moments at various stages associated with the object in locomotion, if that set is considered as just a number of moments.

29. Perhaps each moment in that sequence after the initial moment is or numbers a unit of time.

30. Time is continuous just as a line is continuous, and it is a number if expressed in units like a line when expressed as, say, ten feet. Thus, a moment in time is like a point within a line, and just as the line is continuous at that point, so is time at that moment; or else, just as an object in motion is continuous at some intermediate but indivisible stage, so is a moment within an interval of time. Time is divisible at a moment in an analogous manner; but perhaps this divisibility is potential or in thought.

31. Perhaps he means the object when continuously in motion.

32. Just as an intermediate and indivisible stage of an object in motion divides the prior part of the motion from the posterior, so does a moment in time.

33. That is, not as a beginning of what is to follow and an end of what preceded.

34. Perhaps he means that given one initial moment, then the succeeding number of moments mark time as a number, although the moments themselves do not make up time (just as no number of points make up a line), and the last moment marks time as the number of motion up to that stage.

35. A limit is a limit of some subject; it is incapable of existing apart from that subject. Thus it is an attribute of that subject, like coldness which must exist in a body. It is in this way that points are related to lines, lines to surfaces, surfaces to solids, and moments as limits to time.

12

1. Perhaps by "without qualification" he means a number as defined, namely, a plurality of units numerable by a unit. Such plurality must be divisible, and each ultimate part must be indivisible or taken qua undivided (1020a7–11).

2. An alternative to "qualified" is "particular" or "individual", which is the usual meaning of the Greek word τις.

3. Why "two or one"? How can one line be a qualified or a particular number? One line can be expressed as a number, e.g., if "two feet long" is a predicate of it, but it is not clear whether this is what Aristotle has in mind.

4. Since a magnitude is always divisible, and into magnitudes, there is no smallest magnitude which can be expressed as the smallest number, i.e., as two.

5. The terms "long" and "short" are attributes of what is continuous, but "much" and "little" are attributes of numbers, as in "much time" and "little time", and time is a number. English alternatives to "much" and "little" are "many" and "few" and also "great" and "small", as in "a great number" and "a small number".

6. That is, not numerically the same, although it may be the same in

species as in "two years", which is a predicate of any two consecutive years.

7. By "that by which we count" does he mean the concept "number"?

8. By "one and the same" he means one and the same in species (224a2–15), and that which is the same in species here is one hundred.

9. To know a particular number, such as ten horses, both the nature which underlies the unit must be known and the number of such units.

10. If this sentence is analogous to the preceding, then the motion which we measure by time is analogous to the plurality of horses which is measured by a number, and the time which is measured by a [unit] motion is analogous to the number of horses which is measured by one horse as the unit.

11. Perhaps by "quantitative" he means measurable or numerable, for the continuous can be numbered if some unit of measure is taken.

12. The measurements indicated here seem to be of the whole magnitude traversed, the whole motion over that magnitude, and the total time taken. Once the units of measurement are taken, then the magnitudes are proportional to the corresponding times.

13. The different terms "motion" and "being moved", or "motion" and "being of motion" as given later in the sentence, seem to indicate a distinction. One alternative is that while "motion" signifies just the attribute (i.e., motion) of the body, "being moved" or "being in motion" signifies the body along with the attribute; another alternative, as some commentators indicate, is that while "motion" signifies the attribute, "being moved" or "being in motion" signifies the temporal interval of the existence of that attribute. In each alternative, the corresponding limits of both exist simultaneously.

14. One alternative to "being" is "existence"; another is "essence".

15. By "part" he means a material part, like a unit in a number and a hand in a body; but an *attribute* is like the whiteness or the length, for each of these is said of the whole body. Both kinds are said to belong to a body.

16. It is in sense 2(b) that he is speaking of a motion as being in time. In other words, a motion is said to be in time if there is a number of it (or of its being).

17. Just as there is a (primary) place for a thing in place, so there is a (primary) time, which is a number of a motion for a thing in time.

18. That is, time is a cause of destruction more than of generation.

19. Motion belongs to a thing already existing, not to what will be but does not yet exist. So if time is an attribute (a number) of motion, it is an attribute of what exists; and that which exists will not be generated but may be destroyed as time elapses. Perhaps an argument such as this accounts for Aristotle's expression "time in virtue of itself is a cause rather of destruction".

20. Since they are eternal, no time can exist which is greater than eternity and can contain them, and no unit of measure, however large,

can measure eternity (finitely). Are not the Moon and the stars, although eternal, changing with respect to place? But their particular place at any given time is accidental to their essence, although to be in some place is essential, and they are always in some place.

21. An alternative to "as an attribute" is "as an accident" or "accidentally". Some texts omit this phrase.

The definition of time includes motion, and a motion is numerable, so the connection between time and motion is direct, so to speak. But an object at rest is also in time, and time contains it just as it contains a (finite) motion.

22. 202a3–5.

23. Things in time include also things at rest, as stated earlier.

24. The measurement will be given as a number of motion.

25. Qua a quantity, a thing in motion has also a length, a surface, and a volume, and it is not these which are measurable by time.

26. Are things which are in motion or at rest only as attributes also measurable? For example, if A, which is white, travels from A to B, is its whiteness measurable qua being an attribute of A while in motion? This may be accidental or indirect measurement.

27. What cannot exist cannot be measurable and so cannot be in time. Such are a commensurate diagonal and a number whose square has an odd number of factors.

28. They include things at rest.

29. Perhaps by "destructible and generable" he means things which are essentially so, while things which at one time exist but at another do not exist may not be changeable except as attributes, such as points, lines, whiteness and, in general, whatever has no physical matter (280b26–8, 1034b7–16, 1044b21–4).

30. For example, President Nixon existed and will exist for some time, and he is contained by time.

31. The opposition meant is a contrariety, not a contradiction, for the contradictory of "always" is "not always" and what does not always exist may exist sometime, but the contrary of "always" is "never".

32. Referring to the incommensurable diagonal, or to the fact that the diagonal is incommensurable with the side.

13

1. 220a4–5.

2. Like a point on a finite line, a moment within a finite interval of time preserves the unity of the two parts on both sides. But the point persists for an interval of time while the moment cannot do so.

3. When time is divided at a moment like a line at a point, the moment at which division takes place becomes two moments, the end of the earlier part of time and the beginning of the later part, or else that moment, even if numerically one, is viewed at the end of one part and the beginning of the other part, and, qua being viewed in this manner,

it is defined differently. But if no division has been made, then the moment is neither the end of one part nor the beginning of another except potentially, but it is both numerically and in definition one, and as such it connects the two parts.

4. A line can be divided actually as well as in thought, but it seems that time can be divided in thought but not actually. If so, then it appears that a moment divides potentially an interval of time in thought and not actually.

5. In other words, after division, the point becomes two points, each a limit of a line; but without division, no actual distinctions arise in the point.

6. An alternative to "and" is "or".

7. It is numerically the same point which can be the limit of each of two parts and can also keep the line unified, but its definition as a limit is not the same as its definition as something which keeps the unity of the line.

8. The Greek term for "moment" and "now" is the same.

9. According to some texts, the word should be "will" and not "did"; according to others, the verb is missing.

10. An alternate to "finite" is "limited", whether by moments or by time intervals.

11. That motion always exists is shown in 250b11–2b7.

12. Numerically, the time from (say) 1966 to 1968 cannot be repeated, but an interval of two years can be repeated; and such intervals of time are the same in species, for intervals of two years are the same in species.

13. That is, numerically the same moment ends past time and begins future time, and past and future are numerically distinct times, and since a moment always exists, though it is always distinct, time is always numerically distinct. The analogy with the circle seems to be this: The circumference is the same line or limit with the surface of a circle on its concave side and the surface outside on its convex side. Likewise, the moment is the same limit of past time on one side and future on the other.

14. The same numerical moment cannot be both the beginning and the end of the same interval of time.

15. There is only one Greek term for "presently" and "already"; accordingly, without a change in meaning, we have varied the translation so as to take care of the linguistic discrepancy.

16. Alternatives to "come" are "go" and "arrive".

17. As time passes we become wiser, but we also forget, so whether time should be called "the wisest" or "the stupidest" may be a problem. See Comm. 19, Section 12 of this Book.

18. 221a30–b3.

19. An alternative to "is generated" is "becomes something", and this may be a qualified becoming (or generation), in which case the thing which becomes something (like becoming a doctor) already exists as a

substance or body; and the thing must move or make an effort to become something, whereas by just doing nothing it may still be destroyed.

14

1. Uniform motion is more apparent in locomotion than in the other kinds of motion. It is not specified whether "uniform motion" means a motion along a uniform path (a straight line or a circular line) or a motion with a uniform speed or both (228b15–28).

2. Perhaps he means that time is simultaneous with a thing in motion, whether the thing is *actually* or potentially in motion; for if at rest, the thing is potentially in motion since it is movable, and time applies to motion as well as to its privation (or rest).

3. A number is not just a plurality; it is a plurality numberable by a unit. So it seems that while a plurality (e.g., of trees) exists even if an intellect does not exist, a number requires an intellect since a number is numerable.

Perhaps there is something in a number which depends on the intellect, for a number seems to have unity which depends somehow on the intellect. The height of a tree is a continuous magnitude and not a number, and it is considered to be a number when we specify a unit measure; but the choice of that measure depends on us, so the number itself somehow depends on us. Thus a tree is 40 yards high, but it is also 120 feet, and the two numbers are not the same. Once the unit of measure is specified, the number of the height does not depend on us; nevertheless, the unit does depend on us. In the case of five horses, there is no unity in them but just a plurality, although the essence of each horse is the same in species. But it is we who choose one horse as a unit and it is we who restrict the numbering to just that plurality, which then is a number; so the unity of five horses does depend on the intellect.

Whether Aristotle's view was something like the one given above, I am not sure.

4. Of course, a motion and things in motion always exist (250b11–4b6) even if no man exists, and so does the prior and the posterior in motion. Perhaps by "that" he means the motion, and time is an *attribute* or accident of motion.

5. Since time requires numerability, so do the attributes or parts of time (though indirectly through time), and the prior and posterior in time may be parts (time intervals) or moments.

6. He seems to be saying that the time of each kind of motion is the number of it qua a motion; for example, the time of a certain locomotion is the number of that locomotion but qua motion.

7. An alternative to "other things", according to some texts, is "another thing". Anyway, the problem here is different from that considered in the preceding Commentary; for in that Commentary the problem we were facing was the kinds of motion, but here we are facing the number of motions.

8. In other words, though motions may be distinct, whether numerically or in kind, if the limits (of their existence) coincide, their time is (numerically) one and the same. If their limits do not coincide, their time may be specifically the same, as in the case of a locomotion from 4 P.M. to 6 P.M. and an alteration from 9 P.M. to 11 P.M.

9. Perhaps by "distinct" he means distinct in kind and by "separate" he means motions of separate things, whether the motions are distinct or not.

10. Does time measure a motion in the same sense in which a motion measures time? Perhaps lines 220b14–24 indicate the different senses. To know a number of horses, say ten horses, we need to know the kind of a unit, which is one horse, and the number of such units, which is ten. Perhaps time measures a given motion as being that (number of units) by which the given motion is measured, like the ten horses by ten, while a motion measures time or the time of the given motion as being the unit which measures that time, like a horse, which as a unit measures ten horses.

11. Perhaps he means that the number of a uniform circular locomotion is the most known of the numbers of motion, as in the case of the locomotion of the Sun around the Earth, which makes up the days.

12. 261a28–b26.

13. That is, time as a number is measured by a unit of motion, and this unit is a circular motion of the universe once around the Earth.

14. That which is measured primarily is a continuous circular locomotion but qua a number, and the unit of that number is one revolution of that motion. But that which is measured is not (necessarily) just one revolution, it may be a plurality of such measures or revolutions, e.g., five revolutions of the Sun around the Center.

15. This is a definition of sameness. In general, if G is a genus whose species are S_1 and S_2, then things which come under S_1 are said to be of the same G, but if one comes under S_1 and another under S_2, they are said to be different G's. Time as a number is said to be the same or different in the same or in an analogous way.

16. What is pertinent to its inquiry are its parts and attributes, already considered.

Book E

1

1. Attributes or forms are not in motion or do not change essentially; what is in motion essentially is a body, or an object with matter, and it is in motion with respect to an attribute or a form (224b4–6, 1067b9–12). If a ship is in motion, is a man who stands on deck accidentally in motion (211a17–23)? Yes, for in the ship he is like a part, but he can be in motion essentially, as when he walks on deck.

2. In this case, it is the whole body that is in motion and not just a part of it.

3. For example, the alterable is distinguished from the thing in locomotion in that the motion in the first is one with respect to quality while the motion in the second is one with respect to place.

4. For example, if a mathematician moves a desk, it is not the science of mathematics that causes the motion; mathematics is just an accident of the man who causes the motion.

5. For example, the hand may move the book while the rest of the body remains motionless.

6. When a doctor heals an eye, he begins the motion; but does he do this with his whole medical science or with just a part of it? Perhaps with a part of it, for he does not use all his medical knowledge to heal the eye. As for the hand that strikes, it is a part of the doctor, and it does not begin the motion.

7. Perhaps "the hot" and "the cold" here mean the attributes heat and coldness, respectively; and that which is in motion, the wood, does not include heat or coldness or any intermediate temperature. In this sense, the underlying subject, the form, and the privation are primary (principles).

8. Perhaps this form is the contrary toward which motion proceeds.

9. For example, a motion toward becoming white is named "whitening", that toward becoming a building is named "building", and that toward health is named "becoming healthy" (in the Greek, the name is "healthying", if literally stated). The word "rather" indicates that this is not always the case.

10. 200b25–1b15.

11. What can move is a body, not attributes or forms.

12. Of course, the term "affection" has many senses: It means certain attributes, but also the motions or changes to those attributes (1022b15–21). Thus, both whiteness and whitening are affections, but not in the same sense of the term "affection".

13. He will consider this later (225b13–6a23).

14. By "these" he means the immovable affections in relation to the object in motion. Thus, as an end and in relation to the object which is being whitened, whiteness is essential; but an object of thought is accidental, as when one starts thinking of it when it is white, and a color is a part, for "whiteness" is a species of "color" (1023b12–25), or else, "a color" appears as a part in the definition of whiteness.

15. These distinctions are the same as those in 224a21–8. Perhaps "essentially" indicates that it is a body that causes motion or is moved, whether the whole body (primarily) or a part of it (in virtue of a part or of something else).

16. The movable may not be in motion, but it is in motion when it is in *actuality* qua movable.

17. Anyway, there is no science of accidents (1064b17–9).

18. In generation and destruction also; for here a change is from nonbeing to being and from being to nonbeing respectively.

19. Perhaps he means from an intermediate as well as to an intermediate. The alternatives are these: Change proceeds (a) from a contrary to a contrary (e.g., from white to black, or vice versa), (b) from a contrary to an intermediate or vice versa (from white to yellow, or vice versa), and (c) from an intermediate to an intermediate (from yellow to red, which lie between white and black). In (b) and (c) the ends function like contraries, but only in a qualified sense. For if a motion proceeds from, let us say, red to yellow, then within that motion the colors mostly opposed or most contrary are the ends, red and yellow, which may be said to be contrary in a relative way; and the same applies to a motion whose ends are a contrary and an intermediate.

20. For example, a subject is signified by such a term as "whiteness", "a man", and, in general, by a term under any category, but not by a negative term such as "not-man" or "not-red"; and a subject so signified need not be a body or have matter.

21. For example, from whiteness to blackness.

22. For example, from the white to the not-white, and, in general, from A to not-A, where A is signified by an affirmative term, as stated in Comm. 20.

23. One may consider a change from one not-A to another not-A (e.g., if the first not-A is greenness and the second is curvature, where "A" signifies a man) or from not-A to not-B (where "A" signifies a man and "B" signifies hardness); but such changes may be accidental and are excluded, and if they are not accidental they are already included in alternatives (a) and (b). For example, if "A" and "B" have the meanings already given, a white liquid (which is not-A) may change to a black liquid (which is not-B), and one may say that not-A changes to not-B, but the white liquid does not change qua not-A.

If the opposition is a contrariety, each contrary is signified by an affirmative term, and if a contradiction, as in A and not-A, then one of the contradictories, namely A, is signified by an affirmative term.

24. Such a change would be from not-A to A, not from not-B to A.

25. For example, a change from not-man to a man is an unqualified generation, for a man is a substance.

26. For example, from not-whiteness to whiteness, and whiteness comes under a category other than that of substance.

27. If a man is generated, then this is a change from not-man to a man, from a nonsubject to a subject, and "not-man" is not an affirmative term. But what is not-man? In this case it is a seed (or a fertilized egg, if you wish), which is not-man, and a seed is signified by "a seed", an affirmative term. Is a seed, then, not a substance but only matter, so to speak, or close to it? Or, if it is a substance, should the change from nonsubject to subject be limited to that from not-A to A? For in the latter case, if water changes to air and if both water and air are substances, still the change will have to be stated as that from not-air to air. For Aristotle, air and water and earth and the like are matter or potencies, or close to matter, for there is hardly a numerical unity in

them like that in a man (1040b5–10). Perhaps that which changes to a man is a potency which is a principle as matter and not a substance, and such a principle cannot be signified by an affirmative term if these are limited to the categories only.

28. Such nonbeing would be a false thought, which, as an *attribute*, is without matter and hence is immovable (4a21–b16, 1017a31–5, 1027b25–7).

29. This is potency as matter, which is a principle but not under any category.

30. The term "not-white" signifies a qualified being and may be a predicate of a substance, e.g., a black man, who can be in motion; so the not-white may be in motion, not qua not-white, which is an accident or attribute of him, but qua a body or substance. It is in this sense that the not-white is accidentally in motion, for the man is named by a qualified nonbeing, which is an accident of him.

31. An unqualified non-*this* cannot be a substance or an accident; and so it cannot be in motion, whether in virtue of itself or accidentally, since it cannot be signified by an affirmative term.

32. That is, unqualified nonbeing cannot be in motion, whether accidentally or essentially.

33. By definition, a generation proceeds from nonbeing, and from unqualified nonbeing there is unqualified generation.

34. This is unqualified nonbeing.

35. Since rest is contrary to motion, it can be an attribute only of that which can be in motion. So since unqualified nonbeing cannot be in motion, neither can it be at rest.

36. 225a7–12.

37. The Greek term translates into "white", but this does not signify a privation. Perhaps it should be νωδόν (= "toothless"), as in the *Metaphysics* (1068a7). Of course, "toothless" as an English term gives the appearance of being a negative term, but the Greek term gives the appearance of being an affirmative term.

38. Only eight categories are given; possession and position are omitted. This may be because he often does not complete the list or because he has changed his mind.

From what follows, there is no motion with respect to substance, relation, acting, and the others.

2

1. 3b24–7. A substance changes to a nonsubstance and conversely; and the opposition in such a change is a contradiction, not a contrariety.

2. For example, while retaining the same height and so not changing, John may be taller than Tom today but shorter than Tom a year from now.

3. Of course, the thing which acts may be in motion, and the moving thing is certainly a motion; but the meaning here is, there is no motion

of a moving thing with respect to the attribute of that thing, that is, with respect to its motion, which is another way of saying that there is no motion of the motion of a thing. This is made clear by what follows, namely, by "since there is no motion of a motion, no . . . .".

4. That is, from one kind of change to another kind of change, as from a locomotion to an alteration, or from healing to getting sick. The two kinds of change would be analogous to sickness and health, which are distinct.

5. A generation is a change from nonbeing to being, a destruction is a change from being to nonbeing, and the opposition in these is a contradiction (being and nonbeing are contradictories). But in a motion, the subject remains the same, and the change is from one contrary to another, as when Socrates changes from being healthy to being sick; and the subject is Socrates, not just matter.

6. A change is from a contrary to a contrary or from a contradictory to a contradictory (as in generation and destruction); and if a change changes from one change to another, these changes must be either contraries or contradictories and not any chance changes.

7. If becoming sick is one contrary, then becoming healthy would be the other, just as black is the contrary of white when a subject changes from white to black.

8. If recollecting and forgetting are contrary changes, then the subject in which they exist is a man and not a change, and forgetting does not always follow recollecting (and so it is accidental to it.)

9. If G_1 and G_2 are generations and G_2 is an attribute of G_1 as a subject, there will be a G_3, also a generation, which is an attribute of G_2.

10. Perhaps the argument is as follows. It is assumed that there is a generation G_1 of a generation, and so a G_1 of the simple generation G. If so, then there must be also a generation G_2 of G_1, for G_1 cannot be eternal. Let G take place during the time interval T_1T_2 and G_1 during T_0T_1. Now G is a simple or unqualified generation, and that which is generated at the moment T_2 is a substance, say S. But G_1 is not a simple generation, for G, which comes to be at T_1, is not a substance but something belonging to a substance, and G is a process occupying time T_1T_2. So T_0T_1 is a time prior to T_1T_2. But G_1 will likewise have to be generated by G_2 and during a time earlier than T_0T_1. Since, then, every generation will have to be generated, the series G, G_1, G_2, . . . will never end, and since there is no last G_i in that series to begin the generations, G cannot be generated and so S cannot be generated. Thus, a simple generation, or likewise any motion or change, turns out to be impossible.

11. Perhaps the meaning is as follows. That which is generated can also be destroyed, e.g., a house. So let G be a process of generation during time T_1T_2, and let G be in the process of being destroyed. While still in the process of being destroyed, G must exist as G. So G cannot be in the process of being destroyed before moment T_1 or after moment T_2, for it does not then exist; nor can it be in the process of being destroyed at T_1 or at T_2, for each of these is not a time interval but a limit of G,

and T_1 or T_2 is not the entire G. Hence G must be in the process of being destroyed during T_1T_2. Thus, that which is in the process of generation G during T_1T_2 is at the same time in the process of destruction, and this is impossible.

The argument is strengthened if it is assumed that G is not eternal but destructable and so must be destroyed sometime.

12. A body becomes white or black, a man gets sick, so there is a subject which takes on a form (in the wide sense). What is the subject which becomes a motion? Motion in itself is like an attribute or a form and has no matter.

13. 224a21–34.

14. If so, one may say that he who recovers is running or that recovering is running or something of this sort.

15. 224b26–8.

16. 1020a33–b25.

17. What is a qualified motion? Perhaps one in which there is a variation in degree (the more and the less) within an unqualified motion. For example, in a rectilinear motion, this might be an acceleration or its contrary; in the color red, this might be a change from more brilliant to less brilliant or vice versa; and, in general, in the same unqualified motion, a change with respect to a quality of such a motion.

3

1. These attributes are considered by physics rather than by mathematics because place enters into their definition; and the nature of place is considered by physics, for it is defined in terms of a body, which is considered by physics. Relative place, of course, is also found in mathematics in a qualified way (208b22–5, 322b29–3a3), but it is posterior.

2. Can such things be wholes or unities? Two bodies cannot be (wholly) in the same primary place (211a23–2a21), and two points which touch each other are not bodies and so cannot be in place. It appears, then, that either (a) the things are parts of one body, being together in one primary place in virtue of the whole body which is in one primary place, or (b) they are bodies which, taken together in virtue of their contact, are in one primary place, like the contents in a room.

3. For example, two men at a distance are apart, for the two taken together (just the two of them) cannot be in one primary place.

4. The whole boundaries of two or more things cannot be together; and since boundaries are not bodies, they are not in a place except accidentally, i.e., as attributes of bodies which (bodies) are in a place essentially. Perhaps "coincident" is better than "together"; anyway, "together" must not be confused with "together in a place".

5. Why the use of "at least"? Perhaps one may say that, for example, C is between A and D, if the order is ABCD, and there are four elements here.

6. The musical notes are not continuous, although pitch is continu-

ous. Hence, Aristotle adds "the smallest gap", and this would be the gap between successive notes.

7. In time, the lowest note may be struck right after the highest, but neither of these is an intermediate note. Hence, the phrase "in the thing in which it moves" is needed.

8. A contradiction excludes a middle; there is nothing between A and not-A.

9. This sentence has been transferred here from 227a7–10 to yield continuity in thought.

10. The lines (i.e., curves) connecting points A and B may be infinite, and so may the measures of their lengths; but the shortest line between A and B is unique, a straight line, and there is no longest. So Aristotle uses the shortest line as the principle to define contrariety in place. If various places are to be intermediate or contrary, then they have to lie along a straight line; and if so, the places at the ends of that line will be the contrary places, being most distant from each other.

11. Would not "species" be better than "genus"? Anyway, things in succession must be of the same kind. Thus, in a row of houses, trees may lie between the first and the second house; yet the second house still succeeds the first, by definition.

12. In using "a principle", Aristotle gives a wide definition of succession in order to include all alternatives in physics. This definition, then, is one by analogy, for "a principle" is an analogous term. Lines are not comparable with units or houses, for these three genera are distinct, but order may exist in each of them, and "order" and other terms allied to it are analogous. One may raise the problem of whether "succession" belongs to physics or to metaphysics, for the term is used also in mathematics and in other disciplines. Of course, one may so define succession that its application is limited to physics.

13. In the case of two and one, perhaps *being greater than one* is the principle, for two immediately follows one; in the case of the first and second days of the month, time or a day is the principle, for the second day is posterior in time to or immediately follows the first.

14. There seems to be a difficulty. Succession is an order which we may call "one-dimensional", as in the case of (whole) numbers and the parts of a straight line. But continuity may be one-dimensional, as in the line just mentioned, or it may be what we call "two-dimensional", as in

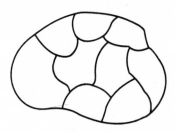

Fig. 15

a surface in which the parts are not one-dimensionally connected (as shown in Fig. 15), or it may even be three-dimensional, as in the parts of a body.

The difficulty is overcome if ἐχόμενον is replaced by ἀπτόμενον, that is, if "consecutive" is replaced by "touching".

15. 1015b36–6a17.

16. First (or prior to all others) in definition and in existence.

17. Of course, succession is prior to consecutiveness and to continuity.

18. Evidently things may be in contact in two ways: when they are parts of a continuous whole and when they touch but are not continuous. Aristotle uses "contact" in two senses, for both the genus and the species (things which touch but are not continuous).

19. Platonists.

20. The Platonists are in difficulties: If the Ideas and/or the Mathematical Objects are not in a place, how can Points (whether these be Ideas or Mathematical Objects) differ from Units. If Points have position (for they need this if they can be in contact), then they are in a place; and if they are not in a place, they do not differ from Units and are equivocally called "points".

21. That is, there need not be anything between numbers, e.g., there is nothing between any two successive numbers, although there is something between two non-successive numbers, e.g., between 3 and 7.

22. He means togetherness in place, for "togetherness" is an analogous term and has other applications also, as in time and in some other things (14b24–5a12).

4

1. From what follows, it appears that by "form of predication" he means the term used to name a given motion; for whitening may be named "whitening", "alteration", "motion", "incomplete actuality", etc.

2. An indivisible species cannot be subdivided into other species.

3. The same in species.

4. This is a conclusion reached by the use of definition (b) and by the entire preceding sentence, which is dialectically accepted.

5. For example, "quadrilateral" is a species of "polygon" but a genus of "square"; so it is not an ultimate or an unqualified species but a qualified species. So squares and parallelograms are specifically one in a qualified way, for both are quadrilaterals, and "quadrilateral" is both a species and a genus. Similarly, "science" is a species of "belief" but a genus of "mathematics" and of "physics" and of other sciences.

6. Why use a point whose motion can be only accidental? Is it (a) in view of what Aristotle calls "clear to us", (b) a concession to mathematicians, or (c) a corruption in Greek?

7. Unlike whitening, which for Aristotle is specifically one motion, a motion from place A to place B may be circular, straight, or mixed; and

since an arc and a straight line are distinct, so will be the motions along these lines (200b32–1a9).

8. By "one in *substance*" he means that the motion must be with respect to just one ultimate species, e.g., a rectilinear motion from, say, A to B (1054a35–b7); and to be numerically one, it must be in one individual, as explained from what follows.

9. This is one of the principles of motion, namely, the subject which is in motion.

10. Motion does not exist apart from bodies, and it must be with respect to something within a category, whether a quality, a quantity, or place; and it is one of the latter which he calls "that in which".

11. There may be some corruption in the Greek, but the thought indicated is clear, and we have translated accordingly.

12. The time must be continuous from, let us say, moment T_1 to moment T_2.

13. Coriscus and the light may be numerically one but in essence two (if Coriscus is light), and so they are accidentally one (in virtue of an attribute, lightness); and while the light in him may be turning dark, he may be walking, and so we have two motions and not one, although both of these are simultaneous and in one numerical subject, i.e., in Coriscus.

14. Here we have a disease which is one in *substance* or in indivisible species, but the disease is common, that is, it is present in more than one subject, for it is present in two men.

15. Perhaps by "numerically one" he means numerically one with that which existed previously but has been destroyed. For example, if a white object alters into black, then into white, and then back to black, then the object is white at two different times, and the problem of whether the two alterations (the two blackenings) are numerically one is shifted to the problem of whether the two whitenesses at different times are numerically one. It appears that they are not, although in species they are the same.

16. The sentences from this point to the end of the paragraph leave out much needed information; and there may be some corruption in the Greek. Our only recourse is to an interpretation. The translation, then, follows the interpretation we have chosen.

17. If, according to Heraclitus and others (1010a7–15), a thing is always in motion or in flux from moment to moment, then it cannot be numerically one and the same at any two moments; and if not numerically one and the same, then no habit or affection, which must exist in a body during an interval, can be numerically one and the same.

18. Perhaps the argument is this: If a man who is always in a state of flux is never the same, then during T_1T_2 he is numerically the same number of times, regardless of whether he is sick or healthy during T_2T_3. In other words, in both cases his state of being during T_2T_3, whether healthy or sick during T_2T_3, is distinct from and does not affect his state of being during T_1T_2 or during T_3T_4. So if one says that Soc-

rates' health during T_1T_2 and T_3T_4 is numerically one when he is healthy during T_2T_3, then he should likewise say that it is numerically one when Socrates is ill during T_2T_3.

19. Perhaps the meaning is this: If it is the same habit that is *actualized* at two different times, like strength (a habit) in lifting 200-pound weights, then even if a man lifts a 200-pound weight at two different times, still he has numerically one habit (strength); for the *actuality* of that habit (not the actual lifting) is numerically one, and so the habit itself is numerically one. But if the habit is numerically one, like the ability which one has in walking, then one need not actually walk only once to have that one ability; for he may walk many times by using that ability, which is numerically one.

20. That is, if health in the morning and health now are taken as being numerically one and the same, whether Socrates is healthy or sick during T_2T_3 (for it makes no difference; see Comm. 18 above), then, assuming that Socrates is sick during T_2T_3, his health during T_1T_2 and his health during T_3T_4 will turn out to be numerically one and the same even if interrupted or destroyed in T_2T_3. Of course, they cannot be numerically one and the same.

21. These *difficulties* seem to lie mainly within Metaphysics. The senses of "one", "many", etc. are needed, and there are such problems as to whether, for example, a thing always changes or not (Book Γ, *Metaphysics*).

22. Should the term be "continuous" or "divisible"? If "continuous", then from what follows, every motion is simply one, and this does not seem to be the intended meaning. But if "divisible", then if the motion is simply one, it is more than divisible; it is continuous.

23. For example, a virtue is not continuous with a line, nor a surface with time.

24. For example, redness or equality has no extremity.

25. Points and lines are extremities of lines and surfaces, respectively, but points and lines are not comparable. The term "extremity" has analogous meanings.

26. Things are consecutive if their extremities touch. What are the extremities that touch in a man at the end of his running and at the beginning of his sickness? The subject is one, but the motions are distinct. Perhaps they are the moments, i.e., the end of the time of the first and the beginning of that of the second, as indicated from what follows. In the torch race, the subject holding the torch changes, and the torch is handed from one to the other at a moment, so there is consecutiveness. Of course, "touch" has analogous senses for time, lines, surfaces, and bodies.

27. If they are consecutive, then they are in succession; and they may be in succession even if there is rest between them.

28. In other words, two or more motions may be specifically one but numerically many.

29. For example, if a stone dropped from a house is caught and not

allowed to reach its natural place, its motion would not be complete, or not so complete as when allowed to reach its place. It is like a part of a motion, which is not quite one. Similarly, there is incomplete ripening or increasing, or an incomplete walk (1016b11–7, 1021b12–2a3).

30. The unity here is in virtue of continuity, though there is no unity qua being a complete motion.

31. This is like a vector in two or three dimensions, analyzable into one-dimensional components as elements or principles which are no longer analyzable. Scientifically speaking, such analysis is necessary (184a10–6).

32. If the motion is a mixture of contraries, then there may be more of one contrary and less of the other; and if more than two elements participate in the mixture or blend, the more and the less may apply to more than two of them, as in vectors. He says "seems to be", for perhaps the investigation of this point belongs to a less universal science, depending on the kind of motion.

33. For example, a part of a straight line can be made to coincide with any other part equal in length, but this is not so in the case of a parabola.

34. It is like whiteness and blackness, which are not differentiae of men or of dogs but are attributes of bodies.

35. One kind of earth may be denser than another, and it may travel faster to its natural place; and likewise with samples of fire.

36. The phrase "to a lesser degree" here does not apply to a thing within the category of quality; it is a predicate of unity, and thus a metaphysical predicate, so to speak.

37. If A is one to a lesser degree than B, then since A is something and B is something but neither is an unqualified nonbeing, A must be opposed to B as a privation; and since this is a privation of unity and the contrary of unity is plurality, B must be somehow a plurality, or a composite of unity and plurality in some sense.

38. Perhaps consecutive in time is meant, for otherwise there may be no contact.

5

1. Some thinkers regarded generations and destructions as motions, and these would be motions to A and from A, respectively, thus being like motions to health and from health (314a6–7, b1–4).

2. This is alternative (d). No verb appears in the Greek, and "may be", which we have supplied, seems to be the proper expression since the two motions as stated may or may not be one.

3. The definition of a change from health differs from that of a change to disease; for the first does not mention disease, and the second does not mention health. Besides, such a change need not be a motion, as when a white thing is generated and its whiteness comes into being

just when the thing is generated or as when a healthy man is killed and the result is not a diseased man.

4. There are two alternative interpretations, and both make sense: If A and C are contraries and B is an intermediate, then (a) a motion from A may be toward C or toward B, so it is not a uniquely determined motion such as to be contrary to just one motion; and (b) a motion from A may be toward B or toward C, and a motion from C may be toward B or toward A, so the two motions from A and from C, which may end at B (and these cannot be unqualified contrary motions), or at C and at A, or at B and at A, or at C and at B, respectively, are not uniquely determined to be contrary.

5. 229b16–21.

6. Perhaps this argument, though dialectical, seems debatable; but one may argue that the loss of a contrary might be a change from being to nonbeing, or a change whose ends are opposites and not necessarily contraries, while in the gain of contraries the end results are contraries and not just contradictories.

7. This is a dialectical argument, based on language which corresponds to fact most of the time or often.

8. This would make alternative (c) be the same as (e).

9. A change from a contrary or a change to a contrary does not explicitly indicate that it is a motion, for a change from health occurs also when a man dies. To be a motion, then, the change must be such that it proceeds from A to B, where these are within a contrariety and are not just opposites (this is considered later in 229b10–4).

10. He probably means falling sick from being healthy, for he often leaves statements incomplete, and the same applies to "being taught" and "being led into a mistake", and to the other examples that follow. Of course, it may be that falling sick, which in Greek is signified by a single word, is defined as a change or a motion from health to disease, and likewise for the other motions.

11. Just as one may get *knowledge* through himself as well as through another, so he may be led into a mistake through himself as well as through another.

12. Since the starting-point is not specified, it is a change since it need not be a motion. It may be called "a qualified generation", as stated in 225a12–7. For example, in a simple generation, e.g., a birth of a baby, the thing generated may be white, and there is no substance which remains the same in that change, so there is no motion. The same applies to a qualified destruction.

13. For example, there is no contrary to a substance, e.g., to a man, and so the birth of Socrates is not a motion but is a change contrary to his death. Are losing and gaining identical to destruction and generation? Perhaps losing or gaining is a qualified destruction or generation respectively, for perhaps there is a subject, and the same subject, which loses or gains respectively.

14. In an unqualified way, the contrary of white is black, and vice versa. But if a completed motion has white and grey as ends, or grey and black, then with respect to that motion the two ends are most different; and whether it is black or white which is the qualified contrary of grey depends on which direction the motion from grey proceeds (224b30–5).

15. 224b30–5.

6

1. This sense is not the unqualified sense just stated and discussed in the preceding section, but a distinct sense yet to be specified.

2. Is *"rest"* a synonym of "rest" or of "rest with respect to place"?

3. The meaning of "subject" is given in 225a34–b5.

4. That is, *rest* at the one place and *rest* at the other.

5. If contrariety in two motions arises in virtue of their place, then certainly contrariety of rest with respect to place should also arise.

If A and B are contraries and a thing has only one contrary, how can rest at A be contrary to rest at B and also to the motion from A to B, or how can the motion from A to B be contrary to that from B to A and also to rest at A? One may argue that one contrariety is within the genus "motion", another within "rest", and a third is an opposition of a motion to rest; so one may distinguish or qualify the kinds of contrarieties and thus avoid confusion.

6. It must be a motion either from disease to health or from health to disease.

7. Whiteness is not the contrary of health, and so rest in whiteness is not the contrary of rest in health; besides, if rest in whiteness were the contrary, so would be rest in strength, rest in virtue, and an indefinite number of other states of rest.

8. If A changes to non-A and A has no contrary, that change is not a motion; and since rest is the privation and not just the denial of motion, there can be no rest (or *rest*) at A or at non-A; but there may be changelessness. Thus A may remain A, and likewise for non-A.

9. For example, if Socrates is the subject, there may be changelessness in both healthy Socrates and nonhealthy Socrates.

10. Since rest belongs only to that to which motion belongs, if rest were to belong to non-A, then "rest" would be a predicate also of what is not a motion, for a change from A to non-A is not a motion but a destruction.

11. The analogy is this: Rest is to the contraries in a motion as changelessness is to the contradictories in a change, provided that not-A as a contradictory is something and not pure nonbeing.

12. Just as rest at A is contrary to the motion from A to its contrary, so changelessness at A is contrary to the change from A to its contradictory.

13. That is, it is not the case that one increase is according to nature while another is contrary to nature.

14. The denial of the two differences (according to nature and contrary to nature) within a kind of change does not imply the denial of that change as being according to nature but not otherwise.

15. A force is a moving cause and goes contrary to the nature of something. For example, stones fall down according to nature, but force prevents them from doing this (1015a26–7) and so acts contrary to their nature.

16. Taken without qualification, a generation is contrary to a destruction. But if a generation (or a destruction) is qualified as being pleasant, then there is another and contrary qualified generation (or destruction), a painful one. Just as there are many kinds of qualifications that may be attached to a generation or to a destruction, so there arise many kinds of qualified contrarieties.

17. The term "the one" refers to a motion or a state of rest.

18. The preceding contrariety is of motions by nature which differ in virtue of the contrary places to which they are directed. Here the contrariety is with respect to a motion by nature and one contrary to nature; and this is clearly exemplified by the same kind of body, like fire, and these motions differ likewise in direction.

19. Here we have a contrariety between rest and motion when rest is contrary to nature but motion is according to nature, and this too, like the preceding case, is clearly exemplified by the same kind of body; and rest contrary to the nature of a body functions like the motion contrary to the nature of that body.

20. There seem to be two parts to the problem: (a) whether a non-eternal state of rest of a body in a place contrary to its nature is essentially generated and (b) whether the generation of such a state of rest is a coming to a stop.

21. Although Aristotle gives no direct answer to the problem, the distinctions he makes seem to suggest at least part of the answer. If the definition of coming to a stop includes faster travelling, then it is restricted to motions according to nature and excludes those contrary to nature. If so, then a body at rest contrary to its nature by definition did not come to a stop; and if coming to a stop is a motion, then the state of rest of that body was not in the process of being essentially generated but was generated, if at all, only accidentally (1027a29–32). Whether coming to a stop or travelling to one's own place would then be the same in definition, or different but occurring at the same time, is left unanswered. The answer depends on whether there is a difference or not and whether the difference or the lack of it is apprehended.

22. This problem, restricted to locomotion here, may be applied also to the other motions.

23. For example, if A starts altering from white to black at moment T, at an intermediate moment T_1 when it is grey it is still partly white,

and that part of white at T_1 has been at rest in the time interval TT_1.

24. To what? Perhaps to the thing in motion. For part of the thing is at rest, as suggested in the preceding Commentary, and the thing is assumed to be in motion, so it is at rest and in motion; or else, since at an intermediate state it has some of the contrary it started out with and also some of the other contrary which it gained, it therefore has both, an apparent contradiction.

25. There is no contradiction; for to say that contraries A and B belong to C at the same time is to say that C is wholly A and wholly B at the same time. In this case C is partly A and partly B, or it possesses contraries in a qualified way.

26. It seems that the term should be ἠρεμία (rest) and not ἠρέμησις (a coming to rest).

In contrary motions, one motion is always losing some thing while the other is always gaining that thing; for example, in blackening, whiteness is constantly being lost, while in whitening it is constantly being gained. But if a thing is resting at whiteness, it is not losing any of it; so blackening and whitening change in opposite directions at a greater rate than blackening and resting at the state of whiteness. Aristotle here aptly uses the comparative "rather".

27. This seems to be the end of Book E. The next paragraph, included by some manuscripts but omitted by others, seems to be out of place. Lines 230b28–1b2 consider whether a state of rest at A is contrary to a motion from A; so there is some reason that lines 231a5–10, which consider whether a motion to A is opposed to a state of rest, should follow lines 230b28–1b2. Lines 231a10–6 seem to state what lines 230b12–6 do. Finally, lines 231a16–7 suggest a result while lines 230b28–1b2 elaborate on it. Perhaps lines 231a5–17 are an earlier draft.

Book z

1

1. 226b18–7a13.

2. Some thinkers had different views about lines or points; some posited indivisible lines (206a17–8, 968a1–972b33), and the Pythagoreans posited points as having magnitude (1080b16–21).

3. By definition, an extremity of a thing is not that thing but is only a part of it; so since a point is indivisible, it has no parts and therefore no extremities. And if no such extremities exist, neither can they be one or together.

The argument is based not on how any two parts of a line are related, but on how the ultimate parts of it are related, if such ultimate parts exist and are indivisible.

4. That the points should be continuous with each other to form a

continuum follows from the definition; but that they should be only in contact seems a weaker argument, for things in contact need not be one (227a6–31).

5. For example, the indivisibles in time are moments.

6. Strictly speaking, indivisibles cannot touch even as wholes, for by definition an indivisible has no parts and so cannot even be a whole (1023b26–4a10). However, the meaning is clear. Instead of "they touch as wholes" we could say "they touch entirely" or "they touch but not in virtue of a part" or something of this sort.

7. Some assumptions are needed. If two points touch as wholes, the result is not continuous (for the reason given). If this result itself touches a third point, what results is again not continuous, and for the same reason. Thus no finite number of points, assumed touching, can form somehing continuous.

As for the set of all the numbers, e.g., 1, 2, 3, etc., which we call "a denumerable infinite set", Aristotle rejects its actuality although he allows it if it is assumed potential or as a process. But a line is something actual and not a process; hence a line does not consist of a denumerable infinite number of points. What about what we call "a non-denumerable set", and in particular, all the points on a finite line? If the existence of this depends on, or is established by, the existence of a denumerable infinite set, it would be rejected at least on this basis.

8. If there is always a line between two points and a line has within it other points, then there are always other points between two points, and so these two points cannot be in succession; for, by definition, if two things are in succession, no thing of the same kind as they are lies between. The same applies to moments.

9. If a line, for example, were composed of points which are indivisible parts, and so material principles, then nothing impossible should result if that line be assumed as having been divided into those parts. But something impossible would follow, as already stated earlier.

10. If things of another genus lie between two points, then the same difficulty follows, though in that other genus; and shifting from one genus to another without end is excluded.

11. St. Thomas Aquinas regards infinite divisibility as an alternative definition of continuity given by Aristotle, but this does not seem to be the case. In lines 200b18–20 Aristotle merely states that some thinkers use infinite divisibility as the definition of continuity; and he himself sometimes uses it, but as a property. Moreover, there is only one definition of a thing (998b12).

One might argue as follows. What is continuous has parts, which are either ultimately indivisible or not ultimately indivisible. If ultimately indivisible, something impossible results, as already shown. Hence the parts are not ultimately indivisible; and if not ultimately indivisible, they are always divisible. Infinite divisibility, then, seems to be a property and not a definition of continuity. This is confirmed also by what follows (231b15–8).

12. In Fig. 6, the parts A, B, and C of line ABC appear as divisible, but in the argument they are assumed as indivisible. The motion D of W is the motion of W over part A, and likewise for the motions E and F.

13. The term "object-in-motion" seems to signify the object with its motion. Since that motion is composed of indivisibles D, E, and F, the object-in-motion itself must be composed of indivisibles W(D), W(E), and W(F), where, for example, W(D) is the composite of W with its motion over A, which composite is not divisible with respect to its motion.

14. If W is in the process of moving over A, it must have moved partly but not wholly over A, and if partly, then its motion over A is divisible, contrary to the assumption; and clearly it cannot at the same time or moment be in the process of moving over A and have moved over A.

15. An impulse would be something indivisible. If we call it "a motion", there would be two kinds of motions, divisible and indivisible. In an impulse, then, an object cannot be in the process of motion, for the impulse would be divisible. We may say that the object *has moved* with or in an impulse, but "has moved" does not signify time which is divisible; otherwise, the impulse would be divisible.

16. If the object W has moved over ABC, since it *has moved* over A in an impulse D but was not in the process of moving over A (and likewise over B and over C), then, since a body must be either at rest or in the process of motion, W must be at rest over A, and likewise over B and over C, and so over the whole line ABC. But how can W be at rest and in motion over ABC at the same time?

17. Whether "each" refers to a length or a motion is not specified. The word πᾶσα seems to indicate a motion, but it may also indicate a length, signified by γραμμή, although Aristotle has just used the neuter μῆκος to signify a length. If "each" refers to a motion, then "A" signifies a motion; if it refers to a length, "A" signifies a length. The argument is valid in either case, but perhaps stronger for a length.

2

1. That is, some but not all greater magnitudes. For example, an object with a triple speed will take less time to traverse double the distance, but more time to traverse four times the distance.

2. Does the definition refer to (a), to (b), to (c), to two of them, or to all of them (848b5–8)?

3. Is this Aristotle's definition of "faster"? He seems to be using sometimes (a) and sometimes (b), but each implies the other (222b33–3a4, 248a25–b3, 848b5–8).

4. And T_1T_4, it may be added, is the time taken by B to traverse S_1S_2, which is less than S_1S_3.

5. This axiom is nowadays stated thus: "If A is greater than B and B is greater than C, then A is greater than C".

6. Is there no fastest motion for Aristotle, like that of the great circle

at the extremity of the universe, which he considers to be rotating about the center of the universe?

7. A and B are assumed to be travelling with uniform speeds.

8. Time and length may be infinite (a) by adding more and more indefinitely, or (b) by dividing indefinitely. In the first case, both time and length will be increasing indefinitely (infinitely); in the second, given a finite length S_1S_2 traversed by an object in finite time T_1T_2, as S_1S_2 is divided indefinitely, T_1T_2 too will be divided indefinitely, and conversely. The first is an infinite with respect to addition and in the direction of the greater; the second is an infinite with respect to division and in the direction of the less.

9. This would be the infinite with respect to addition, in which the extremities become always distinct. Infinity by addition may be of two kinds: (a) The parts added never exceed some given interval, as in the addition by bisecting a unit distance or time, in which we have $\frac{1}{2} + \frac{1}{4} + \frac{1}{8} + \ldots$; (b) the parts added are equal, as in the sum $c + c + c + \ldots$ In both cases, the extremities become always distinct in the direction of increase.

Ross thinks that Aristotle contradicts himself when he allows the sum of the c's to exceed every magnitude but at the same time denies an infinity by extension. The distance traversed in an infinite time, however, say by a point P at the outer great circle of the universe, which rotates about its center (according to Aristotle), does not exceed every distance, for it is the same circle (finite in distance) along which P moves again and again. So while the motion (and so the time) along that distance is infinite, the distance remains actually finite. It is like counting the same man again and again; the counting is indefinite and so is the number, but actually there is just one man.

10. This is the infinite of type (b) in the preceding Commentary. Zeno argues thus: There is no motion; for to move from A_1 to A_2 one would have to traverse first half that distance, then half of what remains, etc., indefinitely, and to traverse an infinity of parts in a finite time is impossible.

For Aristotle, both the distance A_1A_2 and the time T_1T_2 are alike finite and alike infinite. They are finite if a unit measure is taken in each case, and both are finitely measured in this sense; they are infinite in the sense that both are infinitely divisible, and just as there is an infinity of parts in A_1A_2 of type (a) in the preceding Commentary (or an infinity of points), so there is an infinity of parts likewise in T_1T_2 (or of moments). Zeno confuses the types. If he is to say that A_1A_2 is infinite (by division), he should likewise say that T_1T_2 is infinite and not finite.

11. Uniform speed is assumed. What if the speed is not uniform? Thus, if the speed s is given by the formula $s = Me^{-t}$, where $e = 2.718 \ldots$, then an object cannot traverse the distance M in a finite time, for $\int_0^T Me^{-t}dt = M(1 - e^{-T})$, which is less than M for any finite T.

12. That is, the time taken is a finite number of measures, each measure being equal to T_1T_2.

13. Perhaps this is an assumption confirmed by experience.

14. Thus, if some finite magnitude is traversed in a finite time, it can be further shown that also every finite magnitude is traversed in a finite time.

15. These *indivisible* magnitudes (e.g., straight lines) are assumed equal; otherwise, if one can be made to coincide with a part of another, the latter will not be *indivisible*.

16. If such a part of time is not *indivisible*, then in a part of that part the faster will traverse a magnitude which is less than an *indivisible* magnitude, and this cannot be.

17. If T is to be bisected, then T_2T_3, which is between T_1T_2 and T_3T_4, will have to be bisected and so be divisible. But it is assumed to be *indivisible*.

18. If the slower traverses EF (or FG) in a time greater than an *indivisible* time, then in a smaller or equal time it will have to traverse only a part of EF. But EF is *indivisible*.

3

1. An alternative to "of something else" is "of something in virtue of something else". The primary sense of "moment" is that of something indivisible.

2. If T_1T_2 is taken as the past time, he is referring to T_2 as the limit prior to which there is no part of the future, and if T_1T_2 is taken as the future time, he is referring to T_1 as the limit after which there is no part of past time.

3. If the moment is an extremity of the past and also an extremity of the future, do we not have two extremities? But the moment as a division of time exists only potentially (222a14). Numerically it is one and indivisible, and it unites the two parts of time, past and future, just as the point B on line AC unites the parts AB and BC of that line into one line; but in definition the moment is two, for it may be viewed from the past or from the future, like a point in the middle of a line which may be viewed as the end of one part but the beginning of the other part.

By "to be such and to be the same" perhaps he means to be a limit and to be numerically the same.

4. That is, numerically the same.

5. If distinct, they cannot be in succession (perhaps a succession which is consecutive is meant); for of two things in succession one is prior and the other posterior, while the two moments, being indivisible, would have to touch, if at all, as whole to whole and so to be together, and in this case they would not form a continuum (231a21–b20).

6. Between two limits which are apart (and these limits here are moments) there is what we here call "time". But if there were time between, and so also a moment within that time, then (a) the future would not (immediately) succeed the past since there would be an interval of time prior to the future, and (b) the limit of the past and that of the future would not be in (immediate) succession, because in the intermediate time there would be other moments.

7. 232b20–3a21.

8. Why will the moment be divisible, unless it is assumed (the position of St. Thomas Aquinas) that between the two limits, which are assumed to be apart, there is something which is a moment (for it is moments that are taken as being or as not being in succession)? Perhaps the sentence starts another part of the argument. It was just shown that difficulties result if the two limits are distinct. The alternative is that they are numerically one, but that the limit is divisible.

9. If the moment A is the limit of the past just before the future, and B the limit of the future just after the past, and if A and B are apart, then there is time, say AB, from A to B. Since time is divisible, let AB be divisible at M. Since M is after A, AM (or MB) is in the future, and since M is before B, (AM or) MB is in the past. So AM or MB is both in the past and in the future; or, part of the future (say, AM) is in the past and part of the past (say, MB) is in the future, which is impossible.

10. If there is a division of the moment, then "moment" must be taken not in the sense considered here, but in the secondary sense in which it signifies time (222a20–2).

11. This, too, is impossible, especially when a point is indivisible; otherwise, some past time (here, one part of the moment) and some future time (the other part of the moment) will have to coincide or exist at the same time.

12. On the hypothesis that the moment is divisible, since a continuum (here it is a time interval) can be divided in diverse ways or at various moments, the parts of the divided moment which are past and future vary with the manner of division, and the present moment itself which is that (point of) division will vary and not be the same. All these are impossible.

13. In both past and future.

14. If the same moment M belongs to both the past and the future and a thing may be in motion in a moment, and if it be assumed that a thing is in motion during the past and so during the part M and likewise at rest during the future and so during the part M, then that thing will be at the same time in motion and at rest during M.

If M is the present moment, the past may be taken as a finite interval, say LM, and the future as the finite interval MN.

15. That is, there has been no change in the whole thing or in any of its parts.

16. There can be no two (or more) parts in a moment, and so there can be no one part prior to another part.

4

1. 231b28–30.

2. It is at rest or in a state of changelessness (234b5–7).

3. Perhaps by "the first [state]" he means the end toward which the change proceeds, and this end may be some intermediate state and not necessarily a contrary, like a change from black to grey or one from

the center of the Earth to a place other than the extremity of the universe.

4. The divisibility of the changing thing is with respect to the kind of change, that is, with respect to quality or quantity or place or substantial change. Thus, if the ends are white and grey, the thing will be at intermediate stages; if they are places A and B, it will be at intermediate places; and if they are magnitudes C and D, the thing will have intermediate magnitudes.

What about substantial change, if there is no intermediate between being and nonbeing, e.g., no intermediate between man and not-man? There are stages in the process of generation, but all these are nonbeing with respect to the final stage. Of course, he speaks of the thing that is changing and not of the change itself; so perhaps the various stages, with varying degrees of completeness, would be the intermediates, for the process of generation takes time. In destruction, the situation appears more difficult. We may add that in both generation and destruction other kinds of change take place, e.g., a locomotion or an alteration, and at least with respect to these changes there are intermediates.

5. Such division makes possible certain additive properties of moving things. For example, if a thing has a complex (mixed) locomotion, then its entire motion may be analyzed into, and so be calculated by, the motions of the parts. This is like the modern way of calculating the total work, or momentum, or energy, by summing up that of all the parts.

6. 232a18–22.

7. That is, with respect to place or quality or quantity.

8. An alternative to "being-moved" may be "being-in-motion".

9. Not all the five kinds of division are explained. Let the motion of a thing P be from A to D, where A and D may be places or magnitudes or qualities, depending on the kind of motion, and let there be two divisions at B and C. Then there is (1) the division at T_2 and T_3 of the time T_1T_4 taken and into the time intervals T_1T_2, T_2T_3, and T_3T_4, (2) the division of the whole motion into that from A to B, that from B to C, and that from C to D, and (5) the divisions of the interval from A to D, and these may be at B and C, and the intervals are from A to B, from B to C, and from C to D (e.g., in colors, B and C are different colors, and the intervals AB, BC, and CD are bands in the color spectrum); and these three kinds are clear enough.

As for (4), since the divisions are with respect to time, perhaps this is the thing along with the attribute (place or quality or magnitude) at B, and again at C; and as for (3), perhaps this is the thing along with its motion from A to B and from B to C and from C to D, or else the extent or interval of place or of quality or of magnitude traversed from one division to another.

10. If P has a locomotion from A to D, then the distance AD, being a quantity, is essentially divisible; but if A and D are colors, which are

qualities, the division is accidental, that is, one may consider the different colors possessed by P at T_2 and at T_3.

11. Since time is always divisible, so is the motion during this time, and since the motion from A to D is always divisible, so is the time taken.

12. 234b24–5a7.

13. First he considers the length over which a motion proceeds, as in a locomotion, for a length is essentially divisible and is easy to see; then he mentions the others whose division is accidental (see Comm. 10 above).

14. For example, if in the locomotion from A to B the interval AB is expressed in units of distance, it will be finite, and so will the others, that is, the time, the motion, the being-moved, and the thing in motion; and if it is expressed with respect to its infinite division (for it is infinitely divisible), the others too will be likewise infinite. Moreover, just as a division may be essential or accidental, so may the infinite, for the infinite arises by the division of a thing. For example, the magnitude AB is essentially divisible, so the infinite divisibility of AB may be called "direct" or "essential"; but the band in the color-spectrum is accidentally divisible, so the infinite division of that band into an infinity of colors or color-shades may be called "indirect" or "accidental".

15. 234b10–20.

16. 236b19–8b22.

5

1. The word "when" does not necessarily signify an interval of time; the issue is left open, for there are two alternatives, an interval of time and a moment. By "has changed" he means not that the thing has partly changed but that the thing has completed the change. As for "first", see Comm. 14 in this Section.

2. By "the same" it appears that he means the same in formula or definition.

3. Either "from something to something" is included in the formula of a change, or it is an axiom of change (235b6–7). In either case, "to leave" does not appear to include "to something", so perhaps "to leave" is weaker than (or follows from) "to change". It may be a fact or an axiom that if A leaves something it also proceeds to something. Perhaps it is in view of these considerations that Aristotle, rather than take the time to introduce axioms or definitions, mentions the two alternatives, for the outcome will be the same anyway. He does so in other cases similar to this.

4. That is, changing : leaving :: having changed : having left.

5. This is a generation or a destruction (225a12–20).

6. These would be a destruction, an alteration, a locomotion, an increase, and a decrease.

7. The proper term in the case of a locomotion is "somewhere"; but

perhaps no proper terms exist for the other changes, and so he uses an expression which is general and which we translate as "some state".

8. He considers a locomotion as a typical change, and the same applies to the others.

9. Since a change is continuous and the thing has not yet completed the change, to assume that it is not at the end C is to assume that it is still changing; and because of the continuity, C cannot be consecutive to B without changing.

10. In virtue of the preceding Commentary, to assume that the thing has first changed to B is to be faced with the impossibility that the thing simultaneously has changed and is changing (231b28–31).

11. Perhaps "exist" signifies an existence for some interval of time and not just for a moment; otherwise, the change will be going on without having reached an end.

12. In this change the principle of the excluded middle is sufficient (235b13–6), whereas in a motion additional principles are needed, such as the principle that there must be a subject underlying the change. If so, then the change with respect to contradiction appears to be most of all clear *by nature.*

13. At this point, the meaning of "that" is left open; the alternatives are, it is either a moment or an interval of time.

14. If an object has changed at T (where T is a moment or an interval of time), it is still true to say at some later time or moment that it has changed. Now "first" here signifies that if it has changed at T, it has not (yet) changed at a time or moment earlier than T. In general, as he states, by "has changed first" he means that if it is true to say that the thing has changed at T, it is not true to say that it has changed at any part of T.

15. AC here is taken as being time or a moment.

16. And if so, it would not have completed the change.

17. The thing will have changed first not in AC but in a part of it, and this part is prior to the whole with respect to having changed.

18. If not divisible, it is a moment.

19. This is because a generation and a destruction are kinds of changes.

20. It is the beginning of time, during (or in) any part of which it is true to say that the thing has changed.

21. In one sense, it exists in time like a point in a line, but in another, not; for a moment exists as a limit but not during an interval. And since time is continuous, it exists potentially, so to say.

22. There is neither a moment nor a first time at which a change begins; for at a moment there can be neither a motion nor rest, and time is always divisible. One may define a beginning of a change as a moment such that at any moment later some change has taken place, but this definition avoids the issue. Mathematically, Aristotle is saying that if an object is at rest during T_1T_2 and T_2 is the end of its rest, then it is at rest in the closed interval $[T_1, T_2]$ but in motion in, say, $(T_2, T_3]$,

where the latter time interval is open at the left. Thus neither is there a beginning in this interval, nor is there a first part of time in which the thing was changing.

23. BC is hypothetically taken as being the first part (an interval of time or a moment) in which or during which there has been a process of change.

24. Since in BC there has been a process of change, which (process) is continuous and so infinitely divisible, if BC is indivisible, any divisible process of change will consist of smaller parts of process of change, each of which will occur in indivisibles like BC, and these will then be consecutive and add up to an interval of time, which is impossible.

25. Since the process begins with B, and B is the same as BC since BC is assumed indivisible, it is reasonable to assume the object at rest at some time prior to B or to BC.

26. Of course, for Aristotle there is neither a motion nor rest at a moment or at an indivisible in time. Here, however, the hypothesis is that the thing has changed in the indivisible BC; so if there can be a change in BC, there can also be rest in it.

27. If BC is without parts, then B, BC, and C are identical, except in name.

28. Whether the division is into two parts or more, makes no difference in the argument. For simplicity, then, only two parts are considered.

29. If it is in the process of changing in all of it, it has not yet completed the change.

30. For the part in which it has changed is prior to the whole, since the other part is superfluous with respect to having changed.

31. The assumption here is still that BC is not without parts, and since moments are not consecutive, as already stated, infinite divisibility follows.

32. Just as DE, which is a part of DF, is assumed to be the first part which has changed, so it is assumed that in a time interval less than T_1T_2 there is of DE a first part which has changed. Thus the assumption of DE as a first part which has changed leads to a still prior part which has changed; and this being impossible, it follows that there is no first part. In other words, DF has changed or completes the change as a whole and not part by part.

33. By "that" here he means that with respect to which the thing is changing, for example, the quality in the case of an alteration, the place in a locomotion, the quantity in an increase or decrease.

34. The time.

35. Of course, the man is divisible qua a body or a magnitude, not qua a substance.

36. Perhaps "these" refers to things like paleness, and, in general, to qualities, for these are not quantities except accidentally, and the division considered here is that of magnitudes which are quantities.

37. The motion considered here appears to be a locomotion.

38. The expression "has changed" might appear to indicate a completion of a change, but perhaps this is because of the assumption that there is a first part with respect to which a change has taken place or has been completed, not that the whole change has been completed.

39. The division of BC or of any part of it.

40. This would be an increase or a decrease.

41. A quality is not divisible essentially, although it is divisible accidentally. For example, when a white body is divided qua magnitude into halves, each part is white; and it is just as white as the whole body and not half as white. And when a body changes from white to black, even then the division is not of the color, except accidentally.

A problem arises here. In a continuous change from white to black, is there an infinite division of shades of color, even if accidental? It appears so, for at each division of the interval of the occurring change or of the time of change, the color or shade of color at the moment of division will be different. Ross thinks otherwise, for he speaks of "indivisible installments of change" in quality (*Aristotle's Physics,* pp. 650–1), but this seems to lead to difficulties; for example, there will be time intervals in which the color or its shade will not be changing, and so the change will not be continuous.

6

1. A change in time T_1T_2 is primary if it is from moment T_1 to moment T_2; that is, if there is some change in any interval from T_1 to T_2. Hence no interval of changelessness exists in T_1T_2. For example, if a man walked from A to B in one minute, he will have walked some part of AB during any part of that minute.

2. 232b23–3a10.

3. A time other than AC here would be a part of AC.

4. The speeds of the things in motion are assumed to be uniform.

Some premises are lacking. If "a primary motion" is a predicate also of a continuous motion which is partial and if the primary time AC is of that partial motion of the thing which has not yet completed that motion but is in motion, then, assuming that "having moved" applies also to partial motions already completed (as stated in what follows, 237a3–7), when the thing is in motion and is under consideration at the moment C (or at any small time interval near C, for the argument would be similar), it must have moved (perhaps potentially, since it did not rest) at some earlier interval, say AB, where moment B is earlier than C. There are alternative interpretations.

5. If the thing in motion at C has moved earlier in time AB, as indicated in the preceding Commentary, since an infinite number of moments T_1, T_2, T_3, ... lie within AB, there arise an infinite number of intervals AT_1, T_1T_2, T_2T_3, ... , in each of which the thing has moved and so has changed prior to the moment C.

6. An element of time may be either a time interval or a moment.

7. An alternative to "at" is "in", and likewise for each word "at" which follows in this paragraph.

8. 235b6–13.

9. 231b6–10.

10. Since every interval is divisible, there is no first interval, and so for every moment (which is a division) at which the thing has changed there is an earlier time during which the thing was changing.

11. Perhaps the things which are not essentially continuous are meant, such as contrary colors (if the change is from one quality to another) and a generation or destruction. In these, it is the time taken which is infinitely divisible, and so one uses time for the demonstration.

12. Corresponding to each division of time there arises a distinct state of change; for example, there arises a distinct color, if the change is from white to black (for in colors there is an accidental division, though not an essential one), and there arises a distinct partial generation, so to say.

13. Partial change is also included.

14. That is, if any of these is taken, whether something that has changed or a process of change, there is always an earlier process of change or something that has changed respectively.

15. What has become may be partial.

16. In the generation of a house, one need not restrict the term "generation" to the whole house, for he may consider also a partial generation, as of a part, e.g., a foundation or a wall or a roof.

17. According to Ross, "whatever" probably refers to both the time and the state of change; and this may be true. Neither "state of change" nor "time" appears in the Greek.

7

1. The Greek term for "finite" indicates a feminine term, and this may signify either a motion or a line. Ross suggests both, though not so clearly, but perhaps "line" is the correct term; for Aristotle has just spoken of a motion over a magnitude (and a line is the simplest magnitude), and later in 238b17–22 he indicates that what applies to a magnitude applies also to a motion in view of the one-one correspondence.

2. For example, a thing might move over line PQ and then move repeatedly over QR without an end, or it might move over the circumference of a circle without an end.

3. In other words, the length of each part is finite, and so is the number of parts.

4. Is it possible for a thing to move over the first part (which may be taken as a measure of the whole line) in an infinite time? But then it will not traverse the other parts, contrary to the hypothesis.

5. That is, if in time t_1t_2 the part s_1s_2 was traversed, in t_1t_3 (which is longer than t_1t_2) an additional part, say s_2s_3, was traversed, for the thing was always in motion.

6. If the number of parts is finite and each part is finite in extent, the sum is finite in extent.

7. But, one may ask, if $v = 10e^{-t}$, where v is the speed in miles per hour and t is the time in hours, would it not take an infinite time to traverse 10 miles, seeing that $\int_0^\infty 10e^{-t}\,dt = 10$?

The symbol "∞" in the integral should signify a moment in time, and it does not. Thus, beginning with $t = 0$, since an infinite time is a time without an end, and this is Aristotle's meaning of "potental" in the infinite, and since in this way the object will keep on moving, it will never complete its motion. Or else, if we assume that the thing does complete the motion, then it will finally arrive at its destination and do so at a moment, say at t_n. But this is impossible, for then the time t_0t_n will be finite and not infinite.

However, one may truly say that the distance traversed by the object will never exceed ten miles if $v = 10e^{-t}$. Logically, then, Aristotle is still right in saying that no finite line (and such a line must have limits as its ends and not be an open interval at one end) can be traversed in an infinite time, but we cannot be sure whether or not he was aware of decreasing speeds which would prevent an object from surpassing a given length in an infinite time

8. Coming to rest is a decreasing motion, such as $V = 10e^{-t}$.

9. A change starts and also ends. But if a change is always in a process, it will never end. So the expression "always in the process of being destroyed" indicates that the thing will never be destroyed or will always exist; and if it always exists, how can it be in the process of being destroyed?

10. As in Comm. 7, so here we may take $v = (1 - t)^{-1}$, and the distance traversed in one unit of time will be

$$\int_0^1 (1 - t)^{-1}dt = -\ln(1-t)\Big]_0^1 = \infty.$$

The difficulty here lies in the fact that at $t = 1$ there is no meaning in the term "speed", and so the upper limit of the integral is not justified. Further, any value of t such that $t<1$ results in a finite distance; and for Aristotle a time interval without a limit has as little existence as a body without a surface. It is true to say that given any distance, it will be surpassed at some t_0, but it is also true to say that given any t_0 for which the speed is defined, a finite distance will be traversed, and so not all distances will be surpassed.

In general, if the infinite is considered as existing only potentially, Aristotle's argument here cannot be refuted. Thus the difference lies in the different hypotheses concerning the nature and existence of the infinite.

11. The term "traverse" here is used in a wide sense: A traverses B if any of the two moves over the other.

12. Whether A is in motion and B at rest, or B in motion and A at rest,

as long as the speed of one of them is the same in each case the relative position of the two at any moment is the same; and A measures B either when A is moved over B consecutively or when B is moved over A likewise (or when both move in contrary directions).

13. That is, it is impossible for a finite magnitude to go over an infinite magnitude in a finite time.

14. If an infinite magnitude can traverse an infinite magnitude in a finite time, any finite part of the first can traverse the second infinite magnitude (already shown to be impossible).

15. This is done by dividing the finite time into a finite number of small equal parts and showing that in each part, and so in the whole of the finite time, a finite part and so all of the first infinite cannot traverse the other infinite.

16. Perhaps it is granted here that a motion is said to be finite if it is of a finite body and over a finite magnitude and that it is infinite otherwise (whether the body or the magnitude traversed is infinite, or even both).

17. If in place, then a locomotion is from place A to place B, and so over the interval AB, which is finite.

8

1. These would be bodies.

2. Only a body is either in motion or at rest essentially; attributes are neither in motion nor at rest, except accidentally, i.e., as attributes, and attributes are present in bodies when these are in motion or at rest.

3. In other words, a thing which is coming to a stop is either faster than or slower than or takes the same time as another thing which is coming to a stop. The argument is dialectical and is drawn from the manner in which we speak of things which are coming to a stop.

4. If the thing starts coming to a stop at t_1 and stops at t_2, then the interval t_1t_2 is the primary time in which it is coming to a stop.

5. 236b19–32.

6. Perhaps "first" refers to time, although it may also refer to a motion; Aristotle does not specify. Either of the two, however, implies the other in the case of coming to a stop.

7. In other words, if t_1t_n is the primary time in which a thing comes to a stop and if t_1t_3 is any (small) part of t_1t_n, there is always a t_1t_2, which is a part of t_1t_3, in which the thing is coming to a stop or is in motion.

8. The word "that" refers to time. Motion takes time, so a thing can be in motion only in time. But if a thing which can be in motion is not in motion, it is then at rest, and so it is at rest in time, and rest is divisible just as time is.

9. Just as a motion may be in a state of locomotion or of alteration or of change with respect to quantity, so can rest (or a state of rest).

10. To say that a thing has rested is to say that it has not changed from A to B, where A and B are numerically distinct; and in this case

it is two distinct moments which enclose a time interval, and a time interval has parts.

11. 238b31–6.

12. If the motion is a locomotion, "something" refers to a place, and if an alteration or a quantitative motion, it refers to a quality or a quantity, respectively.

13. If it is in motion in virtue of itself, it is the whole thing that moves and not just a part of it.

14. The term "state" refers to some one place or quality or quantity, depending on the kind of motion. To illustrate the meaning, if a body B moves from place P, then there is no place of B which is first (or next) right after P. For, if R is such a place, then since it takes time, let us say t_1t_3, to change from P to R, at moment t_2 within t_1t_3 the body B will have to be either at P or at R, which is impossible (if at P, the body will be resting during t_1t_2, and if at R, the body will be resting at t_2t_3, but the body is assumed in motion and in a direction away from P throughout t_1t_3).

As a matter of fact, B cannot remain at any given place during an interval of time, for it would then be resting; and if so, it changes place continuously.

9

1. The term "part" may refer to a magnitude or a point; here it refers to a point.

2. It is assumed that no distance is travelled in a moment.

3. He mentions this in 233a21–3. Zeno's argument may take two forms, as Fig. 16 indicates. (1) To go from A to B, one must first arrive at

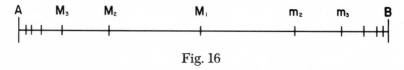

Fig. 16

the midpoint M_1 then at m_2, which is the midpoint of M_1B, then at m_3 likewise, etc., to infinity. (2) To go from A to B, one must first get to M_1, but to get to M_1 one must first get to M_2, and to M_3 before to M_2, and so on to infinity. In both cases, the parts to be traversed are infinite in number, and to traverse these in a finite time is assumed impossible.

It is not specified as to which of the two alternatives Zeno meant. Now (2) is stronger, for in (1) the argument assumes that M_1 has been reached and so that motion took place; but the argument of Achilles, which follows, suggests (1), and this is confirmed by lines 263a4–11.

4. The argument runs thus: When the pursuer who starts at A_0 reaches A_1, the pursued will be at A_2; when the pursuer reaches A_2, the pursued will be at A_3; and so on to infinity. If the distance of A_0A_1 is s and the ratio of the speed of the pursued to that of the pursuer is r,

where $r<1$, then $A_1A_2 = sr$, $A_2A_3 = sr^2$, etc., and the sum S is given by $S = s + sr + sr^2 + \ldots$. But S never reaches $\dfrac{s}{1-r}$; so the pursuer never catches the pursued.

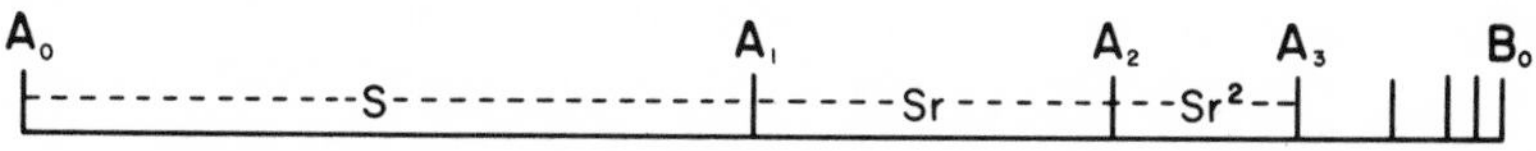

Fig. 17

Aristotle's argument is this: If the distance A_0B_0 is divided as shown in the direction to the right, B_0 will never be reached, and so the pursuer will not overtake the pursued in such division; but if it is granted that the pursued will reach or surpass B_0, and in time this will happen, then the pursued will be overtaken by the pursuer.

5. If a time interval is composed of just moments, then, since the flying arrow is stationary at each moment, it will be stationary throughout the interval. But, just as a line is not composed of just points, so time is not composed of just moments.

6. The terms "half" and "double" in Greek are idiomatic when taken as relatives; lines 6b30–1 and 7b16–21 indicate that the ratio of half to double is 1:2 and not 1:4, and we have translated with this in mind.

7. It is more accurate to say that the left end of C_1 has passed all the B's, etc.

8. In other words, the half is equal to its double, as is stated in Comm. 6.

9. If in Fig. 8(b) the right end of B_1 has passed all four C's, it has travelled a distance of the four C's (so Zeno says), and this is equal to the distance of four A's; and if it has travelled a distance of four A's, which is the distance from the midpoint of the A's to the end of the course, it has reached the end of the course in Fig. 8(c). So at the same time its position is as in Figures 8(b) and 8(c); and since it takes half as long to travel two spaces to the right in Fig. 8(b) as to travel four spaces to the right in Fig. 8(c), the half is equal to its double as before.

10. Ross, St. Thomas Aquinas, and others take the ratio of half to double to be 1:4, and they proceed accordingly. There are also alternatives in representing the relative position of the A's and the B's and the C's. Whatever the case may be, however, Zeno's argument ends in essentially the same thing, namely, "Unequals are equal", which he uses to refute motion.

11. 240a1–4.

12. That is, neither wholly one nor wholly the other. For example, this would be the case if the not-white (whether black or some other color) is in the process of change and at t_1 it is partly white or has a shade of whiteness or is mostly but not entirely white.

13. Each of the terms "white" and "not-white" may have two mean-

ings. If "white" means wholly white and the change from not-white to (wholly) white occurs in the time interval T_1T_2, then the changing thing is not-white during the interval $[T_1, T_2]$, that is, during the whole interval except at the moment T_2; so at each moment it will be true to say of the thing that it is either white or not-white (not both). But if "white" means that the thing is white in the main parts or in most of the parts and if the thing is changing to wholly white, then the thing will first be white at some moment T within T_1T_2 and remain white till T_2; so again at each moment it will be true to say of the thing that it is either white or not white.

The same applies to an unqualified generation. For example, once the meaning of the term "man" is fixed, then it will be true to say of the thing in generation (embryo or fetus or whatever it may be) that at any moment T_1 or time interval T_1T_2 it is either a man or not-man. In the case of a moment, the case is evident; and in the case of the time interval T_1T_2, the thing is not-man if during any part of T_1T_2 it is not a man (unless one wishes to define the thing as a man if it is a man for most of the interval T_1T_2).

14. One might say that a rotating sphere is resting, since the place in which it is (the inner boundary of the body containing it) remains the same. If so, then to say that the rotating sphere is moving with respect to place is false; for, although the parts are moving relative to each other and so their places, which are potential, change, the actual places of the parts qua parts are the place of the whole sphere, and so their place does not change. But if one says that the sphere is moving in virtue of its parts, whether these be surfaces or bodily parts, then this is a qualified motion (a motion of its parts but qua themselves and not qua parts), and the sphere is resting not in virtue of its parts but in virtue of itself as a whole; so it is resting, but not in the same respect.

The argument of the musical man might be as follows. Since a man becomes musical, he changes, but since he remains a man, he does not change. So he changes and does not change at the same time. Yes, he changes, but not in the same respect; for he changes with respect to an attribute, but with respect to *substance* he does not change.

10

1. An alternative to "accidentally" is "as an attribute". For example, that which is in motion by itself as a whole must have physical matter, but whiteness and hardness and things of this sort cannot be in motion by themselves since they are always in something else, in bodies which have physical matter. The same applies to a point, for it exists in a line, which exists in a surface, and a surface exists in a solid, and this in a physical body. So a point exists in a body and cannot exist by itself (it is neither a body nor a substance).

2. A magnitude exists in a body, as pointed out in the preceding Commentary; so a magnitude, too, is in motion but accidentally. In

general, the objects of mathematics are abstracted from physical matter and are immovable (193b22–35, 989b32, 1067b9–12). So in using "a body or a magnitude" perhaps Aristotle leaves the problem (whether magnitudes can move or not) open. The Greek term μέγεθος (= "magnitude") was also used to mean a body.

3. When a body moves, a part of it does not move by itself but in virtue of the motion of the whole body. So just as such a part moves in virtue of the whole, or accidentally, so what is indivisible (e.g., a point or a color) moves in virtue of the whole (which is the thing in which the point or the color exists), or accidentally.

4. The parenthetical statement is intended to show a difference between what is indivisible with respect to quantity and what is divisible. Both a point and a part of a body move accidentally; but a point can never be in motion essentially, while a part of a body can move (when separated from that body) or move potentially.

5. If a sphere rotates around its center, the parts further from the center move with a greater speed than those nearer the center. As for the sphere itself, its place remains the same, though the parts of its surface touch different parts of its place at different moments during, say, one full rotation.

6. Every kind of motion is considered. For simplicity, if it is a locomotion, AB and BC are taken as positions in contact at B.

7. Perhaps by "during the time" he means at any moment within the time interval D, or else at any part of time none of whose limits are those of D.

8. 237a17–b22.

9. If a point moves over a magnitude equal to itself, it will be a magnitude and the least magnitude; and if a magnitude, it will measure the whole line, for every magnitude is exhausted (or measured) by any given magnitude, however small (206b9–12).

10. 232b23–233a10.

11. For example, another meaning of "incapable of being" or "impossible to be" is that which can be but with much difficulty (226b10–5, 280b12–4, 1019b15–30).

12. The contraries of place, let us say of up and down, are the innermost surface of the outer sphere and the Center of the universe. Any qualified contraries, then, like two places with different altitudes, are bounded.

What about the locomotion from A to B, 10 units apart, if the speed is $10e^{-t}$? Apparently, $\int_0^t 10e^{-t}dt = 10(1 - e^{-t})$, which is less than 10 for every t, and so B is never reached although it is approached as t increases indefinitely. So it seems that if no least speed is postulated, an object with a decreasing speed such as $10e^{-t}$ can never complete a certain finite distance; and with such a postulate, Zeno's argument against motion (motion from A to B is impossible) gains some force.

Logically, of course, an interval such as [0, 10), which is open at the end (using the mathematician's language), is not bounded at that end (using Aristotle's sense of "bounded"); but it is bounded in the sense that it is always less than some given interval.

13. The problem is considered at greater length in 261a27–265a12.

14. They do not form one and the same motion numerically.

Book H

1

1. For a discussion of Book H, see *Preface*.

2. This is the principle which causes motion.

3. The assumption is, a thing in motion is caused to be in motion by some thing.

4. In other words, the whole thing (or all of its parts) is taken as being in motion. If only a part of AC is in motion, AC is said to be in motion in a secondary sense, so to say, and this sense presupposes the primary sense. Aristotle is considering the primary sense first, for the secondary sense must be discussed in terms of the primary.

5. If DEF is in motion as a whole (or primarily), it is still possible that a part of it, DE, is caused to be moved by another part, EF, and then DE does not have the principle of causing itself to be in motion. For example, the gravel in a moving truck does not cause itself to be in motion, nor does the flesh of a man in motion. As in the previous Commentary, here, too, Aristotle's first concern is the analysis of a thing no part of which is moved by another part, even if both parts are in motion.

6. Quantitatively divisible (240b8–1a26).

7. AC would not be in motion essentially (not accidentally) and also as a whole (not in virtue of just a part of itself).

8. In that case, it is caused to be moved by something external to itself.

9. It appears that the thing is considered as being in motion primarily, whether the moving cause is external to it or in the thing itself but not in just a part of it.

10. By "motion in place" he seems to mean a locomotion, and a locomotion is prior in existence to all others; hence this motion is the first to be considered.

11. The first mover is not being moved by another thing.

12. In other words, the motions of the mover and the moved are simultaneous, so it makes no difference whether one proceeds in the direction of the movers or in the direction of the things moved.

13. It may be in motion from black to white, which are definite, or from magnitude M to magnitude N, which are definite, or likewise from place P to place Q.

14. 227b3–9a6.

15. 237b23–8a19.

16. Perhaps "EFGH . . ." is better than "EFGH", unless "H" signifies collectively the motions of the infinite things which follow G. The same for "ABCD".

17. If the motions of A, B, C, . . . decrease according to the same ratio, as in a, ar, ar^2, . . . where $r < 1$, all these motions converge to a finite and not to an infinite motion. But the existence of A, B, C, . . . as an actual set and at the same time as something infinite is impossible according to Aristotle, for no thing can have the same attribute both potentially and actually at the same time and in the same respect. In the alternate text, $r \geq 1$, so no problem arises.

18. Namely, that there is a first mover, for an impossibility seems to result if it is assumed that there is an infinity of movable movers without a first mover.

19. But if a finite universe is assumed, then since all movers are actual and finite, there is a mover of least magnitude; and this assumption from physics seems to prove the impossibility of an infinity of movers.

20. Is Aristotle assuming a unity by contact? Then this would be a loose unity, so to say (205a20–1); or else such unity is taken hypothetically for the sake of argument.

21. The two alternatives are (a) ABCD is finite and (b) ABCD is infinite. If infinite, the motion will be infinite, and an infinite magnitude does not exist anyway (207b15–21, 238a20–b22). If finite, see Comms. 17 and 26 of this Section.

22. That thing, of course, might be moved by itself or by an immovable mover, and the immovable mover might be in the self-mover or outside the first thing moved.

23. 32a18–20.

24. Why greater and not less? Since A receives its motion only from B, which is itself in motion, the motion of A cannot be greater than that of B, and it may be less (267a2–10). The motions of B and C are similarly related, and likewise for the rest.

25. In this case, of an infinite number of things in motion.

26. Why the finite? If the motion of the mover is not less than that of the thing moved and if the ratio of the magnitudes of mover to moved is always the same and less than unity, the motion of ABCD . . . will still be infinite.

2

1. This is the proximate mover. If A moves B and B moves C and if B moves C directly and not through an intermediate, then B is the primary or proximate mover of C; and A moves C not primarily but through B.

2. This is the good or the noble (701a7–2b11, 1013a31–3, 1072b1–4).

3. As a moving cause.

4. 260a20–1a26.

5. An example of this is a man, for he can move himself, and the part in him that moves him is in himself.

6. Perhaps by "are referred to these" he means that they come under these as under genera. For example, pulling is referred to locomotion, that is, "locomotion" is a genus of "pulling".

7. Perhaps an example of pushing apart is the splitting of wood.

8. In a generation or destruction, the things that are combined or separated do not remain the same in nature; so we do not have a mere combination or a separation in which that which existed before will again exist. Of course, the term "combination" or "separation" may be given two meanings—a generic one, which includes what takes place in a generation and a destruction, and a specific one for just a locomotion.

9. In modern terms, turning requires two vector forces which are opposite or which contain components which are opposite. An example of turning is what physicists call "a couple".

10. For a discussion of the various versions and perhaps corruptions of a part of this paragraph, see Ross's *Aristotle's Physics*, p. 673.

11. For example, if the Sun heats the water, the last mover is the air which is in contact with the water, and the air itself is heated by the Sun, whether directly or indirectly.

12. An animate thing is or has a body which can receive qualities which bodies receive, but not every body has sensations.

13. That is, an animate thing is aware when a power of sensation in it is affected or when there is sensation.

14. He may mean a sensible quality or a body with such a quality, and in either case this will have to be a mover which causes the alteration. For example, it may be the heat of the water (an attribute) or the hot water itself (subject with attribute) which causes the sensation of heat or the rise in temperature of the body which is being heated.

15. For example, for Aristotle the greenness of grass in daylight moves the air in a certain way, and the surface of this air in contact with the eye moves the eye in a certain way, and the eye itself when so moved causes in turn the sensation of greenness.

16. This is the last or proximate mover; for example, it is not the fragrance in the rose, but that in the air which came from the rose and which is in contact with the organ of smell that affects that organ.

17. Prior to a decrease as a motion, the thing is one by continuity, and that motion ends when a part of the thing is detached. Hence during the motion the part is continuous with the rest of the whole, and there is nothing between two continuous parts since the extremities of those parts are together and even one. The argument for an increase is similar. Perhaps by "that which is causing decrease" he means the proximate part which is continuous with the whole. Of course, this part too is caused (to be detached) by another.

18. By "primary" he means proximate, for there may also be distant

movers, like the hand which moves a stone by means of a stick, which [stick] is an intermediate mover.

19. A genus, being like matter relative to its species or the corresponding differentiae, is like a subject which underlies its attributes (1024a36–b4, 1038a5–8).

20. Apparently, the affection, like heat, for example, is taken as a primary mover.

3

1. In 9a14–27, powers (e.g., natural strength and natural resistance to certain diseases) form a third kind of qualities; but these powers are listed in lines 1019a15–1020a6 as being kinds of habits, and perhaps these lines were written later.

2. Usually, a derivative term differs slightly from the original term in ending (1a12–5). In English, when we call a statue "bronze" we use "bronze" as an adjective and not as a noun.

3. Perhaps by "in a manner similar" he means that, for example, either of the two terms "bronze" and "hot" in an alteration is a predicate of the other as a subject without a change in ending, whereas in the change from wood to a bed the terms "wood" and "bed" (or "wood" and "shape of bed") are not predicates of each other or not in the same way.

4. That is, for example, the two terms "wood" and "bed" are not predicates like the terms "bronze" and "hot" in an alteration. Or else, in a generation, as from wood to bed, "wood" is not a predicate of the bed, but "wooden" is.

5. Of course, this is a dialectical argument resting on the manner of naming things.

6. In other words, an alteration is prior in existence to a generation, for the latter presupposes the former; but for a given individual, it must be generated before it can alter (260b29–33).

7. Just as the process of completing a house is not an alteration but a generation, although an alteration in that process may be or must be involved, so the process to a virtue or to a vice is not an alteration, although alterations may be involved.

8. Perhaps the phrase "in the highest sense" refers to the fact that the figure falls exactly and not approximately under the definition of a circle (all points on the circumference are equidistant from the center), while "best" refers to perfection or excellence or value, like the happiness of a man or the beauty of a circle.

9. For one thing, mixtures and proportions are relations among or between things.

10. Both a virtue and its contrary (a vice) are related or referred to something, for example, to some affection, and perhaps in this sense they are relations (6a36–b6, 11a20–38, 124b15–22).

11. For example, the affections *proper* to both bravery and cowardice are fear and its contrary, courage.

12. They may change accidentally, but not essentially (225b11–3, 1088a29–35).

13. Health, for example, exists primarily not in just a body, but in a body of an animal, that is, it can exist in such a body and only in such a body.

14. For example, an object with color causes seeing, one with sound causes hearing, and these produce pleasure or pain.

15. That is, there is no essential generation, but only an accidental generation of them.

16. We say that *knowledge* is of the *known*, and so *knowledge* and the *known* are relatives (6b32–5).

17. Perhaps this is *knowledge*, or else *knowledge* of the individual (99b34–100b5, 432a3–10, 1087a10–23). It is only when the latter knowledge is formed that knowledge of the universal is also formed; that is, knowledge of the universal is generated from knowledge of the individual in a way similar to that in which a virtue such as temperance is generated from pains and pleasures, which are alterations.

18. Perhaps this is knowledge of the particular.

19. When one knows an individual, e.g., that these two apples and those two apples make four apples, one may also know potentially and universally (which is knowing in another sense) that two units and two units make four units.

20. Both activities and changes (motions, generations, and destructions) are actualities, though activities are ends in themselves and complete while changes are incomplete; and seeing, touching, enjoying, and the like are activities. And just as there is no generation of a change (225b13–6), so there is no generation of an activity (1048b18–36).

21. There is a generation of a *composite* (matter and form), but not of matter or of a form essentially; and *knowing* and thinking wisely or prudently are actualities just as generations are actualities, but they are not *composites*.

22. For example, by force.

23. In both cases, an alteration may be necessary but not sufficient if an activity or use is to occur, but that activity or use is not a part of the alteration, nor is the alteration a part of the activity or of the use.

24. Perhaps they are generated accidentally, like all relations (1088a29–35).

25. We call the shape of the statue not "bronze" but "brazen". Perhaps this is an earlier draft, for a better reason would be to say that we call the statue, which is a *composite* (not just its shape which has no matter), "brazen" rather than "bronze".

26. The term "bronze" here signifies not just the matter of a piece of bronze, but the unity of matter and *form;* for usually that *form* has no name since it is a chance form.

27. By "those things" he means the *form* or the shape or the thing generated (the unity of matter and *form*).

28. For example, as stated earlier, we call the bronze "hot" and the hot "bronze".

29. That is, it is ridiculous to say of the matter which has become a man that it has altered when it became a man. This change is a generation and not an alteration, even if certain alterations took place during the change.

30. By "does not apply to what pertains to habits" perhaps he means that neither are the habits themselves alterations, nor are the generations of those habits alterations.

31. Perhaps a perfection, like an actuality (or a form) which is generated or like the generation itself (an actuality, though incomplete), is not the end product of an alteration or the alteration itself but is something else, although it may require an alteration.

32. We apply the term "circle" to many individuals whose form is close to that of a circle; but we apply that term in the highest degree to the individual whose form fits exactly the definition of a circle as used by mathematicians.

33. Perhaps these are violent causes, like a force of a sort.

4

1. Two motions are said to be comparable if the speed of one is equal to (or like) that of another or if it is faster (or greater) than another or if it is slower (or less) than another.

2. The use of "of like speed" here and "of equal speed" in 248a16 arise from the fact that comparability of two motions is not simple, for quantity is not the only category which may enter. The distinctions unfold as the discussion proceeds.

3. Perhaps "an equal [amount]" is used generically at this point to apply to any interval, whether a length which is in quantity, or a degree of change within a specific quality like red, or any amount which is somehow the same in any change whatever. Of course, the discussion proceeds dialectically.

4. Perhaps "circular" and "straight" apply to motions rather than to lines. If to lines, a difficulty arises (see Comm. 13 of this Section).

5. The term "equal" here seems to be synonymous with "of equal speed" or "of like speed".

6. This would be so because an alteration is a motion with respect to an affection whereas a locomotion is a motion with respect to place (and this motion is over a distance), and the equality of these two motions would seem to imply the equality of an affection to a distance (which is impossible).

7. Equality and inequality (whether greater or less) are not attributes of qualities (6a26–35); so an affection is neither equal nor unequal to a length.

8. It is not specified whether the two kinds of motions have the

same limits; perhaps this is implied from the argument in 248a25–b4, or perhaps it makes no difference in the argument.

9. Perhaps "immediately" indicates that the first motion is taken without proof as being faster, or else as being slower, than the second motion.

10. It is assumed that P moves faster than Q.

11. 222b33–3a4, 232a23–7.

12. If a part of B is equal to C, a part of that part will be less than C; so a straight line may be equal to or less than or greater than some circular line.

13. It is not specified whether "straight" and "circular" apply to lines or to motions along lines. If to motions along lines, the first part of the next sentence has some plausibility, and the second part may mean that not all kinds of motions are comparable; for even if one concedes that straight line M is equal to circular line N, one need not concede that the motion over M is equal to that over N, for there is a difference in direction or vector. But if to lines, a difficulty arises. The differentia of a line (straightness or curvature) does not seem to be relevant to its quantity, and if so, straight lines are comparable to curved lines with respect to equality and inequality; and at least some mathematicians in Aristotle's time took this view, for they were concerned with measuring lengths of curved lines.

There is the alternative that (a) equality of lines for Aristotle meant coincidence of lines, and a straight line cannot coincide with a curved line, or that (b) the argument is dialectical, or that (c) the noncomparability of a straight to a circular line was Aristotle's opinion and perhaps that of some others.

14. Perhaps this sentence should be in the form of a question, thus: "But are all things which are not named equivocally comparable?"

15. One can truly say that the highest note is sharper than the one next to it.

16. If there is some *reason* in truly saying that a circular motion cannot be compared to a rectilinear motion with respect to being faster or slower or of equal speed, then there is a much better *reason* in truly saying that whitening, which is an alteration, cannot be likewise compared to going from Athens to Thebes, which is a locomotion.

17. That is, two quarts of water is double one quart, and likewise for air, but no sample of water can be double a sample of air. The comparison indicated is not with respect to just volumes, but to the substances taken in their entirety. There is no common unit. Of course, the comparison may be made with respect to just an attribute, e.g., volume. Then water and air may be compared with respect to volume.

18. That which is called "much" may be water or air or distance, etc., and so "much" is like the term "one" which has many senses and is not univocal.

19. A line may be equal to a line, a surface to a surface, a volume to a volume, but no line can be equal to a surface or a volume. So "equal"

is equivocal, or better, it is analogous. Thus the axioms concerning equality are analogous (76a37–41).

20. One line is not greater than or less than, nor equal to, one point; and likewise for two lines and two points. 1015b16–7a3, 1052a15–4a19.

21. Perhaps this would be their volume; and it can also be their weight.

22. The term λευκότερον is equivocal; it may be translated as "whiter" and also as "clearer", and "clearer" too is equivocal.

23. The attribute is clearness. We speak of water as being clear and of a voice as being clear, but voice and water are distinct subjects, one a substance and the other a quality, and "clear" is an equivocal predicate of the two.

24. Perhaps the expression "make them" is idiomatic. One interpretation is this: It is possible for P and Q and even other things to be called (equivocally) by the same term "A" and to be one in the sense that they are in numerically the same subject or substance. But P and Q and the others are one numerically and not in definition, and they are distinct subjects relative to A. So "A" has distinct meanings when predicated of P and Q and the others. This is like a pound of sugar, for example, which is one and the same subject; but it is sweet relative to its flavor, white relative to its surface, and equal to a pound of flour relative to its weight, and the same applies if its volume is equal to that of another substance. Now it is possible to use one term to mean sweetness and whiteness and weight, but it would be an equivocal term; and it would be a predicate of one ultimate subject in a sense, of sugar, yet it would be a predicate of distinct proximate subjects, that is, of a flavor, of a surface, and of a weight.

25. For example, curvature belongs to just a line (the term "curvature" is nowadays equivocally applied to a surface or to a space); and a color, to just a physical surface. Thus, if the same term is a predicate of two things which are attributes of two distinct primary subjects, the distinctness of the primary subjects assures us of the distinctness and incomparability of the two things, and so the term is equivocally predicated of the two things.

26. An alternative translation of this sentence is, "things are of like speed if they have moved such-and-such an equal amount in an equal time".

27. If the alternative translation given in the preceding Commentary is correct, then this other part would seem to be equal to the first part.

28. Alterations and locomotions are motions of distinct species; hence, they are not comparable.

29. It is not specified whether "rectilinear" and "circular" apply to motions or to lines. See Comm. 13 of this Section.

30. Perhaps it is taken for granted from the preceding sentence that a rectilinear (motion, or else line) is not comparable to a circular; and if so, the *reason* will be that we have a genus whose species are not comparable. The problem then is, a genus of what?

31. In other words, if two locomotions are not comparable, they are of different species and so "locomotion" is a genus; and if so, there is a difference in the paths over which the locomotions proceed. Conversely, if there is a difference in the paths, there is a difference also in the locomotions.

32. This would mean that the mode, or *that by which,* is accidental to the motion and does not give rise to any species of motion .

33. Same in species.

34. Perhaps "the same" here is general, in the sense that it is applicable to any things of the same species with respect to which (species) motion proceeds. If so, then "and if . . . motion" is given as a principle.

35. This would help us determine which motions are comparable and which are not.

36. In other words, comparison requires things to be not just in one genus, but in one species. With respect to comparability, then, things under the same genus are many and not one, and so a differentiation becomes necessary.

37. For example, "log" means a piece of wood and also a certain mathematical quantity, and the two meanings are far apart. The term "Socrates", however, when applied to Socrates and to a picture of him, is equivocal but there is some similarity in its meaning. As for "equality", it is equivocal by analogy (248b18–9); for lines may be equal to lines and planes to planes, but lines cannot be equal to planes, and the axioms of equality are one by analogy (76a37–b2). Perhaps "motion" as applied to a locomotion and an alteration is equivocal in the sense that the two kinds of motions are close in genus.

38. By "the same thing" perhaps he means that with respect to which something changes, like whiteness, and by "distinct [subject]" perhaps he means the subject or body which is changing.

39. Perhaps he means the definition of a species of motion or the limitations through which we arrive at a species of motion.

40. Alternatives to "and" are "or" and "and/or". The white and the sweet are certainly distinct in species; so if we accept "or", one may raise the question of whether the same attribute (health, or some species of it) in distinct subjects (a dog and a man) gives rise to distinct species of things whose motions are not comparable.

41. Health and whiteness are not the same at all in species, so motions with respect to them are distinct in species. But the same health or whiteness in different subjects may present a problem with respect to quantity, and some distinction should be made (249b14–9).

42. In two alterations, the time taken may be equal and so with regard to their speed the term "equal" is involved. But such motions involve also a quality, and the term "equality" cannot be a predicate of a quality. Thus "of equal speed" does not describe fully alterations which are of the same species and which occur in equal times.

43. This is just a provisional definition, which is taken for the sake of

discussion but which nevertheless does not solve the problem of how we should compare motions.

44. The same in species. For example, recovering from influenza, let us say, by two men.

45. Distinct in species.

46. Becoming white is not the same as nor equal to nor yet similar to recovering from disease, for these relations do not truly apply to qualities of distinct species; and so this distinction or diversity in the species of alteration makes comparison impossible. It is like the case of a motion along a straight line and one around a circle, as mentioned previously.

47. Perhaps the same in species is meant, or else the same in quantity also. Then, if the subjects are the same, affections which are distinct (in species) would give rise to distinct alterations (in species), and affections which are the same would give rise to alterations which are the same.

48. Alterations may be the same with respect to the species of "affection", but one subject undergoing the alteration may be twice as great as another. So this distinction should be expressed in terms of inequality in the quantity and not in terms of otherness or dissimilarity, for these do not apply to quantities qua quantities.

One might observe here that while the elements which give rise to diversity have been considered, the problem of combining them scientifically in the modern sense is still left hanging. For example, if m and M are masses and v and V are velocities having comparable directions (i.e., $V = kv$), comparison of mv to MV requires a further element, the product of mass and velocity and axioms for such products.

49. The term "the same" might apply to a genus which is the same for two or more generations; but the addition of "and *indivisible*" restricts "the same" to an *indivisible* species, like that of men, for a man and a dog do not come under the same *indivisible* species. If so, two generations are equal if during the same time two things in the same species are generated.

50. The term *"distinct"*, from what follows, does not have its usual meaning. A generation is from not-being to being, while in an alteration and the other motions there is always a being which remains but changes with respect to an attribute or with respect to more or less or the like. So there is a difference.

Now just as in equal times one alteration may be faster in virtue of a greater interval of change (if, for example, in an equal time one thing became darker than another), so in generations we might say that in an equal time one may be *faster* than another. But *"faster"* here would have an analogous meaning and not the same meaning. Further, the things generated cannot come under the same indivisible species, for they would then be of equal speed. If so, they come under different or even distinct species, and one of them may require a greater number of steps for its generation in virtue of its greater perfection (this is the position of St. Thomas Aquinas). But there is some difficulty; for the steps in one generation may not be comparable to those of the other. The question then is "How are we to understand precisely the terms "*faster*" and "*otherness*" in generation?" Perhaps some definitions are needed.

51. By "two things", when applied to an alteration, perhaps he means the more and the less in quality, for there is dissimilarity in each of the things. There will be in generation, then, two terms corresponding to "more" and "less" in alteration, and also the term "*otherness*" corresponding to "dissimilarity" in alteration.

52. If two numbers are comparable, their units must be of the same kind. Five men are greater than four men, and the unit is one man; but five points are neither equal nor unequal to four horses, for there is no common unit between a point and a horse (1088a8–14). Hence the generation of four horses in an equal time is not faster or slower than or of equal speed to that of five points.

According to Plato, since the units of two distinct Numbers are not comparable, one Number can be neither equal nor unequal to another. If Plato wishes to compare Numbers, then, he must change his theory (1083a31–5).

53. By "these" perhaps he means the things compared with respect to being greater or less. Such things may be under any category, but both must be of the same *indivisible* species to make comparison possible, e.g., both must be men or horses or in the same ultimate species under the same category; and there is no common univocal name for them, for there is nothing common to distinct categories.

54. Perhaps "these" refers to the generations of numbers. There may be a corruption in the text.

5

1. That is, a mover qua mover in *actuality*.
2. 236b19–7b22.
3. Some quantitative aspects of motion are presented in this section. If A is the mover, B the thing moved, S the interval over which B has moved, and T the time taken, then, taking A to be also the force of A and B to be also the quantity of B,

> (1) in T, A moves B/2 over 2S (250a1–3),
> (2) in T/2, A moves B/2 over S (250a3),
> (3) in T/2, A moves B over S/2 (250a5),
> (4) in T, A/2 moves B/2 over S (250a6–7),
> (5) in T, A/2 may not move B over S/2 (250a9–12),
> (6) if also A_1 moves B_1 over S in T, then $A + A_1$ moves $B + B_1$ over S in T (250a25–8).

Thus, other things being equal, (1) states that, if the object moved is smaller, B is inversely proportional to S, which sounds somewhat like the principle or definition of work, or W = Fs; (2) states that B is proportional to T; (3) states that T is proportional to S; (4) states that, if A is smaller, A is proportional to B; (5) states that, if A is smaller, it may not move B; and (6) states that the sum A + A$_1$ moves the corresponding sum B + B$_1$. No discussion is given concerning the units of measurement for each kind of motion.

4. Although Aristotle observed (5) as a raw fact in nature, he probably made no analysis in which resistance and its coefficient entered as factors into the picture.

5. If Aristotle is to be right, the definition of sound must include both the *actuality* (or disturbance) of air and the ability of such air to cause hearing when someone is present.

6. Perhaps the term "amount" or "interval" would be better, for the more and the less in quality does not seem to admit quantification, unless it is somehow quantified in the modern sense.

7. Twice as much as half that alteration.

8. There may be some corruption in lines 250b4–7, so we translated by analogy, using lines 250a12–9.

Book Θ

1

1. In this Book the existence of an eternal prime mover who is immovable is to be shown. This mover is shown to be eternal, ungenerable, indestructible, without potentiality or matter, hence without parts, and so, simple, always moving in the same way, and so, causing motion eternally (1071b3–3a13). First, then, Aristotle considers whether motion is eternal or not.

Perhaps the term "everlasting" does not necessarily imply continuity; for something can occur repeatedly at intervals forever. If so, then "without the possibility of stopping" adds something new. 404a21–b8.

2. Motion, especially locomotion, is prior in existence to generation or to destruction (243a10–1, 260a20–1a12).

3. For example, Democritus and Leucippus (300b8–11).

4. Translated by John M. Crossett, Jr.

5. This is the prime mover, the first (moving) principle of all motion.

6. 201a9–15.

7. A definition is a statement of the essence of something which exists, so once a definition has been given, the existence of the thing defined is taken for granted.

8. Perhaps the argument is this: Given a motion of a movable object, if the object was generated, then some other change and (therefore) motion must have preceded, and so the given motion cannot be first; hence, if that object was generated and this generation involves a

motion, there can be no first motion. This argument, then, seems to show that motion is eternal, for the hypothesis of a first motion in time leads to a prior motion.

9. The second hypothesis is this: All movable objects always pre-existed without motion, but then a motion began.

10. Whether "this" refers to the thing moved or to the mover is not specified. Perhaps it makes no difference, as indicated from what follows.

11. That is, it changed before the motion which is assumed to be first. If both the mover and the object moved are at rest, then at least one of them must change its disposition of being at rest if it is to act on or be acted upon by the other; and this change is prior to the one assumed as first.

12. This is knowledge through which a doctor, for example, can cause health as well as disease.

13. These would be things, like fire, which act in just one way and are unlike a doctor, who can act in contrary ways; for a doctor can heal a man, and he can also make him sick.

14. If heat is to cause cold, it must depart from the object, and this departure is a prior motion.

15. But this approach is a motion prior to the one assumed to be first.

16. Heat, for example, must approach the object before heating it, and it must depart from it if the object is to be cooled; and heat just causes heat and does not cause another kind of motion, except accidentally.

17. To cause a motion is to move another, and to be moved is to be moved by another; so a mover and the thing moved are related.

18. 219a8–9. Perhaps this is a concession to those who claim that time is a sort of motion.

19. This seems to be a logical argument. If time is as defined (220a24–6), then time cannot exist if motion does not; and if so, since rest is the privation of motion and exists in time (which presupposes motion), things cannot have been at rest even prior to the first motion.

20. *Timaeus*, 37–8. Plato, of course, is inconsistent according to Aristotle; for he posits the generation of Numbers prior to that of the heaven and time, but any essential generation involves a motion and hence time (1084a3–7).

21. Perhaps "some" is better than "in some"; and in the Greek, perhaps it should be ἔν τι rather than ἔν τινι.

22. Perhaps "heated" is a better term than "burned", for we usually think of burning (e.g., of paper) as a kind of destruction, while what we have here is an example of a motion, a rise in temperature.

23. Some manuscripts read "And also the destructible will have to be destroyed, when it is being destroyed,".

If A destroys B and if B's destruction is posited as the last, A's ability to destroy still remains. If so, then since no contradiction should follow if what is possible is posited as being actual, no contradiction should follow if A is posited as actually destroying something else. But if A is posited as actually destroying something else, such destruction would occur after the last destruction, and this is impossible. The argument is similar if the capability of being destroyed is considered rather than the ability to destroy.

24. These consequences are: the positing of a first motion implies a prior motion and the positing of a last motion implies a later motion. If there is a last motion, then there will be no thing that can move and no thing that can be moved. But if in the last motion the thing which was moved will no longer be capable of being moved, it will change from being capable of being moved to being incapable of being moved, and this change will occur after the last motion, contrary to the hypothesis.

25. 250b23–6.

26. For example, fire exists by nature (by its essence or its form), and by its nature fire travels up and not down, unless it be by force. Its form, then, is the cause of its travelling up. So the form of each thing makes it do or be certain things and no others, and this can be known and stated; and perhaps this is what is meant by "order in each thing". If fire, without an outside force, travelled in any direction, then there would be disorder and no definiteness.

In the case of a man, his essence is more complex; nevertheless, there is order here too, though more complex. A science of man, then, is possible.

27. An alternative to "formula" is "ratio", and an alternative to "the infinite" is "the indefinite". He may be referring to Anaxagoras, who posits the togetherness of things for an infinite time prior to the action of *Intelligence* on that togetherness (perhaps for the subsequent infinite time). These two intervals of time have no ratio, or they cannot be explained according to a formula which follows from the nature of the togetherness of things or of *Intelligence*. If *Intelligence* according to Anaxagoras is simple and pure (405a13–9), it must act in one or a simple way, like Aristotle's prime mover, who always acts in the same way. But in being now inactive and then active, *Intelligence* turns out to be complex and not simple.

28. If rest and motion alternate, then at least there is some regularity and order. For example, there is a pattern or a reason in a pendulum which moves now in one direction and now in the contrary direction; and there is a formula for a falling body from rest, namely, $s = \frac{1}{2} gt^2$, even if the speed increases with time. But for Anaxagoras this is not the case (see preceding Commentary).

29. An induction is useful in confirming a universal truth, which is a principle and so cannot be proved, while a demonstration is used to prove a universal truth from principles. In positing a universal statement as a truth, then, like the alternation of rest and motion, one should either induce it from examples or demonstrate it from causes; otherwise, it would be an *unreasonable* axiom.

30. Perhaps by "these hypotheses" he means Empedocles' alternation of motion and rest and Anaxagoras' infinite togetherness prior to the action on it by *Intelligence*. The essence of *Friendship* is not to be active in uniting things at one time and not doing so at another time, and the same may be said of *Strife;* and the action on the togetherness by *Intelligence* after its inaction does not follow from its essence, which is posited as being simple.

31. The use of induction would be at least a reason for the alternate action of *Friendship* and *Strife*. But friendship brings only friends together, not enemies, while for Empedocles it is all the things that are brought together by *Friendship,* and again it is the same things that are separated by *Strife.*

32. The argument needed might be an induction or a proof, for the alternation at equal intervals of time does not follow from the essence of *Friendship* or of *Strife* alone.

33. Principles which are always true (like the axioms of mathematics) are not caused by or cannot be demonstrated from other things; but theorems which are always true are caused by or are demonstrated from such principles. Apparently, Democritus failed to see the distinction.

2

1. Perhaps by "to infinity" he means not in time but to what might be a limit which is infinitely away, although an infinite time may be implied (241a26–b20). The two limits of a change are definite, and so is their interval, like that from black to white or from magnitude A to magnitude B. In some sense, this is an argument from a part to a whole. A change in a thing which is numerically one has limits, and outside those limits the thing is not changing with respect to that change. So one may argue that the whole universe is a thing of this sort.

2. According to almost all thinkers, being cannot be generated from nonbeing (1062b24–6); hence motion cannot be generated from its nonexistence. But we observe the opposite: Some lifeless things which are at rest at one time are in motion or are set in motion at a later time. So a motion can be generated from its nonexistence. If so, what would prevent the universe itself from being at rest at one time and in motion at another time?

3. This argument is even stronger than (2). There is nothing besides the whole universe, and so the universe, if it is to be now at rest and now in motion, has to be moved by itself. But an animal does this, being a small universe, so to say. By induction, then, the whole universe may do this, even if it be infinite (a concession to those who posit an infinite universe, 203b4–15).

4. Since a circular locomotion may exist (and in fact it does, 261b27–5a12), the induction for argument (1) loses its force.

5. 253a22–4b6.

6. And if so, just as there is some part (e.g., the heart) in the animal that is always in motion, so there may be some part in the universe that is always in motion (a dialectical argument).

7. For example, heartbeat and respiration (259b6–14). If some motions in a living thing are caused by outside movers, this seems to be an additional argument for an eternal motion. The problem of a first mover, of course, still remains.

3

1. 253a3–7.

2. Perhaps "not in motion" or "immovable" is better than "at rest", for, by definition, that which is at rest can move; but if all things were *always* at rest, none could be in motion. Of course, the term "rest" ($= \dot{\eta}\rho\epsilon\mu\dot{\iota}a$) may have more than one sense, or else other thinkers may have used the expression "all things are always at rest" (221b12–4, 239a13–6).

3. If alike disposed, perhaps the implication is that things are sometimes in motion and sometimes at rest, not necessarily all at once.

4. Those which admit of both are resting when not in motion, if we use "resting" in its primary sense (221b12–4).

5. This would be common sensation (425a13–b11).

6. To deny motion and so sensation is to deny the possibility of induction and of getting universals of what exists (99b32–100b5, 105a3–7, 185a12–4). The denial of all motion or change, which is the position of Zeno, Parmenides, and Melissus, concerns all beings, and so such denial is a matter to be dealt with by the philosopher and not by the physicist.

7. Physics is about things qua movable, and so if no motion can exist, physics as a science is impossible, for sciences deal with what exists or can exist. Moreover, learning of any kind would be impossible, for learning is a change, and there is a motion in a change.

8. A physicist lays down or accepts the principles of his subject, the existence of motion being one such principle; and any discussion about those principles is the concern of the philosopher or of the philosopher of physics, not of the physicist qua demonstrating theorems from principles.

9. 192b21–3.

10. The existence of motion is more evident than that of rest, for what appears to be resting may be moving slightly and so escape notice.

11. For example, Heraclitus (1078b12–5).

12. Examples are given to contradict the position that all things always move. Thus a man does not continuously increase in weight, for he may not do so during sleep.

13. 250a15–9.

14. After freezing, the object may remain frozen for some time, and so it does not alter or move.

15. If a man is sick at t_1 and if time elapses before he gets well, let t_2 be the first moment he gets well. Then from t_1 to t_2 (exclusive) he is still sick, though partly, and so he is not well. So with respect to sickness he has not moved.

16. If he changes to health, he remains healthy for some time, for if not, he would be changing not to health but to something beyond, since the motion which is posited as one and continuous would not be a motion toward health as its final stage. Besides, a motion cannot proceed beyond the ultimate contrary, e.g., beyond black or beyond hardness in the case of a stone.

17. If earth remains in its proper place for some time, however small, then it is not always moving with respect to its place.

18. 253b11–4a1.

19. It is not clear whether he means an increase by force or just an increase. In a sense, he has included the latter in the previous sentence, but in another (logical) sense he has not. If an increase is continuous and eternal, the thing which is considered increasing will never attain any definite magnitude. Will it then go to infinity? There is the problem of defining increase, whether to infinity or to a never-attained limit. An increase by force is in a sense included in a motion by force.

20. If a thing in motion always moves, it does so always toward something, say, toward B; and so it cannot move away from B. Hence, no thing can have now a natural motion and now a motion contrary to nature, and the distinction between a natural motion and a motion contrary to nature is destroyed.

21. Motion is involved in generation and destruction. If a thing has been generated, a motion toward generation has stopped; but if a motion is eternal and is never completed, no thing can come to be generated. Likewise with destruction. So if the motion of a thing which has been generated has stopped, then the thing has been sometimes in motion and sometimes at rest.

22. Aristotle calls such motion a qualified generation or destruction (190a31–3, 225a12–7).

23. For example, if a body becomes hot from being cold, heat is being generated, but this is a qualified generation.

24. By "that in which" he means a place.

25. Is he referring to 253a24–30 or to Section 1 of this Book?

26. 253a32–b6.

27. Melissus (184b15–6, 185a32–3, b16–7).

28. If the infinite universe is motionless, the parts in it may move, and some parts certainly appear to be in motion.

29. Opinion is of that which may or may not be, and so of that which may change, but not of that which cannot change. But if no thing can change, there can be no opinion but either knowledge or its contrary. Hence, if opinion exists, at least some things do change.

30. The existence of motion is a principle received through sensation, and to deny motion is to deny a principle by means of premises which

are not principles; and such denial is a mark of one who is uneducated in the principles of Analytics.

31. 253b6–4a15. The single conviction indicated is this: Some things are sometimes in motion and sometimes at rest; and if so, not all things can be always in motion or always at rest, nor can some things be always in motion and the others always at rest.

4

1. Whether the expression "are moved" (= κινούμενα) signifies that the things in motion *are moved by something* or not is not specified. Whatever the alternative, Aristotle takes it as a fact that if a thing is in motion, then it is moved by something, by a mover.

2. For example, if a sick man is in motion, we say that his sickness or his finger is accidentally in motion, for his sickness is just an attribute or accident of the man, and his finger is a part and is in motion in virtue of the whole man (211a17–23); and we also say that the man is accidentally in motion when only a part of him is in motion, such as his arm.

A thing is said to cause a motion or to be in motion essentially if it is the whole thing which causes the motion or is in motion.

In 224a21–35 the word "accidentally", which is applied to things in in a change, is used in a narrower sense, that is, in a sense that does not include things which cause a motion or are in motion with respect to a part.

3. Every thing which is essentially in motion must have physical matter.

4. Whether "by force" and "contrary to nature" are synonymous or not is not clear. According to 300a23 the expressions are the same, but whether the same in definition or in genus is not clear. See also 788b27. A thing is moved by force if that which causes it to be in motion is outside of that thing (1110a1–3).

5. By "principle of motion" he means the moving principle. For example, if a man walks, that which as a moving principle causes him to walk is in him, whether this be his soul or a part of his soul (such as his will).

6. Perhaps by "the body" Aristotle here means the animal's body and not any physical body; and if this body is considered in itself and without the soul with which it is united, then it may be in motion by force or contrary to nature, as when the body of a dog is lifted up by a man, or it may be in motion by nature, as when that body is falling when the man lets the dog go.

7. Perhaps the kind of motion meant is locomotion. If so, still the meaning of the sentence is not spelled out. We may interpret it by the following example. If a man who is standing raises his arm, the motion of the arm is contrary to nature, since the arm is denser than the air; but if his position is upside-down, the same relative motion of the arm

is by nature, for it is a downward motion. There are alternative interpretations.

8. For example, when a man hurls a stone upwards or pushes a desk or raises a glass, clearly, the stone and the desk and the glass are caused to be in motion by the man.

9. Clearly, animals can be moved by themselves, as when a dog runs or a man goes upstairs.

10. In an animal, for example, is that which causes its motion a material part or the form or part of the form, and specifically, what is it or what is its nature?

11. These are things generated by art.

12. If "divided" be the correct term (e.g., a man is divided from the ship which he causes to move; and some thinkers posited the mover in things to be a material thing), then the problem is to determine that part of a man which is the mover. An alternative to "divided" is "distinguished", and then the mover need not be a material thing; it might be a form or part of a form.

13. For example, if a man lifts an apple, it is he who causes the apple to go up contrary to [its] nature; and things in motion contrary to their nature are evidently moved by an outside mover (1110a1–3). But if he lets it drop, who or what causes the apple to move down? Is it the man, the place down, the apple itself, or something else?

14. If a thing causes itself to be moved, it must have matter, and so the prime movers who cause only one kind of motion are excluded since they are forms. Now fire when in contact always causes one kind of motion, burning, but it does not cause itself to burn. What about fire causing itself to go up? But this is exactly the problem, whether it is fire that causes itself to go up or something else. Anyway, it is a fact that some physical things (e.g., animals) can cause themselves to move in contrary directions, and others (e.g., inanimate) do not; and this distinction must not be disregarded.

15. Perhaps he means a motion in only one direction, for example, going up but not down or heating but not cooling or expanding but not contracting. An alternative that has not been mentioned is a motion of one kind, e.g., a locomotion, but not an alteration or a motion with respect to quantity.

16. An alternative to συμφυές (="has a natural unity") is "united by nature".

17. From what is said, Aristotle may have in mind that it is a whole that acts or is acted upon, not a part. He may also have in mind the fact that air, fire, and the other elements, and perhaps all homogeneous things, unlike animals, which differ in their parts, show no differences in kind in their parts; so in each of them one material part does not act on another part since this would imply different actualities or functions in the two like parts. Perhaps he has both in mind. Perhaps the argument is dialectical.

18. He is referring to the things which have a uniform nature and perhaps also to the lifeless things.

19. Perhaps the distinct causes meant are those by nature and those contrary to nature.

20. The lever, although a mover, moves things up not by itself but by another, by an outside mover pressing on it in a certain way; but when fire causes cold things to become hot, the primary moving cause is in fire itself, and so it is by [its] nature that fire heats things.

21. A principle of being moved seems to be indicated.

22. A body qua potentially having a certain quality does not necessarily also have potentially a certain quantity, but both may belong to the body as accidents or attributes; for neither is a quality essentially a quantity, nor is a quantity essentially a quality. By "quality" he means a sensible quality. A line is essentially straight or curved, but straightness and curvature are qualities as differentiae and are not sensible qualities (1020a33–b25).

23. Fire and earth are also held by force in places not *proper* to them.

24. When earth is up, it is by force (which is an outside mover) there and not by nature; and it is by nature potentially down not qua a mover but qua being movable.

25. A man may be a potential scientist in two senses: (a) if he has not yet the power (or habit) of investigating but can have it, as when he is learning and so acquiring that habit, and (b) if he has the power but is not exercising it, as when he is asleep or attending to something else.

26. The learner does not yet have the power of investigating, and so he is potentially a man with that power; and when he acquires that habit, he may not be investigating, and so he is potentially an investigator. In a sense, a learner is potentially a man who investigates, but not directly (primarily), for he has to acquire the habit first.

27. Sickness or tiredness or lack of wish or preoccupation with something else might prevent him.

28. Water is potentially air first in a manner similar to that in which a learner is potentially a scientist (with the power of investigating) first. The water must first become air before being in the place where air belongs; but if air is prevented from being in that place, it is potentially in that place but not in the way in which water is potentially there.

29. It is potentially light in the sense that it can be or become air, which is light.

30. Perhaps the meaning is this: The man who moves the supporting pillar moves the object resting on the pillar accidentally just as the wall moves the ball accidentally. But what moves the supported object essentially? In the case of the ball thrown, it is the thrower that moves the ball essentially, and according to St. Thomas Aquinas, in the case

of the supported object the essential mover is that which generated that heavy object and gave it the inclination of going down.

The *actuality* of a scientist while he is investigating is similar to the *actuality* of a heavy body while it is down. Now the scientist may start investigating immediately after that which impedes him is removed; but the heavy object which has been lifted up does not begin to be down immediately after it is released, for it has to go down first. What essentially causes it to go down in this case? Is it still the generator who caused it to become heavy or is it another mover?

5

1. The term "through" indicates a first moving cause. Thus, if it is through itself that the mover moves an object, then the first mover must be in itself or be itself but not outside of itself.

2. In the example just given, the stick is the last mover and the man is the first mover, and the man is not moved by a thing outside of him.

3. An alternative to "and" is "or". If (a) the alternative is "or", perhaps two mutually exclusive *reasons* are given for which the first mover moves the object to a higher degree, but if (b) the alternative is "and", two different *reasons* are given. In (a), either the last mover is directly moved by the first mover, which immediately precedes it, or it is moved directly by an intermediate mover. But in (b), one *reason* is that the first mover moves the last, whether directly or indirectly, but not vice versa; and the other *reason* is that the first mover qua mover is prior in existence to the last mover, and that which is prior as a cause is a cause to a higher degree (993b24–31).

4. The problem of whether the mover, which is moved by itself, is moved by the whole of itself or by a part is left unresolved at this stage. The denial of an infinity of movers, or of causes in general, is assumed here but is discussed in 994a1–b31.

5. If the object P is moved not by the first mover but by another thing as an instrument, say A, then since A is not the first mover, it is moved by another thing, say B, and B likewise by C, etc. Eventually there will be a thing M which is moved by the first mover; otherwise, there will be an infinite series and no first mover.

6. This mover is prior to B, and it is certainly prior to A.

7. If there is always another mover, the process goes to infinity, and this cannot be.

8. An alternative to "the following" is "the same". This alternative is closer to the Greek text, although there are some variations from it. But the difficulties arising in the paragraph after the next indicate a possible corruption in the text. We used consistency in thought as the principle of translation.

9. Whether by "the thing" he means the mover or the thing caused to be in motion is not clear. Perhaps the mover is meant.

10. If motion were an accident of all movers, then nothing impos-

sible should result by positing all movers to be motionless at some time interval T_1T_2. But absence of motion is impossible (250b11–2b6); hence motion could not be an accident of all movers.

11. If motion is not a necessary attribute of a mover, then it is possible for all movers not to be in motion, and so it is possible for motion not to exist. But motion exists of necessity. Hence some mover must always be in motion.

Aristotle may be thinking of such movers which are immediately moved by immovable movers. For example, the outer sphere of the universe for him is always in motion, and it is moved by the prime mover.

12. What does "this result is reasonable" mean? The first two arguments of this Section show that if every mover is moved, there is a mover that moves itself. The last argument shows that not every mover has motion which is an accident and so is non-eternal. One conclusion from these arguments is that there is a mover which is in motion eternally, although whether this mover is moved by itself or by another is not discussed here. Perhaps it is these arguments that suggest the reasonable result which follows.

13. In other words, there exist things in motion which are moved by other things but which are not themselves movers. An object which alters but suffers no other change would be an example.

14. Alternatives to "at the same time" are "together with" or "together with and at the same time". Of course, the mover qua mover and the thing moved qua being moved by that mover exist at the same time (95a22–4); and if both are movable and in motion, contact is necessary and so they are in motion together.

15. A stone cannot initiate a motion by itself, although if moved by another it can cause a motion on some object.

16. What is reasonable, not to say necessary, is this: There exist (a) things which can be in motion but cannot cause motion by themselves (e.g., rocks), (b) things which can both be in motion and cause motion by themselves (e.g., men), and (c) things which can cause motion but cannot be in motion (e.g., God).

17. If *Intelligence* is movable, it can be changed or affected after being moved and can be the source of motion not only of all other things but also of itself, since no other thing can move it; and if it is blended, it is a composite and therefore subject to decomposition and destruction, which is impossible.

18. Lines 256b4–7 seem to indicate that a mover with an essential motion is always in motion.

19. How can one learn that which he already knows and teaches, or how can the medical art be healing itself when healing a patient?

20. The assumption made here is that two motions of the same kind are not repeated; and if so, there will be a mover which is not given a motion by another mover.

21. The argument seems to be this: If A is carried by B, B is altered

by C, C is increased by D, and D is carried by E, then although B is not carried by C, E is a mover of B to a higher degree than C is, for E is prior to C; hence, B is carried to a higher degree than it is altered. It is understood that these motions are simultaneous (95a22–4).

22. In other words, the consequence is that every mover will be moved with the same kind of motion, although indirectly. This is impossible; for the teacher will also be a learner of the same subject, and so the same person will have and not have the same knowledge at the same time.

23. Perhaps by "movable" he means movable with the same species of motion.

24. The alternatives are (a) an object is directly caused to be moved by the same specific motion which it causes on another object, and (b) an object is indirectly caused to be moved, etc. If (a), then the impossible follows (Comm. 22, above); if (b) then, to take an example, the teacher who is teaching is at the same time indirectly (i.e., through a series of movers) being taught by another teacher, and this is fictitious.

25. By "a cause" here he means a moving cause although the statement applies to other causes also (993b23–31). Of movers that can be moved, then, self-movers are first, for they initiate motion; and Plato is partly right when he posits self-movers as first and defines the soul as a self-mover, but he is partly wrong in not pushing his inquiry far enough to an immovable mover.

26. 234b10–20. That which can be essentially in motion is a body, which is continuous and hence infinitely divisible.

27. For example, if a man travels from A to B, he is still a man throughout the motion, so his essence as a man does not move or change.

28. It was already shown that he who is teaching cannot at the same time be learning what he is teaching. The same applies to the other motions, though perhaps less obviously.

29. If A is heating A (i.e., if A is heating itself), then qua causing heat it is already hot, but qua being in the process of being heated it is not yet hot; so it is hot and not hot at the same time. Accordingly, if a contradiction is to be avoided, there must be two distinct parts or aspects in A, that which causes the motion and that which is caused to be in motion.

Also, that which causes the motion exists already in actuality, but that which is caused to be in motion is on its way to an actuality; so there is a difference between the two.

30. If A has parts A_1 and A_2 and if A_1 moves A_2 while A_2 moves A_1, then this causing of motion, which must be simultaneous (95a22–4), goes back and forth infinitely, and there is no first mover. But this is impossible (994a1–b31).

31. If A_1 moves A_2 while A_2 moves A_1, then A_1, by moving A_2, is more of a cause than A_2 and also causes more motion than A_2, and A_2, by moving A_1, is similarly related to A_1, so it turns out that A_1 is more of

a cause than itself and also moves more than itself. This is impossible.

32. 256a4–21.

33. For example, if A moves B, B moves C, C moves D, D moves E, and E is the last thing moved, then B is nearer to A, which is the source of motion, than C or D, each of which lies between B and E.

34. An alternative to "motionless" is "immovable". The term ἀκίνητον means motionless and also immovable (221b12–4, 226b10–5). If a thing is immovable, then it is motionless; if it is motionless, it may be immovable or it may be movable.

35. In other words, if A and B are the two parts and if A does not move B but B moves A, then, assuming B not to move itself primarily, B will be a motionless mover.

36. Perhaps the argument is this: If motion must be eternal, then at least one self-mover with parts A and B is such that the part, say A, which need not be moved by B and which moves B must be either motionless or a self-mover.

37. It is assumed that no other mover is causing C to be in motion.

38. Here he leaves the issue open, but elsewhere he excludes reciprocal contact. In 323a28–33 he says, "we sometimes say that he who gives us pain touches us, but we do not say that we touch him". The term "touch" here is not used in a literal sense. But what is its meaning when an immovable mover is said to touch the body it moves? If that mover is desire or will, which is in a man or an animal, then it is not separate from a body and it somehow affects directly (or *touches*) the body; but if it is separate from a body, like the prime mover who is moving the outer sphere according to Aristotle, the manner in which it *touches* the body is less direct and so more difficult to conceive. One might use an analogy.

39. If a part of it moves itself, then the whole does not move itself primarily.

40. If it is the whole that is being moved in its entirety, then the mover in it is moved also. If so, (a) the mover is movable and (b) there is a part (the mover) which moves itself. Thus, (a) neither will the mover be immovable, and (b) nor will the whole move itself primarily.

41. If, for example, a part of flesh is removed and if that part does not interfere with the power to run or with the parts of the body needed for running, then with the same power the man becomes less tired per unit mile or goes further before getting exhausted. Thus, A remains the same but B changes quantitatively its potentiality of being moved.

The problem of whether a motionless or immovable mover is continuous or not is here left unsolved.

6

1. Shown in 250b11–2b6.

2. Perhaps Aristotle has in mind the motion or motions existing always and continuously. If so, then an immovable mover who exists always is required. The Greek text is not specific in detail.

3. A mover can be immovable and still be destructible, as in the case of the soul of an animal; and it may be subject to accidental change, e.g., if it is a form in a body with locomotion, for a form cannot be essentially in motion or generation or destruction, though it is changed accidentally as a form when the body in which it exists changes, as in the locomotion of an animal. So the mover indicated here is a substance which is separate from matter and cannot be changed essentially or accidentally by anything.

4. 1043b13–21, 1044b21–9.

5. 240b8–1a26.

6. For example, the soul, or a part of it, like the will, each of which is in an animal.

7. There may be movers which are immovable and yet always existing.

8. Perhaps he is thinking not of a temporary mover, like the father of Socrates, but of a mover necessary for the temporary existence of not only Socrates but also his father and each of the preceding temporary movers.

9. For example, an animal can move itself; for it is or it has a body, which can be in motion, and it is or it has a principle which causes motion.

10. That is, from what has been said it does not follow that every mover has magnitude.

11. Perhaps "continuously" here means that at any given time T_1T_2 there is some generation or destruction going on.

12. Whether the process implied is the continuous and eternal circular movement of the heavens or the generation of things is not spelled out. Perhaps he means the latter. Although there is always some generation, still it is not the generation of just one thing. What exists is a set of generations, no one of which is eternal.

13. For example, one man moves one thing while another moves another.

14. Perhaps "a cause" is better than "the cause", for this allows for the possibility of many immovable and eternal movers. The term does not appear in the Greek but is implied.

Socrates' father is a moving cause of Socrates, and the prime mover is also a cause, but in a different sense. The one is proximate; the other is ultimate. But since the proximate cannot exist without the ultimate, the ultimate is prior in existence.

15. Perhaps the point suggested here is not the necessity of one prime eternal mover (for elsewhere he posits many), but the necessity of an eternal mover prior in some sense (e.g., as a moving cause) to other movers.

16. It seems that Aristotle assumes the existence of a motion which is one and eternally continuous; so there is the problem of whether in 250b11–2b6 he has proved the necessity of such a motion or of just some motion at any given time. If just some motion, there is no necessity

for one eternal and continuous motion to exist, unless he assumes it to exist, whether by hypothesis or by the observation of the circular motion of the outer sphere about the Earth, which he considers later (261b27–5a12.)

17. Perhaps by "the principle of movers" he means the two kinds he mentions a little further (259a32–b1), namely, a mover that moves itself among movables, and an immovable mover among all things (movable or not).

18. 253a22–4b6.

19. In other words, of movable things there is a first which is moved by itself and not by another, and this is a self-mover; but of things, whether movable or not, there is a first mover which is immovable (256a4–8b9).

20. 252b17–28, 253a7–11.

21. Locomotion (253a7–15).

22. It is not clear whether "not independently" here means complete or just partial dependence on something outside. If partial, then also the animal contributes, and the nature of what the animal contributes, whether the form of the motion or something else, is another problem.

23. The taking in of food is just a locomotion; when the food, after digestion, becomes a part of the body, there is increase.

24. The first mover of an animal, whether this be the soul or part of it, cannot move essentially, since in itself it has no physical matter; but it moves accidentally, that is, as the body is in motion, we may say that its form or an attribute of it is in motion, but the motion of an attribute is accidental whereas that of a body is essential. Thus "motion" has two senses, a primary and a secondary.

25. Manuscripts differ, and our use of "as if by a lever" may not be the exact meaning intended.

26. Perhaps he means a continuous motion which is eternal.

27. Perhaps by "being" he means the whole universe, or else the outer sphere, which is changeless except for its locomotion.

28. Perhaps by "in the same [state]" he means in a state of changelessness except for its locomotion.

29. If the moving principle stays the same, it must always be acting in the same way; and this suggests that the object acted upon must stay the same somehow. Qua being acted upon, that object cannot be entirely motionless, so except for its motion, which is a circular locomotion, it must stay the same in other respects. Perhaps the object meant is the outer heaven, which, except for its circular locomotion, stays the same; and even that motion is the same, for it is uniform and one and continuous.

30. Perhaps the phrase "be continuous in relation to the principle" means that the relation of the mover to the moved must always or continuously be the same if the mover is to act always in the same way and the object moved is to be acted upon always in the same way.

The circular locomotion leaves the outer heaven in the same state.

The change in position of the parts of the outer heaven does not alter the action of the mover, for (a) that action is on the outer heaven as on a whole object and not separately on the parts, and (b) that whole remains changeless in other respects, i.e., with respect to quantity, size, shape, quality, etc.

31. Perhaps by "some principles" he means either the various spheres except the outer sphere or the eternal objects in those spheres, like the Sun and Moon, but not the prime movers of those spheres. Those movers exist separately from the spheres they move and cannot be like the soul of a man which exists in a body. The Sun, for example, is moved by the immovable mover, which moves the sphere containing the Sun, but it is also moved indirectly by the mover of the outer sphere or by that sphere itself, which transfers its motion to the lower spheres; for the Sun (according to Aristotle) is moved by a number of motions and not by just one.

32. The Sun, for example, changes its distance from the objects on the Earth, and so its effect on those objects is not always the same.

33. 253a22–4.

34. These would be the spheres and their parts, like the stars and the Sun and the Moon.

35. The objects on Earth would be examples of things which change in this manner.

36. For St. Thomas Aquinas, the creation of the universe by the prime mover (God) can take place without any change in the prime mover; for Aristotle, some change in the prime mover for such creation would be necessary (250b11–2b6).

7

1. He means a continuous and eternal motion.

2. From here to 261a26 he shows that locomotions are primary, and the senses of "primary" are given in 260b17–9.

3. Apparently, the kind of increase meant here is not one by, say, contact or gluing together; the thing increased must have a unity, rather an organic unity, and it must be a substance. The growth of a tree or an animal would be an instance.

4. For example, if an animal is increased by means of taking in food, the mere taking in of food does not cause the increase, for it must be digested first; the increase occurs when the food becomes blood or flesh or bone. For example, food is unlike flesh, and, in altering, it becomes flesh or like flesh; and an alteration is from one contrary or intermediate to another contrary or intermediate (416a21–b9).

Is the change from food to flesh an alteration or a substantial change? One might argue that food is destroyed and flesh is generated. In either case, in an unqualified destruction or generation there is also present an alteration.

5. If the material parts of a body are changeless in quantity, as

assumed by some atomists, locomotion of those parts certainly takes place during condensation and rarefaction; and if the parts themselves change in magnitude, still there is locomotion, and in two ways: (a) each part changes its primary place when increasing or decreasing, and (b) at least some parts change their relative distance during condensation or rarefaction.

6. The primary place is meant, that is, the innermost boundary of the body that surrounds the magnitude which decreases or increases.

7. 1018b9–9a14. An alternative to "substance" is *"substance"*. By "primary", of course, he means prior to all the others.

8. Apparently, he is using "continuously" in two senses: To exist continuously is to be either continuous or in succession. The reference is to the motion which always exists. The problem is this: Assuming there is always a motion, does a motion which is continuous and eternal exist or do only motions which succeed one another exist?

9. 1015b36–6a17.

10. 261b27–5a12.

11. What does "primary in time" exactly mean? Assuming that an eternal motion must be a locomotion, then some part of that motion must exist before any other motion; but it will exist both before and after any other motion. So perhaps "prior in time" does not mean that the whole eternal locomotion exists earlier than any other motion. Of course, an eternal locomotion is prior in existence to any other motion.

12. For example, babies just born do not immediately walk; but they grow and change in qualities, and it is later that they are able to walk.

13. A father is not in the process of being generated when he is in the course of begetting a child; there is some locomotion when he is in the course of begetting the child.

14. Given a destructible individual, say Socrates, he is first generated, and the other motions belong to him after he is generated.

15. Perhaps he means a locomotion; or if not, still there is a locomotion involved in any of the other motions.

16. This does not necessarily mean that that individual was generated at an earlier stage; for example, the father of Socrates was generated earlier, but the Sun which contributes as an indirect mover to births was not generated at all (194b13).

17. The argument is not fully stated. If we assume that priority in time is still under discussion, then for any given destructible thing its generation is first and the other motions follow; but all changes in that thing must be preceded by a locomotion. But if generation were primary in time, what is the meaning of "for otherwise all things would be destructible"? It may mean (a) that whatever has any of the other motions must have been generated earlier and is therefore destructible, and this would make the Sun and the other heavenly bodies (assumed indestructible by Aristotle) destructible. Perhaps there are other alternatives.

18. For example, an embryo is on its way to acquiring a form, the

soul of a man, and such a form is a principle of a substance. Of course, without such principles nothing can exist, for substances are prior to attributes and a form is prior to matter. For example, men must exist if babies are to be born and become sick or healthy, etc. (1049b4–1051a3).

19. The baby or the grown man is posterior in time to the sperm or embryo from which it or he developed, but unlike the embryo or the sperm which is incomplete in nature (or form), the baby or the man is complete and has a form; and besides, the sperm or embryo or baby was caused by a man who is complete in form. Moreover, that which is complete is a substance to a higher degree than that which is incomplete.

20. Analogous attributes of prior substances are prior (1018b37–9a1).

21. Apparently, change in place is assumed as affecting a substance less than change in quality or quantity.

22. That which moves itself causes a locomotion above all; so since that which moves itself also causes other things which are not self-movers *to be in* motion or to cause motion and since a cause is prior in *substance* to its effect, an attribute (i.e., a locomotion) of that cause is prior in *substance* to a similar attribute (i.e., any other kind of motion) of that which it causes to be in motion or to be a mover (1018b37–9a1).

23. 260b23–6.

24. That is, rest with respect to the given motion. For example, if a thing is not changing with respect to magnitude but exists, then it keeps the same magnitude or rests with respect to magnitude. Rest is the privation of motion.

25. Perhaps "moving" is better than "changing", and the motion here is assumed to proceed to a contrary, and so circular locomotion is excluded.

26. If rest is the privation of motion, that which is resting is that which can be but is not in motion, and "that" refers to the same thing. But if a thing is destroyed, it is not the same thing any longer, and so destruction is the opposite and not the contrary of generation, for of a pair of contraries one is a possession and the other a privation, like white and black in that which is receptive of them.

27. That is, rest with respect to the motion under consideration.

28. A motion may be opposed in three different respects. It may be opposed just qua motion, without reference to its direction or to its being natural or contrary to nature, and in this respect it is opposed to rest. It may be opposed in direction, and in this respect a motion from A to B is opposed to that from B to A. And it may be opposed with respect to its being natural or contrary to nature, whether qua motion or also with respect to rest; and in this case, a natural motion of an object from A to B may be opposed to rest of that object at A, and a natural motion of an object from A to B is opposed to a motion of that object from B to A, if this be contrary to nature. Evidently, the downward motion of earth is not opposed to the upward motion of fire with respect to its being natural or contrary to nature.

29. The induction here is this: Just as a thing generated must remain generated for some time before being destroyed, so it is natural in the case of any motion that when an object has moved from A to B, it must remain at the B state for some interval of time; for motions are similar in this respect to generations and destructions. Modern scientists do not take the same view. For example, a ball thrown up need not stop at its highest point for an interval of time.

8

1. By "not continuous" he seems to mean not eternally continuous.

2. It is assumed that (a) the rectilinear component of the velocity does not change direction, and (b) the angular direction does not change.

Since in a plane only circular and straight lines are posited as being elementary, perhaps any other line (i.e., a curve in a plane) would be a blend of the two. For example, such would be the parabola whose equation is $y = \sqrt{x}$, for if a point starts from the origin $(0,0)$ and moves along this parabola, then both (a) the x-component always increases and (b) the direction is always clockwise.

3. For Aristotle, an eternal motion along a finite straight line is impossible (233a31–2), for the universe is finite (207b19–21, 286b10–1), and so its greatest length is finite. Thus there can be no eternal rectilinear motion. One may posit an infinite straight line, but the hypothesis is false; and a science deals with being and not with nonbeing.

If the speed s is given by $s = Me^{-t}$, then the distance traversed in an infinite time will be less than M (Comm. 11, Section 2, Book Z). So an eternal rectilinear motion appears to be possible.

4. 227b3–9a6.

5. 227b24–6.

6. The object in motion must be a material substance, but the usage of θεός (= "god" or "divine being") seems curious. Perhaps he is using the term in a popular sense. The term may have been θέον (= "that which runs").

7. If "form" indicates changes with respect to substance, these would be generations and destructions, and if so, he may be using "motion" in a wider sense (15a13–4); but a generation and a destruction may also be taken in a qualified sense (190a31–3, 225a12–7).

8. An alternative to "species" is "kind".

9. If they stop, the contrary motions have equal speeds, the term "speed" to be taken in a sense wide enough to include also alterations and motions with respect to magnitude. Is Aristotle assuming the two motions to belong to the same body? If so, then two movers are acting on the same body but in contrary directions, as in the case of a passenger who walks in one direction while the ship sails in the contrary direction.

10. The meaning is not spelled out. If the contrary motions have uni-

form and equal speeds, the resultant is along the diameter AD and is a simple harmonic motion; but there is an instantaneous change of direction at D (or perhaps at E, the resultant of the two motions), and there is no stop. Does Aristotle mean something else?

11. A lateral motion is one whose components are perpendicular and each of them always has the same direction. Although the two directions are different, they are not contrary.

There seems to be a philosophical difficulty in the case of locomotion. If the three subdivisions of locomotion [up-down, right-left, forward-backward] are species, then perpendicular locomotions should have some contrariety. Perhaps they are not species, but the motion, for example, along the line connecting the Center (down) and the extremity (up), regardless of the direction, is a genus whose ultimate species are the direction upward and the direction downward. In this sense, perpendicular directions are not comparable in species, although they may be comparable with respect to some common attribute, such as speed, which is not a differentia of motion but admits of the predicates "greater" and "less".

12. A motion along a circle is analogous to a motion along a straight line in this respect: The two contrary directions along a straight line correspond to the clockwise and counterclockwise directions along the circle. Aristotle uses "circular locomotion" to mean a motion along a circle in one direction only, and he uses "around a circle" to mean a motion which is sometimes clockwise and sometimes counterclockwise.

13. Is it evident from sensation that a motion must stop before changing to a contrary direction? For modern physicists, a rock thrown up does not (theoretically) rest at the highest point.

14. The argument applies to rectilinear motions as well as to motions along a circle.

15. By "middle" he means any intermediate, not necessarily that whose intervals from the beginning and the end are equal or the same.

16. In other words, if B is a middle, A the beginning, and C the end, then B is both a beginning and an end; it is the beginning relative to C but the end relative to A. As a subject, B is numerically the same, but its definition or formula as an object in relation to C differs from that as an object in relation to A, for to be an end of something is not to be a beginning of something else.

17. For example, the line AC is potentially two or three or more lines, for it can be divided (although it is not yet divided) into two or three or more lines, but it is *actually* one line. Similarly, an intermediate point B exists potentially as the end of AB and as the beginning of BC but is actually the end of AB and the beginning of BC after AC is divided at B.

18. He is not stating his meaning literally enough. If the object P has the motion $M_1M_2M_3$ along line ABC in time T_1T_3, then the division is not of the line at B but of the motion $M_1M_2M_3$ at B; so by "divides the line" Aristotle in this case means that, instead of passing over B and

being at B just for a moment, which is indivisible, P stops at B for a time interval t_1t_2 and so makes B *actually* the end of the preceding motion, of M_1M_2 along AB, and the beginning of the succeeding motion, of M_2M_3 along BC.

19. Here, "to arrive at B" means to terminate the motion at B, in which case P must stay at B for an interval of time. Similarly, "to depart from B" means to use B as the beginning of a motion, in which case P must be resting at B for an interval of time prior to that motion.

20. Since "in" has many senses, there is a sense in which one may say that P is at B in an interval of time, namely, this: Since P is at B at moment T_2, and T_2 is in the whole of time T_1T_3, P is at B in the time T_1T_3. But it is at B primarily at the moment T_2 and secondarily or indirectly in the time T_1T_3.

21. By "simultaneously" he means at a moment, e.g., at T_2.

22. The term σημεῖον has many meanings. It means, among other things, a point or a mark (like a pencil mark) or a limit. We will use the term "cut". Perhaps Aristotle is using it in a generic sense to mean that which potentially divides any one-dimensional continuum. This would be a point within a line or a moment in time. Perhaps "limit" is not the correct translation, for "limit" suggests something after division, while σημεῖον suggests something indivisible, whether as a limit or not.

23. Perhaps the *difficulty* was raised by some thinker, or by Aristotle himself. The details of the *difficulty* are not spelled out, and many interpretations are possible; but in all of them the common but false premise is this: Since an object P, which starts at A and travels continuously along line ABC, must be sometime at point B, it must stop there for a time interval. Perhaps Ross's interpretation is correct, and both the translation given and the bracketed remarks follow this interpretation.

Perhaps there is some corruption in the Greek text. We shall give another interpretation in the next Commentary.

24. The argument is as follows. Let AC = DF, and AB = DE; then BC = EF. Both P and Q start simultaneously from A and D, respectively, with uniform and equal speeds. P is assumed to be at B and so to have arrived there, let us say at moment t_1, while Q is assumed to be continuing toward F from E at t_1 and so using t_1 as if a starting moment in travelling toward F. Since P's arrival at B and departure from B are not simultaneous, P will depart from B at t_2, which is a moment existing later than t_1. Hence, Q will arrive at F before P arrives at C, for EF = BC and Q's speed is equal to that of P.

Another interpretation is as follows. Let B be near A, AC = DF and AB = DE, P arrive at B at t_1 and depart from B at t_2, Q depart from D at t_1 but at t_2 be at a point S beyond E (for E is near D). Then while P uses B as a point of departure at t_2, Q at t_2 uses S as if a point of departure (for Q is taken as always in the process of travelling and not arriving at any point between D and F); and since SF is less than BC, Q arrives at F before P arrives at C.

25. In other words, H will be a point of arrival and a point of

departure; and though it is the same point, not only will it be defined in two different ways, but it will exist at different moments as a point of arrival and as a point of departure.

26. Perhaps the argument is this: Since t_1t_3 is the time during which R rests at H (for to arrive at H implies to rest there for some time), if R is assumed to both arrive and depart at the same moment t_1, then (a) at an intermediate moment t_2 it will be at H qua having arrived at H, but (b) it will not be at H qua having departed from H at t_1, for t_2 comes after t_1 in time.

27. Just as H is an arrival or an end of one time interval but a departure and a beginning of another time interval, so it is an end of one motion but a beginning of another motion.

28. Of course, if an infinite straight line existed, a motion along it might be eternally continuous; but no such line exists, since the universe, according to Aristotle, is finite. A velocity of the form $v = ke^{-t}$ could still make an eternally continuous motion along a finite straight line possible, as pointed out earlier (Book Z, Sec. 2, Comm. 11).

29. 233a21–31, 239b11–4.

30. Perhaps by "the infinite" he means any infinite number of things, and in this case we have an infinite number of halves in the manner described.

31. See Comm. 10, Sec. 2, Book Z.

32. Zeno's argument assumes that the parts to be traversed are *actually* infinite in number. Aristotle's refutation of this argument in 233a21–31 is dialectical; for he makes a concession in assuming the *actuality* of this infinite (even if he denies such *actuality* as a fact) but indicates to his opponent that if a finite length by being bisected in a certain manner is equated to an infinite number of parts, a finite interval of time too will have to be equated to an infinite number of parts for a similar reason. Here, however, Aristotle is concerned with the truth or the fact itself and not with refutation; hence he must proceed with true premises. And it is a fact that if a thing, e.g., a finite line or an interval of time, is one and continuous, it is not *actually* many or an infinite number, and if it is *actually* many, it is not one and continuous.

33. These are possible divisions or possible moments at which division can take place.

34. After the line is divided, there is a break in the line at the point of division, and after each count there is likewise a pause.

35. Evidently, if line ABC is actually divided at B, B as a point of division becomes B_1, which is the end of AB_1, and B_2, which is the beginning of B_2C. But, prior to its division, B exists not as something *actual* in ABC but as something potential. In the case of time, such division is not even possible, for a moment is a division only potentially (222a10–9).

36. Perhaps by "an unqualified infinite" he means an infinite number of actual parts, and a continuous motion is not such a number actually. Perhaps by "accidentally" he means that it can be an infinite number

of actual parts, taking the term "infinite" in a potential sense as discussed in 202b30–8a23; but if the parts are actual, the motion is not essentially one but many.

37. The *substance* of a line is to be a certain kind of a continuous quantity and one such quantity, not a number or an infinite number of things. It is true that a line can become potentially an infinite number of things, but such becoming is an accident or an attribute of the line and not its essence or in its essence. Further, the line exists as one and not as many.

38. For example, in changing from white to black, the thing would be black and white at the same moment unless the moment at which the change to black is made is taken to belong to the thing when it is black but not when it is white or at an intermediate state.

39. Unlike a point within a line, at which [point] a division actually made will divide the line into two lines and two points will result, a moment in time cannot do this but is only a potential division or cut (222a10–20). So it is one numerically, but qua being related to the past time it will not be defined in the same way as it will be defined qua being related to the future time.

40. In other words, if a thing changes from white to black at moment t, then the thing is black at t but not white.

41. In ABC, A stands for a time interval, and so does C, but B stands for the moment which is the end of A and the beginning of C. Thus B is assumed to belong to both A and C.

42. That is, at the moment B the thing is not-white, and it is false to say that it is white.

43. In other words, during A we may speak of P as becoming not-white from being white, and we may also speak of it as being in the process of being destroyed as white.

44. The argument of this paragraph may be summarized as follows. If the process of becoming not-white from white starts at moment T_1 and terminates at T_2 and if the thing is not-white from T_2 to T_3, then the thing is white at T_1 and during T_1T_2, but not at T_2. Or in the mathematician's language, it is white in the interval $[T_1, T_2)$ in which the right hand side is open; and it is not-white in the time interval T_2T_3, including T_2.

45. The argument may be as follows: Since B is next to A and time is assumed divisible into *indivisible* intervals, let A_n be the last *indivisible* interval of A. Then B is next (consecutive) to A_n. Now P is not-white in A_n (or during A_n, if you wish); and it is white first in B. But it takes time for P to become white from not-white, for a generation (whether qualified or unqualified) always takes time. Hence there must be time between A_n and B, contrary to the hypothesis.

One might reply that P was in the process of generation in A_n (or during A_n), but this leads to difficulties. A process is divisible, but A_n was assumed to be *indivisible*. The phrase "during A_n", too, is not correct; for this implies a beginning and an end (and a middle, too), whereas A_n has no distinct parts at all and so no beginning or middle or end. In fact, the hypothesis of ultimate *indivisible* intervals of time makes continuous change impossible.

46. If no *indivisible* interval of time exists, every interval of time is divisible; hence no consecutive *indivisible* time intervals such as A_n and B (in the preceding Commentary) exist. Thus if P is white at moment M_2 and not-white at any earlier moment M_1, there is always a time interval M_1M_2 (for M_1 and M_2 are not consecutive) for a generation to take place.

47. By "that at which" he means the time's last moment at which P first became white. If T_1 and T_2 are the first and last moments respectively of time T_1T_2, then $T_2 + [T_1, T_2)$ is not greater than $[T_1, T_2)$; that is, the addition of a moment to the time interval $[T_1, T_2)$, which is closed at the beginning and open at the end (mathematically speaking), does not make the result greater than that time interval. Just as the sum of a line and a point does not make the result greater than the line itself (regardless of whether the line be taken with or without anyone or both of its end points), so it is in time.

48. A logical argument is one that is based mainly not on truths *proper* to the subject but on common truths from logic (in Aristotle, these are in *Prior* and *Posterior Analytics*) or dialectics or even metaphysics. Logical truths which are applied to one subject are applicable to other subjects also. In the argument that follows, such are the truths that a thing cannot have contraries and therefore contrary motions at the same time.

49. Since the motion is assumed continuous, P would not rest at C but would be there only at one moment.

50. Perhaps the argument is as follows. Since P leaves A, its direction is away from A, let us say eastwards; but since, as just stated (264a9–14), it is travelling toward the same point from beginning to end, and the end is A, then it is travelling toward A, especially after having reached C. So it has contrary motions at the same time, the eastward motion from A and the westward motion to A (229a7–b22).

51. The argument is not spelled out, and two alternatives are: (1) Since in a single motion an object travels from a place at which it has been (for some time) and which cannot be that to which it is travelling, P cannot have been at A, to which it is travelling; but it has been at A, from which it started. (2) Since P is travelling toward A, it must have started from a contrary point, say B, at which it was at rest prior to starting; but there is no such B, for P started from A. Perhaps there are other alternatives.

52. Since impossibilities result by assuming P not to stop at C, the alternative left is that P stops at C; and if so, P has two motions, one from A to C and another from C to A.

53. Locomotion, motion with respect to quality, and motion with respect to quantity, whether increase or decrease (225b5–9).

54. Perhaps the word δὲ in line 264a24 should be omitted.

55. Actually, the thing was resting at A prior to the motion from A. But the motion from C to A, which is a part of the motion (assumed continuous) from A to C and back to A, is not contrary to rest at A. 229b29–230a5.

56. The hypothesis is that the motion is continuous at C. A contradiction results. Hence the motion is not continuous at C.

57. Perhaps the argument is as follows. A thing changes from opposite to opposite, and in particular, from not-white to white; and a change occurs in one continuous time. Thus, if the change from not-white to its opposite occurs in T_1T_2, the thing will be destroyed as not-white and will be white at moment T_2. But if the change is continuous from not-white to white and from white to not-white during T_1T_2, the thing will be not-white at moment T_2. So the thing will be both white and not-white at T_2. Since this is impossible, the thing *rests* when it becomes white, and so there are two changes in the time interval T_1T_2.

The destruction and generation in the alteration just given are qualified (225a13–20).

58. There seems to be no continuity of thought, and premises are needed for the argument. If the motion, assumed continuous, is from black to white in T_1T_2 and back to black in T_2T_3, by "same extremity" does he mean the color of the moving object at T_2 or at T_3? Evidently, the color is white at T_2. One might argue thus: If in one motion the change is to a contrary, then at T_3 the object should be white; but the change in T_2T_3 is to black.

59. In other words, the direction is always clockwise, or always counterclockwise.

60. It would have contrary or contradictory motions if, for example, it changed direction from clockwise to counterclockwise.

61. If the motion from A to A proceeds along the diameter AB from A to B and back to A, the motion from A to B will be contrary to that

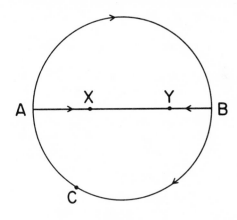

Fig. 18

from B to A, for the ends A and B along the diameter are farthest apart. And if the motion is clockwise along the circumference from A to C and counterclockwise back to A, the two motions along arcs ABC and CBA would be contradictory; for A and C on arc ABC are not farthest apart, since B is farther from A in distance than C is. That which is contrary is contradictory, but the converse is not necessarily true; e.g., the unequal is not equal but that which is not equal may or may not be unequal (a point is neither equal nor unequal to a color).

62. The motion from A to A but along the diameter AB (Fig. 18) lies within the same contrary limits A and B, so one part will be the motion AXYB and the other will be the motion BYXA. The intermediate points X and Y will be crossed twice, first X and then Y if the motion is from A to B, but in reverse order if the motion is from B to A. In fact, the motions AXYB and BYXA are contrary.

But the motion from A back to A along the circumference and in the same direction, let us say clockwise, has no such contrary limits. It returns to the same point A, and no point along the circumference in one rotation is crossed twice. Further, if the motion is along the diameter, the points A and B are contrary and are unique as limits. But in the clockwise circular motion no two points are unique in this manner; the motion may be from A to A, or from B to B, etc. Thus each point along the circumference is alike a point of departure or of arrival, and the distinction which exists in the rectilinear motion (point of departure and point of arrival) does not appear here. It is like saying that the motion is from the same to the same (not to another), and such motion (and "motion" may not quite be the right term) is like an *actuality* which is complete rather than incomplete, or else, which is least incomplete.

If the prime mover, then, is to cause diversity in things but in a manner most proper to Himself (He is simple and complete *actuality*), He will choose to cause a change closest to complete actuality, and such a change is a circular or rotary motion.

63. He means any arc less than the circumference. The end-points of such an arc will be distinct, and the motion along that arc cannot be eternally continuous because it will have to change direction many times.

64. Contrary changes do not necessarily imply contrary limits. The change in the motion along arc ABC in Fig. 18 from clockwise to counterclockwise direction will be contrary, but the points A and C are contradictory (see Comm. 61 of this Section).

65. If a motion along an arc, other than the complete circumference, is one when a distinct end-point is reached, the beginning of that motion cannot coincide with the end.

66. In what sense is the motion complete? If A and B differ in *substance* in that A is nearer to *substance* than B and if analogous attributes of A and B are similarly related, then since of elementary lines the circumference is complete but the straight line is not complete or is

less complete, a motion along the circumference is complete, or else, it is more complete and partakes of *substance* more than a motion along a line with distinct ends (286b10–33, 1016b16–7, 1021b12–2a3).

67. These may be white and black or any two colors A and B. In either case, the limits are distinct, and an alteration from A to B must stop at B if it is to return to A; moreover, the intermediate colors must be repeated, and those from B to A must follow in an order which is the reverse of that in which they follow when the object proceeds from A to B.

68. If, according to these thinkers (Anaxagoras, Cratylus, Heraclitus, etc.), alterations are the primary of changes, then since the ends of an alteration are distinct and an object cannot alter in one direction continuously and eternally but must stop before changing direction, the object in alteration must rest for some time, and so it cannot be always altering (187a32–4, 314a6–15, 987a32–4, 1078b12–5).

69. He means always continuously.

9

1. The senses in which circular locomotions are primary are taken up as the discussion proceeds. See also 260b16–9.

2. 261b28–9. A path which is a blend of the circular and the rectilinear is posterior to the elementary paths in at least two senses: (a) It is posterior in definition or in knowledge, for it must be defined in terms of the others (for example, in the equation $y = \sqrt{x}$ of the parabola, the letter "y" signifies an ordinate, which is a straight line, and likewise for "x"; and the curvature at any point (x, y) is defined in terms of a circular and a straight line); and (b) it is posterior in existence, for the existence of a blend presupposes that of its elements.

3. This is yet to be shown.

4. Since the universe is finite (207b15–21, 208a8–11), no motion can take place along a path whose linear component (such as x in $y = \sqrt{x}$) is infinite in the direction of increase (i.e., by a component which exceeds the length of the universe).

5. An infinite length cannot be traversed in a finite time (233a31–4); hence a motion along such length cannot be completed.

6. If the motion of an object is rectilinear, the object must rest before changing its motion in the contrary direction (264a9–5a12); and if so, one motion ends and another begins, and so we have not one motion but many.

7. Evidently, a rectilinear motion is destructible; for it exists during a finite time, say T_1T_2, and at any moment later than T_2 it does not exist. But in what sense is it incomplete? According to St. Thomas Aquinas, it is incomplete because it is possible to add to it (for example, the motion may still continue further along the extended straight line). Perhaps it is incomplete in another sense; for a motion which has not reached but will reach an end is an incomplete actuality (201b31–3),

for it exists potentially relative to that actuality, while a circular motion was shown in the previous Section to be complete in some sense.

8. That which is complete is prior in nature to that which is incomplete, for it participates in an essence or *substance* more than the incomplete does; and it is prior in formula, for the incomplete is defined in terms of the complete, as a semicircle in terms of a circle and the hand in terms of the man (1035b9–11); and it is also prior in time or in existence, e.g., prior to the baby there existed a father (a complete being), and no baby can be generated without a father.

9. Attributes of prior subjects are prior, and an eternal motion exists in an eternal object, which is prior to a destructible object. Moreover, that which can be eternal is actually eternal (203b30).

10. He means eternally continuous.

11. If it has a beginning and an end, it cannot be eternal.

12. The term "one" may refer to a point on a circle (or a sphere) or to a state of the moving object at a moment.

13. If the object is considered as being always at the beginning or at the end, it is like an object at rest; but if it is never at the beginning or at the end (i.e., if it is in the middle), it is like an object in motion. So in one sense it is at rest and in another sense in motion.

14. Since the rotating sphere is in the same place as a whole, it is not moving to another place and so it is at rest; but the primary place of each part in itself and not qua part changes, and so in this sense the sphere is in motion.

15. An alternative to "beginning" is "principle". It is not specified in what sense the center is a beginning or a principle. Perhaps like a finite straight line, which starts from one end and ends at the other and beyond the latter end no part of the line exists, in a sphere (or a circle), too, one may start from the center and end at the surface (or circumference) and beyond this no part of the sphere (or circle) exists. In another sense, the center usually appears in the definition of a sphere or a circle, and so it functions as a principle. Aristotle would probably not use the center in the definition of a circle; he might posit its existence as a hypothesis.

16. Evidently, the center is the middle of a sphere (or a circle). And the center of a sphere is like the mid-point of a straight line, while the surface as the limit of that sphere is like the end-points of the straight line, which are limits also.

17. It is not specified in what sense the center is an end. In a motion along a (finite) straight line, the starting-point is a limit and the end is not that limit but the other limit, and both starting-point and end are on that line. So if the starting-point in a circle or a sphere is the circumference or the spherical surface, respectively, perhaps the end should be the center, for in the circle or the sphere this is the point which is mostly opposed to the circumference or the spherical surface; and it is the point at which all the radii (which start from the circumference or the sphere) terminate.

18. By "outside of the circumference" he does not mean outside of the circle; he means that the center is not on the circumference.

19. Because of the fact that the center is outside of the circumference (see previous Commentary) and the travelling object will never get to this opposed point, the object will never reach an end-point where it might rest. Perhaps by "extreme" he means the center, for it is this that is opposed to the circumference.

20. Because the center rests, the rotating sphere or circle as a whole is in the same primary place; but the primary places of the parts are in motion because of their rotation.

21. If a thing is primary, it is a measure of the others; and if it is a measure of the others, it is primary. However, the thing's being a measure is not the cause of its being primary, but its being primary is the cause of its being a measure. This difference is brought out by the often used phrases "in view of the fact that" and "because of", for the latter signifies a cause, whereas the former, only a factual connection.

22. The position of a body at rest here is contrary to nature, e.g., for earth it is up, for fire it is down. Thus, if the cause which keeps a body at a place contrary to nature is removed, the body accelerates as it travels to its natural place. And if a body is moved by force to an unnatural place, as when a stone is thrown up, it decelerates (230b24–5). It appears that Aristotle was familiar with the fact of acceleration and retardation of bodies when travelling unimpeded up or down. For him, *down* amounts to the center of the Earth or the center of gravity of the Earth; it does not have the universality customary in modern times.

23. Since an object in a circular motion is by nature neither nearer to nor farther from a starting-point or an end but is always in the same state, it has neither an acceleration nor a retardation but is uniform in speed.

24. By "the principles of motion" he means the moving principles or movers, and from the dialectical arguments that follow in this paragraph, by "this kind of motion" he means locomotion in general and not circular locomotion in particular.

25. This is the position of Empedocles. See 985a21–31; Empedocles, fr. 26, 5–6.

26. 203a19–33, 250b24–6; Empedocles, fr. 12.

27. Leucippus and Democritus (985b4–20; Democritus, fr. 168).

28. Perhaps by "nature" he or they meant the primary bodies or particles, posited by Leucippus and Democritus as indivisible and as principles. These particles suffer no change other than locomotion.

29. He uses "as if a motion in place" because his definition of place is such that it does not apply to a body in a void; for if a body is surrounded by a void, which is not a body, that body is not in contact with a surrounding body, and so it is not in a primary place.

30. In other words, increase and decrease and alterations are reduced to nothing but locomotions. For Aristotle, this is not the case.

31. These thinkers, too, reduce generations and destructions to just locomotions.

32. These are Plato and his followers. (140b2–4, 406b25–7a2; *Phaedrus* 245c–246a).

33. This is a dialectical argument from language. People regard a locomotion as a motion in the main sense, and they regard all other kinds of motion as qualified and not as unqualified motions.

10

1. It is assumed that A and B are finite. Aristotle denies the existence of infinite bodies.

2. If the ratio $A_1 : A$ is equal to the ratio $B_1 : B$, the time should be infinite, but if $A_1 : A$ is less than $B_1 : B$, there is some argument for Aristotle's position. A stronger argument results if it is granted that any given part of the object in motion can be moved in a finite time by some part of the mover, if we assume that all the parts of the mover have uniform power per unit volume.

Cornford's interpretation (*Class. Quart.* 26, 1932, 53–4) runs thus: Since A_1 moves B_1 in less time than it moves B and a time interval which is less than another time interval is finite, A_1 moves B_1 in a finite time.

3. The assumption here is this: If X is less than Y and Y is infinite, then X is finite. Modern mathematicians deny this, but their denial rests on positing an actual infinite, which is denied by Aristotle.

4. Of course, by using A (which is a number of A_1's) to move B_1, the time is even lessened; and it is only when the B_1's are added to exhaust B that the time required is increased.

5. If no finite object can be moved by a finite mover in an infinite time, then certainly no infinite object (if such exists) can be moved by a finite mover in an infinite time. Hence no object (whether finite or infinite) can be so moved.

6. If the Speed S of the object B which is in motion is not uniform but is given by $S = e^{-t}$, then B can be in motion for an infinite time and still not surpass a unit distance, for $\int_0^\infty e^{-t}dt$ cannot be greater than 1. Would Aristotle deny the possibility of such speed?

7. What does "an infinite power" mean? If a finite body has a power, this power is actual, and as such it cannot be infinite, for the infinite is in the process of becoming. Perhaps for dialectical purposes Aristotle is assuming an infinite power to be a power which is greater than any finite power, thus making a concession to those who are using "infinite" in that sense (266b14–5). From his definition of "greater power" which follows, he seems to be using "power" in a somewhat modern sense.

8. Perhaps by "more by this than by another" he means that since a greater power causes the same effect in less time, an infinite power causes the same effect in less time than a finite power does.

9. As an illustration, let the finite magnitude M_1 have an infinite power and cause an effect E in time T_1, and let another finite magnitude M_2 with a finite power cause the same effect in time T_2. Evidently, $T_2 > T_1$; so let $T_2 = 100T_1$. It is also assumed that M_1 and M_2 are alike homogeneous in power, that is, if a part of M_1 is equal in volume to a part of M_2, then both have potentially equal powers. Then as we repeatedly add to M_2 parts equal to M_2, we arrive at $100M_2$, and this will cause the effect E in $1/100$ of T_2, or in T_1. Now the power of $100M_2$ is finite whereas that of M_1 is infinite, but they cause the same effect E in the same time T_1. This cannot be.

10. It makes no difference whether the magnitude is increased by always doubling or by always adding another AB; for if, by doubling n times, T will be divided by 2^n, then by adding $(2^n - 1)$ times the time will still be divided by 2^n. Of course the quotient of T over 2^n can be made less than any assigned value.

The power in AZ is infinite, for if finite, it would move M in a finite time, say t. But for any given t, some finite magnitude in AZ which is a multiple of AB will move M in time t or less. Hence AZ, which is infinite in magnitude, cannot have a finite power.

11. The hypothesis to be refuted is this: AZ is infinite in magnitude but has a finite power. One implicit assumption in the argument is that AZ is homogeneous in power, that is, each unit volume of AZ has an equal power; and the same applies to AB.

Whether AB is a part of AZ or not is not stated; but it makes no difference in the argument. The alternative proof hinted in 266b20–4 seems to suggest that AB is not a part of AZ. So let the power of AB be P and let it be R times the power of a part of AZ equal in magnitude to AB; and let the power of AZ move M over a certain interval I in time t, as in the previous Commentary. Then since some multiple of AB, say n·AB, will move M over the interval I in a time interval equal to or less than t, a part of AZ equal in magnitude to R times n·AB will likewise move M over I in a time interval equal to or less than t. But a part of AZ equal in magnitude to R times n·AB is finite, and the whole of AZ is assumed to move M over I in t. Hence AZ cannot have a finite power.

If the power in AZ is not homogeneous but diminishes by such a factor as e^{-x}, where x is the distance from A, then the argument cannot stand, for the total power, which has the form $\int_0^\infty pe^{-x}dx$, cannot exceed p.

12. By "generically the same" he may mean that the power per unit volume in the finite magnitude which is taken is equal to that per unit volume in AZ.

13. Let the finite power in AZ be P, and let the power in AB be p. Since p measures P, let $P = np$. Then n AB's, which is a finite magnitude, will have the same power as AZ. But the magnitude of AZ is infinite while that of n AB's is finite. Accordingly, AZ cannot have a finite power.

14. In the case of a thing thrown, like a stone, there is a further complication because a stone tends to go down. Perhaps a better example is an object like a ball, caused to be moved horizontally on a surface, or a book which is given a horizontal impulse.

15. That is, the motion of the thing thrown.

16. The argument is as follows: If the first mover A hurls a stone B and if, after A stops being a mover, B is still moved and is moved by C, which was caused to be moved by A, then C itself is in motion without being caused to be in motion by A. And if C is moved by D, etc., the same argument holds, for A has stopped being a mover. Accordingly, when A stops, all should stop simultaneously, and when the last thing caused to be moved is in motion, all the preceding things should be in motion and the first mover should be causing the motion.

17. An alternative to "stone" is "magnetic stone". If the term is "stone", then a stone is an object moved and a mover, as when a man uses a stone to move something; but if the term is "magnetic stone", then this may be the first mover which makes another object (e.g., iron) a mover, as when the iron attracts other objects through the influence of a magnetic stone.

18. Evidently such object must be a physical object with matter, for these alone can by nature be in motion as well as cause motion.

19. Perhaps he means that the object does not stop simultaneously being a mover and also an object moved by the first (or the preceding) mover, for having been caused to be like a mover by the first (or the preceding) mover, it may still cause itself or another object to be in motion.

20. Perhaps he means that the object stops being moved *by another thing* just when that thing stops causing it to be moved, but the object, now having been made to act like a mover, may still cause itself or another object to be moved.

21. If A causes B to be moved and likewise B causes C, C causes D, D causes E, and E does not cause anything else to be moved, the power to cause motion is lessened as the object in motion is further from the first mover A; and the last thing, E, has no power to move but only to be moved.

22. By "these" does he mean (a) the last mover and the object it moves or (b) every consecutive pair of objects in the series so related that one is a mover and the other an object moved by that mover? Perhaps he means (a).

23. If by "the whole motion" Aristotle means the motion of just the last object which is not a mover, this follows from the assumption that there is nothing to move it. But if (using the symbolism of Comm. 21) he means the motions of E, D, C, etc., with the implication that these must stop simultaneously, then there must be a simultaneous cessation of being a mover (both a self-mover and a mover of another object) for all the movers, which is something to be shown. He may mean that eventually the whole motion must stop.

24. A continuous motion is one in which there is one mover, one

object moved, and one continuous interval of time (259a17–20).

25. When an object is given an impulse by a mover and is in motion, it appears that there is one mover, one object moved, and one interval of time, as in throwing a ball. But the object moved need not always be moved by the same mover, and other things are set in motion also; and the object moved as well as other things may be caused to act like movers by their movers which directly precede them.

26. Perhaps he has in mind Plato (*Timaeus*, 79–80) and some others.

27. The solution given by Aristotle resembles somewhat the *Law of Inertia*. If A causes B to be moved but then A stops and if B is to continue in motion, then B must be causing itself to be in motion; and whether one says that B causes itself to be in motion after being set in motion or that it keeps being in motion (with the same velocity, unless acted on by something else), the result is the same as far as the results go, though there is a difference in the analysis. Even the quantitative attribute of that motion is suggested by Aristotle, for this is hinted when he says that the power to cause (an amount of) motion in another is lessened (in modern terms, there is a loss of momentum) as the movers recede from the first mover (267a8–9).

Evidently it is a mistake to attribute to Aristotle the simplified view that, when the mover stops, it is the air behind the object moved which keeps that object in motion.

28. For example, when water is given a rotary motion in a glass, all the parts of the water are movers and objects in motion, and they stop simultaneously, and so one cannot truly say that one part of the water is the first mover. Who is the first mover, then? Perhaps the man who acted on the glass to give the water its rotary motion; and he is not a part of the things in mutual replacement.

29. An eternally continuous motion is meant.

30. 227b21–8a6.

31. It will follow the object which it causes to be in motion, for it will move another by contact.

32. It will be changing, at least with respect to place.

33. It will be moved by something; for everything in motion requires a mover.

34. The place of οὐκ seems to require the translation "does not necessarily change" rather than "of necessity does not change". So either it should be after ἀνάγκη, or it is idiomatic Greek to be translated as we did. Another alternative: he may mean that the mover does not necessarily change accidentally.

35. Of the motions of bodies, the rotation of a sphere about any one line through the center (or center of gravity) is the most regular, if we assume that the angular velocity is always the same; for the place or state of the sphere remains always the same (unlike the place of any other body), and the motion always has the same direction. If there is any change, it is that of the parts (a secondary change) relative to the surrounding parts of the place, and perhaps it is in view of this that the phrase "or more than any other" is added.

36. Since the prime mover does not change, He does not change qua mover, and so He imparts the same motion to the object moved. Hence, the motion of the object is eternal and has a uniform angular velocity.

37. The object remains a sphere. If it changes, it is in virtue of its parts and not as a whole. But the mover acts not on each part separately but on the sphere as a whole, which remains a sphere. Thus the mover is always similarly related to the whole and so gives it a uniform motion.

38. "The circumference" here probably means the spherical surface of the universe, for κύκλος has many meanings.

39. The surface of a sphere is a principle as form (or shape). The center is a principle occupying a unique position. We nowadays call this "the centroid", or "the center of gravity" if the material is uniform in density. The sphere is usually defined in terms of the center; and in this respect, too, the center becomes a principle in the definition.

40. Some texts have κύκλου (= "of the circumference") and others have ὅλου (= "of the whole"). Perhaps the former is correct.

Some explanation is needed. If a sphere rotates around its axis AB, let any plane perpendicular to AB cut the sphere at a circle C. Then the motion of any point on the circumference of C is fastest compared to the motion of any other point in the plane of C. Of course, taking the sphere as a whole, the fastest motion is that of any point on the circumference of C, provided C is a great circle. Perhaps it is something like this that Aristotle had in mind.

41. Literally, the translation should be "so the mover there". Since the prime mover is immovable and is not a body, He cannot be in place. So perhaps Aristotle means that the mover acts on the circumference of the sphere to cause rotation; but Aristotle does not discuss how such action can take place. The difficulty is similar to that of how the immovable part of a man (e.g., the will or something like it) causes the man to move.

42. He seems to mean one motion which is continuous and eternal. Perhaps he has in mind moved movers such as the spheres or celestial bodies.

43. 266b27–7a12.

44. Qua immovable, the prime mover acts in the same way, and qua being also eternal, He always acts in the same way. Moreover, it is possible that there be an object which can be acted upon (be moved) in the same way always, and this object is the outermost sphere, for it can be eternally moved in the same way; and that sphere moves in the same way and eternally (according to Aristotle).

45. 204a8–6a8.

46. 266a24–b6.

47. 266a12–24.

48. It is either divisible or indivisible. If divisible, it will have to be or have a magnitude, finite or infinite; and this is impossible. Hence it is indivisible.

Glossary

In the English-Greek Glossary, if an English term is used in many senses or has one or more synonyms, this is indicated. When convenient, we give the definition of a term, e.g., of the term "motion"; when not convenient, we often give the reference to page and lines according to the Bekker text, as in the case of the terms "one" and "being". In some important cases, a term is slightly changed in appearance to indicate its different senses; this is done by the use of italics or an initial capital letter or both. For example, if a common name has two senses, a wide and a narrow sense, the narrow sense is usually signified by the term in italics, as in "chance" and "*chance*", "knowledge" and "*knowledge*". If a term signifies a principle posited by a philosopher other than Aristotle, it is given in italics with a capital initial letter, as in the terms "*One*" and "*Intelligence*".

In the Greek-English Glossary, English synonyms used for the same Greek term are separated by a comma; for example, the translation of ὑπόθεσις is "hypothesis" or "assumption", and the latter two terms are separated by a comma in the Glossary and are synonymously used. But if separated by a semicolon, the English terms are not synonymously used. For example, the translations of αὐτόματον are "chance" and "*chance*", and these are not synonyms. The same applies to "analogy" and "proportion" for ἀναλογία, and to "number" and "Number" for ἀριθμός. Sometimes it is difficult to know in what sense Aristotle is using a term, and this is subject to interpretation.

English-Greek

a great many   ἄπειρα
absence of motion   ἀκινησία

345

absurd   ἄτοπον

accelerate   ἐπιτείνειν

accident   συμβεβηκός   B is an accident of A if "A is B" is true sometimes, but neither always nor for the most part. For example, to
be a geometrician is an accident of a man, and so is finding a
coin when looking for Socrates. 186b18–20, 1025a14–30.

accident, by   See "by accident".

accidental   See "accidentally".

accidentally   κατά συμβεβηκός

according to   κατά   Synonyms: "with respect to", "in virtue of". 73a27–
b24, 1022a14–35. See "in virtue of".

according to nature   κατὰ φύσιν   192b8–193a1, 199b14–8.

accurate   ἀκριβής   One discipline is more accurate than another if (a)
the first includes the causes of the facts to a higher degree; or, if
(b) the first is concerned with more abstract things; or, if (c) the
second contains additional principles. 87a31–7, 982a25–8,
1078a9–13.

act, v.   ποιεῖν   This is one of the categories, and so an ultimate genus.
1b25–2a10.

act, v.   πράττειν   See "*action*". Synonym: "do".

acted upon, be   πάσχειν   This is one of the categories. 1b25–7,
1017a24–7.

action   πρᾶξις   An action *chosen* for its own sake with understanding
and certainty and without hesitation. 1105a28–33.

active, be   ἐνεργεῖν   Synonym: "be in activity".

activity   ἐνέργεια   Synonym: "*actuality*". 1045b27–1052a11.

activity, be in   ἐνεργεῖν.

actuality   ἐντελέχεια   Probably the same as "activity".

actuality   ἐνέργεια   Synonym: "activity".

affected, be   πάσχειν   The same as "be acted upon".

affection   πάθος   An alterable quality or the actuality of that quality.
1022b15–21.

affirmation   κατάφασις

air   ἀήρ   For the meaning of "air", see "water".

Air   ἀήρ   The material principle for Anaximenes and Diogenes, and
one of the material principles for some other thinkers. 984a5–16.

alike in species or kind   ὁμοειδής

already   ἤδη   222b7–11.

alteration   ἀλλοίωσις   Motion with respect to quality; e.g., becoming
sick. 226a26–9, 270a27–30, 319b10–4.

always   ἀεί

analogy   ἀναλογία

animal ζῷον

another ἄλλο

apart χωρίς P is said to be apart from Q if P and Q are in different primary places. 226b21–3, 1068b26–7.

appear φαίνεσθαι To seem to be as a fact, whether through sensation or imagination or in some other way. 1010b1–9, 1024b21–4.

appropriate οἰκεῖος

argument λόγος A statement or statements aimed at convincing that something is or is not the case.

arrangement διάθεσις

art τέχνη Knowledge of how to produce something, e.g., a building; the thing so produced; the form in the thing so produced. 193a31–3, 1034a21–4.

assertion φάσις

assumption ὑπόθεσις A statement or premise, posited without proof, which signifies that something is or is not the case. 72a14–24.

astronomy ἀστρολογία The science of heavenly bodies, such as the Sun, Moon, stars, etc., mathematically treated. 78b34–40, 194a7–12, 297a2–6, 1073b3–6.

at some time ποτέ

at the same time ἅμα

attribute συμβεβηκός B is an attribute of A if it belongs to A as to a subject and in virtue of A but is not in the *substance* of A. For example, the equality of the three angles to two right angles is an attribute of a triangle. The term "attribute" means also an accident. 186b18–26, 1025a30–4.

attribute πάθος Perhaps "attribute" is a species of "attribute". The expressions "*proper attribute*" and "*essential attribute*" are often used, each signifying that which belongs to a genus as to a subject. Thus, evenness belongs only to numbers, straightness only to lines, contrariety and otherness only to being. 997a7, 1004b5–15, 1078a7.

axiom ἀξίωμα A truth which one must have if he is to learn anything within a science. In a theoretical science, axioms are necessarily true. Axioms are used not as principles with which, but as principles from which theorems are demonstrated, that is, not as premises but as regulative principles. The principles of contradiction and of the excluded middle are axioms, and so is "Equals from equals leave equal remainders". 72a16–8, 76a37–b2, 77a26–31.

bad κακός

be εἶναι Synonym: "exist".

be generated γίγνεσθαι To change from nonbeing to being, whether simply or in a qualified way. Synonym: "become", "come to be". 225a12–7, 1067b21–3.

be in activity ἐνεργεῖν

be in contact See "touch".

be thought δοκεῖν

beautiful καλός

beauty, physical κάλλος

because διά In "A has the attribute C because of B", B is the cause or a cause of the fact that A has C. Synonym: "through".

become Same as "be generated".

before πρότερον

beginning ἀρχή Synonyms: "principle", "source", "starting point". See "principle".

being, n. ὄν Synonyms: "thing", "that which exists". 1017a7–b9.

Being, n. ὄν A principle for some thinkers; the only existing principle for Parmenides and others.

belief ὑπόληψις The term is generic. It is an affection of *thought* about what is or is not the case. Its species are *"knowledge"*, "opinion", "prudence", and their contraries. 427b24–7.

between μεταξύ B is said to be between A and C if, in going from A to C, one must by nature go through B before reaching C. Synonym: "intermediate". 226b23–31, 1057a21–6.

blend μῖξις, μῖγμα A union of bodies, readily adaptable in shape, which have acted upon and so altered each other; for example, a union of coffee and cream, not of salt and pepper. 327a30–328b32.

Blend μῖξις, μῖγμα For Anaxagoras, this is a principle, the unity of all things which existed at first as something motionless before *Intelligence* acted as a moving cause on it to separate distinct things. 250b24–6.

body σῶμα A three-dimensional physical object. For Aristotle, a body may be destructible, as a man or a rock, or it may be indestructible, as the Sun or a star (for him). 1042b4–6, 1073a22–36.

boundary ὅρος, πέρας 1022a4–13.

bringing together σύνωσις A pulling of one thing towards another. 243b5–6.

by accident κατὰ συμβεβηκός

by itself καθ᾽ αὑτό 1022a35–6.

by nature φύσει 192b8–193a2, 199b14–8.

capable δυνατός

capability δύναμις A principle or ability of being moved or of being changed by another thing or by itself qua other.

carried, be φέρεσθαι To be moved with respect to place by another thing.

carry φέρειν To move another thing with respect to place.

carrying ὄχησις, φορά 243b17–244a2.

category κατηγορία Any of the highest genera of things, e.g., "a quantity" or "a quality", generically taken. 1b25–7.

cause αἰτία, αἴτιον Synonyms: *"why"* as a noun, *"reason"*. 194b16–195b30, 983a24–32, 1013a24–1014a25.

cease παύειν

Center μέσον (a) The center of the universe; (b) the inner place of the element (water) which touches (or should be touching by nature) the earth as a whole.

certainty βεβαιότης This term is applied to our state of mind about an object, not to the object itself.

chance αὐτόματον A moving cause which is accidental and hence variable or indefinite. 195b31–198a13.

chance αὐτόματον This is chance (a chance cause) which by nature has no ability of making a *choice*.

change μεταβολή This is a generic term, and its species are "generation", "destruction", and "motion"; and the kinds of motion are locomotion, alteration, increase, and decrease. 225a1–b9.

changelessness ἀμεταβλησία

choice αἵρεσις

choice προαίρεσις A choice of the apparently best of the alternatives deliberated upon. 1113a1–7.

circular περιφερές

clear σαφής The term is applicable to expressions. An expression is *clear* if in a given context it has just one meaning which is known or familiar or definite.

clearly δῆλον

coincident ἅμα

cold, adj. or n. ψυχρόν

Cold ψυχρόν For Parmenides, a principle of sensibles. 986b31–987a2.

color χρῶμα

combination σύγκρισις

combing κέρκισις

come to a standstill or stop ἵστασθαι

come to be γίγνεσθαι Same as "become" or "be generated". See "be generated".

coming to rest ἠρέμησις

commensurable σύμμετρος Two quantities are commensurable if they can be measured by some unit, i.e., if their ratio is a rational number.

common κοινός The same in species or genus or by analogy. 645b20–8. Commonly agreed: ὁμολογούμενον.

comparable συμβλητός Two quantities A and B are said to be comparable if they can be added or subtracted or related to each other with respect to equality and inequality. For example, three men and six men are comparable, but six units and a line are not, nor is a line and a surface.

complete τέλειος (a) That of which no part is outside; (b) that whose virtue within its genus cannot be exceeded, as a complete house or a perfect doctor. Synonym: "perfect". 1021b12–1022a3.

composite σύνολον The parts are matter and form, as in a man or a statue.

composite σύνθετος

compress πιλόω, συμπιλόω

concave κοῖλον

conceive νοεῖν

conclude falsely παραλογίζεσθαι

conclusion συμπέρασμα

consecutive ἐχόμενος A is said to be consecutive to B if A succeeds and touches B. 227a6–7, 1069a1–2.

contact, n. ἁφή, θίξις See "touch".

contact, be in ἅπτεσθαι

continuous συνεχής A and B are said to be continuous if their limits (not necessarily all) are one; a property of continuity is infinite divisibility. 227a10–7, 1069a5–9, 232b24–5, 268a6–7.

contradiction ἀντίφασις Two opposite or contrary statements taken together.

contrariety ἐναντίωσις Complete difference; the two contraries taken together. See "contrary".

contrary ἐναντίος The primary meaning is: contraries are the most different in each genus; e.g., whiteness and blackness, oddness and evenness, justice and injustice. For secondary meanings, see 1018a25–35, 1055a3–b29.

contrary to nature παρὰ φύσιν For example, if a rock is let go, it goes down; but if it is carried up (by force), its motion is contrary to nature, not according to nature.

contrary to reason παράλογον

convex κυρτός

conviction πίστις Sometimes: a strong belief. Also, an attribute of a belief, admitting the more and the less. 125b28–126a2, 126b13–30, 428a19–23, 1146b24–31.

corporeal σωματικός Having physical matter or with physical matter.

curvature καμπύλον

cut, n.   σημεῖον   A point on a line, or a moment in time, but not at the end of the line or of the time interval.

decelerate   ἀνίημι

decrease, n.   φθίσις   Motion with respect to quality, from complete to incomplete, or, in the direction of less. 226a29–32, 241a32–b2.

deficiency   ἔλλειψις   This is the contrary of excess.

Deficiency   ἔλλειψις   Some thinkers posited *Excess* and *Deficiency* as the material principles from which things were generated. 1087b17–8.

definite   ὡρισμένος

definition   ὁρισμός, ὅρος   A formula signifying the whatness or the essence of a thing. The two terms seem to be used synonymously. The term ὅρος signifies also a boundary, like a point at the end of a line, or a limit. 90b3–4, 94a11–4, 1031a11–4.

deliberation   βούλευσις   An inquiry into the means, whether possible or attainable for the most part, by which one would achieve an end. 1112a18–1113a15.

demonstration   ἀπόδειξις   A syllogism of what is necessarily true through its cause. 71b9–18.

demonstration through impossibility   ἀπόδειξις εἰς τὸ ἀδύνατον   This is a demonstration which proves a proposition p by assuming the contradictory of p as a premise and along with other true premises proving a proposition which contradicts an already known true proposition.

denial   ἀπόφασις   A statement signifying that something does not belong to something else; for example, the forms "no A is B" and "some A is not B". The parts "not B" and "is not B" are also called "denials".

dense   πυκνόν   Having its parts relatively close to each other. 10a20–2.

Dense, n.   πυκνόν   Some natural philosophers, e.g., Leucippus, posited the *Dense* and the *Rare* as the principles which cause the forms of all other things. 188a19–22, 985b10–2.

density   βάρος

depth   βάθος

derivative   παρώνυμος   A term somewhat changed from the original term in order to indicate some difference from that term. Thus, "virtuous" differs from the original "virtue", and it signifies (usually) a man who has virtue. 1a12–5.

desire, n.   ὄρεξις   Desire is proper to the genus of animals, and its three kinds are wish, *desire*, and anger. 413b21–4, 414b1–6, 700b22, 701a33–b1, 1369a1–4.

desire, n.   ἐπιθυμία   Desire of the pleasant or of what seems to be pleasant (but is not). 146b36–147a4, 414b5–6.

destruction φθορά Change from being to nonbeing. Such a change is said to be unqualified if it is with respect to substance, as when a man dies, but it is said to be qualified if it is with respect to quality or quantity or place. 225a12–20, 1067b21–5.

differ διαφέρειν See "differentia".

difference διαφορά See "differentia".

different διάφορος A and B are said to be different if, being the same in species or genus or by analogy, but not numerically the same, they are distinct. 1018a12–5, 1054b23–31, 1058a6–8.

differentia διαφορά If A and B are different but under the same genus, those elements in the definitions of A and B which make these distinct are said to be their differentiae. For example, "equilateral" and "scalene" are the differentiae of an equilateral and a scalene triangle.

difficulty ἀπορία Uncertainty as to whether something is or is not the case, especially in view of arguments favoring both sides. Synonym: "problem". 145a33–b20.

dimension διάστημα

direction διάστασις

discipline πραγματεία

discriminate κρίνειν Synonym: "*judge*".

displacement μετάστασις

disposition διάθεσις 8b26–9a13, 1019b5, 1022b1–3.

distinct ἕτερον, ἄλλο If A and B are beings but not the same, then it is said that they are distinct or other or that A is distinct from or other than B. Since things may be the same either numerically or numerically and in definition or just in definition, things may also be distinct or other in as many ways. See "same". 1017b27–1018a19, 1054a32–b25.

distinction διαίρεσις

divine θεῖον Honorable and eternal, or almost so.

division διαίρεσις

division τομή Perhaps the same as "division", or else differing from it slightly.

do πράττειν Synonym: "*act*".

doctrine δόξα A belief of great philosophic or scientific value, true or false, and usually a principle or given without proof. 987a32–4, 996b27–31.

Dyad δυάς For Plato, this is the material principle of all things generated. It also goes by the name "*Indefinite Dyad*".

each ἕκαστος

earlier πρότερος

earth γῆ For its meaning, see "water".

Earth γῆ

Earth γῆ A material principle for Empedocles. 984a8–11.

easy ῥάδιον That which requires little time, effort, pain, or thought, etc. 1363a23, 1422a17–8.

element στοιχεῖον The first constituent in each thing. Thus, the material components which are indivisible in kind into other kinds are elements, and so are the letters of words and the indefinable terms and the syllogisms which are used as forms in geometrical or other demonstrations. 1014a26–b15.

eliminate ἀναιρεῖν

end τέλος This term is narrower than "extreme" or "limit". 1021b25–1022a13.

entire πᾶν; καθόλου (sometimes).

equal in speed ἰσοταχύς

equality ἰσότης Oneness in quantity. 1021a11–2.

equivocal ὁμώνυμος Having or called by the same name. A and B are said to be equivocally named if the term naming them has not the same meaning for both. For example, a man and a picture of him are equivocally called "a man", but a man and a horse are not equivocally called "an animal". 1a1–6.

eristic ἐριστικός Pertaining to an argument which only appears to be valid or to proceed from true premises and which is aimed at victory over the opponent. 171b6–34.

err ἁμαρτάνειν To fail to achieve what is right.

error ἁμαρτία

essence τὶ ἦν εἶναι (a) That which, usually being in a category, is in the thing and in virtue of which the thing remains the same and is univocally called by the same name, for example, the form of a statue or the whiteness of whatever is white insofar as it is white; (b) that in the soul (this exists as *knowledge*) by which we know a thing's essence in sense (a). 1029b1–1030b13.

essential καθ' αὑτό A is said to belong essentially to B if it is a part of the whatness of B (as animality is a part of a man) or if it is provable or demonstrable through B (as the equality of vertical angles through the definition of vertical angles) or if it is an attribute of B and is definable by means of B (as oddness by means of a number and straightness by means of a line). 73a28–b24, 1022a14–36.

essentially καθ' αὑτό

eternal ἀΐδιος That which exists always or necessarily, or, that which exists and is ungenerable and indestructible. 221b3–7, 282a21–3, 337b35–338a1, 1139b22–4.

ether αἰθήρ The medium which exists above the place of fire and in which the heavenly bodies exist.

ethical ἠθικός

even (of a number) ἄρτιος

Even, n. ἄρτιον For the Pythagoreans, the material principle of things. 986a15–21.

evident φανερόν

excess ὑπεροχή If A exceeds B, then A is divisible into a part equal to B and an additional part. 1021a6–7.

Excess ὑπεροχή Some thinkers posited *Excess* and *Deficiency* as the material principles of all things. 1087a17–8.

exhaust ἀναιρεῖν

exist εἶναι

expect ἐλπίζειν

experience, n. ἐμπειρία Knowledge produced by many memories of the same thing; for example, knowledge that Socrates, suffering from disease X, recovered every time he took medicine Y. 980b28–981a12.

expression λόγος

fact πρᾶγμα For example, a sick Socrates (if he is sick) or the equality of vertical angles.

fallacy παραλλογισμός

false ψευδής

falsity ψεῦδος A proposition or belief signifying that something is the case, when it is not, or that something is not, when it is. 1011b25–7, 1051b3–5.

fast ταχύς

faster θᾶττον

few ὀλίγα

fictitious πλασματῶδες That which is forced to agree with a hypothesis or a doctrine. 1082b1–4.

figure σχῆμα

final cause οὗ ἕνεκα That for the sake of which something exists or is generated (the other tenses of time included). This is not limited to animals but extends to plants and to other things. 194b16–195b30, 983a24–b1, 1013a24–b28.

fine (of particles) λεπτός Synonym: "thin".

finite πεπερασμένος Synonym: "limited".

fire πῦρ This is a material element characterized by being hot and dry. See "water".

Fire πῦρ For Hippasus and Heraclitus, *Fire* is the only principle, a material principle, from which the other things are generated. 984a7–8.

first πρῶτος For its various kinds, see "prior". Synonym "primary".

for, conj. γάρ This does not indicate a cause but rather something which confirms a cause, such as a sign or an example.

for the most part ὡς ἐπὶ τὸ πολύ Synonym: "most"

for the sake of ἕνεκα τινός Synonym: "final cause".

force βία (sometimes) Power of hindering (stopping from continuing) or preventing (barring from starting) something from proceeding according to its tendency or *choice*.

form εἶδος Form is contrasted with matter, both being causes; for example, of a bronze statue, bronze is its matter and the shape is its form.

form μορφή Perhaps the same as "form", or close to it. Synonym: *"shape"*.

Form εἶδος For Plato, Forms, which are immovable and changeless, are posited as the causes of sensible or destructible things. Synonym: "Idea". 987a29–b22.

formal ὡς εἶδος Pertaining to form. For example, a formal cause is a cause as form.

formula λόγος A combination of terms; a definition or description, or an expression signifying a being or a nonbeing.

fortunate εὐτυχής One to whom good luck of considerable magnitude has fallen. 197a25–7.

fortune, good εὐτυχία Good luck of considerable magnitude. 197a25–7.

fortune, ill ἀτυχία Bad luck. Perhaps the term is generic, applicable to misfortune as well as to bad luck not of considerable magnitude.

freezing πῆξις

friendship φιλία 1155b17–1156b35.

Friendship φιλία For Empedocles, a principle which causes things to come together. 984b27–985a10.

full πλῆρες The contrary of "empty" or "void".

function ἔργον

futile μάταιος

Gap χάος For Hesiod, this is the first thing that came into existence, as if a necessary condition for anything else to be in. 208b29–33, 984b23–31.

general, in See "in general".

generated, be γίγνεσθαι See "be generated".

generation γένεσις A change from not-being to being. If the generation is to a substance, as when a baby is born, it is called "simple generation" or "unqualified generation", but if to something belonging to a substance, as from not-white to white, it is called "qualified generation". 225a12–7, 1067b21–3. Synonym: "becoming".

genus γένος In the whatness or definition of a thing, the constituent as matter or subject, to which the addition of a differentia produces a species of the same genus.

geometry γεωμετρία The science of magnitudes. 1061a28–b3, 1143a3–4, 1355b30–1.

go through διέναι

godlike δαιμόνιος

good ἀγαθόν That which is chosen or regarded by the intellect as an end in itself or as a means to such an end. 1096a19–29, 1362a21–1363b4.

good fortune See "fortune, good".

good physical condition εὐεξία This is the purpose of gymnastics or physical exercises of the right kind. 113b34–6, 137a3–7.

gray-haired λευκός

great μέγας

Great, n. μέγα For Plato, the Great and Small is (or are) the material principle(s) of things generated. 987b20–2.

great magnitude μέγεθος

great many ἄπειρα

grow φύεσθαι

grow along with each other προσφύειν

grow together συμφύειν Things may grow together by nature, like the parts of a hand (1014b22–6), or not by nature, like siamese twins (1040b13–6).

habit ἕξις A disposition which is hard to displace, whether acquired, like a virtue or scientific knowledge, or natural, such as strength or a disposition to illness. 8b25–9a13, 1022b4–14.

happiness εὐδαιμονία A pleasant life or living according to virtue.

hard σκληρόν 9a24–7.

hardly movable δυσκίνητος 226b10–12.

harmonics ἁρμονική The science of sounds, mathematically treated. 1078a14–6.

harmony ἁρμονία

having the same meaning συνώνυμα Synonym: "univocal".

having the same name ὁμώνυμα

health ὑγίεια 9a21–4, 246b4–6.

heaven οὐρανός 278b9–21.

heavy βαρύς That whose place is by nature at the Center or which by nature moves toward the Center. 269b23.

homogeneous ὁμοιομερής That which is the same or alike in kind as any of its parts or ultimate parts (if the thing has such), and so any two parts are the same or alike in kind; for example, water, air, and fire according to many ancient thinkers, and likewise for the units of a number. 329a3–12. Sometimes the term ὁμοειδής is used.

honor τιμή A sign or an external good conferred (given, bestowed, etc.) upon someone of great worth. 1123b17–21, 1361a27–39.

hot, n. or adj. θερμόν 329b24–32, 378b10–26, 388a20–4, 1070b10–5.

Hot, n. θερμόν For Parmenides, a principle of sensibles. 986b31–7a2.

hypothesis ὑπόθεσις A premise, which is posited as true without proof and which signifies that something is or is not the case. Synonym: "assumption". 72a14–24.

Idea ἰδέα The Ideas were posited by Plato as existing apart from sensible things, as being the causes of those things, as being changeless, and as being the objects of *knowledge*. Synonym: "Form". 987a29–b22.

ill fortune See "fortune, ill"

imagination φαντασία 427b27–429a9.

imitation μίμησις

immediately ἤδη

immovable ἀκίνητος That which cannot by its nature be moved, e.g., whiteness and knowledge, for these have no movable matter. Only bodies can move. 226b10–11.

impossible ἀδύνατον

impulse κίνημα An element of motion, posited as indivisible, for the sake of argument.

in a manner ὡς

in a place ποῦ Synonyms: "somewhere", "whereness". 1b25–2a2.

in a qualified way πῇ

in a simplified way ἁπλῶς

in a way ὡς

in general ὅλως

in itself καθ' αὑτό 1022a14–36, 1029a21–2, 24–5.

in number ἀριθμῷ Synonym: "numerically".

in some way πως

in the highest degree μάλιστα This term is used specifically for qualities which admit the more and the less, and analogically for other things, as when we seek to know the things which are substances in the highest degree. Synonym: "most", "most of all"

in the main sense κυρίως

in vain μάτην For example, if the end of an *action* is not achieved, assuming that it is usually achieved, then we say that the *action* was done in vain.

in virtue of κατά A is said to belong to B, or to C in virtue of B, if A is in the whatness or follows from the whatness of B or C, or if A is defined in terms of B. Synonyms: "according to", "with respect to". 73a27–b24, 1022a14–36.

in virtue of an attribute κατὰ συμβεβηκός For example, if Socrates is smooth, this is in virtue of his bodily surface and not in virtue of his essence as a rational animal.

incommensurable ἀσύμμετρον Quantities A and B are said to be incommensurable if no unit can measure both exactly.

incomparable ἀσύμβλητος The opposite of "comparable". See "comparable".

incorporeal ἀσώματος Not bodily or without physical matter.

increase αὔξησις Motion with respect to quantity and in the direction of complete magnitude or of being greater. 226a29–32, 241a32–b2.

indefinite ἀόριστος

independently κυρίως

individual, n. καθ᾽ ἕκαστον

indivisible ἀδιαίρετος

indivisible ἄτομος

induction ἐπαγωγή

infinite, n. or adj. ἄπειρον Primarily, the infinite is in the genus of what can be gone through, but it cannot be gone through. Thus, a line is a quantity, and one can go through it from one end to the other; but one cannot go through it by successive bisection of what is left. Secondarily, "the infinite" means that which, not being a quantity, cannot be gone through, just as a line is neither virtuous nor vicious (for it is not a man). 204a2–7, 1066a35–b1.

Infinite, n. ἄπειρον The material principle for the Pythagoreans and Plato. 203a1–16.

inquire ζητεῖν

inquiry μέθοδος, πραγματεία Systematic inquiry.

insofar as ᾗ Synonym: "qua". See "qua".

instrumental χρήσιμος

intellect νοῦς The part of the soul which *knows* the principles. 84b35–85a1, 100b5–17, 1140b31–1141a8, 1143a25–b17.

Intelligence νοῦς For Anaxagoras, a moving principle and cause of things. 256b24–7.

intelligible νοητός For example, numbers and universals are intelligible, while the bodies around us are sensible.

intermediate, n. or adj. μεταξύ Synonym: "between". See "between".

interpenetrate συνίημι

interval διάστημα The term is generic, not limited to quantities only.

interval of time χρόνος Synonym: "time". See "time".

investigate θεωρεῖν To seek universal truths for their own sake. Synonym: "speculate".

itself, by καθ' αὐτό

itself, in καθ' αὐτό

joint cause συναιτία

judge, v. λογίζεσθαι To think about things which may or may not come to be. 1139a6–15.

judge, v. κρίνειν A genus of "to sense". For example, sight *judges* colors, the power of hearing *judges* sounds, and some power *judges* that sweetness and whiteness are distinct. Synonym: "discriminate". 111a14–20, 426b8–23.

judging power λογιστικόν

just ὅπερ For example, "a man" signifies *just* a substance, as against "a white man" which signifies a composite of a substance and a color, or as against "whiteness" which signifies a qualified but not a separate being.

kind εἶδος

know γιγνώσκειν, γνωρίζειν

know ἐπίστασθαι See "*knowledge*".

knowledge γνῶσις This term is generic; it may signify true opinion, or that which is necessarily true, or first principles, or sensations.

knowledge ἐπιστήμη This is knowledge of what is necessarily true, whether demonstrable or not.

later ὕστερος

length μῆκος

letter στοιχεῖον The letters of the alphabet are meant.

light, adj. κοῦφον The opposite of heavy. That which is light goes away from the Center.

light, n. φῶς 418b9–10.

like, adj. ὅμοιος Things are said to be like if their quality is one. Synonym: "similar". 1018a15–9, 1021a11–2, 1054b3–14.

limit, n. πέρας, ὅρος 1022a4–13.

limited πεπερασμένος

line γραμμή, μῆκος (sometimes). A one-dimensional limited magnitude. 1016b24–9, 1020a7–14.

little ὀλίγον

locomotion φορά Motion with respect to place. 208a31–2, 226a32–3, 1069b12–3.

logical λογικός For example, a logical argument or refutation would be one which uses principles borrowed mainly from logic, which in Aristotle includes the works usually summarized by the term "organon".

long, adj. μακρός

long ago πάλαι 222b12–4.

luck τύχη Luck or what results from it belongs to what can deliberate, e.g., to men. See "chance", the genus of "luck". 195b31–198a13.

magnitude μέγεθος An infinitely divisible quantity, limited to lines, surfaces, and solids. 1020a7–14.

magnitude, great μέγεθος

mainly κυρίως

make ποιεῖν To generate something by art or *thought* or some power. 1032a25–b21.

man ἄνθρωπος A human being, male or female.

man ἀνήρ A male human being.

many, n. or adj. πολλά, πλῆθος, πλείω The contrary of "one". 1004b27–9, 1054a20–1055a2. Synonym: "plurality". A great many: ἄπειρα

Many πολλά A material principle posited by some thinkers, e.g., Speucippus.

mass ὄγκος

material ὑλικός, ὡς ὕλη Pertaining to matter, e.g., a material object or cause.

mathematical objects μαθήματα, μαθηματικά

Mathematical Objects μαθηματικά For Plato, these are also called "Intermediate Objects" and lie between the Ideas and the sensible objects; they are immovable, eternal, and the objects of the mathematical sciences. For Speucippus, these are first in existence, eternal and immovable, and the objects of the mathematical sciences. For Xenocrates, they are the same as the Ideas.

mathematical sciences μαθήματα

mathematics μαθηματική

matter ὕλη This term is generic. If physical, it may signify prime matter which underlies a form (192a22–34, 1029a20–6, 1042a27–8) or proximate matter like wood and nails in a chair which exist potentially or as parts in the chair but can exist separately (1044a15–32) or as something between (e.g., fire and earth and air, if wood, for example, consists of these). As nonphysical, the premises are said to be matter for the conclusion, the letters are matter for words, the genus is matter for the species, and so on.

may, v. ἐνδέχεσθαι

mean, v. σημαίνειν Synonym: "signify".

measure, n. μέτρον That by which, as first or a principle, a given quantity is known as a number. For example, five men are known by one man as a measure, and ten feet by one foot. 1052b20–7, 1087b33–1088a14.

measure, right See "right measure".

memory μνήμη

middle, n. μέσον

misfortune δυστυχία Bad luck of considerable magnitude. 197a25–7.

mistake ἀπάτη One is said to be mistaken if he thinks that A is B when A is not B or that A is not B when A is B. 1051b17–2a4.

mixture κράσις

moist ὑγρόν

Moist, n. ὑγρόν A principle posited by some thinkers.

moment νῦν A division or a limit of time, considered as indivisible.

moment, present See "present moment".

Moon σελήνη

more μᾶλλον The term is usually used to compare qualities, as when we say that one sample is whiter than another. Sometimes it extends to other things when no special Greek term exists, as when it is said that a man is more of a substance than earth. Synonyms: "to a higher degree", "rather".

most μάλλιστα A superlative for qualities. See "more". Synonyms: "most of all", "in the highest degree".

most ὡς ἐπὶ τὸ πολύ A large majority of the cases, as in "most people get well when taking such-and-such a medicine".

most of all See "most" as a superlative for qualities.

motion κίνησις The actuality of potential being qua potential. The kinds of motion are locomotion, alteration, increase, and decrease. 201a10–1, 1065b16, 33, 1068a8–10.

motionless ἀκίνητος If what is motionless can move, it is said to be at rest when motionless. Hence, rest is the contrary of motion.

motionlessness ἀκινησία

mover κινοῦν That which causes motion. Synonym: "a moving cause".

moving cause See "mover".

much πολύ

mutual replacement ἀντιπερίστασις

name ὄνομα Voice which is significant by convention and no part of which is significant as a part. 16a19–20.

natural φυσικός Synonym: "physical".

natural philosopher φυσιολόγος One who investigates the principles of nature or of physics.

nature φύσις The form of a physical object; the matter of a physical object; the principle of motion present in a physical object. Sometimes, the essence (of a thing), in any category, as when we speak of the nature of a triangle. 192b8–193b21, 1014b16–1015a19.

nature, according to See "according to nature".

nature, by See "by nature".

nature, contrary to   See "contrary to nature".

necessary ἀναγκαῖον The primary meaning: that which cannot be otherwise. For example, vertical angles are necessarily equal, and they can never be unequal. For secondary meanings, see 1015a20–b15.

necessity ἀνάγκη

nonbeing μὴ ὄν, οὐκ ὄν This may be the impossible, as an isosceles triangle with unequal base angles, or the potential yet not existing, as a sitting man when he is actually standing but can sit. Nonbeing in the second way is also called "not-being".

Nonbeing οὐκ ὄν For some thinkers, a principle needed to generate the plurality of things.

not-being μὴ ὄν That which is not but can be; e.g., certain materials are not a house, but they can be made into a house.

nothing μηδέν Synonyms: "nothingness", "zero".

now νῦν Synonym: "present moment".

number ἀριθμός A plurality measured by a unit, or, a discrete quantity. This is what is nowadays called "whole number" or "cardinal number" which is greater than 1. The term closest to the modern term "number" is translated in this work as "quantity". 4b20–31, 1020a8–9, 1057a2–4, 1085b22, 1088a5–8.

Number ἀριθμός For the later Plato, a Number, such as Seven, is also an Idea, and it is generated ultimately from the two principles, the One and the Dyad (also called "Indefinite Dyad"). For Speucippus, Numbers are not Ideas, but they are first in existence and the objects of mathematics. 1075b37–1076a4, 1084a3–7, 1090b13–9.

numerically ἀριθμῷ For example, the President who was assassinated in 1963 and John F. Kennedy are numerically (or in number) one. Synonym: "in number".

object   This term shall signify a being or a nonbeing. There is no such term in Greek (though πρᾶγμα is occasionally so used), but it is signified directly, as in "the thinkable" for "the thinkable object", for the thinkable object may be a being or a nonbeing.

objection ἔνστασις

odd (of a number) περιττός

Odd περιττόν For the Pythagoreans, a principle of all things, mainly a principle as form. 986a15–21.

of equal speed ἰσοταχύς

of like speed ὁμοταχύς

one, n. or adj. ἕν (a) That which is indivisible or undivided, whether numerically (e.g., Socrates and the Athenian philoso-

pher who drank the hemlock) or in formula of a species or genus
(e.g., two horses are one in species and in formula) or in kind or
by analogy. 1015b16–1017a3, 1052a15–1054a19.

One   ἕν   For Plato and others, the *One* is usually a principle as form,
from which other things are generated, such as Numbers and
sensible objects. 987a29–b22, 1084a3–7.

operation   ἔργον

opinion   δόξα   A belief of what may or may not be. For example, "John
is sick". 89a2–3, 100b5–7, 1039b31–1040a1, 1051b10–5.

opposite   ἀντικείμενος   The main kinds are the contradictory, the contrary, the relative, and a privation. 11b16–9, 1018a20–b8.

opposition   ἀντίθεσις

optics   ὀπτική   The mathematical science of light. 997b20–3, 1078a14–
6.

or   ἤ, καί

order   τάξις

Order   τάξις   A principle posited by some philosophers, e.g., Democritus.

other   ἕτερον, ἄλλο   The contrary of "same". The term applies only
to beings. Thus, if A is other than B (or distinct from B), A and B
are beings. A and B may be numerically other, like Socrates and
Plato, or other in species or in genus. Thus, "difference" and
"contrariety" are species of "otherness". Synonym: "distinct".
1018a9–15, 1054b14–32.

packing   σπάθησις

paradox   θέσις   A belief which is contrary to what is accepted by
known philosophers. For example, the belief that contradiction is
impossible is a paradox. 104b19–24.

part   μέρος, μόριον

partless   ἀμερής   Synonym: "without parts".

pattern   παράδειγμα

perfect   τέλειος   Same as "complete".

perish   ἀπόλυσθαι

philosophy   φιλοσοφία   The science of being qua being, or the science
of the highest principles and causes and elements of things.
1003a21–32, 1026a10–32, 1060b31–1061b17, 1064a28–b14.

physical   φυσικός   Synonym "natural".

physical beauty   κάλλος

physicist   φυσικός

physics   φυσική   The science of movable objects qua movable.
1025b18–21, 1061b28–30, 1064a15–6.

place, v.   τίθεσθαι

place, n. τόπος The first inner motionless boundary of a containing body; for example, of a can of tomatoes, the inner surface of the can. 212a20–1.

plain δῆλον

plane, n. or adj. ἐπίπεδον

pleasure ἡδονή 1152b1–1154b34.

plurality πλῆθος, πολλά Synonym: "many". 1004b27–9, 1054a20–1055a2.

point στιγμή, σημεῖον

portrait εἰκών

posit τιθέναι, ποιεῖν To lay down something, usually a principle, as existing or as being true. 72a14–24.

position θέσις Relative place; that which is posited. 6b2–14.

Position θέσις For Democritus, *Shape, Order,* and *Position* are the formal causes of things. 985b4–19.

possession ἕξις

possible δυνατόν Synonym: "potential". 1019a15–1020a6.

possible, be δύνασθαι, ἐνδέχεσθαι

posterior ὕστερον The opposite of prior. If A is prior to B, then B is said to be posterior to A. See "prior".

potency δύναμις Primarily, the principle of motion or of change in another or in the thing itself but qua other. Synonym: "power", "potentiality". 1019a15–1020a6.

potential δυνάμει, δυνατόν

potentiality Same as "potency".

potentially δυνάμει

power Same as "potency".

power of sensation αἴσθησις

predicated of, be κατηγορεῖσθαι

predication κατηγορία

present moment νῦν

presently ἤδη 222b7–11.

primary πρῶτος Synonym: "first".

principally κυρίως

principle ἀρχή The first from which something is or becomes or is known. Synonyms: "beginning", "source", "starting-point". 1012b34–1013a23.

prior πρότερος P is said to be prior to Q with respect to some principle X if P is nearer to X than Q is. For example, if X is existence, then an animal is prior in existence to a man; for if a man exists, so does an animal, but not conversely. 14a26–b23, 1018b9–1019a14.

privation στέρησις (a) Not having, e.g., a sound is deprived of color, that is, it has no color. (b) Not having if by nature it should have, e.g., a blind man is deprived of sight, for qua a man he should possess sight. 1022b22–1023a7.

probability εἰκός That which happens for the most part, or a statement concerning it, e.g., "the envious hate". 70a3–7.

problem ἀπορία Synonym: *"difficulty"*. See *"difficulty"*.

produce ποιεῖν Synonym: "make".

proper ἴδιος

proper οἰκεῖος Perhaps a synonym of "proper", or close to it in meaning.

property ἴδιον A property is an attribute belonging to a thing and to that thing alone.

proportion ἀναλογία

prove συλλογίζεσθαι, δεικνύναι

pulling ἕλξις 244a8–14.

pulsate κυμαίνειν

pushing ὦσις 244a7–8.

pushing along ἔπωσις 243a18–9.

pushing apart δίωσις 243b3–5.

pushing away ἄπωσις 243a19–20.

qua ᾗ An attribute C belongs to it qua B if it belongs to B but to no other genus higher than B. For example, sensation belongs to a man qua an animal, and mobility belongs to a man or a bed qua a body. Synonym: "insofar as". 73b25–74a3.

quality ποιόν This is one of the categories. 8b25–11a38, 1020a33–b25.

quantity ποσόν This is a category, whose primary species are numbers (which we nowadays call "whole numbers", except 1) and magnitudes (lines, surfaces, and solids). There are also accidental quantities, such as time and place, and these presuppose primary quantities. 4b20–6a35, 1020a7–32.

rare μανόν Having its parts relatively at a distance from each other. 10a20–2.

Rare, n. μανόν For some natural philosophers, the *Rare* and the *Dense* were posited as the formal principles of things.

rather μᾶλλον Synonyms: "more", "to a higher degree".

ratio λόγος For example, the ratio 3:2, or 5:4:2 if a thing consists of three elements, e.g., water, air, and earth.

reason λόγος A thought or statement with parts, especially if it is a cause of something else, like the premises when related to the conclusion.

reason same as *"cause"*.

reasonable εὔλογον In agreement with what is commonly accepted, either by all or by most or by a given school of thought, primarily if true.

reasoning λογισμός

reasoning power λογιστικόν

recently ἄρτι 222b12–4.

rectilinear εὐθύς Synonym: "straight".

reduction καθαίρεσις

refer ἀνάγειν To state in terms of ultimate principles or causes or elements.

refute λύειν

regular ὁμαλής Motions may be regular (a) by being over elementary paths (those whose paths fit into each other, e.g., straight or circular or cylindrical lines) or (b) by being of equal speeds or (c) by both. 228b15–28.

reject ἀναιρεῖν

relation πρὸς τι This is a category. A relation involves two things, each of which may be a composite (e.g., when A is between the pair B and C). 6a36–8b24, 1020b26–1021b11.

relative Same as "relation".

remove ἀφαιρεῖν Synonym: "take away".

replacement ἀντιμετάστασις

replacement, mutual ἀντιπερίστασις

rest, n. ἠρεμία, ἠρέμησις Privation of motion of that which by nature can be in motion. 221b12–4, 226b12–6, 1068b22–5.

rest, v. μένειν

rest, n. μονή Perhaps a synonym of "rest", or differing in meaning from it slightly.

revolution περιφορά

right, adj. ὀρθός A genus of "true" and "successful"—the first being a predicate of knowledge, the second, of good actions. 427b8–11.

right measure μέτριον

right proportion συμμετρία

roughness τραχύτης

same ταὐτός One in number or kind or substance or formula. 103a6–39, 1017b27–1018a11, 1054a29–b3, b14–9.

same in kind or species ὁμοειδής

same in kind or genus συγγενής

science ἐπιστήμη Knowledge of that which cannot be otherwise, i.e., of what is necessarily true or a fact. Synonym: "knowledge".

seed σπέρμα

seek ζητεῖν Synonym: "inquire".

seem δοκεῖν Synonym: "thought to be".

segment τμῆμα
sensation αἴσθησις
sensation, power of αἴσθησις
sense Same as "meaning".
separable χωριστός
separate, adj. χωριστός, χωρισμένος
separate, v. χωρίζειν, διακρίνειν
shape σχῆμα Synonym: "figure".
Shape σχῆμα See "*Position*".
shape μορφή Either a synonym of "form", or close to it in meaning.
    Synonym: "*form*".
short βραχύς
show δεικνῦναι
sight ὄψις
sign, n. σημεῖον 70a3–10.
signify σημαίνειν Synonym: "mean".
similar ὅμοιος Same as "like".
similar in species or kind ὁμοειδής
simple ἁπλοῦς
simultaneous ἅμα At the same time or moment.
singly ἁπλῶς
slow βραδύς
small μικρόν
Small μικρόν See "*Great*".
smooth λεῖον
soft μαλακόν 9a24–7.
solid στερεόν An immovable magnitude divisible in three dimensions
    and resulting after the principles of motion (physical matter and
    such qualities as weight and color) have been removed in
    thought; its study belongs to geometry. 1004b13–5, 1016b27–8,
    1077b17–30.
Solid στερεόν For Leucippus and Democritus, a material principle of
    things. 985b4–10.
solve λύειν
somewhere ποῦ This is a category. Synonyms: "whereness", "in a
    place".
sophistry σοφιστική A discipline which is concerned with what ap-
    pears to be wisdom or philosophy but is not. It has as its aim
    honor (by appearing to be philosophy) or making money or just
    winning an argument. The last kind is called "eristics". 165a21–3,
    171b22–34, 1004b17–9.
soul ψυχή The first actuality of a physical organic body. This is the
    form of a physical living being. 412b4–25, 414a4–14.

sound ψόφος

source ἀρχή, ὅθεν Synonyms: "principle", "beginning", "starting-point".

space χώρα

species εἶδος

specific ἴδιος Synonym: "proper".

speculate θεωρεῖν Synonym: "investigate".

speed τάχος

speed, of equal ἰσοταχύς

speed, of like ὁμοταχύς

standstill στάσις

starting-point ἀρχή See "principle".

state of rest ἠρεμία Synonym: "rest".

state of *rest* μονή Synonym: "*rest*".

statement λόγος

stay μένειν Synonym: "stay the same".

stay the same Same as "stay".

stop, v. ἵστασθαι

stop, n. στάσις

straight εὐθύ Synonym: "rectilinear", if used as adjective.

strength ἰσχύς

strife νεῖκος

Strife νεῖκος For Empedocles, a principle which causes things to separate from each other. 984b27–985a10.

strive after ἐφίεσθαι

subject, n. ὑποκείμενον This may be prime matter or an object in any category, but not necessarily a substance, and it is spoken of in relation to that which belongs to it or exists in it, as straightness belongs to a straight line and physical form exists in matter. The term also signifies a part of a statement; for example, in "P is Q", the part "P", of which "Q" is said, is the subject of the statement. Synonym: "underlying subject". 1029a1–9, 1038b2–6.

substance οὐσία This is a generic term. It means (a) a sensible body, physical or heavenly (Sun, Moon, etc.), which is separate, or a part of it (and this may be separable, e.g., a hand); (b) the form or essence of a being in any category, and this is called "a *substance*" (e.g., we may ask What is the *substance* of virtue, or of a triangle?); (c) the subject, which is not said or predicated of another thing but of which other things may be predicated, and this may be matter or form or a *composite* of matter and form; (d) some regard universals and the mathematical objects as eternal and nonsensible and separate and call them "substances" most of all. 2a11–4b19, 1017b10–26, 1028b8–1029a7.

substance οὐσία   See "substance" in sense (b).

succession, in   ἐφεξῆς   A thing is said to be successive or in succession
if, being after a principle and being separate by itself in position
or in kind or in some other way, there is no other thing in the
same genus between it and that which it is said to succeed.
226b34–227a6, 1068b31–9a1.

suddenly   ἐξαίφνης   222b15–6.

Sun   ἥλιος

surface   ἐπιφάνεια, ἐπίπεδον   A magnitude divisible in two dimensions.
1016b26–9.

syllogism   συλλογισμός   An expression (verbal or in thought) in which
a statement (conclusion) follows necessarily from statements
(premises) which are posited as being so or true. 24b8–22,
100a25–7.

symmetry   συμμετρία

take away   ἀφαιρεῖν   Synonym: "remove".

tendency   ὁρμή

that from which   ὅθεν

thin   λεπτός   Synonym: "fine".

thing   ὄν, πρᾶγμα   Synonyms: "being", and sometimes "fact".

think   νοεῖν   The term is generic, and it includes "imagine" as one of
the species.

think διανοεῖν   In thought, to combine or divide or to affirm or deny,
e.g., that the diagonal is not commensurate with the side of a
square or that vertical angles are equal.

this, n.   τόδε τι   This term, in contrast to a universal or a kind, signifies
something separate and a substance which one can point to, but
sometimes something in any category, as a color or a length or
a surface.

thought, n.   νόησις

thought, n.   διάνοια   The result of *thinking*.

thought, be   See "be thought".

through   διά   Synonym: "because". See "because".

throwing   ῥίψις   243a20–b2.

time   χρόνος   A number of motion with respect to before and after.
217b29–220a26. Synonym: "interval of time".

to a higher degree   μᾶλλον   See "more". Synonym: "more", "rather".

together   ἅμα   In the same place (see "place"). For example, your coffee and mine are primarily not together, for they are in different
cups, but they may be secondarily together, if they are in the
same room; and the parts of an apple are primarily together,
since each part qua part has no actual place but its place is that
of the whole apple. 226b21–2, 1068b26.

touch, v. ἅπτεσθαι Things are said to touch if their boundaries (not necessarily all) are together, e.g., two books one on top of the other. 226b23, 323a3–6, 1068b27. Synonym: "be in contact".

touch, n. ἁφή

travel φέρεσθαι To be in motion with respect to place, whether moved by itself or carried by another. 243a11–2.

traverse διεξιέναι, διεξέρχεσθαι

true ἀληθές

truth ἀλήθεια Primarily, a saying or *thinking* of that which is that it is or of that which is not that it is not. 1011b25–7, 1051b3–5.

turning δίνησις 244a2–4.

ugly αἰσχρός

underlie ὑποκεῖσθαι A relation between a subject and an accident or attribute or form. For example, Socrates underlies his sickness, and matter underlies form, and a line underlies its straightness.

underlying subject ὑποκείμενον See "subject". Synonym: "subject".

understand εἰδέναι To know through the causes. 184a10–4, 194b17–20, 981a21–30, 983a25–6.

unequal ἄνισον

uniform ὁμαλής Having the same speed. 228b25–8.

union ἕνωσις

unit μονάς That which is indivisible in every way with respect to quantity and has no position. 1016b17–31. Also, a measure of a quantity, like one foot.

unity ἑνότης

universal καθόλου That which by nature is predicable of or belongs to many things. 17a39–40, 1038b11–2. For Plato, universals are Ideas existing by themselves and being the causes of sensible things and the objects of knowledge.

universally καθόλου

universe κόσμος, τὸ πᾶν It has a spherical shape and includes all, i.e., stars, Sun, Moon, ether, physical objects etc. 212b13–8, 285a27–32.

univocal συνώνυμος Having the same meaning.

unlike ἀνόμοιος The contrary of "like". See "like".

unqualified ἁπλῶς

unreasonable ἄλογον The contrary of "reasonable".

use, n. χρῆσις

useful χρήσιμος The useful is that which exists or becomes for the sake of something else and not for its own sake, e.g., a spoon or money. Thus, the enjoyment of music, being an end in itself, is not useful. 101a25–8, 742a32, 1096a7.

vice κακία The contrary of "virtue".

view, v. θεωρεῖν

virtue ἀρετή Its two kinds are: intellectual and ethical. 1105b19–
    1107a27.

viscous παχύς

void, n. or adj. κενόν A place (or boundary) in which there is no body
    at all, whether light or heavy. 208b25–7, 213a15–9, 214a2–17.

Void, n. κενόν A principle of things, posited by some thinkers.

volume ὄγκος

vortex δίνη

water ὕδωρ As used by Aristotle, the term does not mean what we
    mean by "water" or "H₂O". For him, in terms of attributes, it
    means a body which is cold and moist. "Fire" means a body
    which is hot and dry, "air" means a body which is hot and moist,
    and "earth" means a body which is cold and dry. These are the
    four material elements from which the other sensible bodies (ex-
    cluding the heavenly bodies) are composed. 330a30–b7,
    382b13–5, 388a29–32.

Water ὕδωρ For Thales, the material principle of things; for Em-
    pedocles, one of the material principles. 983b20–4a9.

weight βάρος

weight, excessive βάρος

whatness τὶ ἔστι, τό A formula of what a thing is, primarily of sub-
    stances, secondarily of the things in the other categories, and
    the existence of the thing is presupposed. 92b4–8, 93a16–20.

whenness ποτέ One of the categories. For example, an answer to the
    question When?, such as "yesterday" or "last year", signifies an
    instance of whenness. Synonym: "at some time". 1b25–2a2.

whereness ποῦ One of the categories. Synonyms: "somewhere", "in a
    place". 1b25–2a2.

whirling δίνησις Synonym: "turning".

white, n. or adj. λευκός

whole ὅλος (a) That from which no natural part is absent. (b) That
    which contains what is contained, either (i) actually many (as a
    universal contains the species or the individuals of which it is
    predicated) or (ii) the parts which exist potentially. (c) That in
    which the position of the parts makes a difference, as a whole
    shoe. 1023b26–1024a10.

why, n. διὰ τί, τό The cause of something. Synonyms: "cause",
    "*reason*".

width πλάτος

wisdom σοφία Intellect and science of the most honorable things
    (eternal and divine). Philosophy, then, would be wisdom. In a
    qualified sense, there is wisdom of some part of being, e.g., of

the first principles and some important theorems of physics. 1005b1–2, 1141a9–b8.

wish βούλησις Desire of the good or the apparent good (in the judging part of the soul). The object of wish is an end, not a means to an end. 1113a13–b2, 1369a1–4.

with respect to κατά Synonyms: "in virtue of", "according to". 73a27–b24, 1022a14–35.

without parts ἀμερής Synonym: "partless".

without qualification ἁπλῶς Synonym: "unqualified".

work ἔργον

zero μηδέν Synonyms: "nothing", "nothingness".

Greek-English

ἀγαθόν good
ἀδιαίρετος indivisible
ἀδύνατον impossible
ἀεί always
ἀήρ air; Air
ἀΐδιος eternal
αἰθήρ ether
αἴσθησις sensation; power of sensation
αἰσχρός ugly
αἰτία, αἴτιον cause, *reason*
ἀκίνητος immovable; motionless
ἀκινησία motionlessness, absence of motion
ἀκρίβεια accuracy
ἀλήθεια truth
ἀληθές true
ἄλλο another, other, distinct
ἀλλοίωσις alteration
ἄλογον unreasonable
ἅμα together, coincident, at the same time or moment, simultaneous
ἁμαρτάνειν err
ἁμαρτία error
ἀμερής partless, without parts
ἀμεταβλησία changelessness
ἀναγκαῖον necessary
ἀνάγκη necessity
ἀνάγειν refer

ἀναιρεῖν exhaust; reject; eliminate
ἀναλογία analogy; proportion
ἄνθρωπος man
ἀνίημι decelerate
ἄνισον unequal
ἀνόμοιος unlike
ἀντίθεσις opposition
ἀντικείμενος opposite
ἀντιμετάστασις replacement
ἀντιπερίστασις mutual replacement
ἀντίφασις contradiction
ἀξίωμα axiom
ἀόριστος indefinite
ἀπάτη mistake
ἄπειρον infinite; *Infinite;* a great many
ἁπλοῦς simple
ἁπλῶς unqualified, without qualification; singly; in a simplified way
ἀπόδειξις demonstration
ἀπόδειξις εἰς τὸ ἀδύνατον demonstration through impossibility
ἀπόλλυσθαι perish
ἀπορία problem, *difficulty*
ἀπόφασις denial
ἅπτεσθαι touch, be in contact
ἄπωσις pushing away
ἀρετή virtue
ἀριθμός number; Number
ἀριθμῷ in number, numerically

ἁρμονία harmony

ἁρμονική harmonics

ἄρτι recently

ἄρτιον even (of numbers); *Even*

ἀρχή principle, beginning, source, starting-point

ἀστρολογία astronomy

ἀσύμβλητος incomparable

ἀσύμμετρος incommensurable

ἀσώματος incorporeal

ἄτομος *indivisible*

ἄτοπος absurd

ἀτυχία ill fortune

αὔξησις increase

αὐτόματον chance; *chance*

ἀφαιρεῖν take way, remove

ἀφή contact, touch

βάθος depth

βάρος density; weight; excessive weight

βαρύς heavy

βεβαιότης certainty

βία force

βούλευσις deliberation

βούλησις wish

βραδύς slow

βραχύ short

γάρ for (conj.)

γένεσις generation

γένος genus

γεωμετρία geometry

γῆ earth; Earth; *Earth*

γίγνεσθαι become, be generated, come to be

γιγνώσκειν know

γνωρίζειν know

γνῶσις knowledge

γραμμή line (curve)

δαιμόνιος godlike

δεικνύναι prove; show

δῆλον clearly, plainly

διά because, through

διὰ τί, τό *why*, n.

διάθεσις disposition; arrangement

διαίρεσις division; distinction

διάκρισις separation

διανοεῖν *think*

διάνοια *thought*

διάστασις direction

διάστημα dimension; interval

διαφέρειν differ

διαφορά differentia, difference

διάφορος different

διεξέρχεσθαι traverse

διεξιέναι traverse

διιέναι go through

δίνη vortex

δίνησις turning, whirling

δίωσις pushing apart

δοκεῖν seem, be thought

δόξα opinion; doctrine

δυάς *Dyad*

δυνάμει potential, potentially

δύναμις potentiality, potency, power, capability

δυνατόν potential, possible, capable

δυσκίνητος hardly movable

δυστυχία misfortune

εἰδέναι understand

εἶδος kind; species; form; Form

εἰκός probability

εἰκών portrait

εἶναι be, exist

ἕκαστον each

ἔλλειψις deficiency; *Deficiency*

ἕλξις pulling

ἐλπίζειν expect

ἐμπειρία experience

ἕν one; *One*

ἐναντίος contrary

ἐναντίωσις contrariety

ἐνδέχεσθαι may, be possible

ἕνεκα τινός for the sake of

ἐνέργεια *actuality*, activity

ἐνεργεῖν be active, be in activity

ἑνότης unity

ἔνστασις objection
ἐντελέχεια actuality
ἕνωσις union
ἐξαίφνης suddenly
ἕξις habit, possession
ἐπαγωγή induction
ἐπιθυμία *desire*
ἐπίπεδον plane; surface
ἐπίστασθαι *know*
ἐπιστήμη *knowledge*, science
ἐπιτείνειν accelerate
ἐπιφάνεια surface
ἔπωσις pushing along
ἔργον operation, work, function
ἐριστικός eristic
ἕτερος other, distinct
εὐδαιμονία happiness
εὐεξία good physical condition
εὐθύς straight, rectilinear
εὔλογος reasonable
εὐτυχής fortunate
εὐτυχία good fortune
ἐφεξῆς succession, in succession
ἐφίεσθαι strive after
ἐχόμενος consecutive
ζητεῖν inquire, seek
ζῷον animal
ᾗ qua, insofar as
ἤ or
ἤδη already, immediately, presently
ἡδονή pleasure
ἠθικός ethical
ἥλιος Sun
ἠρέμησις coming to rest; rest, state of rest
ἠρεμία rest, state of rest
θᾶττον faster
θεῖον divine
θερμόν hot (n. or adj.), hotness; *Hot*
θέσις position; paradox; *Position*
θεωρεῖν investigate, speculate; view
θίξις contact
ἰδέα Idea

ἴδιον property
ἴδιος proper, specific
ἰσοταχής of equal speed
ἰσότης equality
ἵστασθαι come to a stop or standstill, stop
ἰσχύς strength, force
καθαίρεσις reduction
καθ' αὑτό essential, essentially; by itself; in itself
καθ' ἕκαστον individual, n.
καθόλου universal, universally; entire
καί and; or
κακία vice
κακός bad
κάλλος physical beauty
καλός beautiful
καμπύλον curvature
κατά with respect to, according to, in virtue of
κατὰ συμβεβηκός accidental, accidentally, by accident, in virtue of an attribute
κατὰ φύσιν according to nature
κατάφασις affirmation
κατηγορία category; predication
κατηγορεῖσθαι be predicated of
κενόν void; *Void*
κέρκισις combing
κίνημα impulse
κίνησις motion
κινοῦν mover, moving cause
κοῖλον concave
κοινός common
κόσμος universe
κοῦφον light (adj.)
κρᾶσις mixture
κρίνειν *judge*, discriminate
κυμαίνειν pulsate
κυρίως mainly, independently, in the main sense, principally
κυρτός convex

λεῖον smooth
λεπτός thin, fine (of particles)
λευκόν white (n. or adj.); gray-haired; light (adj.)
λογικός logical
λογισμός reasoning
λογιστικόν reasoning power, judging power
λόγος formula, statement, expression; reason; argument; ratio
λύειν refute; solve
μαθήματα mathematical sciences; mathematical objects; Mathematical Objects
μαθηματικά mathematical objects
μαθηματική mathematics
μακρόν long
μαλακόν soft
μάλλιστα most, most of all, in the highest degree
μᾶλλον more, rather, to a higher degree
μανόν rare; Rare, n.
ματαῖος futile
μάτην in vain
μέγα great; Great, n.
μέγεθος magnitude; great magnitude
μέθοδος inquiry
μένειν rest, stay, stay the same
μέρος part
μέσον middle; Center
μεταβολή change
μεταξύ between, intermediate
μετάστασις displacement
μέτριον right measure
μέτρον measure
μὴ ὄν nonbeing; not-being
μηδέν nothing, nothingness, zero
μῆκος length; line
μῖγμα blend; Blend
μικρόν small; Small
μίμησις imitation

μίξις blend; Blend
μνήμη memory
μονάς unit
μονή rest, state of rest
μόριον part
μορφή form, shape
νεῖκος Strife; strife
νοεῖν conceive, think
νόησις thought
νοητός intelligible
νοῦς intellect; Intelligence
νῦν moment; now, present moment
ὄγκος volume, mass
ὅθεν that from which, source
οἰκεῖος proper, appropriate
ὀλίγα few
ὀλίγον little
ὅλος whole
ὅλως in general
ὁμαλής uniform; regular
ὁμοειδής alike or same in species or kind, homogeneous
ὁμοιομερής homogeneous
ὅμοιος similar, like
ὁμοταχύς of like speed
ὁμώνυμος equivocal; having the same name
ὄν being, thing; Being
ὄνομα name
ὅπερ just
ὀπτική optics
ὄρεξις desire
ὀρθός right (adj.)
ὁρισμός definition
ὁρμή tendency
ὅρος definition; boundary; limit
οὖ ἕνεκα final cause
οὐκ ὄν nonbeing; Nonbeing
οὐρανός heaven
οὐσία substance; substance
ὄχησις carrying
ὄψις sight
πάθος affection; attribute

πάλαι   long ago
πᾶν   universe; entire thing
παρὰ φύσιν   contrary to nature
παράδειγμα   pattern
παραλογίζεσθαι   conclude falsely
παραλογισμός   fallacy
παράλογον   contrary to reason
παρώνυμος   derivative
πάσχειν   be affected, be acted upon
παύειν   cease
παχύς   viscous
πεπερασμένον   finite, limited
πέρας   limit, boundary
περιττόν   odd; *Odd* (n.)
περιφερές   circular
περιφορά   revolution
πῇ   in a qualified way
πῆξις   freezing
πίστις   conviction
πιλόω   compress
πλασματῶδες   fictitious
πλάτος   width
πλείω   many
πλῆθος   plurality, many
πλῆρες   full
ποιεῖν   act; make, produce; posit
ποιόν   quality
πολύ   much
πολλά   many; *Many*
ποσόν   quantity
ποτέ   whenness, at some time
ποῦ   whereness, somewhere, in a place
πρᾶγμα   thing, fact
πραγματεία   discipline, *inquiry*
πρᾶξις   *action*
πράττειν   *act*, do
προαίρεσις   *choice*
πρὸς τι   relation, relative
προσφύειν   grow along with each other
πρότερος   prior; before, earlier
πρῶτος   first, primary

πυκνόν   dense; *Dense*, n.
πῦρ   fire; *Fire*
πως   in some way
ῥάδιος   easy
ῥίψις   throwing
σαφής   *clear*
σελήνη   Moon
σημαίνειν   signify, mean
σημεῖον   sign; point; cut
σκληρόν   hard
σοφία   wisdom
σοφιστική   sophistry
σπάθησις   packing
σπέρμα   seed
στάσις   stop, standstill
στερεόν   solid; *Solid*
στέρησις   privation
στιγμή   point
στοιχεῖον   element; letter
συγγενής   same in genus or kind
σύγκρισις   combination
συλλογίζεσθαι   prove
συλλογισμός   syllogism
συμβεβηκός   attribute; accident
συμβλητός   comparable
συμμετρία   symmetry; right proportion
σύμμετρος   commensurable
συμπέρασμα   conclusion
συμπιλόω   compress
σύμφυσις   growing together
συναιτία   joint cause
συνεχής   continuous
σύνθετος   composite
συνίημι   interpenetrate
σύνολον   *composite*
συνώνυμος   univocal, having the same meaning
σύνωσις   bringing together
σχῆμα   shape; *Shape;* figure
σῶμα   body
σωματικός   corporeal
τάξις   order; *Order*

ταὐτός same
τάχος speed
ταχύς fast
τέλειος complete, perfect
τέλος end
τέχνη art
τὶ ἔστι, τό whatness
τὶ ἦν εἶναι, τό essence
τιθέναι place; posit
τιμή honor
τμῆμα segment
τόδε τι a *this*
τομή *division*
τόπος place
τραχύτης roughness
τύχη luck
ὑγίεια health
ὑγρόν moist; *Moist* (n.)
ὕδωρ water; *Water*
ὕλη matter
ὑπεροχή excess; *Excess*
ὑπόθεσις hypothesis, assumption
ὑποκείμενον subject, underlying subject
ὑποκεῖσθαι underlie
ὑπολαμβάνειν believe
ὕστερος posterior; later
φαίνεσθαι appear
φανερόν evident
φαντασία imagination
φάσις assertion
φέρειν carry
φέρεσθαι be carried; travel

φθίσις decrease
φθορά destruction
φιλία friendship; *Friendship*
φιλοσοφία philosophy
φορά locomotion; carrying
φύεσθαι grow
φύσει by nature
φυσική physics
φυσικός physical, natural; physicist
φυσιολόγος natural philosopher
φύσις nature; generation towards nature (as form)
φῶς light
χάος *Gap*
χρήσιμος useful, instrumental
χρῆσις use
χρόνος time, interval of time
χρῶμα color
χώρα space
χωρίζειν separate
χωρίς apart
χωρισμένος separate
χωριστός separable; separate
ψευδής false
ψεῦδος falsity
ψόφος sound
ψυχή soul
ψυχρόν cold; *Cold*, n.
ὡρισμένος definite
ὡς in a manner, in a way
ὡς ἐπὶ τὸ πολύ for the most part, most
ὦσις pushing

Index

acceleration: of bodies, 103, 178
accident: definition, 12
according to nature: meaning, 25-26, 39
action:
  and reaction, 45
  by touch, 45
  by touch, necessarily, 135
  not at a distance, 131-37
  with affection, 45
activity: no generation of, 141
actuality: no generation of, 141
after: definition, 87-88
air: as if the form of water, 69
already: definition, 86-87
alteration:
  all at once, sometimes, 154
  definition, 43
  in sensibles and by sensibles only, 137-42
  prior to generation or increase, 167-68
Anaxagoras:
  all things together, at rest, 148
  all were together, 48
  being, as one and many, 13
  Blend, as material principle, 13
  change, had a beginning, 13
  contraries, infinite in kind, 13, 17
  elements, homogeneous, infinite in kind, 13
  elements, infinite by contact, 47-48
  Infinite, keeps itself fixed, 52
  Intelligence, as mover, 48
  Intelligence, caused motion, 148, 151
  Intelligence, moves by locomotion, 178
  Intelligence, pure, unaffected, 160-61
  part, any, a blend of all, like the whole, 48
  void, nonexistent, 69-70
Anaximander: contraries, always blended with matter, 13
ancients: did not mention luck, 32

animal: a mover, of locomotion only, 153
Antiphon: nature, as matter, 26
apart: definition, 95
Archimedes:
  principle of, 109
  principle of, finite exhausted by finite, 54
art:
  as form caused by art, 26
  imitates nature, 28
  imitates or aids nature, 38
  product of, ultimately for us, 28-29
  productive, 29
  productive of matter alone, 28-29
  productive of the ultimately useful, 28-29
  useful, 29
arts: hierarchy in, 28-29
astronomy: closer to physics than geometry, 28
at some time: senses, 86
attribute: senses, 12
axiom: if A>B and B>C, then A>C, 108

beauty: property of, 139-40
because of: indicates a cause, 36
before: definition, 87-88
being:
  as finite, by Parmenides, 10
  as infinite, by Melissus, 10
  by art, 25
  by nature, 25
  essentially, 12
  eternal, not in time, 84
  eternal, possible and actual coincide, 49
  in itself, how possible, 63-64
  senses, 10
  simple, not both mover and moved, 162
between: *see* intermediate
Blend:
  acted on by *Intelligence*, 148
  criticism of, 14

379